Ajax Bible

Ajax Bible

Steven Holzner, PhD

Wiley Publishing, Inc.

Published by
Wiley Publishing, Inc.
10475 Crosspoint Boulevard
Indianapolis, IN 46256
www.wiley.com

ISBN: 978-0-470-10263-3

Manufactured in the United States of America

10 9 8 7 6 5 4 3 2 1

For general information on our other products and services or to obtain technical support, please contact our Customer Care Department within the U.S. at (800) 762-2974, outside the U.S. at (317) 572-3993 or fax (317) 572-4002.

Library of Congress Control Number: 2007920013

About the Author

Steven Holzner is the award-winning author of 102 computer books. He's written many bestsellers, including a number of well-received books on Ajax, such as *Ajax For Dummies* and *Ajax Visual Blueprint*. He is also a former contributing editor at *PC Magazine*, and he's been on the faculty of both MIT and Cornell University. His books have sold several million copies, and been translated into more than 20 languages around the world.

To Nancy, of course.

Credits

Product Development Supervisor
Courtney Allen

Project Editor
Katharine Dvorak

Technical Editor
Steve Wright

Copy Editor
Scott Tullis

Editorial Manager
Robyn Siesky

Business Manager
Amy Knies

Vice President and Executive Group Publisher
Richard Swadley

Vice President and Executive Publisher
Bob Ipsen

Vice President and Publisher
Barry Pruett

Project Coordinator
Patrick Redmond

Graphics and Production Specialists
Carrie A. Foster
Jennifer Mayberry
Barbara Moore
Amanda Spagnuolo

Quality Control Technicians
Laura Albert
Christine Pingleton

Proofreading and Indexing
Linda Seifert
Broccoli Information Management

Contents

Contents

Contents

Contents

Preface

This book is all about making your Web applications look and feel like desktop applications, which is the whole idea behind Ajax. Web applications are becoming more and more popular these days, but there's still that problem with Submit buttons: when you click one, the whole page flickers and refreshes, and you have to wait until the page downloads.

That's exactly where Ajax comes in. With Ajax, you can communicate with the browser behind the scenes, get the data you need, and display it in a Web page. There's no page refresh, no waiting required, no flickering in the browser.

That's cool, because it means your Web applications start to look and feel like desktop applications. As your users' connections to the Internet get faster and faster, soon there will be just about no way to tell a Web application apart from a desktop application.

Ajax is the future of Web programming. With Ajax, applications in a Web browser can work just like those installed on the user's computer. It's no surprise that Ajax is the hottest Web programming topic in years.

About This Book

Everything Ajax is in this book. Part I starts with a guided tour of how Ajax is used today. Along the way you're going to see some very cool applications, as well as some games.

Ajax is based on JavaScript, and there's a section in this part on how to work with JavaScript. If you don't know JavaScript, you're going to need to pick it up, and you can do that here. If you do know JavaScript, you can skip this part of the book and go on to the more advanced topics such as working with Ajax and PHP and security.

Part II then charges into Ajax programming, showing you how to create Ajax-enabled applications from scratch. There are a few chapters on the basics of Ajax, and some on the more advanced, potent aspects. You're also going to see how to save yourself the need for nearly any programming at all when you learn how to work with Ajax frameworks. These frameworks, most of which are available for free, do the Ajax programming for you, letting you create full Ajax applications in a snap.

Ajax involves more than just JavaScript, however. Part III presents the full story on using XML, cascading style sheets, and server-side programming, including a chapter on each of these topics.

Part IV includes chapters on security, as well as chapters on other advanced topics, such as using Web-server filters with Ajax.

All this and more is coming up in this book. In other words, you're going to get the full Ajax story in this book, from soup to nuts. Ajax is going to become a rich toolset for you, ready to be put to work.

Conventions Used in This Book

Some books have many conventions that you need to know before you can even start. Not this one. All you need to know is that when new lines of code are introduced, they appear in bold, like this:

```
function getDataReturnText(url, callback)
{
  var XMLHttpRequestObject = false;

  if (window.XMLHttpRequest) {
    XMLHttpRequestObject = new XMLHttpRequest();
  } else if (window.ActiveXObject) {
    XMLHttpRequestObject = new
     ActiveXObject("Microsoft.XMLHTTP");
  }
        .
        .
        .

}
```

Note also that code that's been omitted has been indicated with three vertical dots.

You can download the code used in this book at www.wiley.com/go/ajaxbible.

What You'll Need

To use this book profitably, you'll need to know some basic HTML — not much, just enough to write a decent Web page. If you need to pick up HTML, take a look at one of the many excellent tutorials on the Internet. The HTML used in this book isn't very advanced, and even if you're not familiar with it, you can probably pick it up just by reading this book.

You're also going to have to know JavaScript. That's not a problem, because all the JavaScript you'll need to know is specifically introduced in this book. However, if you feel you need more, take a look at the JavaScript tutorials online, or check out the *JavaScript Bible*.

Because Ajax involves communicating with the server, there will also be some PHP involved in this book, and in case you're not familiar with PHP, that's also not a problem because the book contains a couple of chapters to bring you up to speed on PHP.

You'll also need a browser, such as Microsoft Internet Explorer or Mozilla Firefox, to use this book. However, because browsers have become so plentiful that you can barely do anything on a computer without bumping into one, that shouldn't be an issue — just use the browser you're accustomed to using.

And that's it! You're ready to go. Turn to Chapter 1 to see Ajax at work.

Acknowledgments

The book you hold in your hands is the product of many people's work. I'd especially like to thank acquisitions editor, Courtney Allen; project editor, Katharine Dvorak; technical editor, Steve Wright; copy editor, Scott Tullis; and project coordinator, Patrick Redmond.

Part I

Fundamental Ajax

Chapter 1

Essential Ajax

Welcome to the *Ajax Bible*! This is the home of all things Ajax. Ajax is the new technology that's blazing through the Internet, igniting Web sites everywhere. The Ajax revolution has come, and it's changing the Internet. In fact, Ajax is the basis of what's being called Web 2.0, the next version of the World Wide Web.

So what's it all about? The central idea is making Web applications look and feel just like desktop applications. For example, take a look at Figure 1.1, where you see the familiar Google search page. Enter a term to search for, such as "Ajax," and click the Google Search button.

Google searches for matches to the term you enter.

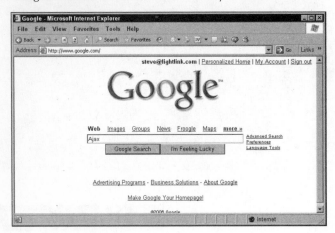

The screen flashes as it's updated with new data, and the matches that Google found to your search term appear, as you see in Figure 1.2.

Google displays the matches it finds.

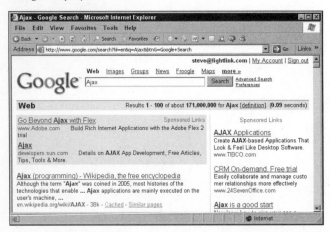

That works OK, but that's not the Ajax way of doing things. Using Ajax, you can work behind the scenes, connecting to the server to get data without causing a page refresh in the browser. For example, take a look at the Google Suggest page at `www.google.com/webhp?complete=1&hl=en`, which is shown in Figure 1.3.

FIGURE 1.3

The Google Suggest page

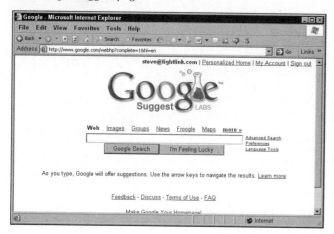

As you type, the page in the browser actually connects to the Google server and looks up matches to the partial search term you entered. For example, type "aj," and you'll see a drop-down list box appear, as in Figure 1.4, with matches found by Google as you're typing.

FIGURE 1.4

Google Suggest looks for matches as you type.

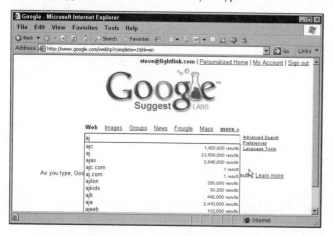

Behind the scenes, using Ajax techniques, the Web page connects to Google Suggest and searches for matches to your search term as you're entering it. It then displays a drop-down list box of the matches it's found to your search term, letting you select from those matches—all without a page refresh. That's the crucial point: no page refresh was necessary. In the old days, when you wanted to send data to the server, you had to click a button, such as the Google Search button. Then you had to wait as the screen flickered and was refreshed. Now, a Web page can send data to the server without creating a page refresh at all, as you see in this example, where your search term was sent to the server automatically and the server sent back data to be displayed in the drop-down list.

No longer do you need to perform a page refresh when you send data to the server, or when you receive data from the server. Instead, Web pages can now act much more like desktop applications, sending data to the server and receiving data back, all behind the scenes.

This conversion of Web applications, making them feel more like desktop applications, is what's meant by Web 2.0. How would you like it if your word processor flashed every time you typed a new character, and the entire document was displayed over again, with the cursor reset to the beginning of the document? Not a very attractive thought. Using Ajax, you can create online word processors that are practically indistinguishable from the desktop version — no flash, no flicker, no resetting the cursor location when you type. Just a smooth word-processing experience, just like the desktop version of the same application.

You can see why Ajax is causing a revolution in Web applications: now it's possible to create online applications that look and feel just like their desktop counterparts.

This chapter gets you started. You'll get an overview of the meaning of the term Ajax, and then a survey of how Ajax is used today. That survey is a very important part of this book because Ajax is turning up in more and more places — sometimes unexpectedly — and if you are familiar with the uses of Ajax, you'll know where you can use it in your own Web applications.

What Does "Ajax" Mean?

So where did the term "Ajax" come from, exactly? Take a look at Figure 1.5, which shows the very important first article written on Ajax, the article that coined the term and started everything. You can find that article at www.adaptivepath.com/publications/essays/archives/ 000385.php. This article is by Adaptive Path's Jesse James Garrett, who was the first to call this technology Ajax.

Here's how that article starts:

> "If anything about current interaction design can be called 'glamorous,' it's creating Web applications. After all, when was the last time you heard someone rave about the inter-action design of a product that wasn't on the Web? (Okay, besides the iPod.) All the cool, innovative new projects are online.

> "Despite this, Web interaction designers can't help but feel a little envious of our col-leagues who create desktop software. Desktop applications have a richness and respon-siveness that has seemed out of reach on the Web. The same simplicity that enabled the Web's rapid proliferation also creates a gap between the experiences we can provide and the experiences users can get from a desktop application.

> "That gap is closing."

FIGURE 1.5

The original Ajax article

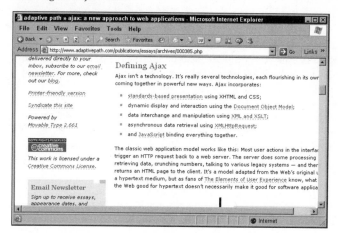

That gap is indeed closing, thanks to Ajax. So, according to the article, what does "Ajax" actually stand for? It stands for *Asynchronous JavaScript and XML*. As you can begin to see from its name, and as you can read in the Jesse James Garrett article, Ajax is really a collection of technologies.

The "asynchronous" part means that the browser isn't going to wait for data to be returned from the server, but can handle that data as it's sent back, when it's sent back. In other words, data transfers take place behind the scenes, without making the browser pause and wait for something to happen. That's a crucial part of Ajax: You can handle data from the server when the server sends you that data. You don't have to put your whole application on hold until that data arrives. If you had to wait for that data, your application would be synchronous; and with slow Internet connections, that could be a problem.

The JavaScript part of the term Ajax is also very important because that's what makes Ajax happen in the browser. Ajax relies on JavaScript in the browser to connect to the server and to handle the data that the server sends back. All the Ajax applications you will develop in this book use JavaScript to connect to the server behind the scenes, uploading and downloading data. And when your data is downloaded, you can use JavaScript in the browser to handle that data, displaying it or crunching it as appropriate.

What about the XML part of the term Ajax? As you probably know, XML has become the lingua franca of the Web, providing a text-based way to send data back and forth across the Internet. The reason XML has become so popular is that it is indeed text-based, which means that you can sling XML around the Internet, because the Internet was designed to handle text-based documents (that is, HTML). For that reason, Ajax applications are often written to handle data sent back from the server using XML. In other words, when you contact the server, it'll send data back to you as an XML document.

In fact, XML is only one of the ways to handle data sent to you from the server. You can also send back plain text as well, and you're going to see both techniques extensively in this book.

Besides JavaScript and XML, Ajax also works with dynamic HTML and Cascading Style Sheets (CSS). Both of these technologies allow you to update the data displayed in a Web page, and, because you don't redraw the entire Web page with Ajax, but just a part of it, you rely on dynamic HTML and CSS quite a bit; both of them allow you to update specific parts of a Web page. You're going to see a lot more on dynamic HTML and CSS in this book because they allow you to refresh just part of a Web page, something that is central to Ajax-enabled applications.

The part of JavaScript that makes Ajax possible is the XMLHttpRequest object. This is a special object built into all modern browsers' version of JavaScript. As you're going to see, this is what makes it possible to connect to the server and handle data sent back from the server behind the scenes. It's not just JavaScript that makes Ajax tick, it's the XMLHttpRequest object inside JavaScript.

So there you have it; Ajax is a collection of technologies, not just a single technology. You use the XMLHttpRequest object built into JavaScript to connect to the server, and then handle the XML — or plain text — the server sends back using JavaScript. And you use dynamic HTML and CSS to display the results in the browser. It's lucky that all the parts of Ajax applications came together as they did — JavaScript, the XMLHttpRequest object, dynamic HTML, and CSS — because all together, they make it possible to make your online applications look like desktop applications.

Actually, the technology for Ajax has been around since 1998, and had already been used by a number of applications such as Microsoft's Outlook Web Access. But it didn't really catch on until early 2005 when some high-profile applications such as Google Suggest put it to work, and Jesse James Garrett wrote his article coining the term Ajax, which put everything under one roof.

Since that time, things have exploded as developers have realized that Web software can finally start acting and behaving like desktop software. So what can you do with Ajax? That's what the rest of this chapter is about.

What Can You Do with Ajax?

There's a great deal you can do with Ajax, and the following pages cover this treasure trove in some detail. Coming up is a good survey of the way Ajax is used today.

Create Ajax live searches

One of the most popular uses of Ajax is to create *live searches*, and you've already seen an example with Google Suggest at the beginning of this chapter. With a live search, the user can enter a partial search term, and using Ajax, the Web application connects to the server and finds matches to that partial search term.

There are plenty of live searches besides Google Suggest available online. For example, take a look at Gollum at `http://gollum.easycp.de/en/`, which is a live search of Wikipedia, the online free encyclopedia at `www.wikipedia.org`. Gollum is shown in Figure 1.6.

FIGURE 1.6

Gollum performs live searches of Wikipedia.

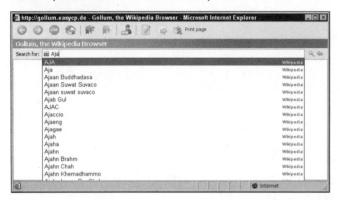

Enter a partial search term in Gollum, such as "Aja" for Ajax, and you can see the results in Figure 1.6, where Gollum has connected to Wikipedia behind the scenes and found matches to your partial search term. Those matches are displayed, as is usual for a live search, in a drop-down list, and you can select the one that you're looking for. When you do, the matching Wikipedia article is opened in your browser.

Create an Ajax-enabled calculator

Any situation where you have to send data to the server and handle the data sent back to you behind the scenes is perfect for Ajax. So how about an Ajax-enabled calculator? You can find one at `www.funwithjustin.com/ajax-toybox-demo/calculator.html`, as shown in Figure 1.7.

To use the calculator, just enter two operands to work with, such as 5 and 7 in Figure 1.7, and click the operation you want to perform — addition, subtraction, multiplication, or division. Using Ajax, this Web page sends your operands to a program on the server that adds, subtracts, multiplies, or divides your numbers as appropriate and sends the results back.

The results then appear in the bottom text field, as you can see in Figure 1.7, where 5 and 7 are added. And it's all done without a page refresh — no browser flicker. This application, like other Ajax applications, looks just as if it's a desktop application.

FIGURE 1.7

An Ajax-enabled calculator

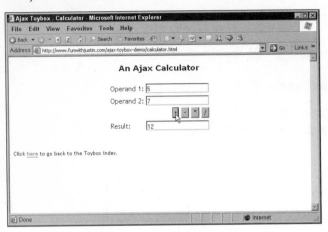

Talk with Ajax chat applications

Ajax is great anywhere intensive updating is required, such as chat applications, where any number of users can type and their text appears automatically to everyone currently logged in. Ajax is a good choice here because the text being displayed is always being updated, and having to watch it flicker as the whole page is updated would be very annoying.

Using Ajax, however, you can update text anywhere in a page easily, no page refresh required. Take a look, for example, at www.phpfreechat.net/demo.en.php, the PHP Free Chat page. This page connects to a PHP script on the server to support a chat application. When you first navigate to PHP Free Chat, it asks you to enter a username, as you see in Figure 1.8.

FIGURE 1.8

Signing in for PHP Free Chat

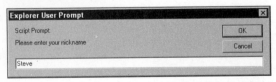

After you've signed in, you can type your text in the text field that appears at the bottom of Figure 1.9; when you press Enter, that text is sent, using Ajax, to the server, which adds that text to the text that others have typed, and the results appear in the chat box, as you can see in Figure 1.9.

PHP Free Chat lets you enter text that others can see.

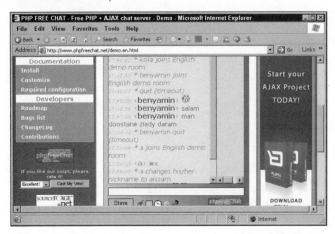

There are many Ajax chat applications around. Take a look at www.plasticshore.com/projects/chat/, for example, which is shown in Figure 1.10. To use this chat application, all you have to do is enter your name (or accept the default name) and your text, and click the Submit button. When you do, your text appears in the chat box, along with everyone else's.

An Ajax-enabled free chat application

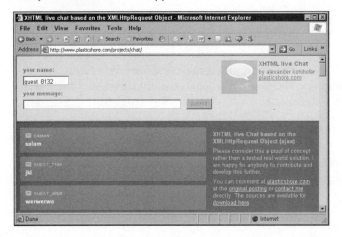

There are many more Ajax-enabled chat applications. For example, take a look at `http://treehouse.ofb.net/chat/?lang=en` for another good one.

Crunch numbers with spreadsheets

More and more desktop-type applications are being migrated to Web, thanks to Ajax. One of the latest is for spreadsheets, which you can now find in a number of places online.

For example, take a look at Num Sum, a free online spreadsheet that works just as a desktop version would, at `http://numsum.com/spreadsheet/new`. You can see Num Sum at work in Figure 1.11.

FIGURE 1.11

Num Sum is an online Ajax spreadsheet application.

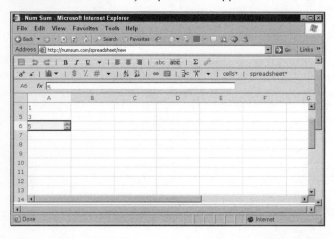

Using Num Sum, you can create real spreadsheets, including the use of formulas, and save your data on the Num Sum server. Using this application is nearly indistinguishable from a desktop version, as you enter data and watch it being updated — all without a browser refresh.

Browse Amazon

Here's a cute one: an application that lets you browse through the products for sale at Amazon.com. This application lets you display everything in Amazon.com using a clickable tree that is updated using Ajax. Just navigate to `http://lmap.co.nr/Amazon1.htm` and click a node to open that node and see the Amazon products, as shown in Figure 1.12.

FIGURE 1.12

Browsing through Amazon.com

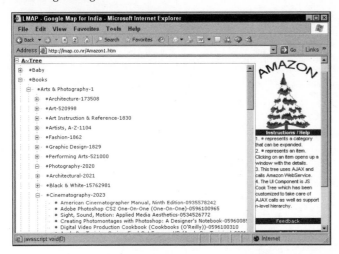

Get the answer with Ajax autocomplete

Ajax autocomplete applications are a lot like live searches. With live searches, you can enter a partial term in a text field. With autocomplete, however, there's no search involved; autocomplete simply offers suggestions to complete the term you're typing (if you do any cell phone text messaging, you're probably familiar with the idea — many cell phones offer suggestions to complete a term as you're typing it).

You can see an autocomplete example at www.papermountain.org/demos/live/, which is shown in Figure 1.13.

Just type a partial English word in the text field as shown in Figure 1.13, and the application sends your partial word to the server, which finds matches to that word and sends back autocomplete suggestions. Those suggestions appear, as you see in Figure 1.13, and you can select among them. When you do, the term you select replaces the partial term you've already typed.

You can find another autocomplete example available for download from SWATO, an Ajax toolkit, at https://swato.dev.java.net/. You can see this example at work in Figure 1.14.

This example matches the names of countries, as shown in Figure 1.14. All you need to do is to type, say, "A", to be shown a set of possible completions, including Algeria, Austria, Australia, and so on.

FIGURE 1.13

Using autocomplete

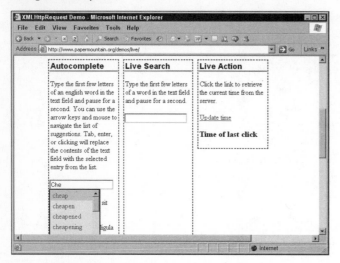

FIGURE 1.14

Using SWATO for autocomplete

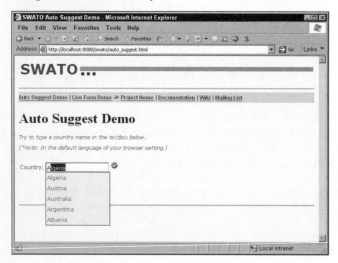

Log in with Ajax

Here's another good one: rather than asking the users to navigate through a couple of pages to log in to a site, you can use Ajax to make the process easier, checking their typed username and password behind the scenes.

For example, take a look at `www.jamesdam.com/ajax_login/login.html`, which is shown in Figure 1.15. This page lets you log in automatically using Ajax, no page refresh required.

FIGURE 1.15

An Ajax-enabled login page

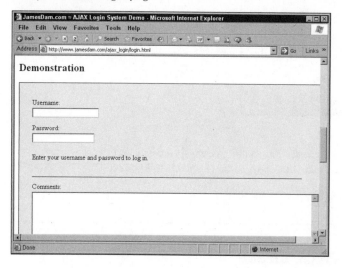

If you enter an incorrect username and password, such as *Steve* and *opensesame* and click the page anywhere, you'll see an error message, as shown in Figure 1.16.

FIGURE 1.16

The login is blocked.

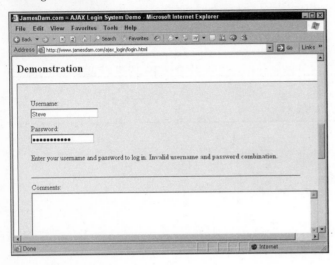

On the other hand, if you enter a correct username and password — user1 and pass1 works here — and click the page, you'll see that you're logged in, as shown in Figure 1.17.

FIGURE 1.17

A successful Ajax-enabled login

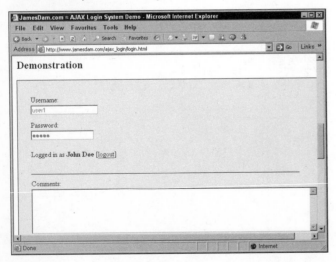

Download images

You can download only text and XML using Ajax. Or can you? One of the examples you're going to see in this book lets you use Ajax together with dynamic HTML to download images. This example is shown in Figure 1.18.

In this example you can download images.

When you click a button, this example downloads and displays an image, as shown in Figure 1.19. So is Ajax really downloading that image? Isn't Ajax limited to downloading text and XML?

In this example you can download a new image without refreshing the page.

What really happens in this example is that Ajax downloads the *name* of the new image to display. Then, the example uses JavaScript to rewrite an HTML <img> element in the Web page, using the name of the file to download. When the browser sees that the <img> element has been rewritten, it downloads the image the <img> element references, through the magic of dynamic HTML.

The end result is that you click a button and a new image appears, no browser refresh needed. That's a combination of Ajax and dynamic HTML at work, and it indicates that you will indeed be able to download binary data using Ajax in this book.

Drag and drop with Ajax

As Web applications become more and more like desktop applications, more and more of what you take for granted in desktop applications is going to start showing up in online applications. For example, drag-and-drop operations can make life a lot easier for the user; and now, when you drag-and-drop items in a Web page, the server can be notified of what you've done behind the scenes. That means the next time you take a look at the page, what you've dragged and dropped appears in the new position you've placed it.

For example, take a look at the refrigerator magnet words at `www.broken-notebook.com/magnetic/`, shown in Figure 1.20.

When you drag a "magnet" to a new location, that new location is sent to the server using Ajax techniques, and that location data is stored. Other people navigating to the page see the magnets in the locations you have set them, and when you come back to the page, the magnets will be where you placed them — unless someone has already moved them.

FIGURE 1.20

The refrigerator magnet words stay where you placed them unless someone else comes along and moves them.

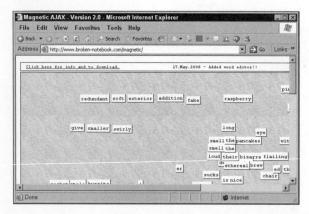

Here's another drag-and-drop example: the mosaic at `thebroth.com`. The idea here is that you and others can drag tiles to create a shared artwork, using Ajax. When you drag a tile, its new location is sent to the server using Ajax, and the tile's position is updated everywhere, in everyone's browser. You can find the mosaic at `www.thebroth.com/mosaic`, and it is shown in Figure 1.21.

FIGURE 1.21

Creating a shared mosaic

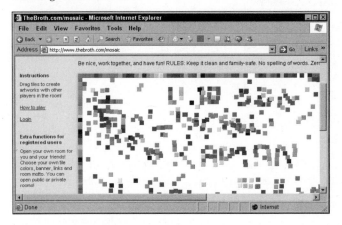

Drag and drop doesn't always have to do with individual items. For example, take a look at Ideo Technologies' datagrid in Figure 1.22, which is located at `http://sweetdev-ria .ideotechnologies.com/sweetdev-ria-demo-1.1-RC3/welcome.do`. The datagrid control lets you rearrange columns by dragging them, as shown in the figure.

When you drag a column, the new column arrangement is sent to the server and stored, which means that when you navigate to other pages for the same datagrid (using the number links under the datagrid), that arrangement is preserved.

One of the biggest uses of dragging and dropping with Ajax is to implement shopping carts. Normally, when you want to add an item to a shopping cart online, you have to go through several pages: when you click the Add to Cart button, you then see a new page corresponding to the shopping cart, and then you must navigate backward to continue shopping.

Wouldn't that be much easier if you never had to leave the page you were shopping on? What if you could simply drag an item to the shopping cart, and the server was notified behind the scenes of your purchase? No fuss, no muss.

FIGURE 1.22

Dragging a column in Ideo Technologies' datagrid

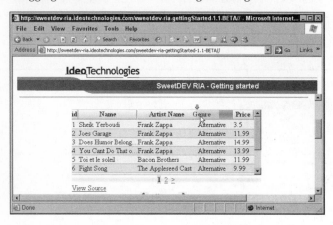

That's the way it works with the shopping cart at `www.puterpet.com/index.php?sel=crafted&menu=crafted&selection=rocks`, which you can see in Figure 1.23.

When you drag and drop an item to the Ajax-enabled shopping cart right in the page, the server is notified of your purchase, and the current total appears in the shopping cart, as shown in Figure 1.24.

FIGURE 1.23

Dragging an item to an Ajax-enabled shopping cart

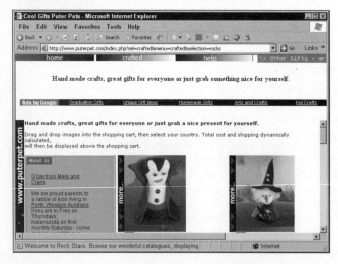

FIGURE 1.24

Adding an item to an Ajax-enabled shopping cart

Play games with Ajax

Here's another fun use of Ajax: a Harry Potter–based "diary" that answers back what you type using Ajax. You can find this one at `http://pandorabots.com/pandora/talk?botid=c96f911b3e35f9e1`, as shown in Figure 1.25.

FIGURE 1.25

Using the Harry Potter–based diary

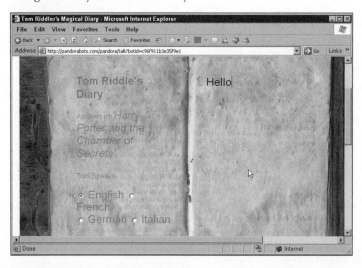

Try typing "Hello" in the diary. The word "Hello" appears momentarily, then disappears, followed by the diary's response — fetched using Ajax — which you see in Figure 1.26.

FIGURE 1.26

The diary responds.

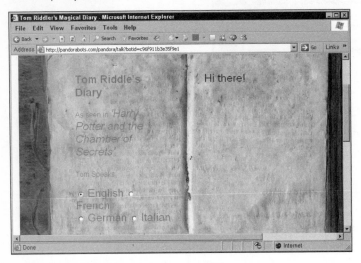

You can ask quite advanced questions of the diary, as shown in Figure 1.27, in which the diary is being asked where it is.

FIGURE 1.27

Asking the diary where it is

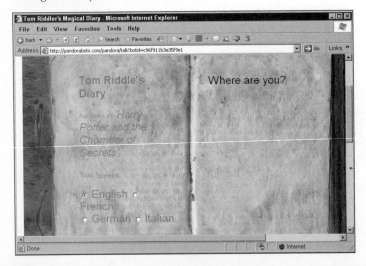

And you can see the diary's response in Figure 1.28.

FIGURE 1.28

The diary indicates where it is.

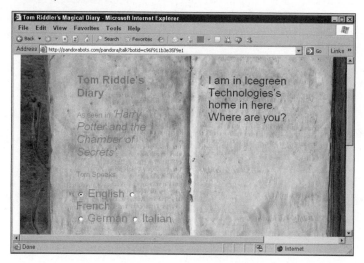

How about a game of Ajax-enabled chess? Take a look at `www.JesperOlsen.Net/PChess/`, which is shown in Figure 1.29. To move a piece, you have only to click it, then click its new position, and the piece is moved automatically. The game sends all the needed data to the server using Ajax, behind the scenes, and gets the data it needs back. Then it uses CSS to move its piece accordingly.

FIGURE 1.29

Playing Ajax chess

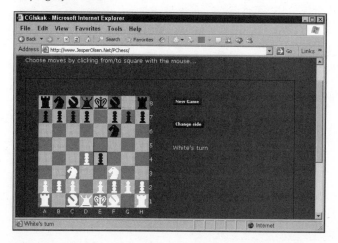

Modify Web pages on the fly

One of the things that Ajax is big on is updating or modifying a Web page as the user watches. Because Ajax applications avoid complete page refreshes, along with the accompanying flicker and flash, you must update specific parts of a Web page in the browser. There are thousands of Ajax applications out there that operate this way, and you're going to be creating some in this book as well.

Here's an example already online: `http://openrico.org/rico/demos.page?demo=`
`ricoAjaxInnerHTML.html`, which you can see in Figure 1.30.

FIGURE 1.30

An Ajax Rolodex

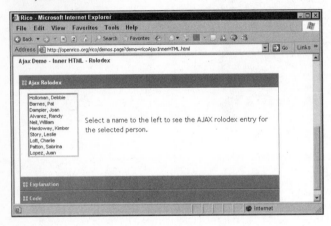

This example is an Ajax-enabled Rolodex. You just have to click a person's name and his or her "card" of information appears, as you see in Figure 1.31.

FIGURE 1.31

Using an Ajax Rolodex

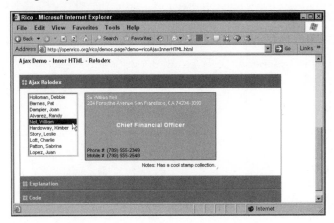

This Rolodex works using CSS to display its data. Each time you click a person's name, the application fetches that person's data from the server, puts together a Rolodex card, and then displays that card using CSS to modify the Web page on the fly.

That's the way it works: You display the results of your actions in a Web page at run time. You don't cause a page refresh to happen.

Another example that shows how to modify a Web page is located at `http://digg.com/spy`, which is shown in Figure 1.32. This site presents news articles that users vote on in real time, and constantly updates itself using a combination of CSS and dynamic HTML. The list of articles you see displayed keeps changing as users vote on them, and each article gets a thumbs-up or thumbs-down icon. It's all done using Ajax to fetch data from the server without causing a page refresh.

FIGURE 1.32

The Digg Spy application updates itself constantly.

The SaneBull Market Monitor is another example that uses Ajax to refresh itself continuously. This page is located at www.sanebull.com and is shown in Figure 1.33.

FIGURE 1.33

SaneBull constantly updates its stock ticker using Ajax.

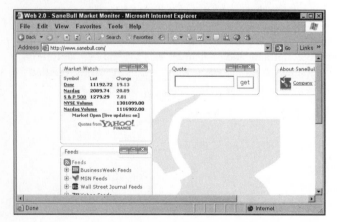

As you watch, the SaneBull monitor updates the Market Watch information at left in the Web page, giving you market quotes by modifying the Web page.

Ajax applications sometimes work by updating HTML controls in the Web page, not just the display in the page itself. You can see an example at `www.jsquery.com/java-jsquery/examples/sql/zipform.jsp`, which is a reverse ZIP code finder. You enter a ZIP code, and the application tells you what city and state the ZIP code is for. You can see the reverse ZIP code finder at work in Figure 1.34.

FIGURE 1.34

A reverse ZIP code finder

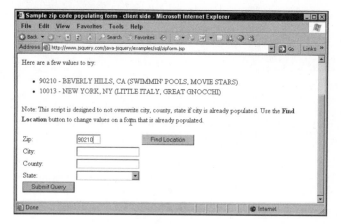

When you click the Find Location button, the city, county, and state matching the ZIP code you've entered appears in the text fields in the Web page, as shown in Figure 1.35, through the magic of Ajax and dynamic HTML.

FIGURE 1.35

Using the reverse ZIP code finder

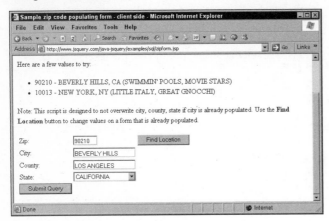

One of the all-time champs of Web page modification, and an application that no review of Ajax should omit, is Writely at `http://docs.google.com`. Writely is a complete online word-processing application of the kind made possible by Ajax, and you can see a sample from Writely's Web site in Figure 1.36.

FIGURE 1.36

A sample Writely page

Writely lets you create and edit documents just as if you were using it on a desktop, and it relies heavily on Ajax to avoid page refreshes as the user works on a document. Writely is another of those applications making the migration from the desktop to the Web. You've already seen an online spreadsheet application; now you've seen an online word processor — both usually desktop applications, now possible online.

Add interactivity to maps

One of the first Ajax applications that started it all is Google Maps, at `http://maps` `.google.com`, which in Figure 1.37 is zooming in on 10 Market Street in San Francisco.

See that popup and the arrow pointing to 10 Market Street? The data for those items is downloaded using Ajax behind the scenes in Google Maps. Cool.

FIGURE 1.37

Using Google Maps

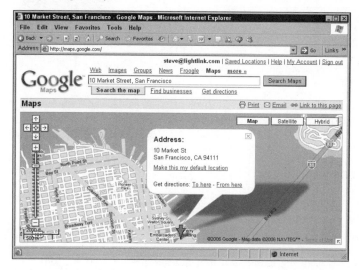

Many other map sites have sprung up since the original Google Maps introduction. For example, take a look at `www.gtraffic.info`, which gives you traffic information in the UK. Those arrows on the map you see in Figure 1.38 are Ajax-enabled.

FIGURE 1.38

Checking traffic conditions in the UK the Ajax way

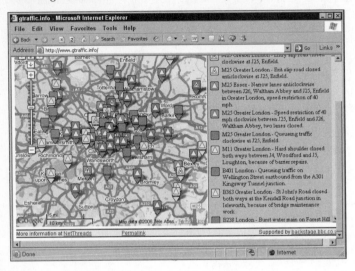

E-mail the Ajax way

Another popular use of Ajax is supporting browser-based e-mail, and you can see an example at `http://demo.nextapp.com/Email/app`, shown in Figure 1.39.

The problem with browser-based e-mail was that you'd see a list of e-mails sent to read, but each time you clicked an e-mail, you'd be taken to an entirely new page. Then you'd have to go back to the e-mail list and scroll down again to check other e-mails.

Handling e-mail the Ajax way is different. You can see the list of e-mails in Figure 1.39; clicking one automatically downloads the e-mail and displays it — without a browser refresh — as you see in Figure 1.40. The body of the e-mail appears at the bottom of the application.

In other words, once again, Ajax has been successful at turning a desktop application into an online one, solving the problems normally faced by online applications.

FIGURE 1.39

Browser-supported e-mail

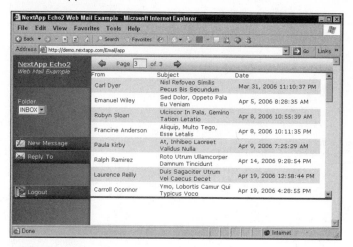

FIGURE 1.40

Using e-mail with Ajax

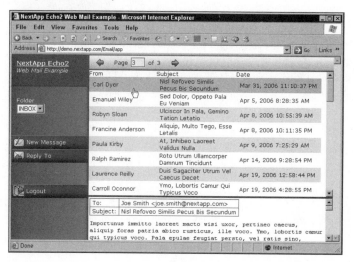

Ajax-enabled pop-ups

Online map applications aren't the only ones using Ajax-enabled pop-ups; you can find them all over. For example, take a look at the Top 100 Netflix titles at `www.netflix.com/Top100`, shown in the following figure.

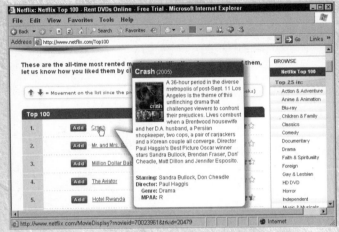

Getting information on the Netflix top 100 movies

All you've got to do to get more information on a movie is to let the mouse cursor rest on the name of the movie, and the application automatically downloads data from the server using Ajax and displays that data in a popup, as you see in the figure. That's Ajax at work, once again: no page refresh needed, and no need to click the Back button in your browser to get back to the original display.

Summary

This chapter gave you an introduction to and overview of how Ajax is used today. As you can see, the emphasis is on making online applications feel like desktop applications, which is what Ajax excels at. A great deal of making that work has to do with using JavaScript in the browser, and that's what the next chapter is about: getting up to speed in JavaScript, the very foundation of Ajax.

Chapter 2

Know Your JavaScript

Ajax is based on JavaScript, and this chapter is all about JavaScript. You're going to need a good foundation in JavaScript to tackle Ajax, and all the JavaScript you'll need to know is in this chapter. If you're already up to speed in JavaScript, you can skip this chapter and turn to Chapter 3, which gets into Ajax in depth.

What Is JavaScript's Place in Ajax?

Where does JavaScript belong in the scheme of things? It turns out that it's absolutely central; JavaScript is what makes Ajax work. To see that, take a look at an example.

This example downloads and displays text from a server. (You'll see what makes it tick in detail in the next chapter.) You can see this example in a Web browser in Figure 2.1.

An Ajax demo

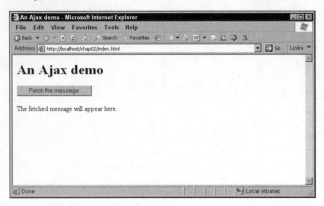

When this application is hosted on a Web server, clicking the Fetch the Message button causes the application to use Ajax techniques behind the scenes to connect to the server and download the contents of a text file, data.txt. Here's what's in data.txt:

> This text was fetched from the server with Ajax.

Clicking the button downloads the message from the server, without any page refresh needed. The downloaded text simply appears, as shown in Figure 2.2.

Downloading text using Ajax

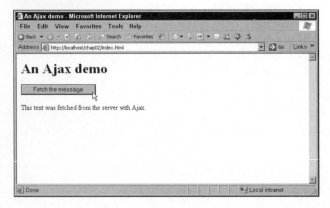

You already know that this example just uses a simple text file, data.txt, on the server, so the whole magic must be in the Web page, index.html, itself. It is, and it's in JavaScript. Here's what that JavaScript looks like in index.html:

```html
<html>
  <head>
    <title>An Ajax demo</title>

    <script language = "javascript">
      var XMLHttpRequestObject = false;

      if (window.XMLHttpRequest) {
        XMLHttpRequestObject = new XMLHttpRequest();
      } else if (window.ActiveXObject) {
        XMLHttpRequestObject = new
          ActiveXObject("Microsoft.XMLHTTP");
      }

      function getData(dataSource, divID)
      {
        if(XMLHttpRequestObject) {
          var obj = document.getElementById(divID);
          XMLHttpRequestObject.open("GET", dataSource);

          XMLHttpRequestObject.onreadystatechange = function()
          {
            if (XMLHttpRequestObject.readyState == 4 &&
              XMLHttpRequestObject.status == 200) {
                obj.innerHTML =
                  XMLHttpRequestObject.responseText;
            }
          }

          XMLHttpRequestObject.send(null);
        }
      }
    </script>
  </head>

<body>

  <H1>An Ajax demo</H1>

  <form>
    <input type = "button" value = "Fetch the message"
      onclick = "getData('data.txt', 'targetDiv')">
  </form>
```

```
<div id="targetDiv">
  <p>The fetched message will appear here.</p>
</div>

</body>
</html>
```

As you can see, nearly all of what's going on here is JavaScript. JavaScript is the basis of this application, as it is of many Ajax applications. In fact, the starting point for any discussion of Ajax programming is JavaScript, so it's time to launch into JavaScript, starting with a little background.

A Brief History of JavaScript

The JavaScript story began in 1995 with a developer named Brendan Eich at Netscape Communications Corporation. He created an early version of JavaScript, originally called LiveScript, but soon renamed JavaScript. The Java programming language was flying high at that time, so one can only assume that led to the name JavaScript because JavaScript itself has very little in common with the Java language. In fact, Sun Microsystems, the creator of Java, had a trademark on the Java name, so the "JavaScript" name is actually a trademark of Sun Microsystems, and JavaScript was announced at a joint press conference of Netscape and Sun in December 1995.

JavaScript caught on; it was fun, it was cool, it was easy to use. Using JavaScript, you could write scripts in Web pages to make all kinds of great effects happen, from responding to mouse rollovers to changing color schemes at the click of the mouse.

That meant that Microsoft had to get in on the deal too. Microsoft was Netscape's competitor in the browser field at that time; it was the Netscape Navigator vs. the Internet Explorer. Microsoft decided to support JavaScript too, but because JavaScript was a product of Netscape, Microsoft created its own version, called JScript.

JScript was released July 16th, 1996, in Internet Explorer 3.0. Now there was both JavaScript and JScript, and the resulting split personality for the language between Netscape and Microsoft has had repercussions that echo down to today. So started the cross-browser and cross-browser version wars that have made life so very interesting for the JavaScript programmer ever since. Programmers started to find that although JScript looked just like JavaScript, some scripts would run in Netscape and not in Internet Explorer, and vice versa.

The result was chaos, and ultimately, both Netscape and Microsoft realized something had to be done. They turned to a third party, the standards body European Computer Manufacturers Association (ECMA). You might expect the standardized language to be called JavaScript, or possibly JScript, but it's not called either. It's called ECMAScript, although the common name is still JavaScript.

The upshot is that although there are still differences, as you're going to see in this book, JavaScript is converging between browsers now — at least the core part of the language matches ECMAScript version 3.0.

All three parties, Microsoft, Netscape, and ECMA, have published reference documents for JavaScript. You can find the JavaScript 1.5 user's guide at `http://web.archive.org/web/20040211195031/devedge.netscape.com/library/manuals/2000/javascript/1.5/guide/`. And you can find the documentation for JScript 5.6 online as well at `http://msdn.microsoft.com/library/default.asp?url=/library/en-us/script56/html/29f83a2c-48c5-49e2-9ae0-7371d2cda2ff.asp`.

The ECMAScript specifications are also online:

- The ECMAScript Language Specification, 3rd edition is at `www.ecma-international.org/publications/standards/Ecma-262.htm`.

- The ECMAScript Components Specification is at `www.ecma-international.org/publications/standards/Ecma-290.htm`.

- The ECMAScript 3rd Edition Compact Profile specification is at `www.ecma-international.org/publications/standards/Ecma-327.htm`.

Getting Started with JavaScript

It's time to get started writing some JavaScript. To write JavaScript, you use the `<script>` element in a Web page like this:

```
<html>
  <head>
    <title>A first JavaScript example</title>

    <script language="javascript">
        .
        .
        .
    </script>
  </head>

  <body>
    <h1>A first JavaScript example</h1>
  </body>
</html>
```

Note that the `<script>` element is an element much like any other HTML element; it even has an attribute, the `language` attribute, which in this case you set to `"javascript"` — including in the Internet Explorer The actual JavaScript code you write goes into the `<script>` element, and the `<script>` element usually goes into the `<head>` section of a Web page.

So what can you do for a first JavaScript example? How about writing a message to the Web page? That sounds like a fine idea. The next question is, of course, how do you access the Web page from inside your JavaScript code?

It turns out that you access the Web page and the browser itself from JavaScript with a variety of built-in *objects*. The objects available for your use include objects like the *document* object (which refers to a Web page), the *window* object (which refers to the browser window), and the *history* object (which refers to a history list that lets the browser navigate forward and backward).

Each of these objects has *methods* and *properties*. You can *call* a method to make something happen (like writing to a Web page) and *set* the value of a property to configure those objects (like setting the background color of a Web page). Following are a few useful object methods:

- `document.write` lets you write text to the current Web page.
- `history.go` moves the browser to a page in the browser's history.
- `window.open` opens a new browser window.

And here are a few of the useful properties that are available:

- `document.bgcolor` holds the background color of the current page.
- `document.fgcolor` holds the foreground color of the current page.
- `document.lastmodified` holds the date the page was last modified.
- `document.title` holds the title of the page.
- `location.hostname` holds the name of the page's host.
- `navigator.appName` holds the type of the browser.

So what does that do for us in the attempt to write to a Web page from JavaScript? You can use the `document.write` method to do just that. Here's what it looks like in JavaScript, in the code file first.html:

```
<html>
  <head>
    <title>A first JavaScript example</title>

    <script language="javascript">
      document.write("You are using JavaScript");
    </script>
  </head>

  <body>
    <h1>A first JavaScript example</h1>
  </body>
</html>
```

That's it, just a single line of JavaScript, designed to write the text "You are using JavaScript" to the Web page. This line of code is executed as soon as the browser encounters it, while it's loading the Web page. The browser encounters the `<head>` section of this page before the `<body>` section, which means that you get the result you see in Figure 2.3, where the text written by your JavaScript ("You are using JavaScript") in the `<head>` section of the page comes before the header ("A first JavaScript example") from the `<body>` section of the page.

A first JavaScript example

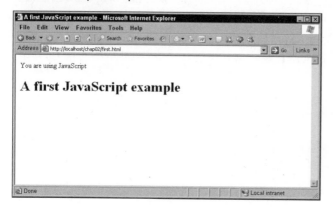

Now you've written to a Web page using a single line of JavaScript. Note that this JavaScript statement ends with a semicolon:

```
<script language="javascript">
  document.write("You are using JavaScript");
</script>
```

All JavaScript statements end with a semicolon like this one does, which is something you have to keep in mind when you're writing JavaScript.

Fixing errors

What if, in one's eagerness to get a program done, one made a programming error? Take a look at this version of the previous example. Can you spot the error?

```
<html>
  <head>
    <title>A first JavaScript example</title>

    <script language="javascript">
      document.writ("You are using JavaScript");
    </script>
  </head>

  <body>
    <h1>A first JavaScript example</h1>
  </body>
</html>
```

If you saw that `document.write` was incorrectly written as `document.writ`, you're correct. Because the document object doesn't have a method named `writ`, no browser is going to be able to run this example. However, the way various browsers handle this issue differs by browser, and that means the tools each browser offers to fix the problem differ.

Internet Explorer gives you the display shown in Figure 2.4. All you see is the `<h1>` heading in the `<body>` element — no output from JavaScript.

FIGURE 2.4

A JavaScript error in Internet Explorer

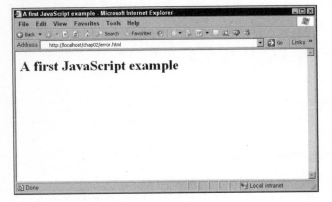

Note in particular the small icon in the lower left corner in the Internet Explorer window, which shows a triangle with an exclamation point. That's Internet Explorer's way of indicating that there's a JavaScript problem. Double-clicking that icon opens a dialog box, as shown in Figure 2.5.

FIGURE 2.5

Examining a JavaScript error in Internet Explorer

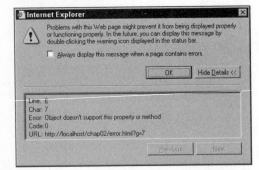

You can see that the error message in Figure 2.5 says, "Object doesn't support this property or method" and indicates the correct line number. Examining your code with this information lets you correct the problem.

Looks like Internet Explorer is going to be helpful debugging JavaScript, right? Unfortunately, it's not. The error message you see in Figure 2.5 is about the only one Internet Explorer displays. Even if your JavaScript is so fouled up that none of it can run, you're still only going to get "Object doesn't support this property or method."

Ajax developers deserve better, and there is better available in Firefox, the alternative to Internet Explorer. You should have Firefox on hand as you develop your Ajax applications, not just because many people use Firefox and so you should develop for that browser in addition to Internet Explorer, but because of its excellent debugging help. Firefox really tells you what's wrong with your script, whereas Internet Explorer only leaves you scratching your head.

This example is shown in Firefox in Figure 2.6. As the figure shows, you're not getting the results you expected; nothing has been written to the browser window using JavaScript.

FIGURE 2.6

A JavaScript problem in Firefox

How can you determine the problem? Select Tools ➪ JavaScript Console to open the JavaScript console, as shown in Figure 2.7.

FIGURE 2.7

Examining a JavaScript problem in Firefox's JavaScript console

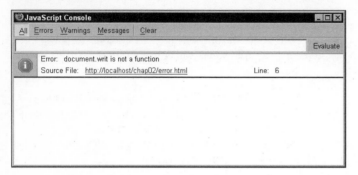

The JavaScript console is a very useful tool because unlike Internet Explorer, it's been written to really pinpoint problems and to tell you about them. As you see, the error message here pinpoints `document.writ` as the problem.

If you're going to be developing lots of JavaScript — and which Ajax developer doesn't? — it's a good idea to get Firefox running on your machine. Doing so can make the debugging process much, much easier.

Commenting your code

As with most programming languages, you can also add *comments* to your JavaScript scripts. A comment is human-readable text that annotates your code. In JavaScript, you can use \\ to start a comment, and adding comments to your code makes it easier for people to understand what's going on in that code.

For example, to add the comment "Use document.write to display a message" to your first script, you could do this:

```
<html>
  <head>
    <title>A first JavaScript example</title>

    <script language="javascript">
      //Use document.write to display a message
      document.write("You are using JavaScript");
    </script>
  </head>

  <body>
    <h1>A first JavaScript example</h1>
  </body>
</html>
```

You can also create a comment at the end of a line using //, like this:

```html
<html>
  <head>
    <title>A first JavaScript example</title>

    <script language="javascript">
      document.write("You are using JavaScript"); //Display
        message
    </script>
  </head>

  <body>
    <h1>A first JavaScript example</h1>
  </body>
</html>
```

There's another kind of comment in JavaScript, the /* */ comment, which lets you divide a comment up over multiple lines. When the browser sees /* in your script, it stops reading until it encounters */, no matter how many lines that takes. In other words, // is for single-line comments, and /* */ is for multi-line comments. Here's an example:

```html
<html>
  <head>
    <title>A first JavaScript example</title>

    <script language="javascript">
      /* Use document.write
         to display
         a message */
      document.write("You are using JavaScript");
    </script>
  </head>

  <body>
    <h1>A first JavaScript example</h1>
  </body>
</html>
```

The // marker prevents the browser from reading any more text from that point to the end of the line, so feel free to sprinkle your code with comments.

Putting your code in external script files

Here's another JavaScript skill you're going to need in this book and when you work with Ajax: placing your JavaScript code in external JavaScript files. Here's how it works: simply place your JavaScript code, which is this single statement here:

```javascript
document.write("You are using JavaScript");
```

in a separate script file named, for example, script.js.

Then you can refer to script.js and include it in your Web page using the `<script>` element's `src` attribute, like this:

```
<html>
  <head>
    <title>A first JavaScript example</title>

    <script language="javascript" src="script.js">
  </head>

  <body>
    <h1>A first JavaScript example</h1>
  </body>
</html>
```

That's all it takes. Now you can store your JavaScript in external files, which is great if your JavaScript is getting long and/or you want to share it between Web pages. As you're also going to see in this book, there are many Ajax frameworks available for free online. Such frameworks do the Ajax programming for you, saving you lots of time and effort, and those frameworks are usually external JavaScript files.

Responding to browser events

So far, the code you've written runs when the Web page containing it loads. That's because the code is simply stored in a `<script>` element:

```
<html>
  <head>
    <title>A first JavaScript example</title>

    <script language="javascript">
      document.write("You are using JavaScript");
    </script>
  </head>

  <body>
    <h1>A first JavaScript example</h1>
  </body>
</html>
```

Code like this that is simply placed directly in a `<script>` element executes immediately when a Web page loads. But that's not the way Ajax applications work. They usually wait until the user does something: clicks a button, types something, and so on. They do that by responding to user events.

An event occurs when something happens in the browser: the mouse moves or is clicked, a scroll bar is scrolled, a button is pressed, and so on. When an event occurs, your JavaScript code can be notified of the event, which means that your code can respond to that event appropriately.

What events are available? Here are some common events you might see in Ajax applications:

- `onabort`: Happens when an action is aborted.
- `onblur`: Happens when an element loses the input focus.
- `onchange`: Happens when data in a control, like a text field, changes.
- `onclick`: Happens when an element is clicked.
- `ondblclick`: Happens when an element is double-clicked.
- `ondragdrop`: Happens when a drag-drop operation is undertaken.
- `onerror`: Happens when there's been a JavaScript error.
- `onfocus`: Happens when an element gets the focus.
- `onkeydown`: Happens when a key goes down.
- `onkeypress`: Happens when a key is pressed and the key code is available.
- `onkeyup`: Happens when a key goes up.
- `onload`: Happens when the page loads.
- `onmousedown`: Happens when a mouse button goes down.
- `onmousemove`: Happens when the mouse moves.
- `onmouseout`: Happens when the mouse leaves an element.
- `onmouseover`: Happens when the mouse moves over an element.
- `onmouseup`: Happens when a mouse button goes up.
- `onreset`: Happens when the user clicks a Reset button.
- `onresize`: Happens when an element or page is resized.
- `onsubmit`: Happens when the user clicks a Submit button.
- `onunload`: Happens when a page is unloaded.

These are event attributes that you use with HTML tags. How does that work? For example, the document itself is represented by the `<body>` element, so you can use an attribute like `onmousedown` to catch when a mouse button is pushed.

So how do you put all this to work? Here's a simple example, making use of the fact that you can create inline scripts in JavaScript — that is, short scripts that you can assign to an event attribute like onmousedown, no <script> element needed. This example uses JavaScript to display a dialog box called an alert box with the text "You clicked the page" in it:

```
<html>
    <head>
        <title>
            Using JavaScript events
        </title>
    </head>

    <body onmousedown="alert('You clicked the page.')">
        <h1>
            Clicking this page will display an alert box.
        </h1>
        Give it a try.
    </body>
</html>
```

This example works this way: the user presses the mouse button, and the onmousedown event occurs, which executes any code connected to that event. In this case, the JavaScript that executes is alert('You clicked the page.'), which displays an alert box as shown in Figure 2.8.

FIGURE 2.8

Handling an onmousedown event

One thing to note about inline scripts like this: Because you assign them to event attributes like onmousedown, you have to enclose them inside quotation marks. If you have to use quotation marks in your code itself, make them single quotation marks, like this:

```
<body onmousedown="alert('You clicked the page.')">
```

Why single quotation marks? JavaScript can handle both single and double quotation marks, and that allows you to alternate them if needed. In other words, this is legal JavaScript:

```
alert('You clicked the page.')
```

and so is this:

```
alert("You clicked the page.")
```

That means you can enclose inline JavaScript inside double quotation marks if you alternate double and single quotation marks. For example, if you used all double quotation marks like this:

```
<body onmousedown="alert("You clicked the page.")">
```

JavaScript would get confused. Where does the quotation begin and where does it end? For that reason, alternate double and single quotation marks like this:

```
<body onmousedown="alert('You clicked the page.')">
```

Okay so far, but inline scripts are designed for very short pieces of code. What if you wanted to connect an event attribute like onmousedown to code in a <script> element? For that, you have to use JavaScript *functions*.

Creating JavaScript Functions

This is the script you developed earlier in this chapter to display a message:

```
<html>
  <head>
    <title>A first JavaScript example</title>

    <script language="javascript">
      document.write("You are using JavaScript");
    </script>
  </head>

  <body>
    <h1>A first JavaScript example</h1>
  </body>
</html>
```

The JavaScript document.write("You are using JavaScript"); is executed as soon as the <head> section is loaded, which means that the message "You are using JavaScript" appears in the Web page before the header, "A first JavaScript example," does, as you saw earlier in Figure 2.3.

That's fine as far as it goes, but isn't that a little backward? After all, shouldn't the header come first? How can you make it work that way?

Here's how: place the <script> element in the <body> of the Web page, which means the code in the <script> element won't be executed until after the header has already been displayed, like this:

```
<html>
  <head>
    <title>A first JavaScript example</title>

  </head>
```

```
<body>
  <h1>A first JavaScript example</h1>
  <script language="javascript">
    document.write("You are using JavaScript");
  </script>
</body>
</html>
```

Here, the header appears first, followed by the text "You are using JavaScript." In other words, where you place your <script> element in a Web page determines when it is executed.

On the other hand, the modern way of doing things is to place the <script> element in the <head> section of a Web page. So how can you make that work? How can you make your code in a <script> element execute only when you want it to?

That's what functions are all about. By placing your code in a function, that code won't be executed until you call the function. A JavaScript *function* is a set of code statements that are specifically executed only when you want them to be. Those statements are set off from the rest of your code by surrounding them with { and } in the body of the function.

> **NOTE**   A function is just like the methods you've already seen — like the `document` object's `write` method — except that a function isn't connected to an object.

For example, say you wanted to create a function named showMessage. That would look like this in the <script> element:

```
<html>
  <head>
    <title>A first JavaScript example</title>

    <script language="javascript">
      function showMessage ()
      {
          .
          .
          .
      }
    </script>
  </head>

  <body>
    <h1>A first JavaScript example</h1>
  </body>
</html>
```

Note how this works: You use the keyword function to define a new function, then give the name of the function, followed by a pair of parentheses (more on what those parentheses are for later in this chapter). Then you use curly braces, { and }, to enclose the JavaScript statements you want to have run when the function is called.

How do you call this function? You just have to use its name as a JavaScript statement. In this case, you can use browser events to call this function. In particular, you want to call the function after the <body> element has been loaded. You can make sure the <body> element has been loaded with the onload event attribute like this:

```html
<html>
  <head>
    <title>A first JavaScript example</title>

    <script language="javascript">
      function showMessage ()
      {
          .
          .
          .
      }
    </script>
  </head>

  <body onload="">
    <h1>A first JavaScript example</h1>
  </body>
</html>
```

So how do you actually call the showMessage function using the onload attribute? You just have to use the name of the function, followed by parentheses, as a JavaScript statement, so you call that function when the <body> element has been fully loaded like this:

```html
<html>
  <head>
    <title>A first JavaScript example</title>

    <script language="javascript">
      function showMessage ()
      {
          .
          .
          .
      }
    </script>
  </head>

  <body onload="showMessage()">
    <h1>A first JavaScript example</h1>
  </body>
</html>
```

Excellent; you're making progress.

You now might be wondering if you can simply place the document.write call in the showMessage function to display the message "You are using JavaScript" like this:

```html
<html>
  <head>
    <title>A first JavaScript example</title>

    <script language="javascript">
      function showMessage ()
      {

        document.write("You are using JavaScript");

      }
    </script>
  </head>

  <body onload="showMessage()">
    <h1>A first JavaScript example</h1>
  </body>
</html>
```

Sadly, the answer is no. The showMessage function will indeed be called after the body of the page loads, and that's fine. But there's a catch: when the body is loaded, you can no longer use the document.write method because the document is considered *closed*. And opening it again to write to it clears any text in it, so that's no good here. All you'd see is the "You are using JavaScript" message because the "A first JavaScript example" header will have been overwritten.

So what can you do? You can do what all Ajax applications do when faced with this issue: you can write the message to a specific part of the Web page. For example, say that you add a <div> element and name it targetDiv, like this:

```html
<html>
  <head>
    <title>A first JavaScript example</title>

    <script language="javascript">
      function showMessage ()
      {
        document.write("You are using JavaScript");
      }
    </script>
  </head>

  <body onload="showMessage()">
    <h1>A first JavaScript example</h1>
```

```
      <div id="targetDiv">
      </div>

   </body>
</html>
```

Now when the showMessage function is called, you can write the message to the targetDiv `<div>` element. You can get a JavaScript object corresponding to that `<div>` element with the JavaScript expression `document.getElementById('targetDiv')`. The object corresponding to the `<div>` element supports a number of properties, such as the innherHTML property, corresponding to the HTML inside the `<div>` element. To rewrite that HTML, and so display the message, you need only to assign the text of the message to the `<div>` element's innerHTML property in messager.html like this:

```
<html>
  <head>
    <title>A first JavaScript example</title>

    <script language="javascript">
      function showMessage ()
      {
        document.getElementById('targetDiv').innerHTML =
          "You are using JavaScript";
      }
    </script>
  </head>

  <body onload="showMessage()">
    <h1>A first JavaScript example</h1>

    <div id="targetDiv">
    </div>

  </body>
</html>
```

You can see the results in Figure 2.9. The message was indeed written to the body of the page after the header, all thanks to the magic of functions, which let you call JavaScript code when you're ready to execute that code.

FIGURE 2.9

Writing a message to a Web page

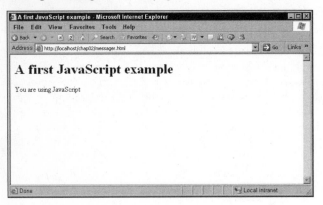

Note the following line of code from earlier in the chapter:

```
document.write("You are using JavaScript");
```

Here, you're writing the text "You are using JavaScript" to a Web page. You do that by passing the text to write to the `write` method. In fact, you can also pass data to the functions you write as well (remember, the difference between a function and a method is simply that a method is a function built into an object), and that's coming up next.

Passing arguments to functions

Being able to pass data to functions is an important part of JavaScript because passing data to functions means those functions can work on that data, and they can even pass you back results. For example, you might have a function that adds two numbers and gives you a result, and to use that function, you have to be able to pass it the two numbers to add.

Say, for example, that you want to pass the message text to display in the Web page to the `showMessage` function rather than simply having that function automatically display the text "You are using JavaScript." How could you do that?

You start by specifying a name you want to refer to the message text by in the body of the function. If you want to refer to that text by the name "message," for example, you do so by placing the name `message` in the parentheses after the name of the `showMessage` function. `message` is now called an *argument* of the `showMessage` function:

```
<html>
  <head>
    <title>Passing function arguments</title>
```

```
    <script language="javascript">
      function showMessage (message)
      {
        document.getElementById('targetDiv').innerHTML =
          "You are using JavaScript";
      }
    </script>
  </head>

  <body onload="showMessage()">
    <h1>Passing function arguments</h1>

    <div id="targetDiv">
    </div>

  </body>
</html>
```

In the body of the showMessage function, you can refer to the text passed to the function using the name message, which means you can assign that text to the targetDiv <div> element like this:

```
<html>
  <head>
    <title>Passing function arguments</title>

    <script language="javascript">
      function showMessage (message)
      {
        document.getElementById('targetDiv').innerHTML = message;
      }
    </script>
  </head>

  <body onload="showMessage()">
    <h1>Passing function arguments</h1>

    <div id="targetDiv">
    </div>

  </body>
</html>
```

Great! This sets up the showMessage function. Now you can pass text to that function simply by placing that text inside the parentheses when you call the function. For example, you might want to display the message "You are seeing this thanks to JavaScript." You could do that like this in the Web page, messagerArguments.html:

```html
<html>
  <head>
    <title>Passing function arguments</title>

    <script language="javascript">
      function showMessage (message)
      {
         document.getElementById('targetDiv').innerHTML = message;
      }
    </script>
  </head>

  <body onload="showMessage(
    'You are seeing this thanks to JavaScript')">
    <h1>Passing function arguments</h1>

    <div id="targetDiv">
    </div>

  </body>
</html>
```

The results are shown in Figure 2.10, where the text you passed to the showMessage function was indeed faithfully displayed. Not bad.

Writing a message to a Web page using function arguments

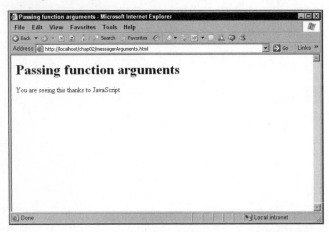

Note that this example uses a <div> element to display text. Another element you'll frequently use in Ajax applications is the <span> element. The <div> element is a block element, which means that it get its own line in the browser's display. The <span> element, on the other hand, is an inline element, which means that you can use it to change the text inside sentences or other text.

Take a look at this example, span.html, which displays text in a <span> element:

```html
<html>
  <head>
    <title>Using a &lt;span&gt; to display text</title>

    <script language="javascript">
      function showMessage (message)
      {
        document.getElementById('targetSpan').innerHTML =
          message;
      }
    </script>
  </head>

  <body onload="showMessage(
    'You are seeing this thanks to JavaScript')">
    <h1>Using a &lt;span&gt; to display text</h1>

    Here is the message: <span id="targetSpan">
    </span>.

  </body>
</html>
```

The results are shown in Figure 2.11. Note that the text of the message appears inline in the sentence at the bottom of the page.

FIGURE 2.11

Writing text using a <span> element

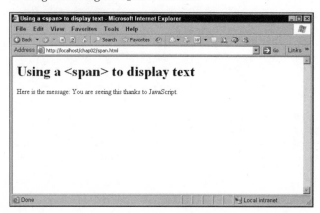

NOTE When you're working with Ajax, it's important to be able to insert data into a Web page where you want that data to go; and one of the most common techniques to do that is to use `<div>` and `<span>` elements, as you've just seen. The `<div>` element is the most popular, but it's a block element, which means it gets its own line in the display; and if you don't want that, you can always use an inline `<span>` element.

There's still more to consider when passing arguments to JavaScript functions. You can pass multiple arguments, not just the single arguments you've seen so far. Handling multiple arguments is just about as easy as handling single arguments: you just list them inside the parentheses, separated by commas, when creating a function. For example, say you wanted to pass the name of the `<div>` element to display text in the `showMessage` function. You could do that like this in a new Web page, multipleArguments.html:

```
<html>
  <head>
    <title>Passing multiple function arguments</title>

    <script language="javascript">
      function showMessage (message, divName)
      {
        document.getElementById(divName).innerHTML = message;
      }
    </script>
  </head>

  <body onload="showMessage(
    'You are seeing this thanks to JavaScript')">
    <h1>Passing multiple function arguments</h1>

    <div id="targetDiv">
    </div>

  </body>
</html>
```

And when you pass multiple arguments to the function, you also separate those arguments with commas:

```
<html>
  <head>
    <title>Passing multiple function arguments</title>

    <script language="javascript">
      function showMessage (message, divName)
      {
        document.getElementById(divName).innerHTML = message;
      }
    </script>
  </head>
```

```
<body onload="showMessage(
  'You are seeing this thanks to JavaScript', 'targetDiv')">
  <h1>Passing multiple function arguments</h1>

  <div id="targetDiv">
  </div>

</body>
</html>
```

And that's all you need. This Web page gives you the same result as the messagerArguments.html Web page did earlier.

There's still more that you can do with functions: you can *return values* from functions.

Returning values from functions

Functions act as self-contained sections of code. As the name indicates, each function is usually designed to have a single function, that is, perform a single task. The idea is that you can divide and conquer your programming by segmenting it up into self-contained functions. You already know that you can pass data to functions so that they perform their tasks. What about letting them communicate the results of those tasks back to you?

That's where returning values from functions comes in. You can let a function handle the data you've sent it and send you back the results of its calculation. For example, say that you want to add two numbers using a function named adder and display the results. To do that, you might create a new function, adder, and pass two numbers to add to that function.

Here's how you might pass two numbers, 5 and 3, to adder and display the results:

```
<html>
  <head>
    <title>Returning values from functions</title>

    <script language="javascript">
      function showMessage ()
      {
        document.getElementById("targetDiv").innerHTML =
          "5 + 3 = " + adder(5, 3);
      }

    </script>
  </head>

  <body onload="showMessage()">
    <h1>Returning values from functions</h1>
```

```
        <div id="targetDiv">
        </div>

    </body>
  </html>
```

There are two things to note here: first, the expression `adder(5, 3)` will be replaced by the results returned from the `adder` function, which is 8. Second, note that you can join strings together in JavaScript by using a +, like this: `"5 + 3 = " + adder(5, 3)`. This gives you `"5 + 3 = 8"`.

What about creating the `adder` function? That looks like this:

```
<html>
  <head>
    <title>Returning values from functions</title>

    <script language="javascript">
      function showMessage ()
      {
        document.getElementById("targetDiv").innerHTML =
          "5 + 3 = " + adder(5, 3);
      }

      function adder(operand1, operand2)
      {
         .
         .
         .
      }
    </script>
  </head>

  <body onload="showMessage()">
    <h1>Returning values from functions</h1>

    <div id="targetDiv">
    </div>

  </body>
</html>
```

So how do you actually add two numbers and return a value from the `adder` function? You can use + in JavaScript to add the two numbers passed to the `adder` function, and you use the `return` statement to return a value from a function, so the `adder` function's body looks like this:

```
<html>
  <head>
    <title>Returning values from functions</title>

    <script language="javascript">
      function showMessage ()
      {
        document.getElementById("targetDiv").innerHTML =
          "5 + 3 = " + adder(5, 3);
      }

      function adder(operand1, operand2)
      {
        return operand1 + operand2;
      }
    </script>
  </head>

  <body onload="showMessage()">
    <h1>Returning values from functions</h1>

    <div id="targetDiv">
    </div>

  </body>
</html>
```

Excellent; that's all you need. You can see the results in Figure 2.12, where 5 and 3 were indeed passed to the adder function, which returned a value of 8.

Returning values from functions

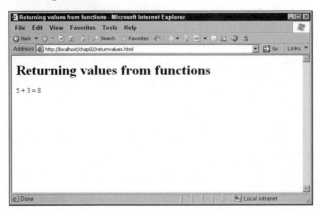

Storing Your Data in Variables

In general, Ajax applications can use JavaScript pretty intensively, and, among other things, that means handling data like the current price of music CDs, the number of LCD monitors in stock, the temperature in San Francisco, and so on. And in JavaScript, you can store data using *variables*.

For example, say that you want to store the message "This data was stored in a variable" in a variable, and use that variable to display that message. You can do it by creating a variable named, for example, `message`, to contain that text. You create a variable using the JavaScript `var` statement; after you've created a variable and assigned a value to it, you can use the variable in statements, like this in variables.html, where the value in the `message` variable is assigned to the target `<div>` element:

```
<html>
  <head>
    <title>Working with variables</title>

    <script language="javascript">

      var message = "This data was stored in a variable.";

      function showMessage ()
      {
        document.getElementById('targetDiv').innerHTML = message
      }
    </script>
  </head>

  <body onload="showMessage()">
    <h1>Working with variables</h1>

    <div id="targetDiv">
    </div>

  </body>
</html>
```

Figure 2.13 shows the results. Now you've stored data in JavaScript variables and retrieved that data in order to display it.

FIGURE 2.13

Storing data in variables

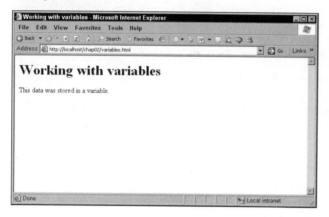

Besides text, you can also store numbers in variables. For example, say you wanted to change the adder function so that it adds the two numbers passed to it in a variable named sum, and then returns the value in that variable from the function? You could do it like this:

```html
<html>
  <head>
    <title>Returning values from functions</title>

    <script language="javascript">
      function showMessage ()
      {
        document.getElementById("targetDiv").innerHTML =
          "5 + 3 = " + adder(5, 3);
      }

      function adder(operand1, operand2)
      {
        var sum = operand1 + operand2;
        return sum;
      }
    </script>
  </head>

  <body onload="showMessage()">
    <h1>Returning values from functions</h1>

    <div id="targetDiv">
    </div>
```

```
    </body>
</html>
```

There is one more point to make about variables, and that has to do with functions. Did you notice that the message variable was declared outside any function?

```
var message = "This data was stored in a variable.";

function showMessage ()
{
  document.getElementById('targetDiv').innerHTML = message

}
```

while the sum variable was declared inside the adder function?

```
function adder(operand1, operand2)
{
  var sum = operand1 + operand2;
  return sum;
}
```

That makes message a *global* variable, while sum is a *local* variable, that is, local to the adder function. Global variables — those declared outside any function — are available anywhere in your code, and local variables — those declared inside a function — are available only in that function.

Here's another thing to know about variables: variables created inside a function will be reset to their original values each time the function is called. Not knowing that has stymied many JavaScript programmers. If you don't want that to happen, place the var statement to create the variables you want to use outside the function.

Operating on Your Data with Operators

You've already seen that you can use + to add two numbers together:

```
function adder(operand1, operand2)
{
  return operand1 + operand2;
}
```

The + here is a JavaScript *operator*, and you use operators to work on your data. There are many JavaScript operators besides +; for example, you can use * to multiply two numbers together:

```
function multiplier(operand1, operand2)
{
  return operand1 * operand2;
}
```

The addition operator is +, the multiplication operator is *, the subtraction operator is −, and the division operator is /. What other operators are available? You can see them all in Table 2.1. (Don't try to memorize what you see there. Come back to this table throughout the book as needed.)

TABLE 2.1

JavaScript Operators

Operator	Description
Arithmetic Operators	
+	Adds two numbers.
++	Increments the value in a variable by one.
-	Subtracts one number from another. Also can change the sign of its operand like this: -variableName.
--	Decrements the value in a variable by one.
*	Multiplies two numbers.
/	Divides two numbers.
%	Evaluates to the remainder after dividing two numbers using integer division.
String Operators	
+	Joins (concatenates) two strings.
+=	Joins (concatenates) two strings and assigns the joined string to the first operand.
Logical Operators	
&&	Evaluates to true if both operands are true; otherwise, evaluates to false.
||	Evaluates to true if either operand is true. However, if both operands are false, evaluates to false.
!	Evaluates to false if its operand is true, true if its operand is false.
Bitwise Operators	
&	Sets a 1 in each bit position of both operands.
^	Sets a 1 in a bit position if the bits of one operand, but not both operands, are one.
|	Sets a 1 in a bit if either operand has a 1 in that position.
~	Flips each bit.
<<	Shifts the bits of its first operand to the left by the number of places specified by the second operand.
>>	Shifts the bits of the first operand to the right by the number of places specified by the second operand.
>>>	Shifts the bits of the first operand to the right by the number of places specified by the second operand, and shifting in zeros from the left.

continued

TABLE 2.1 (continued)

Operator	Description
Assignment Operators	
=	Assigns the value of the second operand to the first operand.
+=	Adds two operands and assigns the result to the first operand.
-=	Subtracts two operands and assigns the result to the first operand.
*=	Multiplies two operands and assigns the result to the first operand.
/=	Divides two operands and assigns the result to the first operand.
%=	Calculates the modulus of two operands and assigns the result to the first operand.
&=	Performs a bitwise AND operation on two operands and assigns the result to the first operand.
^=	Performs a bitwise exclusive OR operation on two operands and assigns the result to the first operand.
|=	Performs a bitwise OR operation on two operands and assigns the result to the first operand.
<<=	Performs a left shift operation on two operands and assigns the result to the first operand.
>>=	Performs a sign-propagating right shift operation on two operands and assigns the result to the first operand.
>>>=	Performs a zero-fill right shift operation on two operands and assigns the result to the first operand.
Comparison Operators	
==	Evaluates to true if the two operands are equal to each other.
!=	Evaluates to true if the two operands are not equal to each other.
===	Evaluates to true if the two operands are both equal and of the same type.
!==	Evaluates to true if the two operands are either not equal and/or not of the same type.
>	Evaluates to true if the first operand's value is greater than the second operand's value.
>=	Evaluates to true if the first operand's value is greater than or equal to the second operand's value.
<	Evaluates to true if the first operand's value is less than the second operand's value.
<=	Less-than-or-equal-to operator. Evaluates to true if the first operand's value is less than or equal to the second operand's value.

Operator	Description
Special Operators	
?:	Performs an "if...else" test.
,	Evaluates two expressions and returns the result of evaluating the second expression.
delete	Deletes an object and removes it from memory, or deletes an object's property, or deletes an element in an array.
function	Creates an anonymous function. (See Chapter 3.)
in	Evaluates to true if the property you're testing is supported by a specific object.
instanceof	Evaluates to true if the given object is an instance of the specified type.
new	Creates a new object from the specified object type.
typeof	Evaluates to the name of the type of the operand.
Void	Allows evaluation of an expression without returning any value.

You can use combination operators, like +=, to perform both an operation and to assign the results of that operation to a variable, all in one step. For example, you could do this to add 5 to the value in temperature:

```
var temperature;
temperature = 72;
temperature = temperature + 5;
```

But you can also use the shortcut operator += to do the addition and assignment together, like this:

```
var temperature;
temperature = 72;
temperature += 5;
```

Similarly, there are -=, *=, and other combination operators.

What about the ==, >, <, <=, operators in Table 2.1? You use them to make decisions in JavaScript, executing some code if a particular condition is true and other code if that condition is false, which is discussed next.

Making Decisions with the If Statement

In JavaScript, you can use the if statement to test whether a certain condition is true and execute code based on the answer. For example, you might want to test whether you have over $1,000 in your bank account, and if so, take appropriate action (time for a party!).

The if statement also includes an optional else clause that holds code to be executed if the test condition was false. Here's what the syntax of this statement looks like, formally speaking (note that the code to execute is between curly braces, { and }, and that the part in standard braces, [and], is optional):

```
if (condition) {
    statements1
}
[else {
    statements2
}]
```

How about an example? Do you have more than $1,000 in your bank account? If so, this next example, if.html, will display the message "Time for a party!":

```
<html>
  <head>
    <title>Using the if statement</title>

    <script language="javascript">

      function showMessage()
      {
        var account = 2000;
        if(account > 1000) {
            document.getElementById('targetDiv').innerHTML =
                "Time for a party!";
        }
      }
    </script>

  </head>

  <body onload="showMessage()">

    <h1>Using the if statement</h1>

    <div id="targetDiv">
    </div>

    </body>
  </html>
```

How does it work? To check the amount in the account variable, this example uses the > greater than operator (see Table 2.1). The expression account > 1000 is true if account holds more than 1000, which it does. That means that the code inside the if statement's body (the part between { and }) executes:

```
var account = 2000;
if(account > 1000) {
  document.getElementById('targetDiv').innerHTML =
    "Time for a party!";
}
```

The results are shown in Figure 2.14. As you can see, it's time for a party.

Using the `if` statement

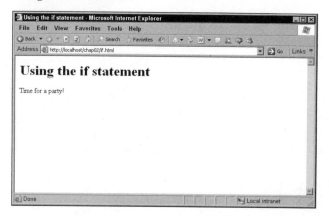

What if the amount in the account is $1,000 or less? You can execute code in that case using an `else` statement. That is, if the condition of the `if` statement is false, the code in the `else` statement, if there is one, executes instead. In that case, there's not going to be a party, and everyone should get back to work. Here's how it looks in code, in else.html—note that the account now holds $900, so the `else` statement will be triggered:

```
<html>
  <head>
    <title>Using the else statement</title>

    <script language="javascript">

      function showMessage()
      {
        var account = 900;
        if(account > 1000) {
            document.getElementById('targetDiv').innerHTML =
                "Time for a party!";
        }
        else {
```

```
            document.getElementById('targetDiv').innerHTML =
                "Get back to work!";
        }
      }
   </script>

 </head>

 <body onload="showMessage()">

   <h1>Using the else statement</h1>

   <div id="targetDiv">
   </div>

   </body>
</html>
```

You can see the results in Figure 2.15. Unfortunately, it's time to get back to work.

FIGURE 2.15

Using the else statement

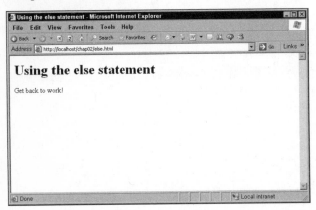

Executing Different Code in Different Browsers

One of the issues with JavaScript, as you're going to see in this book, is that you must deal with different browsers in different ways. This is because the set of objects each browser supports is different, and the way you work with them is different. Fortunately, now that you know about the if statement, you can handle the major browsers in different ways.

The following example works by checking which browser the user has, and executing code accordingly. For example, the way you create an XMLHttpRequest object, which is the very heart of Ajax, is very different in Internet Explorer than in Firefox. To check which browser the user has, you can use the navigator object, which is built into all browsers to support JavaScript. Here are the relevant properties of this object:

- navigator.AppName: The type of the browser.

- navigator.AppVersion: The version of the browser.

- navigator.UserAgent: Additional information about the browser.

For example, here's a script that displays these properties in a Web page, browsers.html:

```html
<html>
    <head>
        <title>
            Getting browser information
        </title>
        <script language="javascript">
            function showMessage()
            {
                var text = "Your browser is " + navigator.appName;
                text += "<br><br>";
                text += "Your browser's version is  " +
                    navigator.appVersion;
                text += "<br><br>";
                text += "Here is the full information: " +
                navigator.userAgent;
                document.getElementById("targetDiv").innerHTML =
                    text;
            }
        </script>
    </head>

    <body onload="showMessage()">

        <h1>Getting browser information</h1>

        <div id="targetDiv">
        </div>
    </body>
</html>
```

You can see what this page looks like in Firefox in Figure 2.16, and in Internet Explorer in Figure 2.17.

FIGURE 2.16

Determining that the user's browser is Firefox

FIGURE 2.17

Determining that the user's browser is Internet Explorer

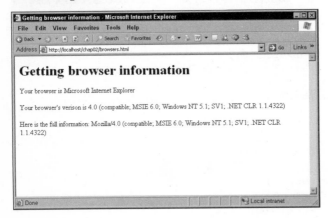

How about executing code depending on which browser the user has? Here's another example that lets you do just that, and it uses the `if` and `else` statements, as well as some JavaScript string-handling properties and methods:

- The `length` property of a string returns the length of the string.

- The `indexOf` method finds the occurrence of a substring in a string and returns the location of the first match, or –1 if there was no match. Note that the first character of a string is considered character 0.

- The `substring` method extracts a substring from a larger string. You pass this method the start and end positions of the substring to extract.

Here's how this example, checkBrowser.html, works: it uses JavaScript to search the `naviga-tor.userAgent` property, which, as you've already seen in this chapter, holds the browser name and version, extracts that information, and displays it. You can see how the code selects browser type with the `if` statements (don't bother to memorize this code, just put it to use in your own Ajax applications). You can easily modify the `if` statements in this example to execute code only for specific browsers — the code in the first `if` statement is executed if the user has Firefox:

```html
<html>
  <head>
    <title>
      Determining browser type and version
    </title>

    <script language="javascript">

    var begin, end

    function showMessage()
    {
      if(navigator.appName == "Netscape") {
        if(navigator.userAgent.indexOf("Firefox") > 0) {
          begin = navigator.userAgent.indexOf("Firefox") +
          "Firefox".length + 1;
          end = navigator.userAgent.length;
          document.getElementById("targetDiv").innerHTML =
            "You are using Firefox " +
            navigator.userAgent.substring(begin, end);
        }
      }
        .
        .
        .
```

And the code in the other `if` statement is executed if the user has Internet Explorer:

```html
<html>
  <head>
    <title>
      Determining browser type and version
    </title>

    <script language="javascript">

    var begin, end

    function showMessage()
    {
      if(navigator.appName == "Netscape") {
        if(navigator.userAgent.indexOf("Firefox") > 0) {
```

```
            begin = navigator.userAgent.indexOf("Firefox") +
            "Firefox".length + 1;
            end = navigator.userAgent.length;
            document.getElementById("targetDiv").innerHTML =
              "You are using Firefox " +
              navigator.userAgent.substring(begin, end);
          }
        }

        if (navigator.appName == "Microsoft Internet Explorer") {
          begin = navigator.userAgent.indexOf("MSIE ") +
          "MSIE ".length;
          if(navigator.userAgent.indexOf(";", begin) > 0) {
            end = navigator.userAgent.indexOf(";", begin);
          } else {
            end = navigator.userAgent.indexOf(")", begin)
              + 2;
          }
          document.getElementById("targetDiv").innerHTML =
            "You are using Internet Explorer " +
            navigator.userAgent.substring(begin, end);
        }
      }
    </script>
  </head>

  <body onload="showMessage()">
    <h1>Determining browser type and version</h1>
      <div ID="targetDiv"></div>
  </body>
</html>
```

As it is, this application uses the `if` statements to display the browser type and version. The results in Firefox are shown in Figure 2.18, and the results for Internet Explorer are shown in Figure 2.19. As you can see, alternate code was executed in those two browsers. Very cool.

Okay, you've seen the `if` statement and the `else` statement, which let you make choices at run time, and execute different code depending on the true/false condition you test. The next step up in JavaScript programming is to start working with loops.

FIGURE 2.18

Determining the user's Firefox version

FIGURE 2.19

Determining the user's Internet Explorer version

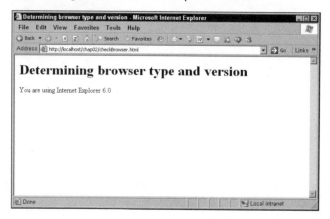

Working with Loops

Loops let you execute the same code over and over; although the code is the same each time through, the data you work on changes. That's particularly important for computers, which are great at handling large sets of data to work on. The first loop you're going to see in this chapter is the most popular one: the for loop.

Looping with the for loop

You might be in charge of inventory for a huge company, and be charged with determining the average price of all items in stock. You could do that handily with a for loop, which lets you loop over a number of items. The for loop is the most commonly used loop in JavaScript, and here's how it works:

```
for ([initial-expression]; [condition]; [increment-expression]) {
    statements
}
```

You usually use a for loop with a loop index, also named a loop counter. A loop index is a variable that keeps track of the number of times the loop has been executed. In the *initial-expression* part, you usually set the loop index to a starting value; in the *condition* part, you test that value to see whether you still want to keep on looping; and the *increment-expression* lets you increment the loop counter.

It's time for an example. Say, for example, that you wanted to add the numbers from 1 to 1,000 and display the result. Here's what that would look like in an example using the for loop, for.html:

```
<html>
  <head>
    <title>Using a for loop</title>

    <script language="javascript">

      function showMessage()
      {
        var loopIndex;
        var total = 0;

        for(loopIndex = 1; loopIndex <= 1000; loopIndex++) {
          total += loopIndex;
        }

        document.getElementById('targetDiv').innerHTML =
          "The total of 1 to 1000 is " + total;
      }
    </script>

  </head>

  <body onload="showMessage()">

    <h1>Using a for loop</h1>

    <div id="targetDiv">
    </div>

  </body>
</html>
```

Here's the for loop in this example:

```
for(loopIndex = 1; loopIndex <= 1000; loopIndex++) {
  total += loopIndex;
}
```

Note how this works: the loop index is initialized to 1, and the body of the loop is executed with that value in loopIndex. After the loop is executed, the expression loopIndex++ is executed; the ++ operator (see Table 2.1) increments its value by 1, so loopIndex ends up holding 2. Then JavaScript tests whether the condition is still true. Because that condition is loopIndex <= 1000 — that is, loopIndex is less than or equal to 1000 — the condition is true, and the body of the loop is executed again. And so the loop keeps going until all the numbers from 1 to 1000 have been added together.

What's the result? You can see the answer in Figure 2.20; adding all the numbers from 1 to 1,000 gives you 500,500.

Imagine doing this calculation by hand. Adding 1 to 1,000 would take a long time, and it's a calculation that's prone to error. But using JavaScript, it's no problem.

Besides the for loop, there's another loop you should know about — the while loop. The while loop lets you keep executing the body of the loop while a test condition is true, and it's coming up next.

FIGURE 2.20

Adding 1 to 1000 with the for loop

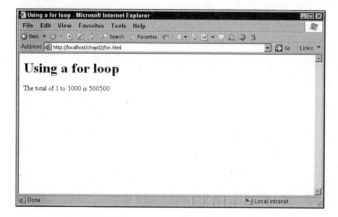

Looping with the while loop

Besides the for loop, you can also use the while loop to loop over code. In fact, the while loop is simpler than the for loop — it just keeps looping while a test condition is true:

```
while (condition) {
    statements
}
```

It's time for an example. This example is going to loop over a number of customers, from Anne to Zack, searching for a particular customer. How can you keep track of your customers? You can use an *array*, another part of JavaScript. Unlike simple variables, arrays can hold multiple data items, and they're indexed with a numeric index. For example, say you wanted to create an array named customers to keep track of your customers; you could do that like this:

```
var customers = new Array(8);
```

This creates an array of eight customers. Now you can address each of the eight as you would a simple variable, using an array index, which is placed inside square braces like this:

```
customers[0] = "Anne";
customers[1] = "Tom";
customers[2] = "Frank";
customers[3] = "Sam";
customers[4] = "Elizabeth";
customers[5] = "Nancy";
customers[6] = "Ralph";
customers[7] = "Zack";
```

Notice that the first customer has array index 0. That's because JavaScript arrays always start with array index 0. Now you can refer to each element in the array by number. For example, customers[1] holds Tom, customers[3] holds Sam, and so on. In this way, an array functions as a collection of simple variables, indexed by number.

Because arrays are indexed with numbers, they're perfect to use with loops because they act as a set of variables you can access by number, and you can increment that number in a loop (for example, that number can be a loop index in a for loop).

In this example, you want to search your customers for a particular customer, say Nancy. That is, you want to keep looping until you find Nancy. To check for equality, you can use the JavaScript == operator like this:

```
customers[loopIndex] == "Nancy"
```

This expression will be true when customers[loopIndex] holds the word "Nancy."

However, that's not exactly what you want in this case. You want to keep looping with the while loop while the current customer is *not* Nancy (the idea is to find Nancy). So you'd want to use the not equals, !=, operator like this as the test condition of the while loop:

```
customers[loopIndex] != "Nancy"
```

Here's what the while loop is going to look like:

```
var loopIndex = 0;

while(customers[loopIndex] != "Nancy"){
  loopIndex++;
}
```

When this loop ends, the `loopIndex` variable should hold the index of the array element that holds Nancy. But there's a problem here: what if there's no Nancy in the customers list? You can put a cap on the value that `loopIndex` can take so that you don't try searching past the end of the array. You do that by determining the number of elements in the array using the array's `length` property; this property returns 8 for the customers array because it has eight elements. However, because this example uses the array index, which goes from 0 to 7, you have to compare that loop index to `customers.length - 1`, not just to `customers.length`.

So how do you add the condition `loopIndex < customers.length - 1` to the `while` loop's current condition, `customers[loopIndex] != "Nancy"`? You can use the `&&` "and" operator (see Table 2.1), which insists that two conditions be true before the overall condition is true; here's what it looks like in the while loop:

```
while(customers[loopIndex] != "Nancy" && loopIndex <
  customers.length - 1){
  loopIndex++;
}
```

There's also an "or" operator, `||`, that makes a condition true if one or the other of two conditions are true — a `||` b is true if either a or b is true, or both a and b; otherwise, it's false.

Okay, this `while` loop is ready to go. Here's what the Web page that searches for Nancy, while.html, looks like:

```
<html>
  <head>
    <title>Using the while loop</title>

    <script language="javascript">

      function showMessage()
      {
        var loopIndex = 0, customers = new Array(6);

        customers[0] = "Anne";
        customers[1] = "Tom";
        customers[2] = "Frank";
        customers[3] = "Sam";
        customers[4] = "Elizabeth";
        customers[5] = "Nancy";
        customers[6] = "Ralph";
        customers[7] = "Zack";

        while(customers[loopIndex] != "Nancy" && loopIndex <
          customers.length - 1){
          loopIndex++;
        }
```

```
      if(loopIndex < customers.length - 1){
        document.getElementById('targetDiv').innerHTML =
        "I found Nancy at customer index " + loopIndex;
      }
      else {
        document.getElementById('targetDiv').innerHTML =
        "I did not find Nancy.";
      }
    }
  </script>

</head>

<body onload="showMessage()">

  <h1>Using the while loop</h1>

  <div id="targetDiv">
  </div>

</body>
</html>
```

So will this Web page be able to find Nancy? Take a look at Figure 2.21. Yes, it did indeed find Nancy.

FIGURE 2.21

Finding Nancy with the while loop

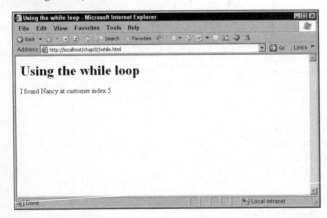

At this point, you've got all the JavaScript you're going to need in this book under your belt. You've seen basic JavaScript, working with variables, operators, the if statement, and the loops. There's just one more skill you're going to need: working with HTML controls such as buttons in Web pages.

Connecting JavaScript to HTML Buttons

When you run an Ajax application, you usually wait for the user to do something; you don't simply execute your code when the page loads, as the examples in this chapter have done so far:

```
<body onload="showMessage()">

  <h1>Using the while loop</h1>

  <div id="targetDiv">
  </div>

</body>
```

To wait for the user to do something, you can wait for a browser event to happen. Events are commonly triggered by HTML controls, such as buttons, list boxes, text fields, checkboxes, and so on.

This example shows how to connect JavaScript code to a button. To create a button, you can use an HTML <input type="button"> element inside an HTML <form> element:

```
<form>
  <input type="button" value="Click Here">
</form>
```

How do you connect this button to a JavaScript function named, for example, showMessage? You do that with the onclick event handler:

```
<form>
  <input type="button" onclick="showMessage()"
    value="Click Here">
</form>
```

That connects the button to the showMessage function, so when the user clicks the button, the showMessage function will be called. In the showMessage function, you can display a message, "You clicked the button," in a <div> element like this in the Web page buttons.html:

```
<html>
    <head>
        <title>Using buttons</title>

        <script language="javascript">
            function showMessage()
            {
              document.getElementById('targetDiv').innerHTML =
              "You clicked the button.";
            }
        </script>

    </head>
```

```
<body>
    <h1>Using buttons</h1>
    <form>
       <input type="button" onclick="showMessage()"
         value="Click Here">
    </form>

    <div id="targetDiv">
    </div>
</body>
</html>
```

You can see what this page looks like in Figure 2.22.

FIGURE 2.22

A JavaScript-enabled button

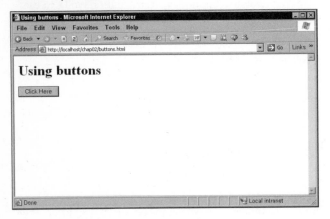

When the user clicks the button, the browser calls the `showMessage` function, which displays the message, as you can see in Figure 2.23. All of which proves that the JavaScript `showMessage` function is indeed connected to the button.

FIGURE 2.23

Responding to a button click

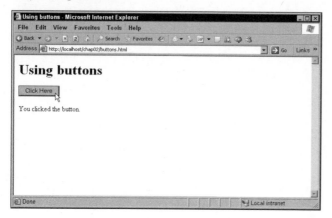

Summary

And that's it! That finishes this chapter on JavaScript. At this point, you have enough JavaScript under your belt to handle the Ajax programming in this book. Ajax is centered on JavaScript, and without JavaScript you can't do any Ajax. But now that you're all set, it's time to get started coding Ajax applications in Chapter 3.

Chapter 3

Creating Ajax Applications

It's time to write some Ajax. In this chapter you see how to write complete Ajax applications from soup to nuts. In particular, you're going to see how to create and work with the XMLHttpRequest object. Because this object is the central object on which Ajax is based, the XMLHttpRequest object is going to be at the very heart of all the Ajax applications you write.

Writing Ajax

This chapter starts by taking an in-depth look at the example you first saw in Chapter 2 — index.html, which is shown in Figure 3.1.

FIGURE 3.1

A first Ajax application

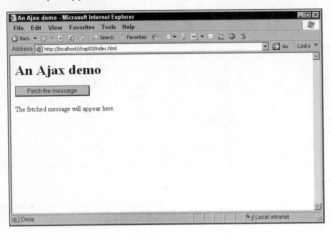

This application boasts a button with the caption "Fetch the Message." When you click that button, the application uses Ajax techniques to download text behind the scenes and display it.

The data that the application reads from the server is stored in a file named data.txt. Here are the contents of that file:

```
This text was fetched from the server with Ajax.
```

When you click the button in this application, the application downloads this text and displays it, all without a page refresh. You can see the results in Figure 3.2.

FIGURE 3.2

Downloading text using Ajax techniques

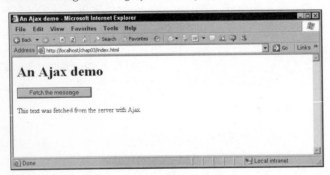

Here's what the code for this application looks like:

```html
<html>
  <head>
    <title>An Ajax demo</title>

    <script language = "javascript">
      var XMLHttpRequestObject = false;

      if (window.XMLHttpRequest) {
        XMLHttpRequestObject = new XMLHttpRequest();
      } else if (window.ActiveXObject) {
        XMLHttpRequestObject = new
          ActiveXObject("Microsoft.XMLHTTP");
      }

      function getData(dataSource, divID)
      {
        if(XMLHttpRequestObject) {
          var obj = document.getElementById(divID);
          XMLHttpRequestObject.open("GET", dataSource);

          XMLHttpRequestObject.onreadystatechange = function()
          {
            if (XMLHttpRequestObject.readyState == 4 &&
              XMLHttpRequestObject.status == 200) {
                obj.innerHTML =
                  XMLHttpRequestObject.responseText;
            }
          }

          XMLHttpRequestObject.send(null);
        }
      }
    </script>
  </head>

  <body>

    <H1>An Ajax demo</H1>

    <form>
      <input type = "button" value = "Fetch the message"
        onclick = "getData('data.txt', 'targetDiv')">
    </form>

    <div id="targetDiv">
      <p>The fetched message will appear here.</p>
    </div>
```

```
      </body>
    </html>
```

We're going to take this code apart now.

Setting up the application

This application starts by displaying the text "The fetched message will appear here" in a `<div>` element that has the ID `targetDiv`. This is where much of the action is going to take place: the code in this application is going to display the text fetched from the server in this `<div>` element. Here's what the `<div>` looks like:

```
    <body>

      <H1>An Ajax demo</H1>

      <form>
        <input type = "button" value = "Fetch the message"
          onclick = "getData('data.txt', 'targetDiv')">
      </form>

      <div id="targetDiv">
        <p>The fetched message will appear here.</p>
      </div>

    </body>
```

There's also a button whose `onclick` event attribute is connected to a JavaScript function named `getData`:

```
    <body>

      <H1>An Ajax demo</H1>

      <form>
        <input type = "button" value = "Fetch the message"
          onclick = "getData('data.txt', 'targetDiv')">
      </form>

      <div id="targetDiv">
        <p>The fetched message will appear here.</p>
      </div>

    </body>
```

Note that the `getData` function is passed two text strings: the name of the file to fetch from the server, and the ID of the `<div>` element to display the results in. So what's the next step? Seeing how the JavaScript in this application does its thing.

Writing the JavaScript

The `getData` function is in the `<script>` element in the application's Web page, and it's set up to accept two arguments: `dataSource` (the name of the file on the server to fetch) and `divID` (the ID of the `<div>` element to display the results in):

```
<script language = "javascript">

  function getData(dataSource, divID)
  {
     .
     .
     .
  }
</script>
```

Then the code checks on a variable named `XMLHttpRequestObject` to see whether it contains an object or null:

```
<script language = "javascript">

  function getData(dataSource, divID)
  {
     if(XMLHttpRequestObject) {
     .
     .
     .
     }
</script>
```

So what is this `XMLHttpRequestObject` object? This is the object that forms the basis of Ajax. The `XMLHttpRequest` object is built into modern browsers, and it lets you communicate with the server behind the scenes.

This example application creates an `XMLHttpRequest` object as soon as its Web page is loaded into the server so that that object will be available in code. All of which means it's time to create your own XMLHtppRequest object.

Creating an XMLHttpRequest object

When this application loads, it creates a variable named `XMLHttpRequestObject` and sets it to `false` like this:

```
<script language = "javascript">

  var XMLHttpRequestObject = false;
```

```
function getData(dataSource, divID)
{
  if(XMLHttpRequestObject) {
    .
    .
    .
  }
</script>
```

This variable is set to false initially so that if the attempt to create an XMLHttpRequest object fails, this variable will still hold false, which is something you can test easily in code.

> **NOTE**   You can also set JavaScript variables to a value of true. True and false are called *Boolean* values in JavaScript.

Netscape Navigator (version 7.0 and later), Apple Safari (version 1.2 and later), and Firefox let you create XMLHttpRequest objects directly with code like this:

```
XMLHttpRequestObject = new XMLHttpRequest();
```

So how do you know whether you're dealing with a browser that can create an XMLHttpRequest object this way? The XMLHttpRequest object is part of the browser's window object; you can test whether it exists using this if statement:

```
<script language = "javascript">

  var XMLHttpRequestObject = false;

  if (window.XMLHttpRequest) {
    .
    .
    .
  }
    .
    .
    .

</script>
```

If the browser can create XMLHttpRequest objects this way, you can create such an object and store it in the XMLHttpRequestObject variable like this:

```
<script language = "javascript">

  var XMLHttpRequestObject = false;
```

```
if (window.XMLHttpRequest) {
  XMLHttpRequestObject = new XMLHttpRequest();
}
  .
  .
  .

</script>
```

That takes care of Navigator, Safari, and Firefox. What if you're dealing with the Microsoft Internet Explorer? In that case, window.XMLHttpRequest is undefined; window.ActiveXObject is what you want to check instead, like this:

```
<script language = "javascript">

var XMLHttpRequestObject = false;

if (window.XMLHttpRequest) {
  XMLHttpRequestObject = new XMLHttpRequest();
} else if (window.ActiveXObject) {
  .
  .
  .
}
  .
  .
  .

</script>
```

If window.ActiveXObject exists, you can create an XMLHttpRequest object in Internet Explorer (version 5.0 and later) this way (you'll see additional ways to create XMLHttpRequest objects in Internet Explorer in the next chapter):

```
<script language = "javascript">

var XMLHttpRequestObject = false;

if (window.XMLHttpRequest) {
  XMLHttpRequestObject = new XMLHttpRequest();
} else if (window.ActiveXObject) {
  XMLHttpRequestObject = new
    ActiveXObject("Microsoft.XMLHTTP");
}
  .
  .
  .

</script>
```

Now you've got an XMLHttpRequest object — great. The basic properties and methods of this object are the same across all browsers that support it, but there are significant differences among the more advanced features of this object in different browsers. So what properties and methods are available in these objects in different browsers? The properties of the Internet Explorer XMLHttpRequest object are listed in Table 3.1, and its methods are listed in Table 3.2. The properties of this object for Mozilla, Netscape Navigator, and Firefox are listed in Table 3.3, and the methods are listed in Table 3.4. As yet, Apple hasn't published a full version of the properties and methods for its XMLHttpRequest object, but it has published a set of commonly used properties, which appear in Table 3.5, and commonly used methods, which appear in Table 3.6.

TABLE 3.1

XMLHttpRequest Object Properties for Internet Explorer

Object Property	Description
onreadystatechange	Contains the name of the event handler that should be called when the value of the readyState property changes. Read/write.
readyState	Contains state of the request. Read-only.
responseBody	Contains a response body, which is one way HTTP responses can be returned. Read-only.
responseStream	Contains a response stream, a binary stream to the server. Read-only.
responseText	Contains the response body as a string. Read-only.
responseXML	Contains the response body as XML. Read-only.
Status	Contains the HTTP status code returned by a request. Read-only.
statusText	Contains the HTTP response status text. Read-only.

TABLE 3.2

XMLHttpRequest Object Methods for Internet Explorer

Object Method	Description
abort	Aborts the HTTP request.
getAllResponseHeaders	Returns all the HTTP headers.
getResponseHeader	Returns the value of an HTTP header.
Open	Opens a request to the server.
Send	Sends an HTTP request to the server.
setRequestHeader	Sets the name and value of an HTTP header.

TABLE 3.3

XMLHttpRequest Object Properties for Mozilla, Firefox, and Netscape Navigator

Object Property	Description
`channel`	Contains the channel used to perform the request. Read-only.
`readyState`	Contains state of the request. Read-only.
`responseText`	Contains the response body as a string. Read-only.
`responseXML`	Contains the response body as XML. Read-only.
`status`	Contains the HTTP status code returned by a request. Read-only.
`statusText`	Contains the HTTP response status text. Read-only.
`onreadystatechange`	Contains the name of the event handler that should be called when the value of the `readyState` property changes. Read/write.

TABLE 3.4

XMLHttpRequest Object Methods for Mozilla, Firefox, and Netscape Navigator

Object Method	Description
`abort`	Aborts the HTTP request.
`getAllResponseHeaders`	Returns all the HTTP headers.
`getResponseHeader`	Returns the value of an HTTP header.
`openRequest`	Native (non-script) method to open a request.
`overrideMimeType`	Overrides the MIME type the server returns.
`Open`	Opens a request to the server.
`Send`	Sends an HTTP request to the server.

TABLE 3.5

XMLHttpRequest Object Properties for Apple Safari

Object Property	Description
onreadystatechange	Contains the name of the event handler that should be called when the value of the readyState property changes. Read/write.
readyState	Contains state of the request. Read-only.
responseText	Contains the response body as a string. Read-only.
responseXML	Contains the response body as XML. Read-only.
status	Contains the HTTP status code returned by a request. Read-only.
statusText	Contains the HTTP response status text. Read-only.

TABLE 3.6

XMLHttpRequest Object Methods for Apple Safari

Object Method	Description
abort	Aborts the HTTP request.
getAllResponseHeaders	Returns all the HTTP headers.
getResponseHeader	Returns the value of an HTTP header.
open	Opens a request to the server.
send	Sends an HTTP request to the server.
setRequestHeader	Sets the name and value of an HTTP header.

Now that you have your required XMLHttpRequest object, how do you actually work with it? You start by opening it, which happens in the getData function.

Opening the XMLHttpRequest object

After creating your XMLHttpRequest object, it's ready for use when the user clicks the button in the application's page. The function tied to that button click is getData:

```
<script language = "javascript">

    function getData(dataSource, divID)
    {
      .
      .
      .
    }
</script>
```

It's time to work with the XMLHttpRequest object you've created, connecting to the server and downloading your data. The getData function starts by checking if you've been able to create a valid XMLHttpRequest object, and if not, just quitting:

```
function getData(dataSource, divID)
{
  if(XMLHttpRequestObject) {
      .
      .
      .
  }
}
```

You can also display an error message to users if their browsers can't handle Ajax (that is, can't create an XMLHttpRequest object). You might do that something like this, where the code is using the ID of the target <div> element to get an object corresponding to that <div> element and setting the HTML in the element to the text "Sorry, your browser can't do Ajax":

```
function getData(dataSource, divID)
{
  if(XMLHttpRequestObject) {
      .
      .
      .
  }
  else {
    var obj = document.getElementById(divID);
    obj.innerHTML = "Sorry, your browser can't do Ajax.";
  }
}
```

The first step in working with an XMLHttpRequest object is to *open* it. Opening an XMLHttpRequest object configures it for use with the server; here's how you use that method (items in square braces, [and], are optional):

```
open("method", "URL"[, asyncFlag[, "userName"[, "password"]]])
```

Here are what these various parameters mean:

- method: The HTTP method used to open the connection, such as GET, POST, PUT, HEAD, or PROPFIND.
- URL: The requested URL.
- asyncFlag: A Boolean value indicating whether the call is asynchronous. The default is true.
- username: The user name.
- password: The password.

Here's how this example uses the XMLHttpRequest object's open method. In this case, it uses the GET method to contact the server, and passes the URL of the file it's looking for, which is passed to the getData function as the divID argument:

```
function getData(dataSource, divID)
{
  if(XMLHttpRequestObject) {
    XMLHttpRequestObject.open("GET", dataSource);
       .
       .
       .

}
```

The two primary HTTP methods to access the server used with Ajax are GET and POST, and this example uses the GET method. You'll see how to use POST later in this chapter; you work with the XMLHttpRequest object slightly differently when you use POST.

Note also that the URL passed to the open method is simply the name of the file, data.txt, which is passed to the getData function when the button is clicked:

```
<form>
  <input type = "button" value = "Fetch the message"
    onclick = "getData('data.txt', 'targetDiv')">
</form>
```

To make this work, make sure that data.txt is in the same directory on the server as the application's Web page, index.html. If it's in another directory, such as the data subdirectory of the directory that index.html is in, you can use that as a URL:

```
<form>
  <input type = "button" value = "Fetch the message"
    onclick = "getData('data/data.txt', 'targetDiv')">
</form>
```

Both "data.txt" and "data/data.txt" are relative URLs. You can also use an absolute URL, which specifies the full path to data.txt, something like this:

```
<form>
  <input type = "button" value = "Fetch the message"
    onclick = "getData('http://localhost/chap03/data.txt',
      'targetDiv')">
</form>
```

However, if you want to access data on a different domain than the one index.html comes from, like this:

```
<form>
  <input type = "button" value = "Fetch the message"
    onclick = "getData('http://www.someOtherHost.com/data.txt',
      'targetDiv')">
</form>
```

you'll have problems because the browser considers this a security risk.

CROSS-REF More on this perceived security risk — and how to get around it — in Chapter 4.

To keep things simple, the examples in this book download data from the same directory that the Ajax-enabled page is in. For this example, that means you have to be sure to place data.txt in the same directory as index.html (they come in the same directory as the downloadable code for the book).

Handling data downloads

The data that comes from the server is handled *asynchronously*, that is, the application doesn't hold everything and wait for it. After all, that's what the big A in Ajax is: Asynchronous, right? What does that mean for you?

It means that you have to set up a *callback* function that will be called when data has been downloaded, or is in the process of being downloaded. The XMLHttpRequest object will call that callback function with news of the download.

You can assign a function to the XMLHttpRequest object's onreadystatechange property to connect a callback function to the XMLHttpRequest object. That might look like this, where you're assigning a function named callbackFunction to the onreadystatechange property:

```
function getData(dataSource, divID)
{
  if(XMLHttpRequestObject) {
    XMLHttpRequestObject.open("GET", dataSource);

    XMLHttpRequestObject.onreadystatechange = callbackFunction;

  }
}

function callbackFunction()
{
    .
    .
    .
}
```

However, that's not the way it's usually done in Ajax applications. In Ajax applications, you typically use an anonymous JavaScript function, which you create in-place with the function keyword, followed by the curly braces that you use to enclose the function's body:

```
function getData(dataSource, divID)
{
  if(XMLHttpRequestObject) {
    XMLHttpRequestObject.open("GET", dataSource);
```

```
XMLHttpRequestObject.onreadystatechange = function()
{
        .

        .

        .
}

    }
}
```

These functions are called *anonymous* because they don't have names: you just supply their code directly, inside the curly braces after the `function` keyword.

This new anonymous function handles data downloads for you; it's notified when something happens, data-wise, with the server. The `XMLHttpRequest` object has two properties to check in the new anonymous function: the `readyState` property and the `status` property.

The `readyState` property tells you how the data downloading is coming. Here are the possible values for this property:

- 0 uninitialized
- 1 loading
- 2 loaded
- 3 interactive
- 4 complete

A value of 4 is what you want to see because that means that the data has been fully downloaded.

The `status` property is the property that contains the actual status of the download. This is actually the normal HTTP status code that you get when you try to download Web pages. For example, if the data you're looking for wasn't found, you'll get a value of 404 in the `status` property. Here are some of the possible values:

- 200 OK
- 201 Created
- 204 No Content
- 205 Reset Content
- 206 Partial Content
- 400 Bad Request
- 401 Unauthorized
- 403 Forbidden
- 404 Not Found

- 405 Method Not Allowed
- 406 Not Acceptable
- 407 Proxy Authentication Required
- 408 Request Timeout
- 411 Length Required
- 413 Requested Entity Too Large
- 414 Requested URL Too Long
- 415 Unsupported Media Type
- 500 Internal Server Error
- 501 Not Implemented
- 502 Bad Gateway
- 503 Service Unavailable
- 504 Gateway Timeout
- 505 HTTP Version Not Supported

NOTE You'll want to see a value of 200 here, which means that the download completed normally.

In the anonymous function, you can start by checking the XMLHttpRequest object's readyState property to make sure that it's 4, which means that the data download is complete:

```javascript
<script language = "javascript">
        .
        .
        .

function getData(dataSource, divID)
{
  if(XMLHttpRequestObject) {

    XMLHttpRequestObject.open("GET", dataSource);

    XMLHttpRequestObject.onreadystatechange = function()
    {
      if (XMLHttpRequestObject.readyState == 4
        .
        .
        .

      }
    }

  }
}
</script>
```

And you can also check that the XMLHttpRequest object's status property holds a value of 200, meaning that the download went okay, like this:

```
<script language = "javascript">
           .
           .
           .

function getData(dataSource, divID)
{
   if(XMLHttpRequestObject) {

     XMLHttpRequestObject.open("GET", dataSource);

     XMLHttpRequestObject.onreadystatechange = function()
     {
       if (XMLHttpRequestObject.readyState == 4 &&
         XMLHttpRequestObject.status == 200) {
         .
         .
         .

       }
     }

     XMLHttpRequestObject.send(null);
   }
}
</script>
```

So the download went okay, and it's complete at this point; you got the data you asked for from the server, using Ajax. So how do you actually get access to that data?

Getting your data

If the XMLHttpRequest object's status property holds 200 and its readyState property holds 4, you've downloaded your data. Cool. Now how do you get that data?

There are two ways, both involving the XMLHttpRequest object:

- If the data you've downloaded is in simple text format, you read it from the XMLHttpRequest object's responseText property, like this: XMLHttpRequestObject.responseText.
- If you've downloaded data in XML format, you use the XMLHttpRequest object's responseXml property, like this: XMLHttpRequestObject.responseXml.

In this case, you've downloaded text data from the data.txt file, so this application uses the responseText property. The goal of this first application is to display the fetched data in the Web page, and you can use a little dynamic HTML to do that. You start by getting a JavaScript object corresponding to the targetDiv <div> element in the Web page, which is where this example displays its text:

```
<script language = "javascript">
      .
      .
      .
   function getData(dataSource, divID)
   {
     if(XMLHttpRequestObject) {
       var obj = document.getElementById(divID);
       XMLHttpRequestObject.open("GET", dataSource);

       XMLHttpRequestObject.onreadystatechange = function()
       {
         if (XMLHttpRequestObject.readyState == 4 &&
           XMLHttpRequestObject.status == 200) {
             .
             .
             .
         }
       }

     }
   }
</script>
```

Then you can display the fetch text, currently residing in the responseText property, in the targetDiv <div> element like this:

```
<script language = "javascript">
      .
      .
      .
   function getData(dataSource, divID)
   {
     if(XMLHttpRequestObject) {
       var obj = document.getElementById(divID);
       XMLHttpRequestObject.open("GET", dataSource);

       XMLHttpRequestObject.onreadystatechange = function()
       {
         if (XMLHttpRequestObject.readyState == 4 &&
           XMLHttpRequestObject.status == 200) {
             obj.innerHTML = XMLHttpRequestObject.responseText;
         }
       }

     }
   }
</script>
```

So is that it? Are you ready to go? Not so fast, there's one more step. You've configured the XMLHttpRequest object to connect to the server and download data.txt, and you've set up the code needed to handle the download when it happens. But you haven't made that download happen yet, and that's coming up next.

Downloading the data

You've configured the XMLHttpRequest object with its open method, and you've assigned an anonymous function to its onreadystatechange property. So how do you actually make the download happen by connecting to the server?

Use the XMLHttpRequest object's send method to send your request to the server. When you use the GET HTTP method to connect to the server, everything is configured in the open method; you just send a value of null to the server using the send method. Here's what that looks like in code:

```
<script language = "javascript">
  var XMLHttpRequestObject = false;

  if (window.XMLHttpRequest) {
    XMLHttpRequestObject = new XMLHttpRequest();
  } else if (window.ActiveXObject) {
    XMLHttpRequestObject = new
      ActiveXObject("Microsoft.XMLHTTP");
  }

  function getData(dataSource, divID)
  {
    if(XMLHttpRequestObject) {
      var obj = document.getElementById(divID);
      XMLHttpRequestObject.open("GET", dataSource);

      XMLHttpRequestObject.onreadystatechange = function()
      {
        if (XMLHttpRequestObject.readyState == 4 &&
          XMLHttpRequestObject.status == 200) {
            obj.innerHTML = XMLHttpRequestObject.responseText;
        }
      }

      XMLHttpRequestObject.send(null);
    }
  }
</script>
```

And that's it! You've created your first Ajax application, and it functions as shown earlier in Figures 3.1 and 3.2.

Here's a review of the steps you followed to create this first, important Ajax application:

1. You created an `XMLHttpRequest` object.
2. You used its `open` method to configure it.
3. You connected an anonymous JavaScript function to handle the download to the `XMLHttpRequest` object's `onreadystatechange` property.
4. Because you were using the GET HTTP method to fetch data, you sent an argument of `null` to the server to actually start the data download.

This process is the essence of Ajax.

Now that you've completed your first Ajax application, it's time to elaborate it. You've gotten a good foundation in the topic, but that's only the beginning. For example, there are other ways of creating `XMLHttpRequest` objects.

More ways to create XMLHttpRequest objects

You've already seen one way of creating `XMLHttpRequest` objects in the Ajax application you've just completed, which looks like this in JavaScript:

```
<script language = "javascript">
  var XMLHttpRequestObject = false;

  if (window.XMLHttpRequest) {
    XMLHttpRequestObject = new XMLHttpRequest();
  } else if (window.ActiveXObject) {
    XMLHttpRequestObject = new
      ActiveXObject("Microsoft.XMLHTTP");
  }
```

In fact, you can elaborate this code because there is more than one way of creating `XMLHttpRequest` objects in Internet Explorer (and there's more to say about creating `XMLHttpRequest` objects in Firefox and Mozilla when you're working with XML, as discussed later in this chapter). This code is sufficient for the purposes in this book, but there are various versions of its `XMLHttpRequest` object available in Internet Explorer. You create the normal version of this object with the `Microsoft.XMLHTTP` ActiveX object, but there's a more recent version available: `MSXML2.XMLHTTP`, and even newer versions, such as `MSXML2.XMLHTTP.3.0`, `MSXML2.XMLHTTP.4.0`, or now `MSXML2.XMLHTTP.5.0`.

The trick is to check whether or not your browser can create these recent `XMLHttpRequest` objects, without bringing the application to a screeching halt if it cannot. You can do that with the JavaScript try/catch construct, which lets you test sensitive code, and continue even if it fails. For example, say that you want to create an `MSXML2.XMLHTTP` object with a `try` statement like this:

```
<script language = "javascript">
  var XMLHttpRequestObject = false;
```

```
try {
  XMLHttpRequestObject = new
    ActiveXObject("MSXML2.XMLHTTP");
}
```

If the code that attempts to create the new XMLHttpRequest object fails, use a JavaScript catch statement. That's how it works in general: if the code in a try statement fails, control passes to the following catch statement. Information, such as the reason the try statement failed, is passed to the catch statement using an exception object, like this:

```
<script language = "javascript">
  var XMLHttpRequestObject = false;

  try {
    XMLHttpRequestObject = new
      ActiveXObject("MSXML2.XMLHTTP");
  } catch (exception1) {
    .
    .
    .
  }
```

If the attempt to create an XMLHttpRequest object with ActiveXObject("MSXML2.XML-HTTP") failed, you can create an XMLHttpRequest object the standard way, using ActiveXObject("Microsoft.XMLHTTP") like this in a new try statement:

```
<script language = "javascript">
  var XMLHttpRequestObject = false;

  try {
    XMLHttpRequestObject = new
      ActiveXObject("MSXML2.XMLHTTP");
  } catch (exception1) {
    try {
      XMLHttpRequestObject = new
        ActiveXObject("Microsoft.XMLHTTP");
    }
  }
```

If that works, fine, you have an XMLHttpRequest object. If not, however, you might want to explicitly set the XMLHttpRequestObject variable to false, which you can do like this:

```
<script language = "javascript">
  var XMLHttpRequestObject = false;

  try {
    XMLHttpRequestObject = new
      ActiveXObject("MSXML2.XMLHTTP");
  } catch (exception1) {
```

```
      try {
        XMLHttpRequestObject = new
         ActiveXObject("Microsoft.XMLHTTP");
      } catch (exception2) {
        XMLHttpRequestObject = false;
      }
    }
```

If the `XMLHttpRequestObject` variable is left with a value of `false` at this point, you know you're not dealing with Internet Explorer, version 5.0 or later. That means you have to create an `XMLHttpRequest` object using the Mozilla/Firefox method this way in the sample application index2.html:

```
    <script language = "javascript">
      var XMLHttpRequestObject = false;

      try {
        XMLHttpRequestObject = new
          ActiveXObject("MSXML2.XMLHTTP");
      } catch (exception1) {
        try {
          XMLHttpRequestObject = new
           ActiveXObject("Microsoft.XMLHTTP");
        } catch (exception2) {
          XMLHttpRequestObject = false;
        }
      }

      if (!XMLHttpRequestObject && window.XMLHttpRequest) {
        XMLHttpRequestObject = new XMLHttpRequest();
      }
```

That's it! This code creates an `MSXML2.XMLHTTP` `XMLHttpRequest` object in Internet Explorer, if possible.

Up to this point, you've downloaded some text from a text file, but Ajax is about more than that. Ajax is all about connecting to the server behind the scenes and interacting with that server. And that means working with programming on the server side.

Interacting with Server-Side Code

The real power of Ajax involves code on the server because that's what Ajax is all about: interacting with the server. And to make things happen on the server, you need to use server-side code. This book uses PHP (hypertext preprocessor) for its server-side code, but don't worry, you won't have to know PHP to read this book (although Chapter 11 introduces PHP and Ajax). The PHP used here is basic, and if you know JavaScript, you'll be able to figure it out.

This book uses PHP because it's the most common choice for connecting to Ajax. PHP is easy to write and easy to use. There are thousands of Web servers that support PHP, so if you want to sign up for one, they're easy to find. Your current server may already support PHP because most do these days _ just ask them. For testing purposes, you can also install PHP on your own machine. You can get PHP for free at www.php.net, complete with installation instructions (on Windows, installing can be as easy as running a .exe file).

For example, say that instead of downloading text from a static file, data.txt, you had this PHP script, data.php, installed on the server:

```
<?php
     echo 'This text was also fetched from the server with Ajax.';
?>
```

This script sends (echoes) the text "This text was also fetched from the server with Ajax" back to the browser, so you should be able to display that text in your Ajax application if you fetch it from the server. Fetching that text from the server is easy; all you need to do is fetch data from the URL data.php, not data.txt, as you see here in index3.html:

```
<html>
  <head>
    <title>An Ajax demo</title>

    <script language = "javascript">
      var XMLHttpRequestObject = false;

      if (window.XMLHttpRequest) {
        XMLHttpRequestObject = new XMLHttpRequest();
      } else if (window.ActiveXObject) {
        XMLHttpRequestObject = new
          ActiveXObject("Microsoft.XMLHTTP");
      }

      function getData(dataSource, divID)
      {
        if(XMLHttpRequestObject) {
          var obj = document.getElementById(divID);
          XMLHttpRequestObject.open("GET", dataSource);

          XMLHttpRequestObject.onreadystatechange = function()
          {
            if (XMLHttpRequestObject.readyState == 4 &&
              XMLHttpRequestObject.status == 200) {
                obj.innerHTML =
                  XMLHttpRequestObject.responseText;
            }
          }
        }
```

```
        XMLHttpRequestObject.send(null);
      }
    }
  </script>
</head>

<body>

  <H1>An Ajax demo</H1>

  <form>
    <input type = "button" value = "Fetch the message"
      onclick = "getData('data.php', 'targetDiv')">
  </form>

  <div id="targetDiv">
    <p>The fetched message will appear here.</p>
  </div>

</body>
</html>
```

You can see this Web page, index3.html, in Figure 3.3.

FIGURE 3.3

Reading text from a PHP script using Ajax

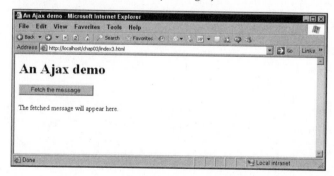

When the user clicks the button in this page, the text from the PHP script, data.php, is downloaded and displayed, as shown in Figure 3.4. Presto! You're working with online server-side scripts and Ajax. Not bad.

FIGURE 3.4

Downloading text from a PHP script

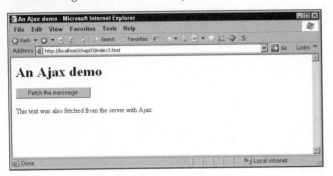

Passing Data to Server-Side Scripts

So data.php works. Still, the text it returns is static. How could it be otherwise, since you're not passing any data to data.php to customize what it returns? But you can pass data to the server, and the way you do that differs if you're using the GET or POST method.

Using GET is easiest, so that's coming up first.

Passing data to the server with GET

Say that you wanted to have two messages returned from the server, depending on data you pass to the server. For example, if you passed a value of 1 to the server, you'd get back 'You sent the server a value of 1', and if you pass a value of 2 to the server, you'd get back 'You sent the server a value of 2' instead.

Arranging this in PHP is easy. When you send data to the server, you assign that data to a parameter. In this case, you might just call that parameter "data" to make life easier. You might call the PHP script datahandler.php in this case, and because you're passing data using the GET HTTP method, you can recover the data you're sending in PHP code using a special PHP array named $_GET. For example, if you assign the parameter data a value of 1 and send that to the datahandler.php script, then the body of this if statement executes:

```
<?
  if ($_GET["data"] == "1") {
    .
    .
    .
  }
?>
```

In this case, you can send the message 'You sent the server a value of 1' back to the browser like this:

```
<?
  if ($_GET["data"] == "1") {
    echo 'You sent the server a value of 1';
  }
?>
```

On the other hand, if you assign the data parameter the value 2, you can send back the message 'You sent the server a value of 2' like this:

```
<?
  if ($_GET["data"] == "1") {
    echo 'You sent the server a value of 1';
  }
  if ($_GET["data"] == "2") {
    echo 'You sent the server a value of 2';
  }
?>
```

That handles the situation in PHP code: when you pass it a parameter named data that's been assigned the value of 1, you get back the first message; when you pass it a value of 2 assigned to the data parameter, you get back the second message.

Now how do you pass data to the server when you're using the GET method and Ajax? When you use the GET method of fetching data from the server, data is sent from Web pages back to the server using *URL encoding*, which means that data is appended to the actual URL that is sent to the server.

For example, if you were using the GET method and you had a standard Web page with a text field named "a" that contained the number 5, a text field named "b" that contained the number 6, and a text field named "c" that contained the text "Now is the time", all that data would be encoded and added to the URL you're accessing. The names of the text fields a, b, and c, are the parameters you're sending to the server, and the text in each text field is the data assigned to each parameter.

When data is URL encoded, a question mark (?) is added to the end of the URL, and the data, in name=data format, is added after that question mark. Spaces in text are converted to a plus sign (+), and you separate pairs of name=data items with ampersands (&). So to encode the data from the "a", "b", and "c" text fields and send it to http://www.servername.com/user/scriptname, you'd use this URL:

```
http://www.servername.com/user/scriptname?a=5&b=6&c=Now+is+the+time
```

NOTE The data you send this way is always text; even if you're sending numbers, they're treated as text.

So that's the way you send data from controls like text fields: by treating the names given to the text fields as parameters and assigning data to those parameters. You don't have any text fields here, however, so this example, datahandler.html, just assigns a value of 1 or 2 to the `data` parameter so the PHP script can get and read that data. For example, this URL assigns a value of 1 to a parameter named `data` and sends it to the datahandler.php script:

```
datahandler.php?data=1
```

Here's how to display two buttons in the datahandler.html application that let the user display the first and second messages:

```html
<html>
  <head>
    <title>An Ajax demo</title>

    <script language = "javascript">
      var XMLHttpRequestObject = false;

      if (window.XMLHttpRequest) {
        XMLHttpRequestObject = new XMLHttpRequest();
      } else if (window.ActiveXObject) {
        XMLHttpRequestObject = new
          ActiveXObject("Microsoft.XMLHTTP");
      }

      function getData(dataSource, divID)
      {
        if(XMLHttpRequestObject) {
          var obj = document.getElementById(divID);
          XMLHttpRequestObject.open("GET", dataSource);

          XMLHttpRequestObject.onreadystatechange = function()
          {
            if (XMLHttpRequestObject.readyState == 4 &&
              XMLHttpRequestObject.status == 200) {
                obj.innerHTML =
                  XMLHttpRequestObject.responseText;
            }
          }

          XMLHttpRequestObject.send(null);
        }
      }
    </script>
  </head>

<body>

  <H1>An Ajax demo</H1>
```

```
<form>
  <input type = "button" value = "Fetch message 1"
    onclick = "getData('datahandler.php?data=1',
      'targetDiv')">
  <input type = "button" value = "Fetch message 2"
    onclick = "getData('datahandler.php?data=2',
      'targetDiv')">
</form>

<div id="targetDiv">
  <p>The fetched message will appear here.</p>
</div>

  </body>
</html>
```

You can see this Web page, index3.html, in Figure 3.5.

Interacting with the server by passing data

When the user clicks a button, the corresponding message is downloaded and displayed, as you see in Figure 3.6. You've now passed data to a server-side script using Ajax and the GET method.

When you use the GET method, things work out fine, but there's one thing to consider: your data is very public. That's because it was attached to the end of the URL you're accessing, which means it could, possibly, be read by others easily. A somewhat more secure method is the POST method, which encodes your data in HTTP headers.

FIGURE 3.6

Retrieving a message from the server

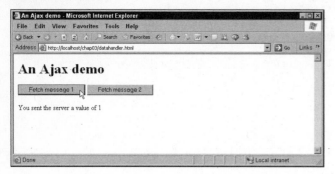

Passing data to the server with POST

Using the POST HTTP method means that any data you send to the server is enclosed in the HTTP request header, so it's not as visible (which doesn't mean it's secure) as with the GET method. In fact, POST is coming to be preferred over GET for that very reason.

When you use the POST method and Ajax, you have to work things a little differently in the code, as you're going to see. And the PHP is different as well; instead of using the $_GET array:

```
<?
  if ($_GET["data"] == "1") {
     echo 'You sent the server a value of 1';
  }
  if ($_GET["data"] == "2") {
     echo 'You sent the server a value of 2';
  }
?>
```

you use the $_POST array, like this in datahandlerpost.php:

```
<?
  if ($_POST["data"] == "1") {
     echo 'You sent the server a value of 1';
  }
  if ($_POST["data"] == "2") {
     echo 'You sent the server a value of 2';
  }
?>
```

Now you have to modify your Ajax application to use POST instead of GET. The first step is obvious: you change this line, where you use the GET method:

```
function getData(dataSource, divID)
{
  if(XMLHttpRequestObject) {
    var obj = document.getElementById(divID);
    XMLHttpRequestObject.open("GET", dataSource);
      .
      .
      .
```

to this, where you use the POST method:

```
function getData(dataSource, divID)
{
  if(XMLHttpRequestObject) {
    var obj = document.getElementById(divID);
    XMLHttpRequestObject.open("POST", dataSource);
      .
      .
      .
```

In order to use the POST method and send data to the server, you also have to set an HTTP request header, the Content-Type request header, to "application/x-www-form-urlencoded". If you don't know what that means, just make sure you include this code:

```
function getData(dataSource, divID)
{
  if(XMLHttpRequestObject) {
    var obj = document.getElementById(divID);
    XMLHttpRequestObject.open("POST", dataSource);
    XMLHttpRequestObject.setRequestHeader('Content-Type',
      'application/x-www-form-urlencoded');
      .
      .
      .
```

Next comes the standard anonymous function to handle the download, and that look like this in datahandlerpost.html:

```
function getData(dataSource, divID)
{
  if(XMLHttpRequestObject) {
    var obj = document.getElementById(divID);
    XMLHttpRequestObject.open("POST", dataSource);
    XMLHttpRequestObject.setRequestHeader('Content-Type',
      'application/x-www-form-urlencoded');
```

```
XMLHttpRequestObject.onreadystatechange = function()
{
  if (XMLHttpRequestObject.readyState == 4 &&
    XMLHttpRequestObject.status == 200) {
      obj.innerHTML =
        XMLHttpRequestObject.responseText;
  }
}
  .
  .
  .
```

So far, so good, but if you can't URL-encode the data you send using the POST method, how do you actually assign the data parameter a value of 1 or 2, depending on which button the user clicks, and send that data to the server?

You might start by changing each button so that it calls the getData function with the number of the message to get, 1 or 2:

```
function getData(dataSource, divID)
{
  if(XMLHttpRequestObject) {
    var obj = document.getElementById(divID);
    XMLHttpRequestObject.open("POST", dataSource);
    XMLHttpRequestObject.setRequestHeader('Content-Type',
      'application/x-www-form-urlencoded');

    XMLHttpRequestObject.onreadystatechange = function()
    {
      if (XMLHttpRequestObject.readyState == 4 &&
        XMLHttpRequestObject.status == 200) {
          obj.innerHTML =
            XMLHttpRequestObject.responseText;
      }
    }
    .
    .
    .

  }
}
    </script>
  </head>

<body>

  <H1>An Ajax demo</H1>
```

```
<form>
  <input type = "button" value = "Fetch message 1"
    onclick = "getData('datahandlerpost.php', 'targetDiv',
      1)">
  <input type = "button" value = "Fetch message 2"
    onclick = "getData('datahandlerpost.php', 'targetDiv',
      2)">
</form>
       .
       .
       .
```

Then you modify the getData function to accept a third parameter, the data parameter, which will be set to 1 or 2, depending on which button was clicked, and therefore which message the user wants to see:

```
function getData(dataSource, divID, data)
{
  if(XMLHttpRequestObject) {
    var obj = document.getElementById(divID);
    XMLHttpRequestObject.open("POST", dataSource);
    XMLHttpRequestObject.setRequestHeader('Content-Type',
      'application/x-www-form-urlencoded');

    XMLHttpRequestObject.onreadystatechange = function()
    {
      if (XMLHttpRequestObject.readyState == 4 &&
        XMLHttpRequestObject.status == 200) {
          obj.innerHTML =
            XMLHttpRequestObject.responseText;
      }
    }
    .
    .
    .
  }
}
```

Here comes the central point: instead of sending a value of null with the send XMLHttpRequest object, as you did when using the GET method, you send the actual data to the server using the send method when you use POST. And you send that data just as you would a URL-encoded string. For example, to send the data assigned to a parameter named data, you do this:

```
function getData(dataSource, divID, data)
{
  if(XMLHttpRequestObject) {
    var obj = document.getElementById(divID);
    XMLHttpRequestObject.open("POST", dataSource);
    XMLHttpRequestObject.setRequestHeader('Content-Type',
      'application/x-www-form-urlencoded');
```

```
XMLHttpRequestObject.onreadystatechange = function()
{
  if (XMLHttpRequestObject.readyState == 4 &&
    XMLHttpRequestObject.status == 200) {
      obj.innerHTML =
        XMLHttpRequestObject.responseText;
  }
}

XMLHttpRequestObject.send("data=" + data);
  }
}
```

And that's it. You're now using POST instead of GET to send data to the server. You can see this Web page, datahandlerpost.html, in Figure 3.7.

FIGURE 3.7

Interacting with the server by passing data using POST

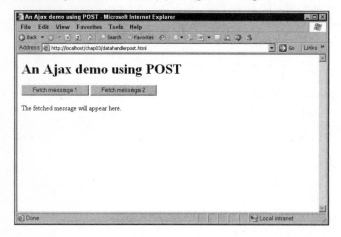

Just as with the GET method, when the user clicks a button, the corresponding message is downloaded and displayed, as you see in Figure 3.8.

FIGURE 3.8

Retrieving a message from the server using POST

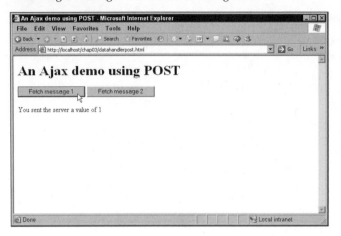

You've gotten a good number of Ajax basics down, but there's still a glaring hole: what about XML? After all, Ajax means Asynchronous JavaScript and XML, doesn't it? XML is coming up next.

Using Ajax with XML

So far, the Ajax examples you've seen in this chapter exchange data with the server using text, but of course you can also send your data in XML format. Doing so involves using the `responseXml` property of the `XMLHttpRequest` object instead of the `responseText` property, but there's more involved. For example, you have to use JavaScript to unravel the XML you receive from the server, and that's by no means trivial. (In fact, Chapter 12 is devoted to the topic.)

How about taking a look at an example that downloads XML from the server, using Ajax? You can see such an example in Figure 3.9, lunch.html.

FIGURE 3.9

The lunch.html page

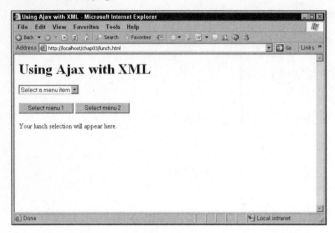

You can use this page to select between two menus. When you select a menu by clicking a button, that menu's items are downloaded in XML format from the server, and displayed in a drop-down list box, as you see in Figure 3.10.

FIGURE 3.10

Retrieving a menu's items from the server using XML

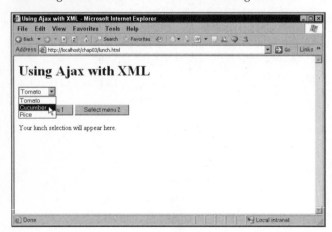

When you select an item from the drop-down list, that item appears in the Web page, as shown in Figure 3.11.

Selecting a menu item

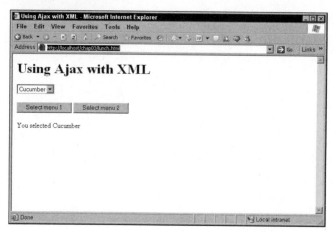

So how does this all work behind the scenes?

Creating the XML

The XML for this example will be stored in two menu XML files: menu1.xml and menu2.xml. Each XML file starts, as any XML file must, with an XML declaration:

```
<?xml version = "1.0" ?>
        .
        .
        .
```

Each menu XML file uses a <menu> item as its document element (in XML, all elements must be contained inside a single document element):

```
<?xml version = "1.0" ?>
<menu>
    .
    .
    .

</menu>
```

Then you list the menu items in each menu using <menuitem> elements, like this in menu1.xml:

```
<?xml version = "1.0" ?>
<menu>
  <menuitem>Ham</menuitem>
  <menuitem>Turkey</menuitem>
  <menuitem>Beef</menuitem>
</menu>
```

Here's what menu2.xml looks like:

```
<?xml version = "1.0" ?>
<menu>
  <menuitem>Tomato</menuitem>
  <menuitem>Cucumber</menuitem>
  <menuitem>Rice</menuitem>
</menu>
```

These XML files go into the same directory on the server as the main Web page, lunch.html. Okay, that prepares the XML. Now how do you download and use it?

Downloading the XML

It's time to write some JavaScript to download and decode the XML in menu1.xml and menu2.xml. The first change from simple text-handling comes early on, during the XMLHttpRequest object-creation process. If you're dealing with a Netscape/Firefox browser, you have to add this line when working with XML:

```
<html>
  <head>

    <title>Using Ajax with XML</title>

    <script language = "javascript">

      var menu;

      var XMLHttpRequestObject = false;

      if (window.XMLHttpRequest) {
        XMLHttpRequestObject = new XMLHttpRequest();
        XMLHttpRequestObject.overrideMimeType("text/xml");
      } else if (window.ActiveXObject) {
        XMLHttpRequestObject = new
          ActiveXObject("Microsoft.XMLHTTP");
      }
        .
        .
        .
```

Why do you need this line of code, and what does it do? In some cases, Mozilla, Firefox, and Netscape can set the type of the data expected by the XMLHttpRequest object to non-XML values, so be sure to use this line to set the expected type of data to XML when you're downloading XML.

Next come the controls you see in this Web page: the drop-down list box, which is a <select> control, two buttons, and a <div> element for displaying the results:

```
<body>

  <h1>Using Ajax with XML</h1>

  <form>
    <select size="1" id="menuList"
      onchange="setmenu()">
      <option>Select a menu item</option>
    </select>
    <br>
    <br>
    <input type = "button" value = "Select menu 1"
      onclick = "getmenu1()">
    <input type = "button" value = "Select menu 2"
      onclick = "getmenu2()">
  </form>

  <div id="targetDiv" width =100 height=100>Your lunch
    selection will appear here.</div>

</body>
```

Note the JavaScript functions these controls are tied to: the two buttons, which let the user select between menu 1 and menu 2 are connected to the functions getmenu1 and getmenu2. And the drop-down list, which shows the menu items for selection, is tied to a function named setmenu, which displays the user's menu selection in the <div> element.

So how do the getmenu1 and getmenu2 functions look? You start getmenu1 by configuring an XMLHttpRequest object to get menu1.xml like this:

```
function getmenu1()
{
  if(XMLHttpRequestObject) {
    XMLHttpRequestObject.open("GET", "menu1.xml");
    .
    .
    .
```

When the response comes back you want to use the `responseXML` property, not `responseText`; here's how that's handled in the code, where the XML is stored in a variable named `xmlDocument`:

```
function getmenu1()
{
  if(XMLHttpRequestObject) {
    XMLHttpRequestObject.open("GET", "menu1.xml");

    XMLHttpRequestObject.onreadystatechange = function()
    {
      if (XMLHttpRequestObject.readyState == 4 &&
        XMLHttpRequestObject.status == 200) {
      var xmlDocument = XMLHttpRequestObject.responseXML;
        .

        .

        .
      }
    }

    XMLHttpRequestObject.send(null);
  }
}
```

The XML you download is stored in JavaScript XML document object form, and you're going to see how to handle that XML throughout this book. In this case, the XML you've downloaded looks like this:

```
<?xml version = "1.0" ?>
<menu>
  <menuitem>Ham</menuitem>
  <menuitem>Turkey</menuitem>
  <menuitem>Beef</menuitem>
</menu>
```

The trick is to extract the data in the `<menuitem>` elements here and to display that data in the drop-down list. You can get an array of `<menuitem>` elements by using the `getElementsByTagName` method, passing it the element name `"menuitem"`:

```
function getmenu1()
{
  if(XMLHttpRequestObject) {
    XMLHttpRequestObject.open("GET", "menu1.xml");

    XMLHttpRequestObject.onreadystatechange = function()
    {
      if (XMLHttpRequestObject.readyState == 4 &&
        XMLHttpRequestObject.status == 200) {
      var xmlDocument = XMLHttpRequestObject.responseXML;
      menu = xmlDocument.getElementsByTagName("menuitem");
```

```
                .
                .
                .
              }
            }

          XMLHttpRequestObject.send(null);
        }
      }
```

Now you need to extract the names of the menu items from the menu object, which contains the
<menuitem> elements. Might as well do that in a new function, listmenu:

```
function getmenu1()
{
  if(XMLHttpRequestObject) {
    XMLHttpRequestObject.open("GET", "menu1.xml");

    XMLHttpRequestObject.onreadystatechange = function()
    {
      if (XMLHttpRequestObject.readyState == 4 &&
        XMLHttpRequestObject.status == 200) {
      var xmlDocument = XMLHttpRequestObject.responseXML;
      menu = xmlDocument.getElementsByTagName("menuitem");
      listmenu();
      }
    }

    XMLHttpRequestObject.send(null);
  }
}
```

In the listmenu function, you can loop over the <menuitem> elements in the menu array:

```
function listmenu ()
{
  var loopIndex;

  for (loopIndex = 0; loopIndex < menu.length; loopIndex++
)
    {
      .
      .
      .
    }
}
```

Inside this loop is where you want to store the new menu items in the drop-down <select> control. You can access the <select> control's items using the control's options array like this:

```
function listmenu ()
{
  var loopIndex;
  var selectControl = document.getElementById('menuList');

  for (loopIndex = 0; loopIndex < menu.length; loopIndex++
)
  {
      selectControl.options[loopIndex] =
      .
      .
      .
  }
}
```

All that remains is to extract the names of each menu item from the <menuitem> elements:

```
<menuitem>Ham</menuitem>
<menuitem>Turkey</menuitem>
<menuitem>Beef</menuitem>
```

Here's where you need some knowledge of XML. For example, the text "Ham" in the first <menuitem> element is actually considered a text node, and it's the first child node of the <menuitem> element. So to access that text node, you'd use this expression: menu[0].first Child. But you're not done yet; you still have to access the data in the text node to recover the "Ham" text, and you do that with this expression: menu[0].firstChild.data.

All that means is that you can recover the menu item's text and place it in the <select> control like this:

```
function listmenu ()
{
  var loopIndex;
  var selectControl = document.getElementById('menuList');

  for (loopIndex = 0; loopIndex < menu.length; loopIndex++
)
  {
      selectControl.options[loopIndex] = new
        Option(menu[loopIndex].firstChild.data);
  }
}
```

That populates the drop-down list with the menu items recovered from the server using XML.

The last bit of code for this example is the `setmenu` function, which handles selections in the drop-down list. When users select a menu item, you should display their selection, as shown earlier in Figure 3.11. Here's how the `setmenu` function does its thing:

```
function setmenu()
{
  document.getElementById('targetDiv').innerHTML =
    "You selected " + menu[document.getElementById
      ('menuList').selectedIndex].firstChild.data;
}
```

And that's it; this example is complete.

On the other hand, this example used static XML files. What if you wanted to interact with the server, sending it data and getting XML back? For example, what if you wanted to convert this example from using two XML files, menu1.xml and menu2.xml, to using one PHP file, menus.php? The menus.php file can pass back the data for both menus to the browser. All you have to do is pass it a parameter named menu, set to 1 for menu 1 and 2 for menu 2.

The menus.php file starts by setting the Content-type header of the data it's going to send back to the browser to `text/xml` so the browser knows it will be XML:

```
<?
header("Content-type: text/xml");
    .
    .
    .

?>
```

Next, menus.php creates an array of menu items depending on the value of the menu parameter:

```
<?
header("Content-type: text/xml");
if ($_GET["menu"] == "1")
  $menuitems = array('Ham', 'Turkey', 'Beef');
if ($_GET["menu"] == "2")
  $menuitems = array('Tomato', 'Cucumber', 'Rice');
      .
      .
      .

?>
```

Finally, this PHP script loops over the array, creating the XML text to send back to the browser:

```php
<?
header("Content-type: text/xml");
if ($_GET["menu"] == "1")
  $menuitems = array('Ham', 'Turkey', 'Beef');
if ($_GET["menu"] == "2")
  $menuitems = array('Tomato', 'Cucumber', 'Rice');
echo '<?xml version="1.0" ?>';
echo '<menu>';
foreach ($menuitems as $value)
{
  echo '<menuitem>';
  echo $value;
  echo '</menuitem>';
}
echo '</menu>';
?>
```

That takes care of the PHP side of things. What about the Ajax application itself, which you might call lunch2.html?

The changes here are easy: instead of getmenu1 and getmenu2 functions, you can put everything together into a single getmenu function to which you pass the number of the menu you want. Then you just call getmenu with the correct menu number when the user clicks a button:

```html
<form>
  <select size="1" id="menuList"
    onchange="setmenu()">
    <option>Select a menu item</option>
  </select>
  <br>
  <br>
  <input type = "button" value = "Select menu 1"
    onclick = "getmenu('1')">
  <input type = "button" value = "Select menu 2"
    onclick = "getmenu('2')">
</form>
```

In the getmenu function, you can URL-encode the number of the menu to fetch and pass that number to menus.php like this:

```javascript
function getmenu(menuNumber)
{
  if(XMLHttpRequestObject) {
    XMLHttpRequestObject.open("GET", "menus.php?menu=" +
      menuNumber);
```

```
    XMLHttpRequestObject.onreadystatechange = function()
    {
      if (XMLHttpRequestObject.readyState == 4 &&
        XMLHttpRequestObject.status == 200) {
      var xmlDocument = XMLHttpRequestObject.responseXML;
      menu = xmlDocument.getElementsByTagName("menuitem");
      listmenu();
      }
    }

    XMLHttpRequestObject.send(null);
  }
}
```

And that's all it takes. Now when the user requests menu 1, menu 1 will be fetched; when the user requests menu 2, menu 2 will be fetched. Cool. Now you're fetching dynamic XML data from the server.

Summary

In this chapter, you got an overview of how to create XMLHttpRequest objects, and how to begin creating Ajax applications. You saw how to fetch text using both the GET and POST methods, as well as how to begin working with XML. This material provides you with a good foundation for the rest of the book.

Chapter 4

Serious Ajax Programming

In Chapter 3 you got your feet wet with Ajax by writing complete Ajax applications. This chapter takes over from there, giving you a working knowledge of the skills you'll need to work through the rest of this book. In other words, you're going to see some serious Ajax here.

This chapter starts by working with multiple XMLHttpRequest objects. For example, if you present the user with two buttons, each of which downloads different data from the server, you can't count on the user to not press both buttons and wait for the results from the server. That's a problem, because Ajax is *asynchronous*, remember? It doesn't block execution of your code until it gets a result from the server. So if you have only one XMLHttpRequest object, and each time the user clicks a button you connect an anonymous function to its onreadystatechange property, which XMLHttpRequest request are you responding to — the one from the first button click or the second button click? You'll tackle that problem first in this chapter.

You're also going to see that in addition to text and XML data, some Ajax applications return JavaScript for you to execute. That's often the case when you connect to a large-scale, Ajax-based interface, such as Google Suggest. You can often connect to these applications using Ajax yourself, and a number of them return JavaScript for you to execute instead of simple text or XML data. (The JavaScript you get from Google Suggest displays the drop-down list of matches.) You'll see how that works in this chapter.

CROSS-REF For an example of Google Suggest at work, see the example in Chapter 1, which used Google Suggest to display a drop-down list of possible matches to a partial search term. You can also find Google Suggest at www.google.com/webhp?complete=1&hl=en.

In addition, you're going to see how to use Ajax with HTTP head requests, allowing you to check whether files exist on the server, what their length and creation date is, and more. And you'll also see how to defeat caching in browsers like Microsoft Internet Explorer, and many other topics as you start getting into serious Ajax programming.

Working with Multiple Concurrent XMLHttpRequest Requests

As you may recall, Chapter 3 ended with a lunch example that let users download their choice of menus using Ajax. There's a subtle flaw with that example: it displayed two buttons, one for lunch menu 1, the other for lunch menu 2. Clicking button 1 displayed the items in menu 1 in the drop-down list, and clicking button 2 displayed the items in menu 2.

So far, so good. But there's a problem. What if the user gets impatient and clicks button 2 after clicking button 1 but doesn't wait until the menu data for button 1 is downloaded? The lunch example used only one `XMLHttpRequest` object to connect to the server, so when the response comes back from the server, which request is the response for? Taking a look at the code reveals the problem: there's only one `XMLHttpRequest` object, but two buttons that make use of it:

```html
<html>
  <head>

    <title>Using Ajax with XML</title>

    <script language = "javascript">

      var menu;

      var XMLHttpRequestObject = false;

      if (window.XMLHttpRequest) {
        XMLHttpRequestObject = new XMLHttpRequest();
        XMLHttpRequestObject.overrideMimeType("text/xml");
      } else if (window.ActiveXObject) {
        XMLHttpRequestObject = new
          ActiveXObject("Microsoft.XMLHTTP");
      }

      function getmenu1()
      {
        if(XMLHttpRequestObject) {
          XMLHttpRequestObject.open("GET", "menu1.xml");

          XMLHttpRequestObject.onreadystatechange = function()
          {
            if (XMLHttpRequestObject.readyState == 4 &&
```

```
                XMLHttpRequestObject.status == 200) {
            var xmlDocument = XMLHttpRequestObject.responseXML;
            menu = xmlDocument.getElementsByTagName("menuitem");
            listmenu();
            }
        }

        XMLHttpRequestObject.send(null);
    }
}

function getmenu2()
{
    if(XMLHttpRequestObject) {
        XMLHttpRequestObject.open("GET", "menu2.xml");

        XMLHttpRequestObject.onreadystatechange = function()
        {
            if (XMLHttpRequestObject.readyState == 4 &&
                XMLHttpRequestObject.status == 200) {
            var xmlDocument = XMLHttpRequestObject.responseXML;
            menu = xmlDocument.getElementsByTagName("menuitem");
            listmenu();
            }
        }

        XMLHttpRequestObject.send(null);
    }
}

function listmenu ()
{
    var loopIndex;
    var selectControl = document.getElementById('menuList');

    for (loopIndex = 0; loopIndex < menu.length; loopIndex++
)
    {
        selectControl.options[loopIndex] = new
            Option(menu[loopIndex].firstChild.data);
    }
}

function setmenu()
{
    document.getElementById('targetDiv').innerHTML =
        "You selected " + menu[document.getElementById
        ('menuList').selectedIndex].firstChild.data;
}
```

```
      </script>
   </head>

   <body>

      <h1>Using Ajax with XML</h1>

      <form>
        <select size="1" id="menuList"
          onchange="setmenu()">
          <option>Select a menu item</option>
        </select>
        <br>
        <br>
        <input type = "button" value = "Select menu 1"
          onclick = "getmenu1()">
        <input type = "button" value = "Select menu 2"
          onclick = "getmenu2()">
      </form>

      <div id="targetDiv" width =100 height=100>Your lunch
        selection will appear here.</div>

   </body>

</html>
```

You can see the issue: both getmenu1 and getmenu2 use the same XMLHttpRequest object, which is probably fine for most purposes, but not all. You can run into cases where the response from the server is slow, and an impatient user clicks the other button. And then you're not sure which XMLHttpRequest the server is responding to.

So what's the answer? One solution is to use multiple XMLHttpRequest objects.

Using multiple XMLHttpRequest objects

One solution to the problem of having multiple choices is to create one XMLHttpRequest object per request. For example, you might modify lunch.html into, for example, double.html, which creates two XMLHttpRequest objects: XMLHttpRequestObject and XMLHttpRequestObject2, like this:

```
         var XMLHttpRequestObject = false;

         if (window.XMLHttpRequest) {
           XMLHttpRequestObject = new XMLHttpRequest();
           XMLHttpRequestObject.overrideMimeType("text/xml");
         } else if (window.ActiveXObject) {
           XMLHttpRequestObject = new
             ActiveXObject("Microsoft.XMLHTTP");
         }
```

```
var XMLHttpRequestObject2 = false;

if (window.XMLHttpRequest2) {
  XMLHttpRequestObject2 = new XMLHttpRequest();
  XMLHttpRequestObject2.overrideMimeType("text/xml");
} else if (window.ActiveXObject) {
  XMLHttpRequestObject2 = new
    ActiveXObject("Microsoft.XMLHTTP");
}
```

This way, when the user clicks one button, one XMLHttpRequest object responds. Because there are two buttons and two XMLHttpRequest objects, you've improved the odds that you won't have any confusion between requests. Here's what the new code, double.html, looks like:

```
<html>
  <head>

    <title>Using two XMLHttpRequest objects</title>

    <script language = "javascript">

      var menu;

      var XMLHttpRequestObject = false;

      if (window.XMLHttpRequest) {
        XMLHttpRequestObject = new XMLHttpRequest();
        XMLHttpRequestObject.overrideMimeType("text/xml");
      } else if (window.ActiveXObject) {
        XMLHttpRequestObject = new
          ActiveXObject("Microsoft.XMLHTTP");
      }

      var XMLHttpRequestObject2 = false;

      if (window.XMLHttpRequest2) {
        XMLHttpRequestObject2 = new XMLHttpRequest();
        XMLHttpRequestObject2.overrideMimeType("text/xml");
      } else if (window.ActiveXObject) {
        XMLHttpRequestObject2 = new
          ActiveXObject("Microsoft.XMLHTTP");
      }

      function getmenu1()
      {
        if(XMLHttpRequestObject) {
          XMLHttpRequestObject.open("GET", "menu1.xml");
```

```
          XMLHttpRequestObject.onreadystatechange = function()
          {
            if (XMLHttpRequestObject.readyState == 4 &&
              XMLHttpRequestObject.status == 200) {
            var xmlDocument = XMLHttpRequestObject.responseXML;
            menu = xmlDocument.getElementsByTagName("menuitem");
            listmenu();
            }
          }

          XMLHttpRequestObject.send(null);
        }
      }

      function getmenu2()
      {
        if(XMLHttpRequestObject2) {
          XMLHttpRequestObject2.open("GET", "menu2.xml");

          XMLHttpRequestObject2.onreadystatechange = function()
          {
            if (XMLHttpRequestObject2.readyState == 4 &&
              XMLHttpRequestObject2.status == 200) {
            var xmlDocument = XMLHttpRequestObject2.responseXML;
            menu = xmlDocument.getElementsByTagName("menuitem");
            listmenu();
            }
          }

          XMLHttpRequestObject2.send(null);
        }
      }

      function listmenu ()
      {
        var loopIndex;
        var selectControl = document.getElementById('menuList');

        for (loopIndex = 0; loopIndex < menu.length; loopIndex++
      )
        {
            selectControl.options[loopIndex] = new
               Option(menu[loopIndex].firstChild.data);
        }
      }
```

```
function setmenu()
{
  document.getElementById('targetDiv').innerHTML =
    "You selected " + menu[document.getElementById
      ('menuList').selectedIndex].firstChild.data;
}

</script>
</head>

<body>

  <h1>Using two XMLHttpRequest objects</h1>

  <form>
    <select size="1" id="menuList"
      onchange="setmenu()">
      <option>Select a menu item</option>
    </select>
    <br>
    <br>
    <input type = "button" value = "Select menu 1"
      onclick = "getmenu1()">
    <input type = "button" value = "Select menu 2"
      onclick = "getmenu2()">
  </form>

  <div id="targetDiv" width =100 height=100>Your lunch
    selection will appear here.</div>

</body>

</html>
```

This way of doing things works, as you can see in Figure 4.1.

Even this solution is somewhat problematic, however. You don't really want to have to write explicit code for each XMLHttpRequest object; what if your application used a hundred such objects? A better way of doing things is to store the objects in an array and create new XMLHttpRequest objects as needed.

FIGURE 4.1

Using two XMLHttpRequest objects

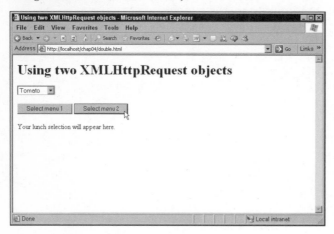

Storing XMLHttpRequest objects in an array

Creating two XMLHttpRequest objects can alleviate the problem of multiple concurrent requests, but what if you need dozens of such objects? One solution is to place them in an object array, as shown in objectarray.html.

You can start by creating an array of XMLHttpRequest objects named XMLHttpRequestObjects:

```
<script language = "javascript">

  var menu;

  var XMLHttpRequestObjects = new Array();
    .
    .
    .
```

Then, in getmenu1 and getmenu2, you can create a new XMLHttpRequest object and add it to the XMLHttpRequestObjects array using that array's built-in push method (which adds an object to the end of the array), as well as adding the index of the current XMLHttpRequest object to the array:

```
function getmenu1()
{
  if (window.XMLHttpRequest) {
    XMLHttpRequestObjects.push(new XMLHttpRequest());
  } else if (window.ActiveXObject) {
```

```
XMLHttpRequestObjects.push(new
  ActiveXObject("Microsoft.XMLHTTP"));
}

index = XMLHttpRequestObjects.length - 1;
  .
  .
  .
```

From then on, you can refer to the new XMLHttpRequest object as
XMLHttpRequestObjects[index] and you're guaranteed to have a fresh XMLHttpRequest
object for each request. Here's how that works in objectarray.html:

```
<html>
  <head>

    <title>Using an array of XMLHTTPRequest objects</title>

    <script language = "javascript">

      var menu;
      var index = 0;

      var XMLHttpRequestObjects = new Array();

      function getmenu1()
      {
        if (window.XMLHttpRequest) {
          XMLHttpRequestObjects.push(new XMLHttpRequest());
        } else if (window.ActiveXObject) {
        XMLHttpRequestObjects.push(new
          ActiveXObject("Microsoft.XMLHTTP"));
        }

        index = XMLHttpRequestObjects.length - 1;

        if(XMLHttpRequestObjects[index]) {
          XMLHttpRequestObjects[index].open("GET", "menu1.xml");

          XMLHttpRequestObjects[index].onreadystatechange =
          function()
          {
            if (XMLHttpRequestObjects[index].readyState == 4 &&
              XMLHttpRequestObjects[index].status == 200) {
            var xmlDocument =
              XMLHttpRequestObjects[index].responseXML;
            menu = xmlDocument.getElementsByTagName("menuitem");
            listmenu();
            }
          }
```

```
        XMLHttpRequestObjects[index].send(null);
      }
    }

  function getmenu2()
  {
    if (window.XMLHttpRequest) {
      XMLHttpRequestObjects.push(new XMLHttpRequest());
    } else if (window.ActiveXObject) {
    XMLHttpRequestObjects.push(new
      ActiveXObject("Microsoft.XMLHTTP"));
    }

    index = XMLHttpRequestObjects.length - 1;

    if(XMLHttpRequestObjects[index]) {
      XMLHttpRequestObjects[index].open("GET", "menu2.xml");

      XMLHttpRequestObjects[index].onreadystatechange =
      function()
      {
        if (XMLHttpRequestObjects[index].readyState == 4 &&
          XMLHttpRequestObjects[index].status == 200) {
        var xmlDocument =
        XMLHttpRequestObjects[index].responseXML;
        menu = xmlDocument.getElementsByTagName("menuitem");
        listmenu();
        }
      }

      XMLHttpRequestObjects[index].send(null);
    }
  }

  function listmenu ()
  {
    var loopIndex;
    var selectControl = document.getElementById('menuList');

    for (loopIndex = 0; loopIndex < menu.length; loopIndex++
  )

    {
        selectControl.options[loopIndex] = new
          Option(menu[loopIndex].firstChild.data);
    }
  }

  function setmenu()
  {
```

```
        document.getElementById('targetDiv').innerHTML =
          "You selected " + menu[document.getElementById
            ('menuList').selectedIndex].firstChild.data;
      }

    </script>
  </head>

<body>

  <h1>Using an array of XMLHTTPRequest objects</h1>

  <form>
    <select size="1" id="menuList"
      onchange="setmenu()">
      <option>Select a menu item</option>
    </select>
    <br>
    <br>
    <input type = "button" value = "Select menu 1"
      onclick = "getmenu1()">
    <input type = "button" value = "Select menu 2"
      onclick = "getmenu2()">
  </form>

  <div id="targetDiv" width =100 height=100>Your lunch
    selection will appear here.</div>

  </body>

</html>
```

This way of doing things also works, as you can see in Figure 4.2.

FIGURE 4.2

Using an array of `XMLHttpRequest` objects

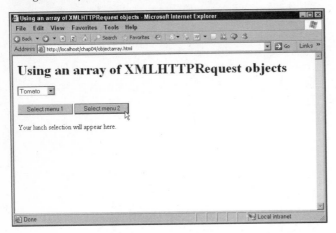

Creating an array of `XMLHttpRequest` objects like this lets you handle multiple `XMLHttp` requests without getting them all mixed up. But this is a little awkward, and you're going to end up with a big array of `XMLHttpRequest` objects unless you start deleting them from the array when they're no longer needed.

It turns out that there's a better way to handle multiple `XMLHttpRequest` objects than even an array of such objects, and that's using *inner functions* in JavaScript.

Using inner functions

The way you usually handle multiple `XMLHttpRequest` requests is through the use of inner functions in Ajax. A JavaScript inner function is just a function defined inside another function. Here's an example, where the function named `inner` is an inner function:

```
function outer(data)
{
  var variable1 = data;

  function inner(variable2)
  {
    alert(variable1 + variable2)
  }
}
```

Now say you call the outer function with a value of 4 like this: `outer(4)`. That sets the variable `variable1` in this function to 4. The inner function has access to the outer function's data, even after the call to the outer function has finished. So if you were now to call the inner function, passing a value of 5, that would set `variable2` in the inner function to 5 — and `variable1` is still set to 4. So the result of calling the inner function would be 4 + 5 = 9, which is the value that the JavaScript `alert` function would display in this case.

Here's the good part: every time you call the outer function, a *new* copy of that function is created, which means a new value will be stored as `variable1`. And the inner function will have access to that value. So if you make the shift from thinking in terms of `variable1` and start thinking in terms of the variable `XMLHttpRequestObject`, you can see that each time a function like this is called, JavaScript creates a new copy of the function with a new `XMLHttpRequest` object, and that object is available to any inner functions.

That's what you want in this case, because the code you've been writing already uses an anonymous inner function, connected to the `onreadystatechange` property in the `getData` function. Here's how it works: the `XMLHttpRequest` object is created, and then it's used inside the anonymous inner function this way:

```
var XMLHttpRequestObject = false;

if (window.XMLHttpRequest) {
  XMLHttpRequestObject = new XMLHttpRequest();
} else if (window.ActiveXObject) {
  XMLHttpRequestObject = new
    ActiveXObject("Microsoft.XMLHTTP");
}

function getData(dataSource, divID)
{
  if(XMLHttpRequestObject) {
    var obj = document.getElementById(divID);
    XMLHttpRequestObject.open("GET", dataSource);

    XMLHttpRequestObject.onreadystatechange = function()
    {
      if (XMLHttpRequestObject.readyState == 4 &&
        XMLHttpRequestObject.status == 200) {
          obj.innerHTML =
            XMLHttpRequestObject.responseText;
      }
    }

    XMLHttpRequestObject.send(null);
  }
}
```

To use a new `XMLHttpRequest` object for each request, move the section of the code where the `XMLHttpRequest` object is created *inside* the `getData` function, because the `getData` function is the outer function that encloses the anonymous inner function. Doing so creates a new `XMLHttpRequest` object to be used by the anonymous inner function each time `getData` is called. And each time `getData` is called, a new copy of `getData` is created. That's what you want: a new `XMLHttpRequest` object for each new request, created automatically.

Here's what it looks like in code:

```
function getData(dataSource, divID)
{
  var XMLHttpRequestObject = false;

  if (window.XMLHttpRequest) {
    XMLHttpRequestObject = new XMLHttpRequest();
  } else if (window.ActiveXObject) {
    XMLHttpRequestObject = new
      ActiveXObject("Microsoft.XMLHTTP");
  }

  if(XMLHttpRequestObject) {
    var obj = document.getElementById(divID);
    XMLHttpRequestObject.open("GET", dataSource);

    XMLHttpRequestObject.onreadystatechange = function()
    {
      if (XMLHttpRequestObject.readyState == 4 &&
        XMLHttpRequestObject.status == 200) {
          obj.innerHTML =
            XMLHttpRequestObject.responseText;
      }
    }

    XMLHttpRequestObject.send(null);
  }
}
```

That's it — you're done. By moving the creation code inside the getData function, this application can now handle multiple concurrent XMLHttpRequest requests, no matter how many times users click the various buttons in your Web page. Each time, the getData function is called, a new copy of the function is created, with a new XMLHttpRequest object, and you're good to go.

This is perfect for the lunch menu application, so perfect that you don't even need two functions, getmenu1 and getmenu2, anymore (because you don't need to rely on separate functions creating separate XMLHttpRequest objects). All you need is one function, getmenu, in this new version of the lunch application, inner.html:

```
<html>
  <head>

    <title>Using multiple XMLHttpRequest objects</title>

    <script language = "javascript">

      var menu;
```

```
var XMLHttpRequestObject = false;

if (window.XMLHttpRequest) {
  XMLHttpRequestObject = new XMLHttpRequest();
  XMLHttpRequestObject.overrideMimeType("text/xml");
} else if (window.ActiveXObject) {
  XMLHttpRequestObject = new
    ActiveXObject("Microsoft.XMLHTTP");
}

function getmenu(menuNumber)
{
  if(XMLHttpRequestObject) {
    XMLHttpRequestObject.open("GET", "menus.php?menu=" +
      menuNumber);

    XMLHttpRequestObject.onreadystatechange = function()
    {
      if (XMLHttpRequestObject.readyState == 4 &&
        XMLHttpRequestObject.status == 200) {
      var xmlDocument = XMLHttpRequestObject.responseXML;
      menu = xmlDocument.getElementsByTagName("menuitem");
      listmenu();
      }
    }

    XMLHttpRequestObject.send(null);
  }
}

function listmenu ()
{
  var loopIndex;
  var selectControl = document.getElementById('menuList');

  for (loopIndex = 0; loopIndex < menu.length; loopIndex++
  )
  {
      selectControl.options[loopIndex] = new
        Option(menu[loopIndex].firstChild.data);
  }
}

function setmenu()
{
  document.getElementById('targetDiv').innerHTML =
    "You selected " + menu[document.getElementById
      ('menuList').selectedIndex].firstChild.data;
}
```

```
        </script>
    </head>

<body>

    <h1>Using multiple XMLHttpRequest objects</h1>

    <form>
      <select size="1" id="menuList"
        onchange="setmenu()">
        <option>Select a menu item</option>
      </select>
      <br>
      <br>
      <input type = "button" value = "Select menu 1"
        onclick = "getmenu('1')">
      <input type = "button" value = "Select menu 2"
        onclick = "getmenu('2')">
    </form>

    <div id="targetDiv" width =100 height=100>Your lunch
      selection will appear here.</div>

  </body>

</html>
```

To handle multiple concurrent XMLHttpRequest requests, just move the XMLHttpRequest object inside the getmenu function, and you're done with inner.html:

```
<html>
  <head>

    <title>Using multiple XMLHttpRequest objects</title>

    <script language = "javascript">

      var menu;

      function getmenu(menuNumber)
      {
        var XMLHttpRequestObject = false;

        if (window.XMLHttpRequest) {
          XMLHttpRequestObject = new XMLHttpRequest();
          XMLHttpRequestObject.overrideMimeType("text/xml");
        } else if (window.ActiveXObject) {
          XMLHttpRequestObject = new
            ActiveXObject("Microsoft.XMLHTTP");
        }
```

```
        if(XMLHttpRequestObject) {
          XMLHttpRequestObject.open("GET", "menus.php?menu=" +
            menuNumber);

          XMLHttpRequestObject.onreadystatechange = function()
          {
            if (XMLHttpRequestObject.readyState == 4 &&
              XMLHttpRequestObject.status == 200) {
            var xmlDocument = XMLHttpRequestObject.responseXML;
            menu = xmlDocument.getElementsByTagName("menuitem");
            listmenu();
            }
          }

          XMLHttpRequestObject.send(null);
        }
      }

    function listmenu ()
    {
      var loopIndex;
      var selectControl = document.getElementById('menuList');

      for (loopIndex = 0; loopIndex < menu.length; loopIndex++
)

      {
          selectControl.options[loopIndex] = new
            Option(menu[loopIndex].firstChild.data);
      }
    }

    function setmenu()
    {
      document.getElementById('targetDiv').innerHTML =
        "You selected " + menu[document.getElementById
          ('menuList').selectedIndex].firstChild.data;
    }

    </script>
  </head>

<body>

  <h1>Using multiple XMLHttpRequest objects</h1>

  <form>
    <select size="1" id="menuList"
      onchange="setmenu()">
      <option>Select a menu item</option>
```

143

```
        </select>
        <br>
        <br>
        <input type = "button" value = "Select menu 1"
          onclick = "getmenu('1')">
        <input type = "button" value = "Select menu 2"
          onclick = "getmenu('2')">
      </form>

      <div id="targetDiv" width =100 height=100>Your lunch
        selection will appear here.</div>

    </body>

  </html>
```

And here's the PHP script this application interacts with, menus.php:

```
<?
header("Content-type: text/xml");
if ($_GET["menu"] == "1")
    $menuitems = array('Ham', 'Turkey', 'Beef');
if ($_GET["menu"] == "2")
    $menuitems = array('Tomato', 'Cucumber', 'Rice');
echo '<?xml version="1.0" ?>';
echo '<menu>';
foreach ($menuitems as $value)
{
  echo '<menuitem>';
  echo $value;
  echo '</menuitem>';
}
echo '</menu>';
?>
```

You can see the end result in Figure 4.3. Feel free to click the buttons as many times as you like; the XMLHttpRequests you send to the server won't get confused.

NOTE Although this technique keeps XMLHttpRequest requests separate, there's still no guarantee that the server won't respond to those requests out of order, especially if the user is into rapid-fire button clicking. There's a technique that Ajax developers sometimes use to handle this problem: instead of executing code to handle (possibly out-of-order) data sent back from the server, they send back the actual JavaScript to execute. In many cases, this technique can make sure that your application does the right thing. It's also a technique used by many big-time online applications with Application Programming Interfaces (APIs) that let you connect to them.

CROSS-REF You'll see how to connect to Google Suggest using such an API later in this chapter. Google Suggest sends back JavaScript for you to execute, so it's worthwhile getting to know how to handle that kind of Ajax result.

FIGURE 4.3

Using multiple XMLHttpRequest objects

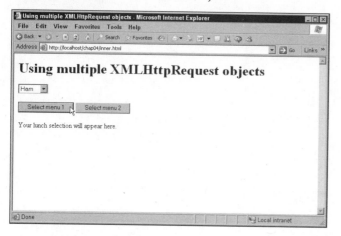

Handling JavaScript Sent from the Server

Sending the actual JavaScript back from the server for you to execute is a fairly common Ajax technique, and it's used by many of the larger online APIs. However, I don't really recommend this technique. There's no real reason the server-side code should have to know the details of your client-side (browser-side, that is) code, and splitting things up this way can make your application harder to maintain and debug. But there certainly is one case where handling JavaScript sent to you from the server is unavoidable: when you're dealing with a server-side API over which you have no control, like Google Suggest. In such a case, you have no choice: you have to be able to download and deal with JavaScript.

Returning JavaScript

You can see an example, javascript.html, in Figure 4.4. This example downloads JavaScript generated from a PHP script, javascript.php, and executes it.

FIGURE 4.4

Downloading JavaScript

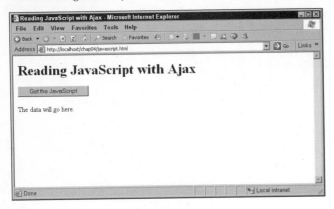

When you click the button in this application, the code connects using Ajax to the server-side script javascript.php, and downloads the JavaScript to execute. In this case, the JavaScript to execute is simply a call to a function, `display` (which is already written in the Web page); here's what javascript.php looks like:

```php
<?php
    echo 'display()';
?>
```

The application in the browser downloads the code to execute (`'display()';`) and executes it, calling the `display` function, which displays a message, as you can see in Figure 4.5.

FIGURE 4.5

Executing JavaScript

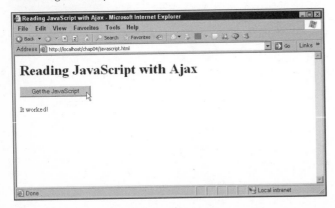

This application starts with the button you see in Figure 4.4:

```
<body>

  <H1>Reading JavaScript with Ajax</H1>

  <form>
    <input type = "button" value = "Get the JavaScript"
      onclick = "getData('javascript.php')">
  </form>

  <div id="targetDiv">
    <p>The data will go here.</p>
  </div>

</body>
```

This button is connected to a JavaScript function named getData, and passes to that function the relative URL of the script to call on the server, javascript.php. Here's how that function calls that PHP script:

```
<html>
  <head>
    <title>Reading JavaScript with Ajax</title>

    <script language = "javascript">

      function getData(dataSource)
      {
        var XMLHttpRequestObject = false;

        if (window.XMLHttpRequest) {
          XMLHttpRequestObject = new XMLHttpRequest();
        } else if (window.ActiveXObject) {
          XMLHttpRequestObject = new
            ActiveXObject("Microsoft.XMLHTTP");
        }

        if(XMLHttpRequestObject) {

          XMLHttpRequestObject.open("GET", dataSource);

          XMLHttpRequestObject.onreadystatechange = function()
          {
            if (XMLHttpRequestObject.readyState == 4 &&
              XMLHttpRequestObject.status == 200) {
                .
                .
                .
            }
          }
```

```
              XMLHttpRequestObject.send(null);
          }
      }
          .
          .
          .
```

The javascript.php script returns the text `'display()'`; as you've seen:

```
<?php
    echo 'display()';
?>
```

How can you execute this JavaScript? You can use the JavaScript `eval` function, which is designed to do exactly that: execute JavaScript that you pass to it in text form. In this case, you can simply pass the text returned from the server in the `responseText` property to the `eval` function:

```
        function getData(dataSource)
        {
          var XMLHttpRequestObject = false;

          if (window.XMLHttpRequest) {
            XMLHttpRequestObject = new XMLHttpRequest();
          } else if (window.ActiveXObject) {
            XMLHttpRequestObject = new
              ActiveXObject("Microsoft.XMLHTTP");
          }

          if(XMLHttpRequestObject) {

            XMLHttpRequestObject.open("GET", dataSource);

            XMLHttpRequestObject.onreadystatechange = function()
            {
              if (XMLHttpRequestObject.readyState == 4 &&
                XMLHttpRequestObject.status == 200) {

                eval(XMLHttpRequestObject.responseText);
              }
            }

            XMLHttpRequestObject.send(null);
          }
        }
```

This call to eval executes the JavaScript returned from the server, `'display();'`, which calls the `display` method. That method looks like this in the Web page javascript.html:

```
function display()
{
    .
    .
    .
}
```

In this function, you can display the message "It worked!" in a `<div>` element in the Web page like this:

```
function display()
{
    var targetDiv = document.getElementById("targetDiv");

    targetDiv.innerHTML = "It worked!";
}
```

And you can see the result in Figure 4.5. It does indeed work, thanks to the JavaScript eval function.

It turns out you can do more than just return JavaScript to execute. You can also return JavaScript objects from the server.

Returning JavaScript objects

So how can you return JavaScript objects from the server? Can you only return text and XML from the server? That's correct, but you can actually format a JavaScript object as text, and convert it back to an object after you've downloaded it.

Here's what that looks like in code. Say that you have a function named `multiplier` that accepts two operands, multiplies them, and displays the results in a `<div>` element:

```
function multiplier(operand1, operand2)
{
  var product = operand1 * operand2;
  var targetDiv = document.getElementById("targetDiv");
  targetDiv.innerHTML = operand1 + " x " + operand2 + " = "
    + product;
}
```

Now say you wanted to create an object that holds the name of the function to call, `multiplier`, and the two operands to pass to that function; this is the kind of object a server-side program might pass back to you. In this case, the object being passed back to your script might have these three properties:

- `function`: The function to call, `multiplier`
- `variable1`: The first operand to pass to the `multiplier` function
- `variable2`: The second operand to pass to the `multiplier` function

It's easy enough to create an object with these three properties from text in JavaScript. Set up a variable named `text` to hold the text to use while creating the object, and create a variable named `object` to hold the object to be created, listing the setting for the three properties, `function`, `variable1`, and `variable2`:

```
var text = "{function: 'multiplier', operand1: 2, operand2: 3};";
var object;
```

You can use the JavaScript `eval` function to create the new object and assign it to the object variable like this:

```
eval('object = ' + text);
```

Then you can call the `multiplier` function using the data stored in the new object:

```
<html>
  <head>
    <title>
      Converting text to a JavaScript object
    </title>

    <script>
      function convert()
      {
        var text = "{method: 'multiplier', operand1: 2, operand2:
          3};";
        var object;

        eval('object = '+ text);

        eval(object.method + '(' + object.operand1 + ',' +
          object.operand2 + ');');
      }

      function multiplier(operand1, operand2)
      {
        var product = operand1 * operand2;
        var targetDiv = document.getElementById("targetDiv");
        targetDiv.innerHTML = operand1 + " x " + operand2 + " = "
          + product;
      }
    </script>
  </head>

  <body>
    <h1>
      Converting text to a JavaScript object
    </h1>
    <form>
      <input type = "button" value =
        "Create JavaScript object from text"
```

```
            onclick = "convert()">
        </form>

        <div id="targetDiv">
        </div>
    </body>
</html>
```

When the user clicks the button, the convert function is called, which creates the JavaScript object from text. Then the method, multiplier, is accessible by name like this: object.method, and the two operands, operand1 and operand2, are accessible as object.operand1 and object.operand2. So as you can see, you can indeed created (limited) objects from text, and of course in Ajax applications, that text can be downloaded from the server.

One well-known Ajax application online that sends you JavaScript to execute is Google Suggest, which is discussed next.

Connecting to Google Suggest

Among famous Ajax applications, there are a few that stand out, such as Google Suggest (`www.google.com/webhp?complete=1&hl=en`). It is shown in Figure 4.6.

FIGURE 4.6

Google Suggest

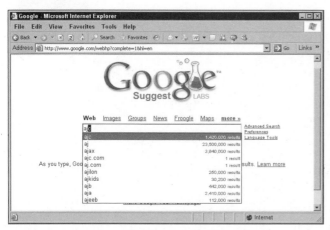

When you enter a partial search term, as shown in the figure, Google Suggest connects, using Ajax, to the Google servers and finds possible matches to your partial search term and displays them — no page refresh needed. Clicking a hyperlink in the drop-down list opens the corresponding search page in Google.

You can create a search page yourself that connects to Google Suggest, and download JavaScript from Google Suggest to do so. You can see this example at work in Figure 4.7.

FIGUrE 4.7

Connecting to Google Suggest with a custom page

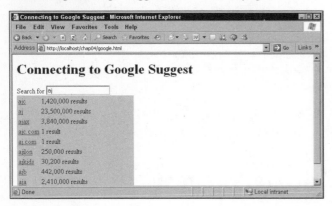

So how can you connect to Google Suggest? Say that you've stored the partial search term in a variable named `searchTerm`. You could then connect to Google Suggest at:

```
http://www.google.com/complete/search?hl=en&js=true&qu=" +
searchTerm;
```

How does Google Suggest communicate with you? It sends back JavaScript code that calls a function named `sendRPCDone`. Here are the parameters passed to that function:

```
sendRPCDone(unusedVariable, searchTerm, arrayTerm, arrayResults,
unusedArray)
```

So what does the JavaScript call you get back from Google Suggest actually look like? If you're searching for `ajax`, this is the kind of JavaScript you'll get back from Google:

```
sendRPCDone(frameElement, "ajax", new Array("ajax", "ajax
amsterdam",
"ajax fc", "ajax ontario", "ajax grips", "ajax football club",
"ajax public library", "ajax football", "ajax soccer", "ajax
pickering transit"), new Array("3,840,000 results", "502,000
results", "710,000 results", "275,000 results", "8,860 results",
"573,000 results", "40,500 results", "454,000 results", "437,000
results", "10,700
results"), new Array(""));
```

You take it from there, writing your own `sendRPCDone` function that displays the results sent back to you from Google Suggest.

It's time to create google.html. The action starts when the user enters a search term in the search text field, which has the ID textField:

```
<body>

  <H1>Connecting to Google Suggest</H1>

  Search for <input id = "textField" type = "text"
    name = "textField" onkeyup = "connectGoogleSuggest(event)">

    <div id = "targetDiv"><div></div></div>

</body>
```

Note how this works. Every time a key goes up, the onkeyup event attribute calls a function named connectGoogleSuggest, which means that you can watch what users type as they type it. Every time the user types a key, the connectGoogleSuggest function is called:

```
function connectGoogleSuggest(keyEvent)
{
  .
  .
  .
}
```

You can start the connectGoogleSuggest function by creating an object that corresponds to the input text field that the user has been typing into:

```
function connectGoogleSuggest(keyEvent)
{
  var input = document.getElementById("textField");
  .
  .
  .
}
```

Next, you can check whether that text field contains any text, and if not, you can clear the target <div> element, which displays the drop-down list of items from Google Suggest:

```
function connectGoogleSuggest(keyEvent)
{
  var input = document.getElementById("textField");

  if (input.value) {
    .
    .
    .
  }
  else {
    var targetDiv = document.getElementById("targetDiv");
```

```
        targetDiv.innerHTML = "<div></div>";
      }
    }
```

If, on the other hand, the input text field does contain text, you can pass that text on to the getData function to connect to Google Suggest and get suggestions. You pass a relative URL, google.php?qu= and the search term, to getData like this:

```
function connectGoogleSuggest(keyEvent)
{
  var input = document.getElementById("textField");

  if (input.value) {
    getData("google.php?qu=" + input.value);
  }
  else {
    var targetDiv = document.getElementById("targetDiv");

    targetDiv.innerHTML = "<div></div>";
  }
}
```

The getData function creates an XMLHttpRequest object in the usual way:

```
function getData(dataSource)
{
  var XMLHttpRequestObject = false;

  if (window.XMLHttpRequest) {
    XMLHttpRequestObject = new XMLHttpRequest();
  } else if (window.ActiveXObject) {
    XMLHttpRequestObject = new
      ActiveXObject("Microsoft.XMLHTTP");
  }
      .
      .
      .
  }
}
```

and then connects to the relative URL passed to it, which is google.php?qu= and the search term:

```
function getData(dataSource)
{
  var XMLHttpRequestObject = false;

  if (window.XMLHttpRequest) {
    XMLHttpRequestObject = new XMLHttpRequest();
  } else if (window.ActiveXObject) {
```

```
    XMLHttpRequestObject = new
      ActiveXObject("Microsoft.XMLHTTP");
  }

  if(XMLHttpRequestObject) {
    XMLHttpRequestObject.open("GET", dataSource);

    XMLHttpRequestObject.onreadystatechange = function()
    {
          .
          .
          .
    }

    XMLHttpRequestObject.send(null);
  }
}
```

The text returned from Google Suggest will be JavaScript to execute, and you can execute that JavaScript using the eval function:

```
function getData(dataSource)
{
  var XMLHttpRequestObject = false;

  if (window.XMLHttpRequest) {
    XMLHttpRequestObject = new XMLHttpRequest();
  } else if (window.ActiveXObject) {
    XMLHttpRequestObject = new
      ActiveXObject("Microsoft.XMLHTTP");
  }

  if(XMLHttpRequestObject) {
    XMLHttpRequestObject.open("GET", dataSource);

    XMLHttpRequestObject.onreadystatechange = function()
    {
      if (XMLHttpRequestObject.readyState == 4 &&
        XMLHttpRequestObject.status == 200) {
          eval(XMLHttpRequestObject.responseText);
      }
    }

    XMLHttpRequestObject.send(null);
  }
}
```

As you know, the JavaScript Google Suggest sends back is a call to a function named
sendRPCDone, and it passes an array of search term matches and the number of such matches to
call sendRPCDone with, so this is the way to start writing sendRPCDone:

```
function sendRPCDone(unusedVariable, searchTerm, arrayTerm,
  arrayResults, unusedArray)
{
  .
  .
  .
}
```

In this application, the results that come back from Google Suggest are displayed in a <div> element with the ID targetDiv, using an HTML table. To assemble the text that should go into that
table, the sendRPCDone function creates a variable named data and starts by storing a <table>
tag in the data variable:

```
function sendRPCDone(unusedVariable, searchTerm, arrayTerm,
  arrayResults, unusedArray)
{
  var data = "<table>";
  .
  .
  .
}
```

To add the items to the table, you can loop over the arrays passed to you, adding a new table row
and cell for each array item:

```
function sendRPCDone(unusedVariable, searchTerm, arrayTerm,
  arrayResults, unusedArray)
{
  var data = "<table>";
  var loopIndex;

  if (arrayResults.length != 0) {
    for (var loopIndex = 0; loopIndex <
      arrayResults.length;
      loopIndex++) {
      data += "<tr><td>" +
      .
      .
      .

    }
  }
}
```

Each match to the search term should be a hyperlink that, when clicked, takes the user to Google, so you can format each match to the partial search term this way in the drop-down list:

```
function sendRPCDone(unusedVariable, searchTerm, arrayTerm,
  arrayResults, unusedArray)
{
  var data = "<table>";
  var loopIndex;

  if (arrayResults.length != 0) {
     for (var loopIndex = 0; loopIndex <
arrayResults.length;
        loopIndex++) {
        data += "<tr><td>" +
        "<a href='http://www.google.com/search?q=" +
        arrayTerm[loopIndex] + "'>" + arrayTerm[loopIndex] +
        '</a></td><td>' + arrayResults[loopIndex] +
           "</td></tr>";
     }
  }
}
```

Finally, you finish the table with a `</table>` tag, and display the table in the `<div>` element, giving the impression of a drop-down list:

```
function sendRPCDone(unusedVariable, searchTerm, arrayTerm,
  arrayResults, unusedArray)
{
  var data = "<table>";
  var loopIndex;

  if (arrayResults.length != 0) {
    for (var loopIndex = 0; loopIndex <
      arrayResults.length;
      loopIndex++) {
      data += "<tr><td>" +
      "<a href='http://www.google.com/search?q=" +
      arrayTerm[loopIndex] + "'>" + arrayTerm[loopIndex] +
      '</a></td><td>' + arrayResults[loopIndex] +
         "</td></tr>";
    }
  }

  data += "</table>";

  var targetDiv = document.getElementById("targetDiv");

  targetDiv.innerHTML = data;
}
```

The target `<div>` element is colored light red to stand out like this in the `<style>` element:

```
<html>
  <head>

    <title>Connecting to Google Suggest</title>

    <style>
    #targetDiv {
      background-color: #FFAAAA;
      width: 40%;
    }
    </style>
         .
         .
         .
```

All that remains is the PHP script, google.php; you use this script to connect to Google Suggest. You start by putting together the URL to open, which is `www.google.com/complete/ search?hl=en&js=true&qu=`, where you append the term to search for at the end. That term is passed to google.php as a parameter named qu, so you can recover the term to search for as `$_GET["qu"]` and cobble together the URL to open this way (the PHP dot operator (.) joins two strings):

```
http://www.google.com/complete/search?hl=en&js=true&qu=" .
    $_GET["qu"]
```

In PHP, you can open URLs as files, using the `fopen` function, which returns a file handle that you use to read from the URL. Note the second parameter, `r`, which means that you're opening the URL for reading:

```
<?php
  $filehandle =
    fopen("http://www.google.com/complete/search?hl=en&js=true&qu=" .
      $_GET["qu"], "r");
         .
         .
         .
?>
```

Then you can keep reading from the URL with a `while` loop and the `feof` function, which returns `true` when you're at the end of a file. You want to keep looping while you're *not* at the end of the file, so you use `!feof` (as in JavaScript, the `!` operator reverses the logical sense of its operand):

```
<?php
  $filehandle =
    fopen("http://www.google.com/complete/search?hl=en&js=true&qu=" .
```

```
        $_GET["qu"], "r");
  while (!feof($filehandle)){
        .
        .
        .
  }
?>
```

To get data from Google Suggest and echo it back to the browser, you can use the PHP `fgets` function to read data and the `echo` function to send it back to the browser:

```
<?php
  $filehandle =

fopen("http://www.google.com/complete/search?hl=en&js=true&qu=" .
      $_GET["qu"], "r");
  while (!feof($filehandle)){
    $download = fgets($filehandle);
    echo $download;
  }
?>
```

Finally, you close the file handle with the `fclose` function:

```
<?php
  $filehandle =

fopen("http://www.google.com/complete/search?hl=en&js=true&qu=" .
      $_GET["qu"], "r");
  while (!feof($filehandle)){
    $download = fgets($filehandle);
    echo $download;
  }
  fclose($filehandle);
?>
```

That echoes the data sent to you from Google Suggest. But why did you need to use google.php at all? Why couldn't you have simply accessed the URL www.google.com/complete/ search?hl=en&js=true&qu=" . $_GET["qu"] directly from the browser, in google.html? The answer has to do with the way the browser lets you call domains in Ajax, which is coming up next.

Calling Another Domain in Ajax

You'll find that if you try to access Google Suggest directly from an Ajax-enabled Web page that there's going to be an issue: your browser will display a warning message in a dialog box. In other words, when an Ajax script tries to access a Web domain that it didn't come from (such as www.google.com), browsers get suspicious for security reasons. (If it tries to access the domain it came from, there's no problem.)

However, living with a warning dialog box each time someone uses your script isn't an option, either. So what can you do? You'll find all kinds of suggestions in the Ajax community, such as changing the security settings of your browser. Clearly, that's not a viable option either; how are you going to convince your millions of users to alter their browser's security settings?

The solution is to use a server-side script to access the sensitive domain for you. Because it's not your browser that's accessing that domain, there's no problem. You already saw this at work with google.php, which is what accessed Google Suggest for you:

```php
<?php
  $filehandle =

fopen("http://www.google.com/complete/search?hl=en&js=true&qu=" .
    $_GET["qu"], "r");
  while (!feof($filehandle)){
    $download = fgets($filehandle);
    echo $download;
  }
?>
```

That's the way to get around the problem. If you need to access a domain other than the one that your Ajax page came from, use server-side code to do the actual accessing.

A Login Example

Note that the Google Suggest application discussed earlier indicates a new use of Ajax: you can now check every key as it's typed. You might not want to do that everywhere in your application; checking every key can be quite a bottleneck, but you might need it in special cases, as when users enter a password or username and you want to tell that what they're typing has already been used.

Take a look at an example in the downloadable code for this book: username.html and username.php. The username.html document asks users to enter the username they want, as you see in Figure 4.8.

FIGURE 4.8

FIGURE 4.8

Checking a user's suggested username

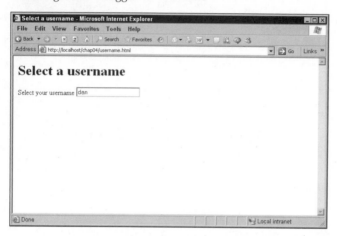

If users take a username that's already taken, such as nancy, the application informs them immediately that their username is not available, as you see in Figure 4.9.

FIGURE 4.9

Rejecting a user's suggested username

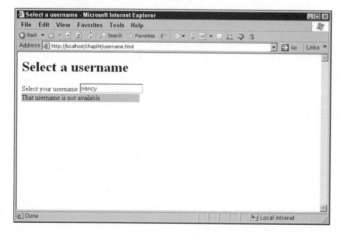

The username.php script is easy enough; all it does is echo no if the username is nancy, and yes otherwise:

```php
<?php
    if ($_GET["qu"] == "nancy"){
      echo "no";
    }
    else {
      echo "yes";
    }
?>
```

How does username.html work? It just watches as the user types keystrokes, calling a function named checkUsername for each keystroke:

```html
<body>

    <H1>Select a username</H1>

    Select your username <input id = "username" type = "text"
      name = "username" onkeyup = "checkUsername(event)">

    <div id = "targetDiv"><div></div></div>

</body>
```

In the checkUsername function, the user's entered username is passed on to the username.php function as the parameter named qu:

```javascript
function checkUsername(keyEvent)
{
  var targetDiv = document.getElementById("targetDiv");
  targetDiv.innerHTML = "<div></div>";
  var input = document.getElementById("username");

  if (input.value) {
    getData("username.php?qu=" + input.value);
  }
}
```

All that's left is to handle the value returned from username.php, yes or no, which is done in the getData function:

```javascript
function getData(dataSource)
{
  var XMLHttpRequestObject = false;
```

```
if (window.XMLHttpRequest) {
  XMLHttpRequestObject = new XMLHttpRequest();
} else if (window.ActiveXObject) {
  XMLHttpRequestObject = new
    ActiveXObject("Microsoft.XMLHTTP");
}

if(XMLHttpRequestObject) {
  XMLHttpRequestObject.open("GET", dataSource);

  XMLHttpRequestObject.onreadystatechange = function()
  {
    if (XMLHttpRequestObject.readyState == 4 &&
      XMLHttpRequestObject.status == 200) {
        if(XMLHttpRequestObject.responseText == "no"){
          var targetDiv =
            document.getElementById("targetDiv");

          targetDiv.innerHTML =
            "<div>That username is not available.</div>";
        }
    }
  }

  XMLHttpRequestObject.send(null);
}
}
```

Working with Ajax and Head Requests

Up to this point, you've used the GET and POST HTTP methods to interact with the server, but there are other methods as well, such as the HEAD method, which retrieves data about documents on a server. You can make a HEAD request just by using "HEAD" as the HTTP method to interact with the server.

Getting all head data

Take a look at the example Figure 4.10, which is making a HEAD request for the file data.txt on the server. You can see a wealth of information returned from the server in the figure.

FIGURE 4.10

A HEAD request

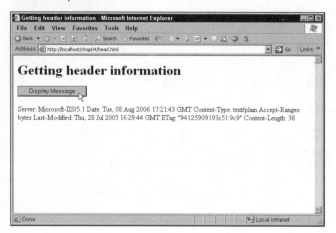

Here's the data returned from this HEAD request on data.txt:

```
Server: Microsoft-IIS/5.1 Date: Tue, 08 Aug 2006 17:21:43 GMT
Content-Type: text/plain Accept-Ranges: bytes Last-Modified: Thu,
28
Jul 2006 16:29:44 GMT ETag: "94125909193c51:9c9" Content-Length:
38
```

As you can see, a HEAD request gives you data about the server as well as about the document you're accessing.

This example, head.html, works by sending a HEAD request this way:

```
function getData(dataSource, divID)
{
  var XMLHttpRequestObject = false;

  if (window.XMLHttpRequest) {
    XMLHttpRequestObject = new XMLHttpRequest();
  } else if (window.ActiveXObject) {
    XMLHttpRequestObject = new
      ActiveXObject("Microsoft.XMLHTTP");
  }

  if(XMLHttpRequestObject) {
    XMLHttpRequestObject.open("HEAD", dataSource);
```

```
        XMLHttpRequestObject.onreadystatechange = function()
        {
          if (XMLHttpRequestObject.readyState == 4 &&
            XMLHttpRequestObject.status == 200) {
              .
              .
              .

          }
        }

        XMLHttpRequestObject.send(null);
      }
    }
```

To retrieve the HEAD data, you use the XMLHttpRequest object's getAllResponseHeaders method like this:

```
    function getData(dataSource, divID)
    {
      var XMLHttpRequestObject = false;

      if (window.XMLHttpRequest) {
        XMLHttpRequestObject = new XMLHttpRequest();
      } else if (window.ActiveXObject) {
        XMLHttpRequestObject = new
          ActiveXObject("Microsoft.XMLHTTP");
      }

      if(XMLHttpRequestObject) {
        var obj = document.getElementById(divID);
        XMLHttpRequestObject.open("HEAD", dataSource);

        XMLHttpRequestObject.onreadystatechange = function()
        {
          if (XMLHttpRequestObject.readyState == 4 &&
            XMLHttpRequestObject.status == 200) {
              obj.innerHTML =
                XMLHttpRequestObject.getAllResponseHeaders();
          }
        }

        XMLHttpRequestObject.send(null);
      }
    }
```

And that's all you need. Now the HEAD information is displayed in the Web page.

Getting specific head data

The `getAllResponseHeaders` method is a good one for getting all response headers, and there's also a method for getting just the particular response header you're interested in, `getResponseHeader`. For example, you might want to find the date a file, such as data.txt, was last modified. And you can do that with the `Last-Modified` header.

Take a look at headdate.html in Figure 4.11, which gets the `Last-Modified` header for data.txt.

FIGURE 4.11

Getting specific HEAD data

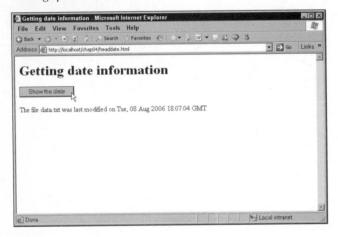

This example simply gets the HEAD data for the data.txt file and then uses `getResponseHeader` method to get the `Last-Modified` data:

```
function getData(dataSource, divID)
{
  if(XMLHttpRequestObject) {
    var obj = document.getElementById(divID);
    XMLHttpRequestObject.open("HEAD", dataSource);

    XMLHttpRequestObject.onreadystatechange = function()
    {
      if (XMLHttpRequestObject.readyState == 4 &&
        XMLHttpRequestObject.status == 200) {
          obj.innerHTML =
            "The file data.txt was last modified on " +
            XMLHttpRequestObject.getResponseHeader(
              "Last-Modified");
      }
    }
```

```
            XMLHttpRequestObject.send(null);
        }
    }
```

You can see the results in Figure 4.11.

Eliminate Caching

One of the stickiest problems when you're developing your own Ajax applications is browser *caching*. Caching takes place when the browser, especially Internet Explorer, has already visited a URL; it stores a copy of the response from the server and doesn't actually access the URL again directly.

That can be maddening when you're changing the output of, say, a PHP script and *want* the browser to read the new data sent back by that script. Say for example that you're accessing javascript.php in this example earlier in the chapter:

```
<body>

    <H1>Reading JavaScript with Ajax</H1>

    <form>
        <input type = "button" value = "Get the JavaScript"
            onclick = "getData('javascript.php)">
    </form>

    <div id="targetDiv">
        <p>The data will go here.</p>
    </div>

</body>
```

If you're debugging javascript.php, you want the browser to keep reading data from it. But, because it has cached javascript.php, it doesn't; you keep getting your old data, time after time. How can you fix this? The most popular solution among Ajax programmers is to modify the URL itself with some nonsense data; because the browser hasn't seen that URL before, it'll go back to the server rather than the cache to update the data from that URL. For example, you could just add ?r=6 to the end of the javascript.php relative URL like this:

```
<body>

    <H1>Reading JavaScript with Ajax</H1>

    <form>
        <input type = "button" value = "Get the JavaScript"
            onclick = "getData('javascript.php?r=6')">
    </form>
```

167

```
<div id="targetDiv">
  <p>The data will go here.</p>
</div>

</body>
```

The r parameter isn't used by javascript.php, but including it changes the URL enough so that the browser thinks that `javascript.php` is a different URL from `javascript.php?r=6`, and so doesn't go to the cache for data but instead accesses the URL directly.

That's fine for debugging purposes because you can keep updating the r parameter's value, creating new URLs. But what about a for-release version of your code? If caching is a problem, that is, if you need to keep going back to a server-side script that's going to send you new data, you can use the current time as an URL parameter, like this:

```
<body>

  <H1>Reading JavaScript with Ajax</H1>

  <form>
    <input type = "button" value = "Get the JavaScript"
      onclick = "getData('javascript.php?r=' +
        new Date().getTime())">
  </form>

  <div id="targetDiv">
    <p>The data will go here.</p>
  </div>

</body>
```

Summary

This chapter showed you some serious Ajax programming, starting by creating multiple XMLHttpRequest objects. You saw how to use two XMLHttpRequest objects and how to use an array of such objects. Then you saw the way this issue is handled most often in Ajax programming, using inner functions. In addition, you saw how to call other domains in Ajax, how to defeat caching, and how to make HEAD requests.

Part II

Ajax in Depth

Chapter 5

Introducing Ajax Frameworks

Want to avoid the whole business of writing Ajax code yourself? If so, you're in luck because there are literally dozens of Ajax frameworks out there that will do the work for you. An Ajax *framework* contains the code you need to support Ajax, and that code has already been written for you. All you have to do to use an Ajax framework is download it and put it to work (most are free). Want to save time using Ajax? Use an Ajax framework.

The majority of Ajax frameworks, as you're going to see in this and the next chapter, are client-side JavaScript code libraries that you can add to your own pages. After doing so, all you do is call functions in those libraries to work with Ajax. The other types of Ajax frameworks are server-side frameworks, and you'll get a look at them in Chapter 7.

Because these Ajax frameworks are free, and are often developed by hobbyists, they're sometimes not developed with the best programming practices in mind. For that reason, this discussion starts with a special Ajax framework, the Ajax Utility Library, developed for this book, and which uses good programming practices. The Ajax Utility Library is easy to use and simple to install.

IN THIS CHAPTER

Building the Ajax Utility Library

Creating the `getText` function

Creating the `getXml` function

Creating the `postDatagetText` function

Creating the `postDatagetXml` function

Using the `libXmlRequest` Ajax framework

Using the AJAXLib Ajax framework

Using the Ajax Utility Library

Take a look at Figure 5.1, which shows a page that uses the Ajax Utility Library. To download text using the Ajax Utility Library, you just have to click a button.

FIGURE 5.1

Using the Ajax Utility Library

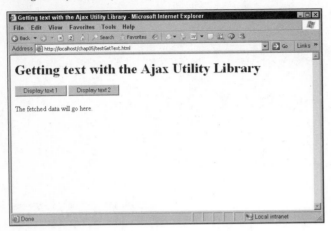

When you do click a button, the Ajax Utility Library springs into action, downloading text, as you see in Figure 5.2.

FIGURE 5.2

Downloading text using the Ajax Utility Library

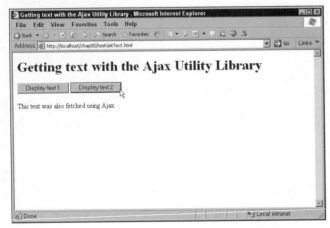

That's the first Ajax framework covered in this book, and it will be developed in this chapter. How easy is it to use this Ajax framework? Just include the JavaScript file ajaxutility.js in your Web page, like this:

```
<script type = "text/javascript" src = "ajaxutility.js"></script>
```

This assumes that ajaxutility.js is in the same directory on the server as the Web page you're including it in; otherwise, be sure to give the full URL to "ajaxutility.js" or your browser won't be able to find it.

Now you're free to use ajaxutility.js functions like getText to get text from the server using Ajax techniques. To call getText, you just supply the URL of the data to get (which can be a relative URL), and the name of a callback function. The Ajax Utility functions call that callback function with your downloaded data.

For example, in the page you see in Figure 5.1, the buttons are tied to the Ajax Utility getText function to download data.txt or data1.txt, with the callback functions callbackMessage1 and callbackMessage2:

```
<H1>Getting text with the Ajax Utility Library</H1>

<form>
  <input type = "button" value = "Display text 1"
    onclick = "getText('data.txt', callbackMessage1)">
  <input type = "button" value = "Display text 2"
    onclick = "getText('data2.txt', callbackMessage2)">
</form>
```

Then you only have to create the callback functions. For example, in callbackMessage1, which is passed the downloaded text when data.txt is downloaded, you can display that text in a <div> element named targetDiv:

```
<script language = "javascript">

  function callbackMessage1(text)
  {
    document.getElementById("targetDiv").innerHTML = text;
  }
         .
         .
         .
</script>
```

And you add the targetDiv element to the <body> element:

```
<body>

  <H1>Getting text with the Ajax Utility Library</H1>
```

```
<form>
  <input type = "button" value = "Display text 1"
    onclick = "getText('data.txt', callbackMessage1)">
  <input type = "button" value = "Display text 2"
    onclick = "getText('data2.txt', callbackMessage2)">
</form>

<div id="targetDiv">
  <p>The fetched data will go here.</p>
</div>

</body>
```

Similarly, you can set up the `callbackMessage2` function, which is passed the text downloaded from data2.txt:

```
<script language = "javascript">
  function callbackMessage1(text)
  {
    document.getElementById("targetDiv").innerHTML = text;
  }

  function callbackMessage2(text)
  {
    document.getElementById("targetDiv").innerHTML = text;
  }
</script>
```

Now you're using an Ajax framework and you don't have to write any Ajax code. You just include ajaxutility.js in your Web page and then call the Ajax Utility functions.

What functions does ajaxutility.js support? There are four functions in ajaxutility.js, two for getting text and XML using the GET method, and two for getting text and XML using POST to send data to the server. Here are those functions:

- `getText(urlToCall, functionToCallBack)`: Uses the GET method to get text from the server.

- `getXml(urlToCall, functionToCallBack)`: Uses the GET method to get XML from the server.

- `postDataGetText(urlToCall, dataToSend, functionToCallBack)`: Uses the POST method to send `dataToSend` to the server, gets text back. Pass the data to send in parameter/value pairs like this: `value=100`.

- `postDataGetXml(urlToCall, dataToSend, functionToCallBack)`: Uses the POST method to send `dataToSend` to the server, gets XML back. Pass the data to send in parameter/value pairs like this: `value=100`.

How do these functions work in ajaxutility.js? The details are coming up next.

CROSS-REF For more information on passing data to the server with the GET method, see Chapter 3.

Get text from the server with getText

The first function in the Ajax Utility Library is getText function, which simply downloads text from the server. To use this function, you pass the URL you want to access, and the name of the callback function you want called with the downloaded text when the download is complete. This function uses the GET method to communicate with the server.

Here's how the code starts: by creating the getText function, complete with the parameters you pass to it (the URL to call, and the function to call back with the downloaded text):

```
function getText(urlToCall, functionToCallBack)
{
    .
    .
    .
}
```

The next step is to create the XMLHttpRequest object that this function uses to communicate with the server behind the scenes:

```
function getText(urlToCall, functionToCallBack)
{
  var XMLHttpRequestObject = false;
    .
    .
    .
}
```

NOTE The XMLHttpRequest creation process is inside the getText function itself, which means you can call getText or any other function in the Ajax Utility Library as many times as you want, in whatever succession you want, and each function will still use its own XMLHttpRequest object, even if it's called multiple times.

First, getText attempts to create an XMLHttpRequest object for the Internet Explorer 7/ Netscape/Firefox brand of browsers:

```
function getText(urlToCall, functionToCallBack)
{
  var XMLHttpRequestObject = false;

  if (window.XMLHttpRequest) {
    XMLHttpRequestObject = new XMLHttpRequest();
  }
    .
    .
    .
}
```

And if that doesn't work, `getText` attempts to create an `XMLHttpRequest` object in Microsoft Internet Explorer:

```
function getText(urlToCall, functionToCallBack)
{
  var XMLHttpRequestObject = false;

  if (window.XMLHttpRequest) {
    XMLHttpRequestObject = new XMLHttpRequest();
  } else if (window.ActiveXObject) {
    XMLHttpRequestObject = new
     ActiveXObject("Microsoft.XMLHTTP");
  }
      .
      .
      .

}
```

The rest of the code in the `getText` function is surrounded by an `if` statement to make sure that an `XMLHttpRequest` object was created before it attempts to do anything further:

```
function getText(urlToCall, functionToCallBack)
{
  var XMLHttpRequestObject = false;

  if (window.XMLHttpRequest) {
    XMLHttpRequestObject = new XMLHttpRequest();
  } else if (window.ActiveXObject) {
    XMLHttpRequestObject = new
     ActiveXObject("Microsoft.XMLHTTP");
  }

  if(XMLHttpRequestObject) {
        .
        .
        .

  }
}
```

If an `XMLHttpRequest` object exists, the `getText` function opens the `XMLHttpRequest` object, configuring it with the GET method and the URL to call, like this:

```
function getText(urlToCall, functionToCallBack)
{
  var XMLHttpRequestObject = false;

  if (window.XMLHttpRequest) {
    XMLHttpRequestObject = new XMLHttpRequest();
  } else if (window.ActiveXObject) {
```

```
    XMLHttpRequestObject = new
     ActiveXObject("Microsoft.XMLHTTP");
  }

  if(XMLHttpRequestObject) {
   XMLHttpRequestObject.open("GET", urlToCall);
              .
              .
              .

  }
}
```

Next, the code connects the XMLHttpRequest object's onreadystatechange property to an anonymous inner function:

```
function getText(urlToCall, functionToCallBack)
{
  var XMLHttpRequestObject = false;

  if (window.XMLHttpRequest) {
    XMLHttpRequestObject = new XMLHttpRequest();
  } else if (window.ActiveXObject) {
    XMLHttpRequestObject = new
      ActiveXObject("Microsoft.XMLHTTP");
  }

  if(XMLHttpRequestObject) {
    XMLHttpRequestObject.open("GET", urlToCall);

    XMLHttpRequestObject.onreadystatechange = function()
    {
              .
              .
              .

    }
  }
}
```

In this function, you wait until the XMLHttpRequest object's readyState property holds 4 and its status property holds 200 to make sure the data has been downloaded correctly:

```
function getText(urlToCall, functionToCallBack)
{
  var XMLHttpRequestObject = false;

  if (window.XMLHttpRequest) {
    XMLHttpRequestObject = new XMLHttpRequest();
  } else if (window.ActiveXObject) {
    XMLHttpRequestObject = new
      ActiveXObject("Microsoft.XMLHTTP");
  }
```

```
      if(XMLHttpRequestObject) {
        XMLHttpRequestObject.open("GET", urlToCall);

        XMLHttpRequestObject.onreadystatechange = function()
        {
          if (XMLHttpRequestObject.readyState == 4 &&
            XMLHttpRequestObject.status == 200) {
            .
            .
            .

          }
        }
      }
    }
```

Here's the crux of this function: when the text data has been downloaded, it calls the callback function with that text data:

```
    function getText(urlToCall, functionToCallBack)
    {
      var XMLHttpRequestObject = false;

      if (window.XMLHttpRequest) {
        XMLHttpRequestObject = new XMLHttpRequest();
      } else if (window.ActiveXObject) {
        XMLHttpRequestObject = new
          ActiveXObject("Microsoft.XMLHTTP");
      }

      if(XMLHttpRequestObject) {
        XMLHttpRequestObject.open("GET", urlToCall);

        XMLHttpRequestObject.onreadystatechange = function()
        {
          if (XMLHttpRequestObject.readyState == 4 &&
            XMLHttpRequestObject.status == 200) {
            functionToCallBack(XMLHttpRequestObject.responseText);
            .
            .
            .

          }
        }
      }
    }
```

To make sure that the XMLHttpRequest object doesn't hang around after it's not needed anymore, the code deletes it this way:

```
    function getText(urlToCall, functionToCallBack)
    {
      var XMLHttpRequestObject = false;
```

```
if (window.XMLHttpRequest) {
  XMLHttpRequestObject = new XMLHttpRequest();
} else if (window.ActiveXObject) {
  XMLHttpRequestObject = new
   ActiveXObject("Microsoft.XMLHTTP");
}

if(XMLHttpRequestObject) {
  XMLHttpRequestObject.open("GET", urlToCall);

  XMLHttpRequestObject.onreadystatechange = function()
  {
    if (XMLHttpRequestObject.readyState == 4 &&
      XMLHttpRequestObject.status == 200) {
        functionToCallBack(XMLHttpRequestObject.responseText);
        delete XMLHttpRequestObject;
        XMLHttpRequestObject = null;
    }
  }
 }
}
```

Finally, you send a value of null to the server, as you always do when using the GET method:

```
function getText(urlToCall, functionToCallBack)
{
  var XMLHttpRequestObject = false;
        .
        .
        .
  XMLHttpRequestObject.onreadystatechange = function()
  {
    if (XMLHttpRequestObject.readyState == 4 &&
      XMLHttpRequestObject.status == 200) {
        functionToCallBack(XMLHttpRequestObject.responseText);
        delete XMLHttpRequestObject;
        XMLHttpRequestObject = null;
    }
  }

  XMLHttpRequestObject.send(null);
 }
}
```

You've already seen how to put the `getText` function to work in the document testGetText.html (shown earlier in Figure 5.1). It's easy: you simply call that function with the URL to fetch from the server and the callback function:

```
<form>
  <input type = "button" value = "Display text 1"
    onclick = "getText('data.txt', callbackMessage1)">
  <input type = "button" value = "Display text 2"
    onclick = "getText('data2.txt', callbackMessage2)">
</form>
```

The callback function is passed the downloaded text, and you can put that text to work any way you want it, such as displaying it in your Web page:

```
<script language = "javascript">
  function callbackMessage1(text)
  {
    document.getElementById("targetDiv").innerHTML = text;
  }

  function callbackMessage2(text)
  {
    document.getElementById("targetDiv").innerHTML = text;
  }
</script>
```

That handles the simplest case: getting text from the server. How about getting some XML? That's what the Ajax Utility Library `getXML` function is for.

Get XML from the server with getXml

The Ajax Utility Library `getXML` function lets you use the GET method to download XML from the server. Like `getText`, all you have to pass it is the URL of the source for the XML, and a callback function to call with the downloaded XML.

Here's how this function starts in ajaxutility.js:

```
function getXml(urlToCall, functionToCallBack)
{
    .
    .
    .
}
```

As you might expect, this function works similarly to `getText`, with a few differences because it handles XML, not straight text.

In particular, it uses the `responseXML` property of the `XMLHttpRequest` object to read the downloaded XML:

```
function getXml(urlToCall, functionToCallBack)
{
  var XMLHttpRequestObject = false;

  if (window.XMLHttpRequest) {
    XMLHttpRequestObject = new XMLHttpRequest();
  } else if (window.ActiveXObject) {
    XMLHttpRequestObject = new
     ActiveXObject("Microsoft.XMLHTTP");
  }

  if(XMLHttpRequestObject) {
    XMLHttpRequestObject.open("GET", urlToCall);

    XMLHttpRequestObject.onreadystatechange = function()
    {
      if (XMLHttpRequestObject.readyState == 4 &&
        XMLHttpRequestObject.status == 200) {
          functionToCallBack(XMLHttpRequestObject.responseXML);
          delete XMLHttpRequestObject;
          XMLHttpRequestObject = null;
      }
    }

    XMLHttpRequestObject.send(null);
  }
}
```

And that's it! That completes the `getXml` function.

How about putting this function to work? For example, you might modify the Chapter 3 page lunch.html that downloaded two XML documents, menu1.xml and menu2.xml, and displayed the menu items in those documents in a drop-down list control.

To start this new page, textGetXml.html, you include ajaxutility.js:

```
<html>
  <head>

    <title>Getting XML with the Ajax Utility Library</title>

    <script type = "text/javascript" src =
      "ajaxutility.js"></script>
        .

        .

        .
```

Next, you add the controls you'll need: a `<select>` control to display the menu items, two buttons that allow the user to select between menus, and a `<div>` element in which to display the item the user selects for their lunch:

```
<form>
  <select size="1" id="menuList"
    onchange="setmenu()">
    <option>Select a menu item</option>
  </select>
  <br>
  <br>
  <input type = "button" value = "Select menu 1"
    onclick = "getXml('menu1.xml', getmenu1)">
  <input type = "button" value = "Select menu 2"
    onclick = "getXml('menu2.xml', getmenu2)">
</form>

<div id="targetDiv" width =100 height=100>Your lunch
  selection will appear here.</div>
```

> **NOTE** Each button is tied to the `getXml` function, directing that function to download menu1.xml or menu2.xml, and using `getmenu1` or `getmenu2` as the callback function.

The `getmenu1` and `getmenu2` callback functions are passed the XML downloaded from the server, in JavaScript XML document form. They decode that XML and pass it on to a function named `listmenu`, which displays the menu selections in the `<select>` control:

```
<html>
  <head>

    <title>Getting XML with the Ajax Utility Library</title>

    <script type = "text/javascript" src =
      "ajaxutility.js"></script>

    <script language = "javascript">
      var menu;

      function getmenu1(xmlDocument)
      {
        menu = xmlDocument.getElementsByTagName("menuitem");
        listmenu();
      }

      function getmenu2(xmlDocument)
      {
        menu = xmlDocument.getElementsByTagName("menuitem");
        listmenu();
      }
```

```
        function listmenu ()
        {
          var loopIndex;
          var selectControl = document.getElementById('menuList');

          for (loopIndex = 0; loopIndex < menu.length; loopIndex++
    )
          {
              selectControl.options[loopIndex] = new
                 Option(menu[loopIndex].firstChild.data);
          }
        }
                    .
                    .
                    .
```

Finally, all that's left is the `setmenu` function, which the `<select>` control calls when the user has made a menu choice and it needs to display that choice in the Web page:

```
<html>
  <head>

    <title>Getting XML with the Ajax Utility Library</title>

    <script type = "text/javascript" src =
      "ajaxutility.js"></script>

    <script language = "javascript">
      var menu;

      function getmenu1(xmlDocument)
      {
        menu = xmlDocument.getElementsByTagName("menuitem");
        listmenu();
      }

      function getmenu2(xmlDocument)
      {
        menu = xmlDocument.getElementsByTagName("menuitem");
        listmenu();
      }

      function listmenu ()
      {
        var loopIndex;
        var selectControl = document.getElementById('menuList');
```

```
        for (loopIndex = 0; loopIndex < menu.length; loopIndex++
    )

        {
            selectControl.options[loopIndex] = new
                Option(menu[loopIndex].firstChild.data);
        }
    }

    function setmenu()
    {
      document.getElementById('targetDiv').innerHTML =
        "You selected " + menu[document.getElementById
          ('menuList').selectedIndex].firstChild.data;
    }
```

What do the two menus look like? The menu1.xml document contains the items ham, turkey, and beef:

```
<?xml version = "1.0" ?>
<menu>
   <menuitem>Ham</menuitem>
   <menuitem>Turkey</menuitem>
   <menuitem>Beef</menuitem>
</menu>
```

and the menu2.xml document contains tomato, cucumber, and rice:

```
<?xml version = "1.0" ?>
<menu>
   <menuitem>Tomato</menuitem>
   <menuitem>Cucumber</menuitem>
   <menuitem>Rice</menuitem>
</menu>
```

You can see this new page, testGetXml.html, at work in a browser in Figure 5.3.

FIGURe 5.3 ⁰

Downloading XML using the Ajax Utility Library

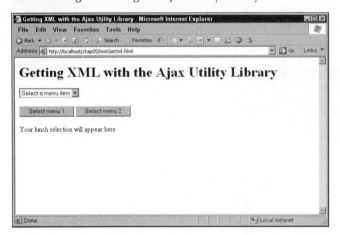

When the user clicks the Select menu 1 button, menu 1 — ham, turkey, and beef — appears in the drop-down list, as you can see in Figure 5.4.

FIGURE 5.4

Downloading menu 1

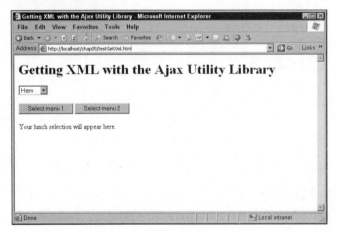

And when the user clicks the Select menu 2 button, the second menu — tomato, cucumber, and rice — appears in the drop-down list, as shown as Figure 5.5.

FIGURE 5.5

Downloading menu 2

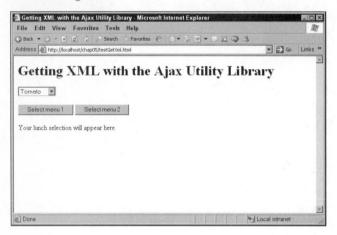

As you can see, the Ajax Utility Library can download XML from the server, and pass that XML on to your own code. Of course, you have to know how to handle that XML yourself because it'll be in JavaScript XML document object form.

One way to make the fetched XML easier to work with is to add auxiliary convenience functions to the Ajax Utility Library. For example, you could add a function named `getElements`, which would unpack the XML document object, returning an array of the elements you're looking for. You could pass the name of the elements you're searching for to the `getElements` function:

```
function getElements(elementName)
{
    .
    .
    .
}
```

And that function would use the XML document object's `getElementsByTagName` method to search that object and return an array of the requested elements, or `null` if no such elements were found, like this:

```
function getElements(elementName)
{
    return xmlDocument.getElementsByTagName(elementName);
}
```

You've seen how to get text and XML from the server, using the `getText` and `getXml` functions. How about posting some data to the server and getting text back?

Post data to the server and get text back

As you know, Ajax applications usually send some data to the server and then get data back. The Ajax Utility Library supports this process with two functions: `postDataGetText` and `postDataGetXml`. First, the `postDataGetText` function: this function lets you post data to the server and get text data back.

> **TIP**   You don't need to send data using the **POST** method. You can also use the Ajax Utility Library's **getText** and **getXML** functions to pass data to the server. You just have to URL-encode that data and append it to the end of the URL used with **GET** like this: **scripter.php?data=Now+is+the_time**.

You pass the `postDataGetText` function the URL you want to access, the data to send to that URL, and the function to call back:

```
function postDataGetText(urlToCall, dataToSend,
functionToCallBack)
{
        .
        .
        .

}
```

As with the other functions in the Ajax Utility Library, `postDataGetText` starts by creating an `XMLHttpRequest` object:

```
function postDataGetText(urlToCall, dataToSend,
functionToCallBack)
{
  var XMLHttpRequestObject = false;

  if (window.XMLHttpRequest) {
    XMLHttpRequestObject = new XMLHttpRequest();
  } else if (window.ActiveXObject) {
    XMLHttpRequestObject = new
     ActiveXObject("Microsoft.XMLHTTP");
  }
      .
      .
      .

}
```

And the code checks to make sure that the `XMLHttpRequest` creation process was successful:

```
function postDataGetText(urlToCall, dataToSend,
functionToCallBack)
```

```
  {
    var XMLHttpRequestObject = false;

    if (window.XMLHttpRequest) {
      XMLHttpRequestObject = new XMLHttpRequest();
    } else if (window.ActiveXObject) {
      XMLHttpRequestObject = new
        ActiveXObject("Microsoft.XMLHTTP");
    }

    if(XMLHttpRequestObject) {
      .
      .
      .
    }
  }
```

Connecting to the server starts with the XMLHttpRequest object's open method, where you indicate you're using the POST method, and configuring the XMLHttpRequest object to connect to the URL passed to the postDataGetText function:

```
function postDataGetText(urlToCall, dataToSend,
functionToCallBack)
  {
    var XMLHttpRequestObject = false;

    if (window.XMLHttpRequest) {
      XMLHttpRequestObject = new XMLHttpRequest();
    } else if (window.ActiveXObject) {
      XMLHttpRequestObject = new
        ActiveXObject("Microsoft.XMLHTTP");
    }

    if(XMLHttpRequestObject) {
      XMLHttpRequestObject.open("POST", urlToCall);
        .
        .
        .
  }
```

When you're using the POST method with Ajax, you also set the Content-Type request header to application/x-www-form-urlencoded, like this:

```
function postDataGetText(urlToCall, dataToSend,
functionToCallBack)
  {
    var XMLHttpRequestObject = false;
```

```
if (window.XMLHttpRequest) {
  XMLHttpRequestObject = new XMLHttpRequest();
} else if (window.ActiveXObject) {
  XMLHttpRequestObject = new
    ActiveXObject("Microsoft.XMLHTTP");
}

if(XMLHttpRequestObject) {
  XMLHttpRequestObject.open("POST", urlToCall);
  XMLHttpRequestObject.setRequestHeader('Content-Type',
    'application/x-www-form-urlencoded');
    .
    .
    .

}
}
```

Now you're ready to connect an anonymous inner function to the XMLHttpRequest object's onreadystatechange property, and wait for the download to occur:

```
function postDataGetText(urlToCall, dataToSend,
functionToCallBack)
{
  var XMLHttpRequestObject = false;

  if (window.XMLHttpRequest) {
    XMLHttpRequestObject = new XMLHttpRequest();
  } else if (window.ActiveXObject) {
    XMLHttpRequestObject = new
      ActiveXObject("Microsoft.XMLHTTP");
  }

  if(XMLHttpRequestObject) {
    XMLHttpRequestObject.open("POST", urlToCall);
    XMLHttpRequestObject.setRequestHeader('Content-Type',
      'application/x-www-form-urlencoded');

    XMLHttpRequestObject.onreadystatechange = function()
    {
      if (XMLHttpRequestObject.readyState == 4 &&
        XMLHttpRequestObject.status == 200) {
        .
        .
        .

      }
    }
  }
}
```

After downloading the data, the postDataGetText function passes it to the callback function you've specified, and then deletes the XMLHttpRequest object:

```
function postDataGetText(urlToCall, dataToSend,
functionToCallBack)
{
  var XMLHttpRequestObject = false;

  if (window.XMLHttpRequest) {
    XMLHttpRequestObject = new XMLHttpRequest();
  } else if (window.ActiveXObject) {
    XMLHttpRequestObject = new
     ActiveXObject("Microsoft.XMLHTTP");
  }

  if(XMLHttpRequestObject) {
    XMLHttpRequestObject.open("POST", urlToCall);
    XMLHttpRequestObject.setRequestHeader('Content-Type',
      'application/x-www-form-urlencoded');

    XMLHttpRequestObject.onreadystatechange = function()
    {
      if (XMLHttpRequestObject.readyState == 4 &&
        XMLHttpRequestObject.status == 200) {
          functionToCallBack(XMLHttpRequestObject.responseText);
          delete XMLHttpRequestObject;
          XMLHttpRequestObject = null;
      }
    }
      .
      .
      .

  }
}
```

Everything's set up. All you need to do is pass the data to send to the server, and that looks like this:

```
function postDataGetText(urlToCall, dataToSend,
functionToCallBack)
{
  var XMLHttpRequestObject = false;
      .
      .
      .

    XMLHttpRequestObject.onreadystatechange = function()
    {
```

```
      if (XMLHttpRequestObject.readyState == 4 &&
        XMLHttpRequestObject.status == 200) {
          functionToCallBack(XMLHttpRequestObject.responseText);
          delete XMLHttpRequestObject;
          XMLHttpRequestObject = null;
      }
    }

    XMLHttpRequestObject.send(dataToSend);
  }
}
```

That completes the postDataGetText function. How about putting it to work?

You can test the postDataGetText function with the testpostDataGetText.html file, which is included in the downloaded files for this chapter. This page simply posts text to a small PHP script, echoer.php, under the parameter message, and that script echoes the text back. Here's what echoer.php looks like:

```
<?
echo ($_POST["message"]);
?>
```

So what does the test page, testpostDataGetText.html, look like? It starts by including the Ajax Utility Library, making the postDataGetText function available to its JavaScript:

```
<html>
  <head>

    <title>Posting data and getting text with the Ajax
      Utility library</title>

    <script type = "text/javascript" src =
      "ajaxutility.js"></script>
         .
         .
         .
```

Then it displays a "Get the text" button, connected to the postDataGetText function. The page passes the URL to post data to, echoer.php, as well as the data to send. Because you post data in the parameter=value format, this example posts the data message=Hello from Ajax Utility to echoer.php. And you also pass the name of the callback function that is passed the downloaded data, called display in this case:

```
<body>

  <h1>Posting data and getting text with the Ajax
    Utility library</h1>
```

```
<form>
  <input type = "button" value = "Get the text"
  onclick = "postDataGetText('echoer.php',
    'message=Hello from Ajax Utility.', display)">
</form>
        .
        .
        .

</body>
```

When the user clicks the button, the data message=Hello from Ajax Utility is passed to echoer.php, which echoes back Hello from Ajax Utility, and the postDataGetText function passes that text to the callback function display. The display function displays the downloaded text in a <div> element:

```
<html>
  <head>

    <title>Posting data and getting text with the Ajax
      Utility library</title>

    <script type = "text/javascript" src =
      "ajaxutility.js"></script>

    <script language = "javascript">

      function display(text)
      {
        document.getElementById('targetDiv').innerHTML = text;
      }

    </script>
  </head>
```

Here's what it looks like in action. You can see the testpostDataGetText.html page at work in Figure 5.6.

There's one more function to add to the Ajax Utility Library — postDataGetXml — which posts data to the server and gets XML back.

FIGURE 5.6

Posting text and getting it back

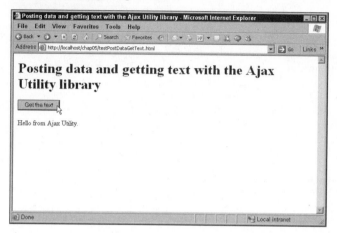

Post data to the server and get XML back

Sometimes you may want to post data to the server and get back XML, not text. The Ajax Utility Library is up to the task with the `postDataGetXml` function. You pass this function the URL to access, the data to post, and the function to call back, like this:

```
function postDataGetXml(urlToCall, dataToSend,
functionToCallBack)
{
    .
    .
    .
}
```

As with the other functions, the code starts by creating an `XMLHttpRequest` object:

```
function postDataGetXml(urlToCall, dataToSend,
functionToCallBack)
{
  var XMLHttpRequestObject = false;

  if (window.XMLHttpRequest) {
    XMLHttpRequestObject = new XMLHttpRequest();
  } else if (window.ActiveXObject) {
    XMLHttpRequestObject = new
      ActiveXObject("Microsoft.XMLHTTP");
```

```
    }
                  .
                  .
                  .
    }
```

If the XMLHttpRequest object was created, the code opens the XMLHttpRequest object, setting the method to POST and configuring that object to connect to the URL passed to the postDataGetXml function:

```
function postDataGetXml(urlToCall, dataToSend,
functionToCallBack)
{
  var XMLHttpRequestObject = false;

  if (window.XMLHttpRequest) {
    XMLHttpRequestObject = new XMLHttpRequest();
  } else if (window.ActiveXObject) {
    XMLHttpRequestObject = new
     ActiveXObject("Microsoft.XMLHTTP");
  }

  if(XMLHttpRequestObject) {
    XMLHttpRequestObject.open("POST", urlToCall);
    XMLHttpRequestObject.setRequestHeader('Content-Type',
      'application/x-www-form-urlencoded');
        .
        .
        .
  }
}
```

Next, you connect an anonymous inner function to the XMLHttpRequest object's onreadystatechange property:

```
function postDataGetXml(urlToCall, dataToSend,
functionToCallBack)
{
  var XMLHttpRequestObject = false;

  if (window.XMLHttpRequest) {
    XMLHttpRequestObject = new XMLHttpRequest();
  } else if (window.ActiveXObject) {
    XMLHttpRequestObject = new
     ActiveXObject("Microsoft.XMLHTTP");
  }
```

```
if(XMLHttpRequestObject) {
  XMLHttpRequestObject.open("POST", urlToCall);
  XMLHttpRequestObject.setRequestHeader('Content-Type',
    'application/x-www-form-urlencoded');

  XMLHttpRequestObject.onreadystatechange = function()
  {
    if (XMLHttpRequestObject.readyState == 4 &&
      XMLHttpRequestObject.status == 200) {
      .
      .
      .
    }
  }
}
}
```

When the XML has been downloaded, the code passes it to the callback function, and then deletes the XMLHttpRequest object:

```
function postDataGetXml(urlToCall, dataToSend,
functionToCallBack)
{
  var XMLHttpRequestObject = false;

  if (window.XMLHttpRequest) {
    XMLHttpRequestObject = new XMLHttpRequest();
  } else if (window.ActiveXObject) {
    XMLHttpRequestObject = new
     ActiveXObject("Microsoft.XMLHTTP");
  }

  if(XMLHttpRequestObject) {
    XMLHttpRequestObject.open("POST", urlToCall);
    XMLHttpRequestObject.setRequestHeader('Content-Type',
      'application/x-www-form-urlencoded');

    XMLHttpRequestObject.onreadystatechange = function()
    {
      if (XMLHttpRequestObject.readyState == 4 &&
        XMLHttpRequestObject.status == 200) {
        functionToCallBack(XMLHttpRequestObject.responseXML);
        delete XMLHttpRequestObject;
        XMLHttpRequestObject = null;
      }
    }
  }
}
```

All that's left is to actually send the data to the server, and that looks like this:

```
function postDataGetXml(urlToCall, dataToSend,
functionToCallBack)
{
  var XMLHttpRequestObject = false;
      .
      .
      .

    XMLHttpRequestObject.onreadystatechange = function()
    {
      if (XMLHttpRequestObject.readyState == 4 &&
        XMLHttpRequestObject.status == 200) {
          functionToCallBack(XMLHttpRequestObject.responseXML);
          delete XMLHttpRequestObject;
          XMLHttpRequestObject = null;
      }
    }

    XMLHttpRequestObject.send(dataToSend);
  }
}
```

This completes the `postDataGetXml` function. Time to put it to the test in a new page,
testPostDataGetText.html, which is included in the downloaded files for this chapter. You might
create a test script, menus.php, that you can pass data to and get back the XML you've already seen
for the two menus. For example, if you pass a parameter named menu set to 1 to menus.php,
you'll get back the first menu:

```
<?
header("Content-type: text/xml");
if ($_POST["menu"] == "1")
  $menuitems = array('Ham', 'Turkey', 'Beef');
      .
      .
      .

?>
```

If you pass the menu parameter set to 2, you'll get the second menu:

```
<?
header("Content-type: text/xml");
if ($_POST["menu"] == "1")
  $menuitems = array('Ham', 'Turkey', 'Beef');
if ($_POST["menu"] == "2")
  $menuitems = array('Tomato', 'Cucumber', 'Rice');
      .
      .
      .

?>
```

And all that remains is to store the menu in XML form and pass it back to the browser:

```php
<?
header("Content-type: text/xml");
if ($_POST["menu"] == "1")
   $menuitems = array('Ham', 'Turkey', 'Beef');
if ($_POST["menu"] == "2")
   $menuitems = array('Tomato', 'Cucumber', 'Rice');
echo '<?xml version="1.0" ?>';
echo '<menu>';
foreach ($menuitems as $value)
{
   echo '<menuitem>';
   echo $value;
   echo '</menuitem>';
}
echo '</menu>';
?>
```

So if you pass menu=1 to menus.php, you get menu 1 back; if you pass menu=2 to menus.php, you get menu 2 back.

All that's left is to write the Web page, testPostDataGetXml.html, that puts menus.php and postDataGetXml to work. You might start by adding the HTML for the <select> control that displays the menus:

```html
<form>
  <select size="1" id="menuList"
    onchange="setmenu()">
    <option>Select a menu item</option>
  </select>
       .
       .
       .
</form>
```

And you can follow that up with the HTML for the two buttons that let the user select between the menus:

```html
<form>
  <select size="1" id="menuList"
    onchange="setmenu()">
    <option>Select a menu item</option>
  </select>
  <br>
  <br>
  <input type = "button" value = "Select menu 1"
```

```
      onclick = "postDataGetXml('menus.php', 'menu=1',
        getmenu)">
  <input type = "button" value = "Select menu 2"
    onclick = "postDataGetXml('menus.php', 'menu=2',
      getmenu)">
</form>
```

NOTE These buttons differ in the data you pass to **postDataGetXml**; one passes **menu=1** and the other **menu=2**, making menus.php return the correct menu.

Finally, you need the <div> element to display the user's selection from the displayed menu:

```
<form>
  <select size="1" id="menuList"
    onchange="setmenu()">
    <option>Select a menu item</option>
  </select>
  <br>
  <br>
  <input type = "button" value = "Select menu 1"
    onclick = "postDataGetXml('menus.php', 'menu=1',
      getmenu)">
  <input type = "button" value = "Select menu 2"
    onclick = "postDataGetXml('menus.php', 'menu=2',
      getmenu)">
</form>

<div id="targetDiv" width =100 height=100>Your lunch
  selection will appear here.</div>
```

That's it for the HTML controls. The Ajax Utility function postDataGetXml does most of the work here, of course, passing the data to the server and getting the XML response; you just use the postDataGetXml function to include ajaxutility.js:

```
<html>
  <head>

    <title>Posting data and getting XML with the Ajax
      Utility Library</title>

    <script type = "text/javascript" src =
      "ajaxutility.js"></script>
        .
        .
        .
```

The callback function, which is getmenu here, is passed a JavaScript XML document holding the XML from the server:

```html
<html>
  <head>

    <title>Posting data and getting XML with the Ajax
      Utility Library</title>

    <script type = "text/javascript" src =
      "ajaxutility.js"></script>

    <script language = "javascript">

      function getmenu(xmlDocument)
      {
        .
        .
        .
      }
        .
        .
        .
```

In getmenu, you can recover the <menuitem> elements, store them in an array named menus, and then call a function named listmenu to handle the work of stocking the <select> control with the menu items:

```html
<html>
  <head>

    <title>Posting data and getting XML with the Ajax
      Utility Library</title>

    <script type = "text/javascript" src =
      "ajaxutility.js"></script>

    <script language = "javascript">

      var menu;

      function getmenu(xmlDocument)
      {
        menu = xmlDocument.getElementsByTagName("menuitem");
        listmenu();
      }
        .
        .
        .
```

The listmenu function stores the menu items in the <select> control this way:

```
<html>
  <head>

    <title>Posting data and getting XML with the Ajax
      Utility Library</title>

    <script type = "text/javascript" src =
      "ajaxutility.js"></script>

    <script language = "javascript">

      var menu;

      function getmenu(xmlDocument)
      {
          menu = xmlDocument.getElementsByTagName("menuitem");
          listmenu();
      }

      function listmenu ()
      {
        var loopIndex;
        var selectControl = document.getElementById('menuList');

        for (loopIndex = 0; loopIndex < menu.length; loopIndex++
)
        {
            selectControl.options[loopIndex] = new
                Option(menu[loopIndex].firstChild.data);
        }
      }
        .
        .
        .
```

When the user makes a menu selection, the <select> control calls a function named setmenu:

```
<html>
  <head>

    <title>Posting data and getting XML with the Ajax
      Utility Library</title>

    <script type = "text/javascript" src =
      "ajaxutility.js"></script>
```

```
<script language = "javascript">
    .
    .
    .
function setmenu()
{
  document.getElementById('targetDiv').innerHTML =
    "You selected " + menu[document.getElementById
      ('menuList').selectedIndex].firstChild.data;
}

</script>
</head>
```

You can see testPostDataGetXml.html at work in Figure 5.7.

Posting data and getting XML back

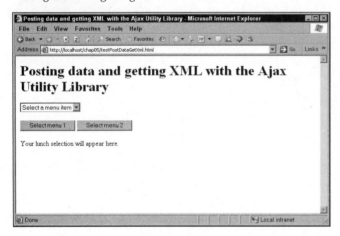

You get menu 1 back from menus.php in XML format by clicking the first button, as shown in Figure 5.8. To get menu 2, click the second button, as shown in Figure 5.9.

FIGURE 5.8

Getting menu 1

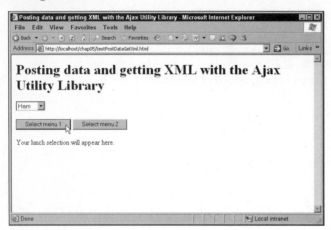

FIGURE 5.9

Getting menu 2

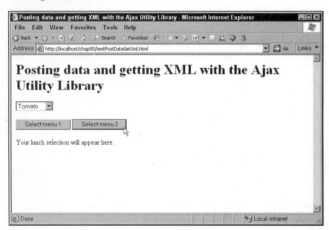

Congratulations! You've got the `postDataGetXml` function working, and with it, the Ajax Utility Library.

As you can see, the Ajax Utility Library is a useful one for working with Ajax. All the Ajax programming is done for you; there's no need to write it yourself. You've only got to select the function you want to use to connect to the server behind the scenes, and the Ajax Utility Library does the rest. Here are the functions to select from:

- `getText(urlToCall, functionToCallBack)`
- `getXml(urlToCall, functionToCallBack)`
- `postDataGetText(urlToCall, dataToSend, functionToCallBack)`
- `postDataGetXml(urlToCall, dataToSend, functionToCallBack)`

That's the idea behind Ajax frameworks: the Ajax code is already written for you, and all you've got to do is make the calls to the frameworks' functions. The Ajax Utility Library is an example of one Ajax framework, and next you'll see others available for free which you might like better, starting with `libXmlRequest`.

Using libXmlRequest to Download XML

One of the popular Ajax frameworks is the Ajax `libXmlRequest` framework, and you can pick it up for free at `www.whitefrost.com/reference/2003/06/17/libXmlRequest.html`. What you actually download is libXmlRequest.js, a JavaScript library of functions much like ajaxutility.js.

The `libXmlRequest` framework revolves around two main Ajax functions: `getXML` and `postXML`. This library is XML-centric, and contains a number of functions that let you handle XML. Here's an overview of the Ajax functions in the `libXmlRequest` library:

- `getXml(url)`: This is a *synchronous* GET request, and it returns `null` or an XML document object.
- `getXml(url, handler,1)`: This is an asynchronous GET request. This call returns 1 if the request was made successfully, and calls the callback function handler when the XML is downloaded.
- `postXml(url, data)`: This is a *synchronous* POST request, and it returns `null` or an XML document object.
- `postXml(url, data, handler, 1)`: This is an asynchronous POST request, and this call returns 1 if the request was made successfully, and calls the callback function handler when the XML is downloaded.

The callback functions, called *handler* here, are called with two parameters, and the second parameter is the one you're interested in because it contains the downloaded XML. The xdom property of that parameter is the XML object that contains your data.

When you use this library, you must preface the names of these functions with `org.cote.js.xml.` to call them. For example, if you want to call the `postXml` function, for example, you'd call `org.cote.js.xml.postXml`.

How about putting the `libXmlRequest` framework to work in an example, testlibXmlRequest.html? For example, you might want to read the text inside the `<text>` element inside a file named message.xml:

```
<?xml version = "1.0" ?>
<text>
This text was fetched using libXmlRequest.
</text>
```

So how do you download and recover the data in message.xml using the `libXmlRequest` framework? You start, naturally enough, by including the libXmlRequest.js library in testlibXmlRequest.html:

```
<html>
  <head>
    <title>Using the libXmlRequest Ajax framework</title>

    <script src = "libXmlRequest.js"></script>
      .
      .
      .
```

Next, you can add a button with the caption `Get the message`:

```
<form>
  <input type = "button" value = "Get the message"
    .
    .
    .
</form>
```

When the user clicks that button, you can call the asynchronous version of the `org.cote.js`
`.xml.getXml` function to download message.xml, calling a callback function simply named callback:

```
<form>
  <input type = "button" value = "Get the message"
    onclick = "org.cote.js.xml.getXml('message.xml',
      callback, 1)">
</form>
```

And you might add a `<div>` element to display the downloaded data in, like this:

```
<form>
  <input type = "button" value = "Get the message"
    onclick = "org.cote.js.xml.getXml('message.xml',
      callback, 1)">
</form>
```

```
<div id="targetDiv">
  <p>The fetched data will go here.</p>
</div>
```

The callback function will be called with two parameters:

```
<html>
  <head>
    <title>Using the libXmlRequest Ajax framework</title>

    <script src = "libXmlRequest.js"></script>

    <script language = "javascript">

      function callback(a, b)
      {
          .
          .
          .
      }
    </script>
  </head>
```

The second parameter is the one of interest; its xdom property gives you access to the downloaded XML. You can use the getElementsByTagName method to get an array of XML elements; in this example, the only XML element is the <text> element, so you can get an array of <text> elements like this:

```
<html>
  <head>
    <title>Using the libXmlRequest Ajax framework</title>

    <script src = "libXmlRequest.js"></script>

    <script language = "javascript">

      function callback(a, b)
      {
        var xmlData = b.xdom.getElementsByTagName("text");
          .
          .
          .

      }
    </script>
  </head>
```

This array should contain only one <text> element, in fact, because there is only one <text> element in messages.xml. You can access that <text> element as xmlData[0]. The text inside that element is stored in a text node, which is the first child node of xmlData[0]. And you can access the text inside the text node with its `data` property, all of which means that you can recover the text inside the `<text>` element and display that text like this:

```
<html>
  <head>
    <title>Using the libXmlRequest Ajax framework</title>

    <script src = "libXmlRequest.js"></script>

    <script language = "javascript">

      function callback(a, b)
      {
        var xmlData = b.xdom.getElementsByTagName("text");

        var div = document.getElementById('targetDiv');

        div.innerHTML = xmlData[0].firstChild.data;

      }
    </script>
  </head>
```

But does it work? Take a look at Figure 5.10, which shows testlibXmlRequest.html at work. When you click the button, the `libXmlRequest` function `getXML` operates behind the scenes and fetches the data from message.xml, which is displayed.

Downloading XML data using `libXmlRequest`

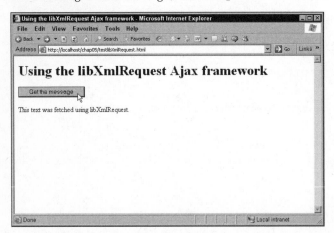

The libXmlRequest library is one Ajax framework. How about another? Take a look at AJAXLib, which is discussed next.

Using AJAXLib to Download XML

AJAXLib is a very simple Ajax framework that you can pick up for free at `http://karaszewski` `.com/tools/ajaxlib/`. The actual framework's JavaScript library is named ajaxlib.js.

How do you use it? This framework is easy to use: All you have to do is pass this library's `loadXMLDoc` function, passing that function the URL to your XML source, the callback function to call after the XML is downloaded, and a `true`/`false` parameter that lets you remove white space in the downloaded XML (`true` means AJAXLib should remove white space). When the XML is downloaded, the XML will be accessible in a variable named `resultXML`.

How about an example? Say you wanted to read the text from a new XML document, message2.xml, which contains these contents:

```
<?xml version = "1.0" ?>
<text>
This text was fetched using AJAXLib.
</text>
```

Doing so using the AJAXLib library is simple. You start, as you'd expect, by including `ajaxlib.js` in your Web page, testAJAXLib.html:

```
<html>
  <head>
    <title>Using the AJAXLib Ajax framework</title>

    <script src = "ajaxlib.js"></script>
         .
         .
         .
```

To download the XML, you can connect a button to the `AJAXLib loadXMLDoc` function, indicating that you want to download message2.xml, call a function named `callback` when the XML has been downloaded, and not remove white space in the XML:

```
<body>

    <H1>Using the AJAXLib Ajax framework</H1>

    <form>
      <input type = "button" value = "Get the message"
        onclick = "loadXMLDoc('message2.xml', callback, false)">
    </form>
```

You'll also need a `<div>` element to display the downloaded XML data:

```
<form>
  <input type = "button" value = "Get the message"
    onclick = "loadXMLDoc('message2.xml', callback, false)">
</form>
```

```
<div id="targetDiv">
  <p>The fetched data will go here.</p>
</div>
```

The `loadXMLDoc` function does its thing and, if successful, calls the `callback` function. In that function, you can access the `resultXML` variable, introduced into your page by AJAXLib. That variable holds the downloaded XML, stored as a JavaScript XML document object, so you can use the `getElementsByTagName` method to recover all the `<text>` elements that have been downloaded:

```
<html>
  <head>
    <title>Using the AJAXLib Ajax framework</title>

    <script src = "ajaxlib.js"></script>

    <script language = "javascript">

      function callback()
      {
        var xmlData = resultXML.getElementsByTagName("text");
            .
            .
            .

      }
    </script>
  </head>
```

Because there's only one `<text>` element in the array created using `getElementsByTagName`, you can access that element as `xmlData[0]`. The rest of the process for extracting the text data from that element is the same as with the libXmlRequest library, so here's how you can display the downloaded data:

```
<html>
  <head>
    <title>Using the AJAXLib Ajax framework</title>

    <script src = "ajaxlib.js"></script>

    <script language = "javascript">

      function callback()
      {
        var xmlData = resultXML.getElementsByTagName("text");

        var div = document.getElementById('targetDiv');

        div.innerHTML = xmlData[0].firstChild.data;
```

```
        }
    </script>
</head>
```

How does it look in practice? As you'd expect. Take a look at Figure 5.11, where the user has clicked the button and the `loadXMLDoc` function has done its thing, downloading the data, which has been displayed by the page. Very nice.

FIGURE 5.11

Downloading XML data using `AJAXLib`

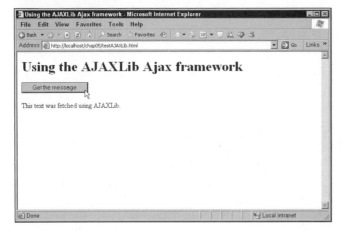

Summary

This chapter covered three Ajax frameworks: the Ajax Utility framework, the `libXmlRequest` framework, and the `AJAXLib` framework. Those are just three of the wide variety of such frameworks available; more are coming up in the next two chapters.

Chapter 6

More Advanced Ajax Frameworks

Many client-side Ajax frameworks are available free for the downloading, and this chapter takes a look at some of the most popular. The frameworks reviewed in this chapter are all JavaScript libraries. You use them by adding them to your Web page with a <script> element. When you've done so, you can call the functions in those libraries, which means you don't have to write any Ajax code for yourself.

JavaScript Ajax frameworks run the full spectrum from thin Ajax clients to complete online application "solutions" complete with rich client controls, such as database grids, ready for you to work with. These frameworks offer a varying degree of effort to install and use; you can read about them in this chapter, and you can judge for yourself.

Let's get started with an easy client-side Ajax framework: Majax.

Using the Majax Framework

What does *Majax* stand for? It stands for "Minimalistic Ajax," and this package comes pretty close to implementing just that — an easy way of using Ajax. There are two primary Ajax-enabled functions here: `majax_get`, which uses the GET method to download Ajax content, and `majax_post`, which uses the POST method.

> **ON the WEB** You can get Majax for free at `http://sourceforge`
> `.net/projects/unips/`. Click the green Download
> unips — Universal Portal Scripting button — and download the unips package,
> which unzips to give you majax.js.

How about an example putting Majax to work? For example, say you wanted to download this text from the file majax.txt on the server:

```
This text was downloaded with Majax.
```

You might put together a Web page called testMajax.html to use the Majax framework to download this text. You start testMajax.html by including majax.js like this:

```
<html>
  <head>
    <title>Testing the Majax framework</title>

    <script type="text/javascript" src="majax.js"></script>
        .
        .
        .
```

Doing so gives you access to the `majax_get` and `majax_post` functions. To get the action started, add a button with the caption `Display the text` to the Web page:

```
<H1>Testing the Majax framework</H1>

<form>
  <input type = "button" value = "Display the text"
      .
      .
      .
</form>
```

And you can connect this new button to a function named, for example, `useMajax`, to put Majax to work downloading the text when the user clicks the button:

```
<H1>Testing the Majax framework</H1>

<form>
  <input type = "button" value = "Display the text"
      onclick = "useMajax()">
</form>
```

You'll also need a `<div>` element in which to display the results:

```
<H1>Testing the Majax framework</H1>

<form>
  <input type = "button" value = "Display the text"
      onclick = "useMajax()">
</form>

<div id="targetDiv">
  <p>The fetched data will go here.</p>
</div>
```

Next, add the useMajax function to a <script> element in the page:

```
<html>
  <head>
    <title>Testing the Majax framework</title>

    <script type="text/javascript" src="majax.js"></script>

    <script language = "javascript">

      function useMajax()
      {
        .
        .
        .
      }
```

Getting text from the server is easy: simply use a function such as majax_get. Start by declaring a variable containing the URL you want to access:

```
<html>
  <head>
    <title>Testing the Majax framework</title>

    <script type="text/javascript" src="majax.js"></script>

    <script language = "javascript">

      function useMajax()
      {
        var url = "majax.txt";
        .
        .
        .
      }
```

then call majax_get with the URL and the data to send to the server, which is null when you use the GET method:

```
<html>
  <head>
    <title>Testing the Majax framework</title>

    <script type="text/javascript" src="majax.js"></script>

    <script language = "javascript">

      function useMajax()
      {
```

```
            var url = "majax.txt";
            majax_get (url, null);
        }
                .
                .
                .
```

Similarly, if you wanted to post data to the server, you could use majax_post(url, data).

How do you read data downloaded from the server? As with most client-side Ajax frameworks, you use a callback function. In this case, you might name the callback function "handler":

```
        <script language = "javascript">

            function useMajax()
            {
              var url = "majax.txt";
              majax_get (url, null);
            }

            function handler()
            {
                .
                .
                .
            }

        </script>
```

Register the callback function with Majax using the MAJAXCM_COMPLETE.register method:

```
        <script language = "javascript">

            function useMajax()
            {
              var url = "majax.txt";
              majax_get (url, null);
            }

            function handler()
            {
                .
                .
                .
            }

            MAJAXCM_COMPLETE.register(handler);

        </script>
```

The downloaded data is stored in a variable named MAJAX_RESPONSE, and when the handler function is called, that data is ready to be used. This example simply displays the downloaded text, and you can do that like this in the handler function:

```
<script language = "javascript">

  function useMajax()
  {
    var url = "majax.txt";
    majax_get (url, null);
  }

  function handler()
  {
    var div = document.getElementById ("targetDiv");
    div.innerHTML = MAJAX_RESPONSE;
  }

  MAJAXCM_COMPLETE.register(handler);

</script>
```

That completes testMajax.html, which you can see at work in Figure 6.1.

FIGURE 6.1

Using the Majax Ajax framework

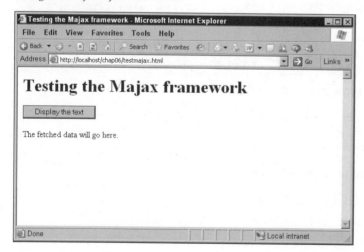

When the user clicks the button, the text in majax.txt is downloaded and displayed, as you can see in Figure 6.2.

FIGURE 6.2

Downloading text with the Majax Ajax framework

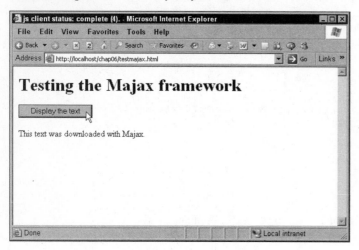

Majax is just one of the JavaScript client-side frameworks available. Another popular framework is the Sack framework, which is discussed next.

Using the Sack Framework

The Sack Ajax framework is a popular one, and it's also free and ready to download.

ON the WEB   Sack, which stands for Simple Ajax Code Kit, is available for free at `http://twilightuniverse.com/resources/code/sack/`. The actual JavaScript library that you use is called tw-sack.js.

Here are the main functions you use with the Sack framework:

- `sack`: Initializing function for the `Sack` object
  - Use: `object sack(file)`
- `file` (**optional**): The name of the file to be accessed using XMLHttpRequest
- `setVar`: Enables you to add data to the URL in the form of a name/value pair. Does not encode the data
  - Use: `void setVar(name, value)`

- name: The name of the data that you want passed
- value: The corresponding data that you want passed
- runAJAX: Runs the AJAX request and fills class variables with appropriate responses
  - Use: string runAJAX(url)
- url (optional): A string of name/value pairs formatted in the GET URL String style (for example, var1=data1&var2=data2)

Here's an example, testSack.html, that reads and downloads the file sack.txt, which has these contents on the server:

```
This text was downloaded with Sack.
```

The testSack.html page starts with a "Display the text" button, connected to a JavaScript function named useSack:

```
<H1>Testing the Sack framework</H1>

<form>
  <input type = "button" value = "Display the text"
    onclick = "useSack()">
</form>
```

And there's also a <div> element in which to display the downloaded text:

```
<H1>Testing the Sack framework</H1>

<form>
  <input type = "button" value = "Display the text"
    onclick = "useSack()">
</form>

<div id="targetDiv">
  <p>The fetched data will go here.</p>
</div>
```

You have to include the Sack JavaScript library as well, of course, and that's tw-sack.js:

```
<html>
  <head>
    <title>Testing the Sack framework</title>

    <script src = "tw-sack.js"></script>
       .
       .
       .
```

You also add the useSack function, which is connected to the button in this Web page:

```
<html>
  <head>
    <title>Testing the Sack framework</title>

    <script src = "tw-sack.js"></script>

    <script language = "javascript">

      function useSack()
      {
        .
        .
        .
      }
    </script>
```

Next, create a Sack object, using the initializing function named sack like this:

```
<html>
  <head>
    <title>Testing the Sack framework</title>

    <script src = "tw-sack.js"></script>

    <script language = "javascript">

      function useSack()
      {
        var sackObject = new sack();
        .
        .
        .
      }
    </script>
```

To use Sack, configure the Sack object and then call its runAjax method. Configure the Sack object by setting the following properties:

- AjaxFailedAlert: Holds a warning message used to alert users that their browser does not support XMLHttpRequest objects. To turn off the warning, set this property to null. Contains a default warning message.

- element: The element whose contents should be replaced with the contents of the response text.

- encodeURIString: Set to true/false; indicates whether to escape the data in the URL string. Set to false to escape the text yourself. The default is true.

- execute: Set to true if you want to evaluate the response text as if it was JavaScript code and run it. The default is false.

- ■ `failed`: Allows you to detect whether the software supports `XMLHttpRequest` objects (`true`) or not (`false`).

- ■ `method`: Sets the `HTTP` method used to communicate with the URL. You can use any valid method; `GET` and `POST` will probably be most common. The default is `POST`.

- ■ `onCompletion`: Set this property to a JavaScript function (without arguments) that you want to run when the download is completed.

- ■ `onInteractive`: Set this property to a JavaScript function (without arguments) that you want to run when the code is connected to the server.

- ■ `onLoaded`: Set this property to a JavaScript function (without arguments) that you want to run when the data has been downloaded.

- ■ `onLoading`: Set this property to a JavaScript function (without arguments) that you want to run when the data is downloading.

- ■ `requestFile`: Set to the URL that the request will be sent to.

- ■ `response`: Contains the response text sent from the server.

- ■ `responseStatus`: An array of the response status returned. 0 index is the response code (for example, 404, 300, and so on) and the 1 index is the text description.

- ■ `responseXML`: Contains the response XML received from the server.

- ■ `URLString`: Contains a list of parameters and values in name/value pairs.

For example, to download the file sack.txt, set the `Sack` object's `requestFile` property to sack.txt:

```html
<html>
  <head>
    <title>Testing the Sack framework</title>

    <script src = "tw-sack.js"></script>

    <script language = "javascript">

      function useSack()
      {
        var sackObject = new sack();

        sackObject.requestFile = "sack.txt";
        .
        .
        .
      }
    </script>
```

You can also set the `HTTP` method to use when communicating with the server to `GET` using the `Sack` object's `method` property:

```
<html>
  <head>
    <title>Testing the Sack framework</title>

    <script src = "tw-sack.js"></script>

    <script language = "javascript">

      function useSack()
      {
        var sackObject = new sack();

        sackObject.requestFile = "sack.txt";
        sackObject.method = "GET";
        .
        .
        .

      }
    </script>
```

In fact, you can even specify the HTML element whose content should be replaced with the down-loaded text. In this example, that's the targetDiv element, so you can tell Sack to place the downloaded text in the targetDiv element like this:

```
<html>
  <head>
    <title>Testing the Sack framework</title>

    <script src = "tw-sack.js"></script>

    <script language = "javascript">

      function useSack()
      {
        var sackObject = new sack();

        sackObject.requestFile = "sack.txt";
        sackObject.method = "GET";
        sackObject.element = "targetDiv";
        .
        .
        .

      }
    </script>
```

All that's left is to call the Sack object's runAjax method, passing it an empty string so it won't send any data to the server:

```
<html>
  <head>
```

```
<title>Testing the Sack framework</title>

<script src = "tw-sack.js"></script>

<script language = "javascript">

  function useSack()
  {
    var sackObject = new sack();

    sackObject.requestFile = "sack.txt";
    sackObject.method = "GET";
    sackObject.element = "targetDiv";
    sackObject.runAJAX("");
  }
</script>
```

That's all you need. Sack takes it from here, downloading sack.txt and displaying the contents of that file in the target <div> element. You can see testSack.html at work in Figure 6.3. Click the button to see this example download sack.txt and display the contents of that file.

Downloading text with the Sack Ajax framework

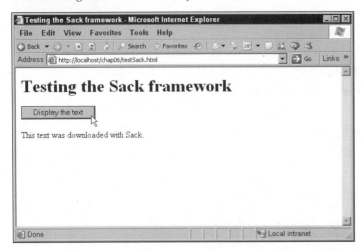

Using the XHConn Framework

The JavaScript-based XHConn framework is similar to the Sack framework. This framework is an easy one to use: just create an XHConn object and call its connect method. It'll call your callback function with the downloaded data.

ON the WEB You can pick up the XHConn framework for free at `http://xkr.us/code/` `javascript/XHConn/`.

To use this framework, you must include the JavaScript file XHConn.js in your Web page and put it to work.

Here's an example. In this case, the code downloads the file xhconn.txt, which contains this text on the server:

```
This text was downloaded with XHConn.
```

The code for this example starts with a button as before, this time connected to a function named useXHConn:

```
<h1>Testing the XHConn framework</h1>

<form>
  <input type = "button" value = "Display the text"
    onclick = "useXHConn()">
</form>
```

You'll need a `<div>` element to display the downloaded text in:

```
<h1>Testing the XHConn framework</h1>

<form>
  <input type = "button" value = "Display the text"
    onclick = "useXHConn()">
</form>

<div id="targetDiv">
  <p>The fetched data will go here.</p>
</div>
```

To work with XHConn, you need to include the file XHConn.js in your page like this:

```
<html>
  <head>

    <title>Testing the XHConn framework</title>

    <script src = "XHConn.js"></script>
         .
         .
         .
```

The button in this Web page is connected to a function named useXHConn. Start with XHConn by creating an XHConn object:

```
<head>

   <title>Testing the XHConn framework</title>

   <script src = "XHConn.js"></script>

   <script language = "javascript">

     function useXHConn()
     {
       var xhconnObject = new XHConn();
         .
         .
         .
     }

   </script>
</head>
```

And if that object wasn't created, XHConn recommends that you alert the user like this:

```
<head>

   <title>Testing the XHConn framework</title>

   <script src = "XHConn.js"></script>

   <script language = "javascript">

     function useXHConn()
     {
       var xhconnObject = new XHConn();

       if (!xhconnObject) {
         alert("XHConn object creation failed.");
       }
         .
         .
         .
     }

   </script>
</head>
```

If everything's okay, you can use the XHConn object's connect method to connect to the server and download your data:

```
xhconnObject.connect(url, method, data, callback);
```

The arguments to this method include:

- url: The URL to connect to.
- method: The HTTP method, which is either GET or POST.
- data: A string of parameter/value pairs, encoded in the form parameter1=data1& parameter2=data2& . . . . This is the data that is submitted to the server.
- callback: The function that is called when the data is downloaded. One argument, the XMLHttpRequest object, is passed to the function.

Here's what the call to the connect method looks like in this example in order to download the text in xhconn.txt:

```
<head>

  <title>Testing the XHConn framework</title>

  <script src = "XHConn.js"></script>

  <script language = "javascript">

    function useXHConn()
    {
      var xhconnObject = new XHConn();

      if (!xhconnObject) {
        alert("XHConn object creation failed.");
      }

      xhconnObject.connect("xhconn.txt", "GET", "", callback);
    }

  </script>
</head>
```

You're also going to need a callback function, which is called with the XMLHttpRequest object like this:

```
<head>

  <title>Testing the XHConn framework</title>

  <script src = "XHConn.js"></script>

  <script language = "javascript">

    function useXHConn()
    {
```

```
    var xhconnObject = new XHConn();

    if (!xhconnObject) {
      alert("XHConn object creation failed.");
    }

    xhconnObject.connect("xhconn.txt", "GET", "", callback);
  }

  function callback(XMLHttpRequestObject)
  {
    .
    .
    .
  }

</script>
</head>
```

Finally, you can use the XMLHttpRequest object passed to the callback function to recover the response text and display it like this:

```
<head>

  <title>Testing the XHConn framework</title>

  <script src = "XHConn.js"></script>

  <script language = "javascript">

    function useXHConn()
    {
      var xhconnObject = new XHConn();

      if (!xhconnObject) {
        alert("XHConn object creation failed.");
      }

      xhconnObject.connect("xhconn.txt", "GET", "", callback);
    }

    function callback(XMLHttpRequestObject)
    {
      document.getElementById("targetDiv").innerHTML
        = XMLHttpRequestObject.responseText;
    }

  </script>
</head>
```

You're done! Figure 6.4 shows this page, testXHConn.html, at work.

225

FIGURE 6.4

Downloading text with the XHConn Ajax framework

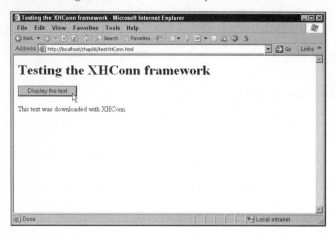

As you can see from the previous example, XHConn is an easy-to-use Ajax framework. Just create an XHConn object and use its connect method. Another, similar framework — the uniAjax framework — is up next.

Using the uniAjax Framework

ON the WEB   The uniAjax framework is available for free at `http://aka-fotos.de/web/?ajax/uniajax`. Download uniAjax.js, and you're in business.

Putting uniAjax to work is simple. For example, say you want to download the text in the file uniAjax.txt, which has these contents:

```
This text was downloaded with uniAjax.
```

This example will be called "testUniAjax.html." As described in earlier examples, you create a button, this time connected to a function named useUniAjax. You also need a <div> element to display the downloaded data:

```
<form>
  <input type = "button" value = "Display the text"
    onclick = "useUniAjax()">
</form>

<div id="targetDiv">
  <p>The fetched data will go here.</p>
</div>
```

Start this example by including uniAjax.js, like this:

```
<head>

  <title>Testing the uniAjax framework</title>

  <script language="JavaScript" src="uniAjax.js"></script>
               .
               .
               .
```

The button is tied to the useUniAjax function. In this function, create a new uniAjax object:

```
<head>

  <title>Testing the uniAjax framework</title>

  <script language="JavaScript" src="uniAjax.js"></script>

  <script language = "javascript">

    function useUniAjax()
    {
      ajax = new uniAjax();
          .
          .
          .
    }

  </script>
</head>
```

Then call the uniAjax object's request method, passing it the URL to access and the callback function. The uniAjax request method uses JavaScript-named parameters, which you pass like this: 'url': 'uniAjax.txt'.

Here's what the call to the request method looks like:

```
<head>

  <title>Testing the uniAjax framework</title>

  <script language="JavaScript" src="uniAjax.js"></script>

  <script language = "javascript">

    function useUniAjax()
    {
      ajax = new uniAjax();
      ajax.request({'url': 'uniAjax.txt', 'func': callback});
```

```
        }

    </script>
</head>
```

You also need a `callback` function to handle the response text from the server and display that text. Here's what that looks like:

```
<head>

    <title>Testing the uniAjax framework</title>

    <script language="JavaScript" src="uniAjax.js"></script>

    <script language = "javascript">

      function useUniAjax()
      {
        ajax = new uniAjax();
        ajax.request({'url': 'uniAjax.txt', 'func': callback});
      }

      function callback(response, id)
      {
        document.getElementById("targetDiv").innerHTML
          = response;
      }

    </script>
</head>
```

You can see this page, testUniAjax.html, at work in Figure 6.5.

FIGURE 6.5

Downloading text with the uniAjax Ajax framework

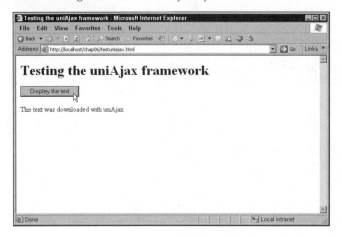

Using the AjaxGear Framework

AjaxGear is an easy-to-use, powerful framework that includes support for Ajax auto-complete, a form validator, a progress bar control, and more.

ON the WEB You can get AjaGear for free at www.ajaxgear.com.

Here's an example showing how AjaxGear works. Say you want to download the contents of AjaxGear.txt:

```
This text was downloaded with AjaxGear.
```

You might start, as with the previous examples, by connecting a button to a JavaScript function, this time named useAjaxGear. You can display the downloaded text in a `<div>` element like this:

```
<form>
  <input type = "button" value = "Display the text"
    onclick = "useAjaxGear()">
</form>

<div id="targetDiv">
  <p>The fetched data will go here.</p>
</div>
```

AjaxGear comes with a number of JavaScript libraries specialized by function. The one to use in this example is AjaxGear.Core.js. Include it in this example, testAjaxGear.html, like this:

```
<head>

  <title>Testing the AjaxGear framework</title>

  <script language="JavaScript"
    src="AjaxGear.Core.js"></script>
      .
      .
      .
```

The button is connected to a function named useAjaxGear, which is started by creating a new Ajax object using the AjaxGear Ajax function:

```
<head>

  <title>Testing the AjaxGear framework</title>

  <script language="JavaScript"
    src="AjaxGear.Core.js"></script>

  <script language = "javascript">

    var ajax;

    function useAjaxGear()
    {
      ajax = new AjaxGear.Ajax();
        .
        .
        .
    }

  </script>
</head>
```

Next, you can configure the ajax object. Following are the available members you can work with:

- getIsAsynchronous: Indicates whether or not the call is asynchronous. The default value is true.
- getMethod: Contains the HTTP method used.
- getRequestData: Contains the data sent to the server.
- getResponseText: Contains the text data read from the server.
- getResponseXml: Contains the xml data read from the server.
- onRequestComplete: Calls an assigned function when the download is complete.

- `setIsAsynchronous`: Sets whether or not the call is asynchronous.
- `setMethod`: Sets the HTTP method to be used for request. AjaxGear supports both GET and POST methods.
- `setPagePath`: Sets the URL you want to access.
- `setRequestData`: Sets the data that will be passed to the server. Use this property also for query strings when you use the GET method.
- `startRequest`: Starts the asynchronous communication with the server.

To set the HTTP method to use to connect to the server, use the `setMethod` method:

```
<head>

  <title>Testing the AjaxGear framework</title>

  <script language="JavaScript"
    src="AjaxGear.Core.js"></script>

  <script language = "javascript">

    var ajax;

    function useAjaxGear()
    {
      ajax = new AjaxGear.Ajax();
      ajax.setMethod("GET");
        .
        .
        .
    }

  </script>
</head>
```

Use the `setPagePath` method to set the URL to access ajaxGear.txt:

```
<head>
    .
    .
    .
  <script language = "javascript">

    var ajax;

    function useAjaxGear()
    {
      ajax = new AjaxGear.Ajax();
      ajax.setMethod("GET");
```

```
        ajax.setPagePath("ajaxGear.txt");
            .
            .
            .
        }

    </script>
</head>
```

And you can connect a callback function to the ajax object with the onRequestComplete property. This example simply uses a callback function named callback:

```
<head>
    .
    .
    .
  <script language = "javascript">

    var ajax;

    function useAjaxGear()
    {
      ajax = new AjaxGear.Ajax();
      ajax.setMethod("GET");
      ajax.setPagePath("ajaxGear.txt");
      ajax.onRequestComplete = callback;
            .
            .
            .
      }

    </script>
</head>
```

Finally, start the Ajax download with the startRequest method:

```
<head>
    .
    .
    .
  <script language = "javascript">

    var ajax;

    function useAjaxGear()
    {
      ajax = new AjaxGear.Ajax();
      ajax.setMethod("GET");
      ajax.setPagePath("ajaxGear.txt");
      ajax.onRequestComplete = callback;
```

```
    ajax.startRequest();
  }

</script>
</head>
```

How do you handle the data when it's been downloaded? The `ajax` object supports a method, `getResponseText`, that lets you access the `responseText` property. Here's how you can display that downloaded text in the Web page:

```
<head>

  <title>Testing the AjaxGear framework</title>

  <script language="JavaScript"
    src="AjaxGear.Core.js"></script>

  <script language = "javascript">

    var ajax;

    function useAjaxGear()
    {
      ajax = new AjaxGear.Ajax();
      ajax.setMethod("GET");
      ajax.setPagePath("ajaxGear.txt");
      ajax.onRequestComplete = callback;
      ajax.startRequest();
    }

    function callback()
    {
      document.getElementById("targetDiv").innerHTML
        = ajax.getResponseText();
    }

  </script>
</head>
```

That's all you need. You can see this page, testAjaxGear.html, at work in Figure 6.6.

Another JavaScript-based framework is the AjaxRequest framework, and it's got a very handy feature for Ajax developers.

FIGURE 6.6

Downloading text with the AjaxGear Ajax framework

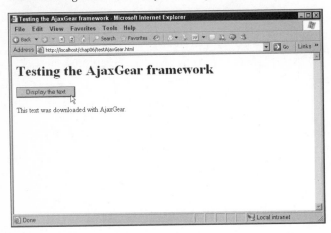

Using the AjaxRequest Framework

A handy feature Ajax applications could use is some way of handling *timeouts*, which is when the server doesn't answer a request. This feature is built into the AjaxRequest framework.

ON the WEB   Download the AjaxRequest framework from www.ajaxtoolbox.com.

Here's how it works. For example, say you want to download the following text, from the file, AjaxRequest.txt:

```
This text was downloaded with AjaxRequest.
```

You can start as you did in the previous examples, with a button, this time connected to a JavaScript function named useAjaxRequest and a <div> element:

```
<form>
  <input type = "button" value = "Display the text"
    onclick = "useAjaxRequest()">
</form>

<div id="targetDiv">
  <p>The fetched data will go here.</p>
</div>
```

The JavaScript library here is AjaxRequest.js, and you can include that in a Web page, testAjaxRequest.html:

```
<head>

  <title>Testing the AjaxRequest framework</title>

  <script src = "AjaxRequest.js"></script>
      .
      .
      .
```

You can use the AjaxRequest library without creating any object; just call the `AjaxRequest.get` method. The button is tied to a function named `useAjaxRequest`, and you can call `AjaxRequest.get` in that function:

```
<head>
    .
    .
    .
  <script language = "javascript">

    function useAjaxRequest()
    {
      AjaxRequest.get(
      {
        .
        .
        .
      }
      );
    }

  </script>
</head>
```

The `AjaxRequest.get` method uses named parameters, just as the uniAjax `request` method did. Start by setting the URL to access like this:

```
<head>
    .
    .
    .
  <script language = "javascript">

    function useAjaxRequest()
    {
      AjaxRequest.get(
      {
```

```
        'url':'AjaxRequest.txt',
           .
           .
           .
      }
      );
   }

   </script>
</head>
```

You can also connect a `callback` function with the `onSuccess` named parameter:

```
<head>
   .
   .
   .
   <script language = "javascript">

     function useAjaxRequest()
     {
       AjaxRequest.get(
       {
         'url':'AjaxRequest.txt',
         'onSuccess': callback,
            .
            .
            .
       }
       );
     }

   </script>
</head>
```

You can also set a timeout using `AjaxRequest`. For example, to set the timeout to 1000 milliseconds (that is, one second), you can use this code:

```
<head>
   .
   .
   .
   <script language = "javascript">

     function useAjaxRequest()
     {
       AjaxRequest.get(
       {
```

```
        'url':'AjaxRequest.txt',
        'onSuccess': callback,
        'timeout':1000,

              .
              .
              .
      }
      );
    }

  </script>
</head>
```

How does AjaxRequest handle timeouts? You can connect a function to the onTimeout named parameter. Here's an example connecting an anonymous inner function to that parameter, which displays an alert box:

```
<head>
    .
    .
    .
<script language = "javascript">

  function useAjaxRequest()
  {
    AjaxRequest.get(
    {
      'url':'AjaxRequest.txt',
      'onSuccess': callback,
      'timeout':1000,
      'onTimeout':function(){alert('Sorry, it timed out.');}
    }
    );
  }

  function callback(XMLHttpRequestObject)
  {
    document.getElementById("targetDiv").innerHTML
      = XMLHttpRequestObject.responseText;
  }

  </script>
</head>
```

Next comes the callback function, which is passed to the XMLHttpRequest object when the data you've requested is downloaded. Because this is a real XMLHttpRequest object, you can simply use its responseText property to recover the downloaded text:

```
<head>
    .
    .
    .
  <script language = "javascript">

    function useAjaxRequest()
    {
      AjaxRequest.get(
      {
        'url':'AjaxRequest.txt',
        'onSuccess': callback,
        'timeout':1000,
        'onTimeout':function(){alert('Sorry, it timed out.');}
      }
      );
    }

    function callback(XMLHttpRequestObject)
    {
      document.getElementById("targetDiv").innerHTML
        = XMLHttpRequestObject.responseText;
    }

  </script>
</head>
```

This example is ready to go. You can see this page, testAjaxRequest.html, at work in Figure 6.7.

FIGURE 6.7

Downloading text with the AjaxRequest Ajax framework

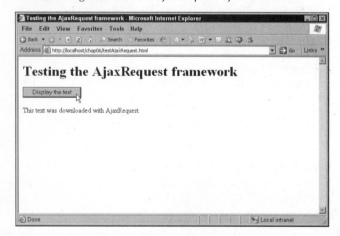

Using the Http Framework to Avoid Caching

Browsers like Microsoft Internet Explorer cache the data you read from a server, which means that you often see the same data over and over when you try to download a URL. That's a problem if the data from that URL has changed, as when a database has been modified and is sending you new data, but Internet Explorer displays the old, cached data. That's only a problem with the GET method; the POST method shouldn't be cached.

As discussed in Chapter 4, you can add the date to a URL to make Internet Explorer avoid caching data read from the server, and the Http framework does that for you.

ON the WEB You can get the Http framework for free at **http://adamv.com/dev/ javascript/http_request**. Just download request.js and put it to work.

Here's an example called testHttp.html. This example downloads the following text from the server in a file named request.txt:

```
This text was downloaded with the Http framework.
```

You start, as before, with a button tied to a function — named useRequest in this case — and a <div> element in which to display the downloaded text:

```
<form>
  <input type = "button" value = "Display the text"
    onclick = "useRequest()">
</form>

<div id="targetDiv">
  <p>The fetched data will go here.</p>
</div>
```

You'll need the request.js library, so start by including that:

```
<html>
  <head>

    <title>Testing the Http Ajax framework</title>

    <script language="JavaScript" src="request.js"></script>
        .
        .
        .
```

You can use the Http.get method in the useRequest function to connect to the server. Like some of the other frameworks in this chapter, the Http framework uses named parameters, so you set the URL to access request.txt like this:

```
<head>

  <title>Testing the Http Ajax framework</title>

  <script language="JavaScript" src="request.js"></script>

  <script language = "javascript">

    function useRequest()
    {
        Http.get({'url':'request.txt',
          .
          .
          .
    }

  </script>
</head>
```

You can set caching level to "no cache" to avoid caching in browsers like Internet Explorer:

```
<head>

  <title>Testing the Http Ajax framework</title>

  <script language="JavaScript" src="request.js"></script>

  <script language = "javascript">

    function useRequest()
    {
        Http.get({'url':'request.txt',
        'cache':Http.Cache.GetNoCache,
          .
          .
          .
    }

  </script>
</head>
```

Following are the caching options:

- `Http.Cache.Get`: Executes a normal request and does not add the result to the local cache. In Internet Explorer, requesting the same URL using GET multiple times causes Internet Explorer to cache the result internally.

- `Http.Cache.GetCache`: Executes a request and caches the result if successful. If the requested URL's response is already cached locally, do not execute the server request.

- `Http.Cache.GetNoCache`: Executes a request and adds a time-based variable to the query string to force Internet Explorer not to cache the result. The result is not placed in the local cache.

- `Http.Cache.FromCache`: Calls the supplied callback on the locally cached version if the requested URL's response has already been cached.

Finally, you set the `callback` function like this:

```
<head>

  <title>Testing the Http Ajax framework</title>

  <script language="JavaScript" src="request.js"></script>

  <script language = "javascript">

    function useRequest()
    {
        Http.get({'url':'request.txt',
        'cache':Http.Cache.GetNoCache,
        'callback':callback});
    }

  </script>
</head>
```

The other named parameter you can use with Http.get is `method`, which lets you set the HTTP method for accessing the server. You can set that parameter to GET or POST.

When you're using the Http framework, the `callback` function is called with the `XMLHttpRequest` object. All you need to do is to use that object's `responseText` property to retrieve the fetched text like this:

```
<head>

  <title>Testing the Http Ajax framework</title>

  <script language="JavaScript" src="request.js"></script>

  <script language = "javascript">

    function useRequest()
    {
        Http.get({'url':'request.txt',
        'cache':Http.Cache.GetNoCache,
        'callback':callback});
    }

    function callback(XMLHttpRquestObject)
```

```
        {
          document.getElementById("targetDiv").innerHTML
            = XMLHttpRquestObject.responseText;
        }

      </script>
  </head>
```

And you're done. You can see this non-caching page at work in Figure 6.8.

Downloading text with the Http Ajax framework

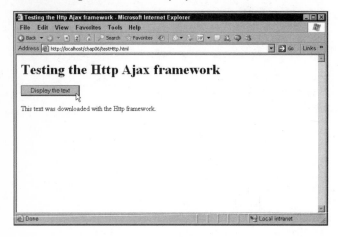

Using the Sarissa Framework to Handle XML

Sarissa is an XML-handling JavaScript library that lets you extract data from XML documents, use Extensible Stylesheet Language (XSLT) to transform XML into other formats like HTML, use XML's XPath to address the data in XML documents, and more. Sarissa also lets you use `XMLHttpRequest` to download data using Ajax.

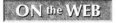 You can get Sarissa from `https://sourceforge.net/projects/sarissa/`.

The Sarissa framework can be a good choice because it lets you work with the XML you've downloaded easily. Here's an example, testSarissa.html, that lets you download and extract the data in the `<data>` element in an XML document, sarissa.xml:

```xml
<?xml version="1.0" ?>
<ajax>
  <response>
    <data>This text was downloaded with Sarissa.</data>
  </response>
</ajax>
```

As usual, you need a button connected to a JavaScript function, useSarissa this time, and a <div> element in which to display the results:

```html
<form>
  <input type = "button" value = "Display the text"
    onclick = "useSarissa()">
</form>

<div id="targetDiv">
  <p>The fetched data will go here.</p>
</div>
```

You need to include two of the JavaScript libraries that come with Sarissa: sarissa.js and sarissa_ieemu_xpath.js:

```html
<head>
  <title>Testing the Sarissa framework</title>

  <script src = "sarissa.js"></script>
  <script src = "sarissa_ieemu_xpath.js">
      .
      .
      .
```

The useSarissa function starts by creating a Sarissa DomDocument object, which is the way that Sarissa handles XML:

```html
<head>
  <title>Testing the Sarissa framework</title>

  <script src = "sarissa.js"></script>
  <script src = "sarissa_ieemu_xpath.js">

  </script>

  <script language = "javascript">

    function useSarissa()
    {
      var domDocument = Sarissa.getDomDocument();
      .
      .
```

```
          .
       }
    </script>
  </head>
```

To work with Ajax, set the DomDocument object's async property to true:

```
<head>
  <title>Testing the Sarissa framework</title>

  <script src = "sarissa.js"></script>
  <script src = "sarissa_ieemu_xpath.js">

  </script>

  <script language = "javascript">

    function useSarissa()
    {
      var domDocument = Sarissa.getDomDocument();
      domDocument.async = true;
      .
      .
      .
    }
  </script>
</head>
```

then connect an anonymous function to the DomDocument object's onreadystatechange to handle the download:

```
<head>
  <title>Testing the Sarissa framework</title>

  <script src = "sarissa.js"></script>
  <script src = "sarissa_ieemu_xpath.js">

  </script>

  <script language = "javascript">

    function useSarissa()
    {
      var domDocument = Sarissa.getDomDocument();
      domDocument.async = true;

      domDocument.onreadystatechange = function ()
      {
        if (domDocument.readyState == 4) {
```

```
                                 .
                                 .
                                 .
                     }
                 }

             }
         </script>
     </head>
```

To recover the data from the <data> element, use the Sarissa method, selectSingleNode, passing that method the XPath expression that points to the <data> element, //data:

```
<head>
    <title>Testing the Sarissa framework</title>

    <script src = "sarissa.js"></script>
    <script src = "sarissa_ieemu_xpath.js">

    </script>

    <script language = "javascript">

      function useSarissa()
      {
        var domDocument = Sarissa.getDomDocument();
        domDocument.async = true;

        domDocument.onreadystatechange = function ()
        {
          if (domDocument.readyState == 4) {
            var element = domDocument.selectSingleNode("//data");
                 .
                 .
                 .
          }
        }

      }
    </script>
</head>
```

Having isolated the <data> element, you can extract the text from that element using the Sarissa serialize method and display that text like this:

```
<head>
    <title>Testing the Sarissa framework</title>

    <script src = "sarissa.js"></script>
```

```
    <script src = "sarissa_ieemu_xpath.js">

    </script>

    <script language = "javascript">

      function useSarissa()
      {
        var domDocument = Sarissa.getDomDocument();
        domDocument.async = true;

        domDocument.onreadystatechange = function ()
        {
          if (domDocument.readyState == 4) {
            var element = domDocument.selectSingleNode("//data");
            document.getElementById("targetDiv").innerHTML =
              Sarissa.serialize(element);
          }
        }

      }
    </script>
  </head>
```

All that's left is to connect to the server, using the Sarissa `load` method:

```
  <head>
    <title>Testing the Sarissa framework</title>

    <script src = "sarissa.js"></script>
    <script src = "sarissa_ieemu_xpath.js">

    </script>

    <script language = "javascript">

      function useSarissa()
      {
        var domDocument = Sarissa.getDomDocument();
        domDocument.async = true;

        domDocument.onreadystatechange = function ()
        {
          if (domDocument.readyState == 4) {
            var element = domDocument.selectSingleNode("//data");
            document.getElementById("targetDiv").innerHTML =
              Sarissa.serialize(element);
          }
```

```
        }

        domDocument.load("sarissa.xml");
      }
    </script>
  </head>
```

And you're done. You can see this Sarissa page at work in Figure 6.9.

FIGURE 6.9

Downloading XML with the Sarissa framework

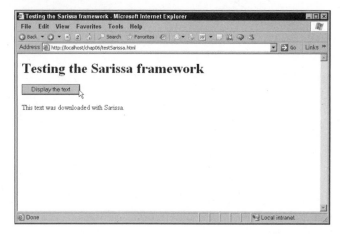

Another framework that specializes in handling XML — the Interactive Website Framework — is discussed next.

Using the Interactive Website Framework to Handle XML

The Interactive Website Framework (IWF) is another framework that specializes in handling XML, and also has Ajax capabilities built in.

ON the WEB   **You can get IWF for free at http://sourceforge.net/projects/iwf/.**

This framework allows multiple XMLHttp requests at the same time, and prevents caching by sending unique URLs to the server. Its custom XML parser can make it easier to handle XML, so that you can extract data from an XML document using syntax like this in JavaScript:

```
var dressing = doc.pizza.topping[0].dressing;
```

instead of something like this:

```
var dressing = doc.documentElement.firstChild
.getAttribute("dressing");
```

CROSS-REF   See Chapter 9 for more information on extracting XML data from XML documents using JavaScript.

IWF gives you many built-in tools, such as functions that let you move elements around a Web page to support drag-and-drop operations, or functions that let you grab XML data and insert it into an HTML element in a Web page.

Here's an example. You need to use certain XML elements to work with IWF, as in this XML document, iwf.xml:

```
<?xml version="1.0" ?>
<response>
  <action type='html'>
    This text was downloaded using IWF.
  </action>
</response>
```

The example page, testIWF.html, downloads and extracts the text in this document. Start with a button, connected to a function named useIWF:

```
<input type = "button" value = "Display the text"
  onclick = "useIWF()">
</form>
```

Instead of the usual <div> element, give the <div> element in this page a special name — iwfContent — which is the name IWF will look for:

```
<input type = "button" value = "Display the text"
  onclick = "useIWF()">
</form>

<div id='iwfContent'>The fetched text will
  appear here.</div>
```

Then include the IWF JavaScript libraries, iwfcore.js, iwfxml.js, and iwfajax.js:

```
<html>
  <head>
```

```
<title>Testing IWF</title>

<script src='iwfcore.js'></script>
<script src='iwfxml.js'></script>
<script src='iwfajax.js'></script>
        .
        .
        .
```

The rest is easy. Just call the `iwfRequest` function, passing it the URL to download, like this:

```
<html>
  <head>
    <title>Testing IWF</title>

    <script src='iwfcore.js'></script>
    <script src='iwfxml.js'></script>
    <script src='iwfajax.js'></script>

    <script>
      function useIWF()
      {
        iwfRequest('iwf.xml')
      }
    </script>
  </head>
```

When iwf.xml is downloaded, IWF unpacks the data itself and displays it in the HTML element that has the ID `iwfContent`. That's all there is to it. You can see this page at work in Figure 6.10.

FIGURE 6.10

Downloading XML with the IWF framework

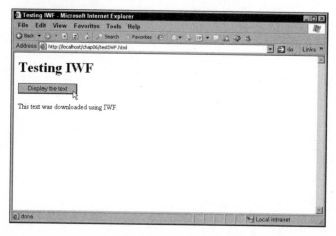

Summary

As you can see, the client-side Ajax frameworks have plenty of power. There are a good number of client-side frameworks available for you to use — picking one is a matter of your personal preference. In fact, there's even more power in server-side Ajax frameworks, which are coming up in the next chapter.

Chapter 7

Using Server-Side Ajax Frameworks

B esides the client-side Ajax frameworks you've seen in the previous two chapters, there are a number of server-side Ajax frameworks as well, and this chapter is about them.

Server-side Ajax frameworks make life easier for you by helping with both the server-side programming and the client-side programming of an Ajax application. They can generate the JavaScript you'll need in the browser automatically. For example, all you need to do is write your server-side code — the framework does the rest.

Server-side Ajax frameworks are available in many different languages. Perhaps the most popular is the server-side scripting language PHP, so this chapter starts with a discussion of PHP-based server-side frameworks. You'll also see Java-based server-side frameworks as well as Ruby on Rails frameworks in this chapter.

Working with PHP-Based Frameworks

One of the most popular server-side scripting languages is PHP. It is especially suited for Web development and can be embedded in to HTML.

Using Sajax and PHP

Sajax is a server-side Ajax framework that lets you create the JavaScript needed in an Ajax application on the server. All you need is server-side code, which can be in many different programming languages, including ASP, ColdFusion, Io, Lua, Perl, PHP, Python, or Ruby. Sajax works with all of them.

ON the WEB You can get Sajax for free at `http://www.modernmethod.com/sajax/`. All you have to do is download the latest version of Sajax and place it on your server.

Here is how Sajax works: you use it to create JavaScript functions in your Web pages. Sajax can connect those JavaScript functions to code you write for server-side programs. The JavaScript that Sajax creates for you takes the data entered in the Web page and sends it to your server-side code to be processed.

So when the user navigates to a PHP-based Web page that uses Sajax, Sajax creates that Web page on the server and creates all the JavaScript needed to connect your client-side code to code on the server. For example, if you have a PHP function named `adder` on the server, Sajax can create the JavaScript needed to pass the data the user enters in a Web page to that function on the server.

Because Sajax creates the JavaScript for your application, you only need to write a little JavaScript yourself. Sajax handles the connection between the Web page and the code on the server by itself, sending the data to the server-side code and reading the results that code passes back to the browser.

For example, take a look at the Web page shown in Figure 7.1, which uses the Sajax framework. When you click the Add button in this example, the two numbers in the text fields are added and the results are displayed, as you see in the figure.

FIGURE 7.1

Adding two numbers with the Sajax Ajax framework

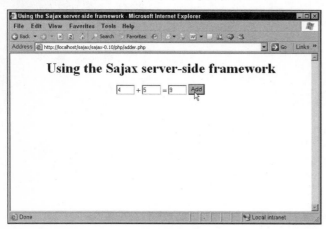

How does this example work? It starts in PHP in the file adder.php, where you include Sajax support by requiring the Sajax.php file:

```
<?
   require("Sajax.php");
          .
          .
          .

?>
```

CROSS-REF Take a look at Chapter 11 for an introduction to PHP. (Don't worry, you won't need to know much PHP to work through the examples in this chapter.)

This example creates a server-side PHP function named adder that adds the two values together and returns the result. You pass the two operands to add to this function:

```
<?
   require("Sajax.php");

   function adder($operand1, $operand2)
   {
          .
          .
          .

   }

?>
```

The adder function adds the two operands and returns the result to create the adder function:

```
<?
   require("Sajax.php");

   function adder($operand1, $operand2)
   {
      return $operand1 + $operand2;
   }

?>
```

How do you connect this function to client-side code in the browser so that the user can add numbers? You start by calling the sajax_init function to set up Sajax:

```
<?
   require("Sajax.php");

   function adder($operand1, $operand2)
   {
      return $operand1 + $operand2;
```

```
  }

sajax_init();
        .
        .
        .

?>
```

then you *export* the adder function, making it available to your Web pages, using the sajax_export function:

```
<?
  require("Sajax.php");

  function adder($operand1, $operand2)
  {
    return $operand1 + $operand2;
  }

  sajax_init();
  sajax_export("adder");
        .
        .
        .

?>
```

The code then calls the sajax_handle_client_request method to connect the adder function to Sajax and start setting up the JavaScript that will appear in the browser:

```
<?
  require("Sajax.php");

  function adder($operand1, $operand2)
  {
    return $operand1 + $operand2;
  }
  sajax_init();
  sajax_export("adder");
  sajax_handle_client_request();

?>
```

How does the adder function get connected to JavaScript in your Web page? Start the HTML portion of this page with a <script> element:

```
<?
  require("Sajax.php");

  function adder($operand1, $operand2)
```

```
    {
      return $operand1 + $operand2;
    }

    sajax_init();
    sajax_export("adder");
    sajax_handle_client_request();

?>
<html>
  <head>
    <title>Using the Sajax server-side framework</title>
    <script>
        .
        .
        .
```

then insert some PHP inside the `<script>` element, which is done by adding a call to the Sajax `sajax_show_javascript` function like this:

```
<?
    require("Sajax.php");

    function adder($operand1, $operand2)
    {
      return $operand1 + $operand2;
    }

    sajax_init();
    sajax_export("adder");
    sajax_handle_client_request();

?>
<html>
  <head>
    <title>Using the Sajax server-side framework</title>
    <script>
      <?
        sajax_show_javascript();
      ?>
        .
        .
        .
```

This call causes Sajax to write the JavaScript needed to connect to the `adder` function on the server.

It's time to supply the `adder` function with some data. As you see in Figure 7.1, this application displays two text fields to let the user enter the numbers to add; here's what they look like in HTML:

```
<body>
  <center>
    <h1>Using the Sajax server-side framework</h1>
    <input type="text" name="operand1" id="operand1" value="4"
      size="3">
    +
    <input type="text" name="operand2" id="operand2" value="5"
      size="3">
    =
    .
    .
    .
  </center>
</body>
```

You'll need a text field in which to display the answer, and that text field is called `result` in this example:

```
<body>
  <center>
    <h1>Using the Sajax server-side framework</h1>
    <input type="text" name="operand1" id="operand1" value="4"
      size="3">
    +
    <input type="text" name="operand2" id="operand2" value="5"
      size="3">
    =
    <input type="text" name="result" id="result" value=""
      size="3">
    .
    .
    .
  </center>
</body>
```

Finally, you can write the HTML Add button that sends the numbers to the `adder` function on the server. That button is tied to a JavaScript function named `do_adder` in this example:

```
<body>
  <center>
    <h1>Using the Sajax server-side framework</h1>
    <input type="text" name="operand1" id="operand1" value="4"
      size="3">
    +
    <input type="text" name="operand2" id="operand2" value="5"
      size="3">
    =
    <input type="text" name="result" id="result" value=""
      size="3">
```

```
        <input type="button" name="check" value="Add"
          onclick="do_adder(); return false;">
      </center>
    </body>
```

When the user clicks the Add button, the do_adder function is called; in that function, the two operands to add are stored in the variables operand1 and operand2:

```
<?
  require("Sajax.php");

  function adder($operand1, $operand2)
  {
    return $operand1 + $operand2;
  }
          .
          .
          .
?>
<html>
  <head>
    <title>Using the Sajax server-side framework</title>
    <script>
      <?
        sajax_show_javascript();
      ?>

      function do_adder()
      {
        var operand1, operand2;

        operand1 = document.getElementById("operand1").value;
        operand2 = document.getElementById("operand2").value;
          .
          .
          .
      }
    </script>

  </head>
```

How do you actually pass those operands to the adder function on the server? Call a function named x_adder, which is the name Sajax has given the PHP function in JavaScript, like this:

```
<?
  require("Sajax.php");

  function adder($operand1, $operand2)
  {
```

```
      return $operand1 + $operand2;
   }

   sajax_init();
   sajax_export("adder");
   sajax_handle_client_request();

?>
<html>
   <head>
      <title>Using the Sajax server-side framework</title>
      <script>
        <?
           sajax_show_javascript();
        ?>

        function do_adder()
        {
          var operand1, operand2;

          operand1 = document.getElementById("operand1").value;
          operand2 = document.getElementById("operand2").value;
          x_adder(operand1, operand2, show_results);
        }
      </script>

   </head>
```

Note how this works: you pass the two operands that will be passed to the PHP adder function on the server, and a function, show_results, that will be passed the value returned by the adder function. All that's left is to create the show_results function. In this function, you can simply display the sum in the results text field like this:

```
<?
   require("Sajax.php");

   function adder($operand1, $operand2)
   {
      return $operand1 + $operand2;
   }

   sajax_init();
   sajax_export("adder");
   sajax_handle_client_request();

?>
<html>
   <head>
      <title>Using the Sajax server-side framework</title>
      <script>
```

```
<?
  sajax_show_javascript();
?>

function show_results(result)
{
  document.getElementById("result").value = result;
}

function do_adder()
{
  var operand1, operand2;

  operand1 = document.getElementById("operand1").value;
  operand2 = document.getElementById("operand2").value;
  x_adder(operand1, operand2, show_results);
}
</script>

</head>
```

And there you have it. You pass the numbers to add to the x_adder function, and they're passed to the PHP adder function on the server. The sum is passed back to the callback function show_results.

> **NOTE** Sajax is for more than simple Ajax downloading. Take a look at http://cyberdummy .co.uk/test/dd.php, which you see in Figure 7.2. In this example Sajax is used to support Ajax-enabled dragging and dropping.

FIGURE 7.2

Dragging and dropping with Sajax

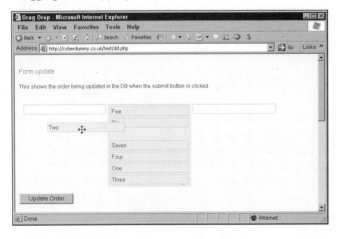

Using Xajax and PHP

Similar to Sajax, Xajax is a server-side Ajax framework that can use PHP on the server to support Ajax in browsers. In contrast to using Sajax, which enables you to use several different programming languages, you need to use PHP to work with Xajax.

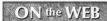 You can pick up Xajax at **http://xajax.sf.net**.

Take a look at the Web page in Figure 7.3, which uses the Xajax server-side framework to add two numbers. When the user clicks the Add button, the two numbers are passed to the server using Ajax techniques, and the sum is sent back to the browser, to be displayed in the third text field, as you see in the figure.

FIGURE 7.3

Using the Xajax framework to add numbers

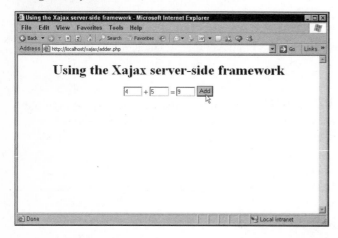

How does this Web page work? You start with PHP, requiring the xajax.inc.php library:

```php
<?php
  require("xajax.inc.php");
        .
        .
        .
?>
```

Next, you can create the PHP `adder` function, which adds two operands passed to it:

```php
<?php
  require("xajax.inc.php");

  function adder($operand1, $operand2)
```

```
{
      .
      .
      .
}

?>
```

To return a result back to the browser in Xajax, you need an `XajaxResponse` object, so you start the `adder` function by creating that object, `$response`:

```php
<?php
require("xajax.inc.php");

function adder($operand1, $operand2)
{
  $response = new xajaxResponse();
      .
      .
      .
}

?>
```

To add a result to the `$response` object, you use the object's `addAssign` method. You pass this method the ID of the HTML control that should hold the answer, the HTML property of that control that should be used to store the answer, and the value to display. Because the answer should appear in a text field that will be called `result`, and you use a text field's `value` property to display text, here's how you pass the sum of the two operands back to the browser:

```php
<?php
require("xajax.inc.php");

function adder($operand1, $operand2)
{
  $response = new xajaxResponse();
  $response->addAssign("result", "value", $operand1 +
    $operand2);
      .
      .
      .
}

?>
```

Having primed the `$response` object, you return its results in XML format, and you can get that XML using the `$response` object's `getXML` method, so here's how you return the result to the browser:

```php
<?php
  require("xajax.inc.php");

  function adder($operand1, $operand2)
  {
    $response = new xajaxResponse();
    $response->addAssign("result", "value", $operand1 +
      $operand2);
    return $response->getXML();
  }

?>
```

Now you've got to register the new `adder` function with Xajax. To do that, create a new Xajax object named `$xajax`:

```php
<?php
  require("xajax.inc.php");

  function adder($operand1, $operand2)
  {
    $response = new xajaxResponse();
    $response->addAssign("result", "value", $operand1 +
      $operand2);
    return $response->getXML();
  }

  $xajax = new xajax();
      .
      .
      .
?>
```

then register the `adder` function with the `$xajax` object:

```php
<?php
  require("xajax.inc.php");

  function adder($operand1, $operand2)
  {
    $response = new xajaxResponse();
    $response->addAssign("result", "value", $operand1 +
      $operand2);
    return $response->getXML();
  }

  $xajax = new xajax();
```

```
$xajax->registerFunction("adder");
        .
        .
        .
?>
```

To tell Xajax to connect to JavaScript in the Web page, use the Xajax method `processRequests` like this:

```
<?php
  require("xajax.inc.php");

  function adder($operand1, $operand2)
  {
    $response = new xajaxResponse();
    $response->addAssign("result", "value", $operand1 +
      $operand2);
    return $response->getXML();
  }

  $xajax = new xajax();
  $xajax->registerFunction("adder");
  $xajax->processRequests();

?>
```

You're almost done with the PHP. All that remains is to call the PHP `printJavascript` method inside the <head> element of the page to allow Xajax to write the JavaScript that connects your Web page with the server:

```
<?php
  require("xajax.inc.php");

  function adder($operand1, $operand2)
  {
    $response = new xajaxResponse();
    $response->addAssign("result", "value", $operand1 +
      $operand2);
    return $response->getXML();
  }

  $xajax = new xajax();
  $xajax->registerFunction("adder");
  $xajax->processRequests();

?>
<html>
  <head>
    <title>Using the Xajax server-side framework</title>
```

```
<?php
  $xajax->printJavascript();
?>
</head>
    .
    .
    .
```

The HTML in the page creates the two text fields that will hold the numbers to add:

```
<body>
  <center>
    <h1>Using the Xajax server-side framework</h1>
    <input type="text" name="operand1" id="operand1" value="4"
      size="3" />
    +
    <input type="text" name="operand2" id="operand2" value="5"
      size="3" />
    =
      .
      .
      .
  </body>
```

You've already told Xajax to display the answer in a text field named `result`, so you'll need that text field as well:

```
<body>
  <center>
    <h1>Using the Xajax server-side framework</h1>
    <input type="text" name="operand1" id="operand1" value="4"
      size="3" />
    +
    <input type="text" name="operand2" id="operand2" value="5"
      size="3" />
    =
    <input type="text" name="result" id="result" value=""
      size="3" />
      .
      .
      .
  </body>
```

Finally, you can add a button connected to a JavaScript function named `useAjax` that will be called when the user clicks that button:

```
<body>
  <center>
    <h1>Using the Xajax server-side framework</h1>
```

```
      <input type="text" name="operand1" id="operand1" value="4"
        size="3" />
      +
      <input type="text" name="operand2" id="operand2" value="5"
        size="3" />
      =
      <input type="text" name="result" id="result" value=""
        size="3" />
      <input type="button" value="Add"
      onclick="useXajax();return false;" />
    </body>
```

Here's where the connection to the server is. Xajax has created a JavaScript function named `xajax_adder` that calls the PHP `adder` function on the server. All you have to do is pass the two operands to add to `xajax_adder` like this in `useXAjax`, which is called when the user clicks the Add button:

```
<html>
  <head>
    <title>Using the Xajax server-side framework</title>
    <?php
      $xajax->printJavascript();
    ?>
    <script>
      function useXajax()
      {
        xajax_adder(document.getElementById('operand1').value,
          document.getElementById('operand2').value);
      }
    </script>
  </head>
```

And there you have it. You've connected the `adder` function on the server to `xajax_adder` in the browser. Your Ajax application is ready to go.

Using LibAjax and PHP

LibAjax is a PHP-based server-side Ajax framework that works in a similar way to Sajax and Xajax. The details and syntax are different, but the main idea — that you write PHP on the server and allow the framework to generate JavaScript — should already be familiar to you.

ON the WEB You can get LibAjax for free from `http://sourceforge.net/projects/libajax`.

You can see LibAjax at work in Figure 7.4, where it's adding numbers together for the user.

FIGURE 7.4

Using the LibAjax framework to add numbers

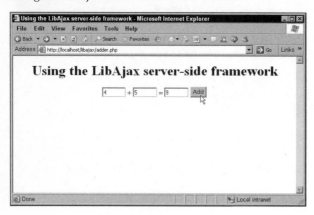

Here's how it works. The LibAjax download includes the PHP support for the framework, libajax.php, and you include that in the PHP for the page, adder.php:

```php
<?php
    require("libajax.php");
        .
        .
        .
?>
```

then you can write the PHP function that actually does the adding of the two operands, the `adder` function:

```php
<?php
    require("libajax.php");

    function adder($operand1, $operand2)
    {
      print $operand1 + $operand2;
    }

?>
```

To connect this function to LibAjax, you create an Ajax object, `$ajax`:

```php
<?php
    require("libajax.php");

    function adder($operand1, $operand2)
```

```
  {
    print $operand1 + $operand2;
  }

  $ajax = new Ajax();
            .
            .
            .

?>
```

You can configure this object by setting its properties. For example, to set the HTTP method this example uses, set the mode property:

```
<?php
  require("libajax.php");

  function adder($operand1, $operand2)
  {
    print $operand1 + $operand2;
  }

  $ajax = new Ajax();
  $ajax->mode = "GET";
            .
            .
            .

?>
```

And you can export the adder function, making it available to your Web page; to export functions in LibAjax, you pass an array of those functions to the export method. In this case, the array contains only one function, the adder function:

```
<?php
  require("libajax.php");

  function adder($operand1, $operand2)
  {
    print $operand1 + $operand2;
  }

  $ajax = new Ajax();
  $ajax->mode = "GET";
  $ajax->export = array("adder");
            .
            .
            .

?>
```

Now you let LibAjax take over. Call its `client_request` method to let it start handling client requests, like this:

```php
<?php
  require("libajax.php");

  function adder($operand1, $operand2)
  {
    print $operand1 + $operand2;
  }

  $ajax = new Ajax();
  $ajax->mode = "GET";
  $ajax->export = array("adder");
  $ajax->client_request();
?>
```

To complete the PHP, call the $ajax object's `output` method to write the JavaScript interface between server and browser:

```php
<?php
  require("libajax.php");

  function adder($operand1, $operand2)
  {
    print $operand1 + $operand2;
  }

  $ajax = new Ajax();
  $ajax->mode = "GET";
  $ajax->export = array("adder");
  $ajax->client_request();
?>
<html>
  <head>
    <title>Using the LibAjax server-side framework</title>
    <script>

      <?php
        $ajax->output();
      ?>

          .

          .

          .

    </script>
```

> **NOTE** The $ajax->output method is called inside a <script> element so that the JavaScript it writes can be executed by the browser.

In the <body> element, add the HTML for the two text fields that will hold the numbers to add:

```
<body>
  <center>
    <h1>Using the LibAjax server-side framework</h1>
    <form>
      <input type="text" name="operand1" id="operand1"
        value="4"
        size="5">
      +
      <input type="text" name="operand2" id="operand2"
        value="5"
        size="5">
      =
        .
        .
        .
    </form>
  </center>
</body>
```

And you can store the answer in a text field named `result`, as before:

```
<body>
  <center>
    <h1>Using the LibAjax server-side framework</h1>
    <form>
      <input type="text" name="operand1" id="operand1"
        value="4"
        size="5">
      +
      <input type="text" name="operand2" id="operand2"
        value="5"
        size="5">
      =
      <input type="text" name="result" id="result" value=""
        size="5">
        .
        .
        .
    </form>
  </center>
</body>
```

The Add button shown in Figure 7.4 is connected to a JavaScript function named `useLibAjax`:

```
<body>
  <center>
```

```
<h1>Using the LibAjax server-side framework</h1>
        .
        .
        .
  <input type="text" name="result" id="result" value=""
    size="5">
  <input type="button" name="check" value="Add"
    onclick="useLibAjax()">
  </form>
 </center>
</body>
```

In the useLibAjax method, you read the two numbers to be added, and pass them on to the JavaScript interface function that LibAjax has created, which is called ajax_adder. You also pass a callback function, called display here, which will be called with the sum of the two numbers:

```
<html>
  <head>
    <title>Using the LibAjax server-side framework</title>
    <script>

      <?php
        $ajax->output();
      ?>

      function useLibAjax()
      {
        var operand1 = document.getElementById("operand1").value;
        var operand2 = document.getElementById("operand2").value;
        ajax_adder(operand1, operand2, display);
      }
    </script>

  </head>
```

All that's left is to add the display callback function:

```
<html>
  <head>
    <title>Using the LibAjax server-side framework</title>
    <script>

      <?php
        $ajax->output();
      ?>

      function display(result)
      {
```

```
      document.getElementById("result").value = result;
    }

    function useLibAjax()
    {
      var operand1 = document.getElementById("operand1").value;
      var operand2 = document.getElementById("operand2").value;
      ajax_adder(operand1, operand2, display);
    }
  </script>

</head>
```

And that's it. Your Ajax application is ready to go.

Working with Java-Based Frameworks

You've gotten the gist of how things work with PHP-based frameworks: you write your PHP and then let the framework generate the JavaScript that connects that PHP to your code in the browser. It's time now to take a look at Java-based frameworks.

Using Direct Web Remoting and Java

Direct Web Remoting (DWR) is an Ajax framework that lets you call Java methods on the server, using JavaScript code to call those methods. Using DWR, you can access the full power of Java on the server behind the scenes—which is great, because Java is a far more powerful language than JavaScript, and includes all kinds of support for databases.

ON the WEB You can pick up DWR at `http://getahead.ltd.uk/dwr` for free and read the documentation at `http://getahead.ltd.uk/dwr/documentation`. There's also an introduction at `www.getahead.ltd.uk/dwr/intro.html`.

DWR works much like the PHP frameworks you've already seen in this chapter: you can call server-side code, and DWR handles the details of connecting your code to those functions. After your data has been downloaded, DWR calls the callback function you've specified.

Take a look at the DWR example shown in Figure 7.5, which you can access at `http://getahead.ltd.uk/dwr/examples/text`. This example downloads and displays information about the server behind the scenes, using Ajax, and displays that information in the Web page.

FIGURE 7.5

Using DWR

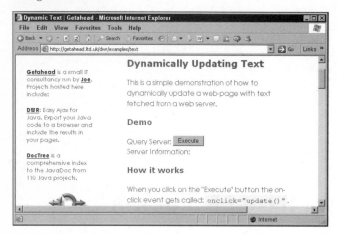

When you click the Execute button, the server information is downloaded and displayed, as you can see in Figure 7.6.

FIGURE 7.6

Using DWR to download text

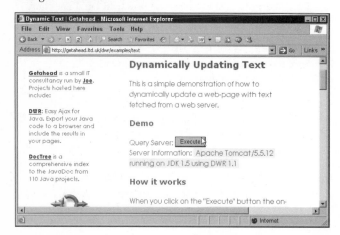

There's also an Ajax chat example on the DWR Web site at `http://getahead.ltd.uk/dwr/examples/chat`. You can see this example in Figure 7.7. Just type your message in the text field and click the Send button.

FIGURE 7.7

The DWR chat application

When you do, your message appears in the chat box, all without a page refresh (Figure 7.8).

FIGURE 7.8

Using the DWR chat application

Another DWR example is available at `http://getahead.ltd.uk/dwr/examples/table`. This example allows you to edit the text in a table in your browser, and make changes without a page refresh. To edit a record, just click that record's Edit button, which loads the data into the editing fields as shown in Figure 7.9.

After you make your edits, click the Save button, which loads the new data into the table, as you see in Figure 7.10 — all without a page refresh.

FIGURE 7.9

Editing a table in the DWR table application

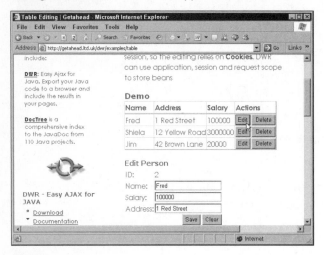

FIGURE 7.10

Saving a change in the DWR table application

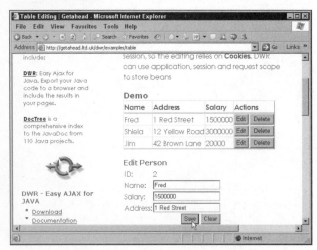

One more example, located at `http://getahead.ltd.uk/dwr/examples/lists`, displays a set of numbers in a drop-down list box, as shown in Figure 7.11. When you check the Big Numbers checkbox, however, a set of big numbers are loaded into the list box using Ajax techniques, as shown in Figure 7.12.

FIGURE 7.11

The DWR list application

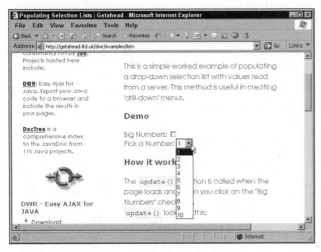

FIGURE 7.12

Reloading the list box in the DWR list application

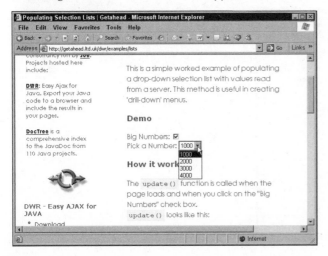

As you can see, DWR offers all the Ajax functionality, this time using Java on the server.

Using Ajax Tags and Java

Another Java Ajax framework is the Ajax Tag Library, which is an Ajax framework that relies on JavaServer Pages (JSP) custom tags to create the JavaScript you need.

ON the WEB You can get the Ajax Tag Library at `http://ajaxtags.sourceforge.net`.

The Ajax Tag Library comes with the following set of JSP tags ready to use in Ajax applications:

- **Autocomplete:** Gets a list of terms that matches the text the user has entered into a field for autocompletion.
- **Callout:** Displays a pop-up balloon connected to an element in a Web page.
- **Select/dropdown:** Sets the contents of a drop-down control according to the user's selection in another drop-down control.
- **Toggle:** Lets you switch between two different images.
- **Update Field:** Updates the text in a field based on the data the user enters in another field.

You can see demos of the Ajax Tag Library at `http://ajaxtags.no-ip.info`. For example, one demo displays a drop-down list of car types when you enter a partial search term, as shown in Figure 7.13. When you select an item in the drop-down list, the specific car make appears in the lower text field, as shown in Figure 7.14.

FIGURE 7.13

The Ajax Tag Library cars application

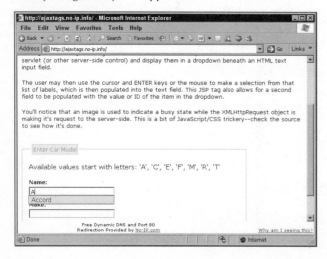

FIGURE 7.14

Selecting a car make in the Ajax Tag Library application

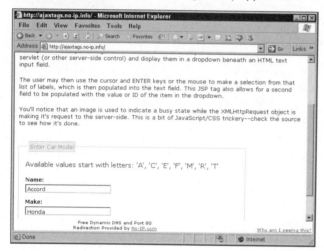

Another example is shown in Figure 7.15 — a speed converter that translates from miles per hour to kilometers per hour. When you enter a speed to convert in miles per hour and click the Calculate button, the results appear in the Web page, as shown in Figure 7.16.

FIGURE 7.15

Using the Ajax Tag Library speed converter

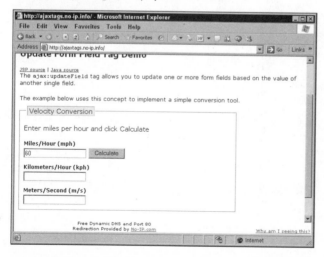

Converting a speed with the Ajax Tag Library speed converter

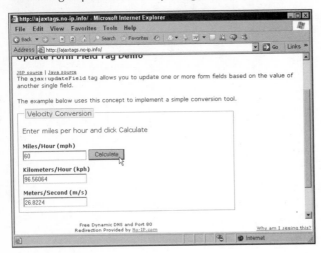

You can also create Ajax-enabled callouts with the Ajax Tag Library, as shown in Figure 7.17, where you see a balloon appear when the mouse hovers over a hyperlink. The text in that balloon was fetched using Ajax.

Callouts created with the Ajax Tag Library

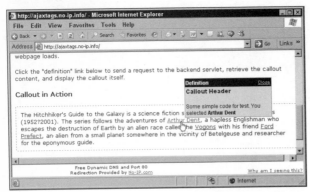

Using SWATO with Java

Another Java-based Ajax framework is SWATO. SWATO comes with built-in components for common Ajax operations, such as an autocomplete text field, a live form, live lists, and so on. You can see the autocomplete control in an example that comes with SWATO in Figure 7.18.

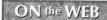 **ON the WEB** You can get SWATO from `https://swato.dev.java.net`. For an introduction to SWATO, go to `https://swato.dev.java.net/doc/html/quickstart.html`.

FIGURE 7.18

A SWATO autocomplete example

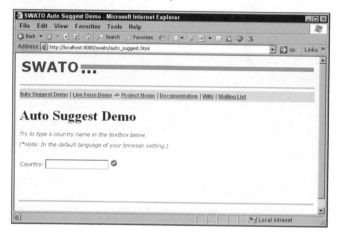

When you enter a partial search term, corresponding to a partial country name, in the search box, this example searches for matches and displays them, as you see in Figure 7.19.

FIGURE 7.19.

Matches are displayed.

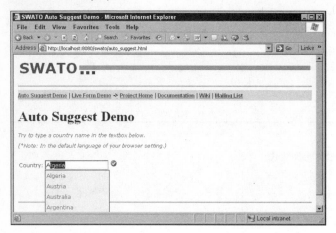

Another SWATO example — an Ajax form example — is shown in Figure 7.20. When you enter data in a text field in this form and click outside the text field, the data sent to the server is displayed in the Web page, as you see in Figure 7.21.

FIGURE 7.20

Using SWATO in an Ajax form example

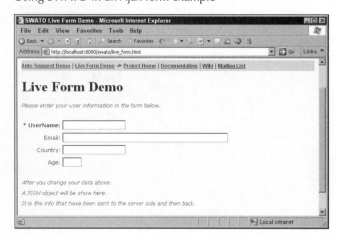

FIGURE 7.21

Data is displayed.

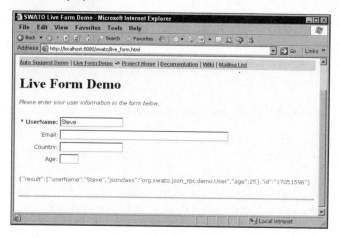

That does it for PHP and Java-based Ajax frameworks. Are there any other ones? There sure are — plenty, including Ruby on Rails, coming up next.

Working with Ajax and Ruby on Rails

Ruby on Rails is an online application framework that comes with Ajax support built in. Ruby is a stand-alone language that's become popular in recent years, and Rails is the Web framework that allows you to put Ruby online.

ON the WEB You can download Ruby on Rails for free from `http://www.rubyonrails.com/down.`

Installing Ruby on Rails is easy: just follow the directions at `http://www.rubyonrails.com/down`. For example, there's a handy one-click installer for Ruby for Windows at `http://rubyinstaller.rubyforge.org`. How much easier could it get than that? Just use the download link, and run the installing program. That's it — you've got Ruby.

Setting up Rails in Windows is just about as easy. Just open a DOS command-prompt window and type this at the command prompt:

```
gem install rails --include-dependencies
```

And that's it; you've got Ruby, and you've got Rails.

Installing on other platforms is as easy — or easier. For example, as of Mac OS X version 10.4, installation is more than easy: Ruby comes built in. To download Rails on the Mac, you're going to need RubyGems, which you can pick up at `http://docs.rubygems.org`. After downloading RubyGems, go to the directory containing the download in the Terminal application and enter this at the command prompt:

```
tar xzf rubygems-0.8.10.tar.gz
cd rubygems-0.8.10
sudo ruby setup.rb
```

The final step is to use RubyGems to download Rails, so enter this command:

```
sudo gem install rails --include-dependencies
```

That's it; you should be on Rails.

If you're using Linux or Unix, it's probable that you already have Ruby installed (if not, take a look at `www.rubyonrails.com/down`). You're also going to need Rails, which is most easily installed with RubyGems. To get RubyGems, go to `http://docs.rubygems.org` and click the downloads link. Then go to the directory containing the download and follow the directions described earlier for the Mac.

Downloading text with Ajax

Time to take a look at a Ruby on Rails example. In the code that follows, the % sign stands for your command prompt, whether you're using Windows, the Mac, or Linux/Unix. To start, you need to create a new Rails application, which is easily done. To create an application named Ajax, just enter this at the command prompt (in whatever directory you want to create the application):

```
%rails ajax
```

That makes Rails create the new Ajax application:

```
%rails ajax
      create
      create   app/controllers
      create   app/helpers
      create   app/models
      create   app/views/layouts
      create   config/environments
      create   components
      create   db
      create   doc
      create   lib
         .
         .
         .
      create   public/javascripts/prototype.js
      create   public/javascripts/effects.js
```

```
create   public/javascripts/dragdrop.js
create   public/javascripts/controls.js
create   public/javascripts/application.js
create   doc/README_FOR_APP
create   log/server.log
create   log/production.log
create   log/development.log
create   log/test.log
```

Next, change directories to the new ajax directory:

```
%cd ajax
```

Now you create a controller named Look for the Ajax application; the *controller* handles the interaction with the user and routes the flow of the application to the correct parts of the application. Here's how you create the controller:

```
%ruby script/generate controller Look
        exists   app/controllers/
        exists   app/helpers/
        create   app/views/look
        exists   test/functional/
        create   app/controllers/look_controller.rb
        create   test/functional/look_controller_test.rb
        create   app/helpers/look_helper.rb
```

Then you edit the file ajax\app\controllers\look_controller.rb, creating an action named at. *Actions* are called by the controller to execute specific tasks in Ruby on Rails applications. Add this code to look_controller.rb:

```
class LookController < ApplicationController

  def at
  end

end
```

Now you can create the application's *view*. The view is a Ruby-enabled HTML page with the extension .rhtml that users see in their browser. Create ajax\app\views\look\at.rhtml now, and place this code in it (you'll see how this code works a little bit later in this chapter):

```
<html>
  <head>
    <title>Using Ajax</title>
    <%= javascript_include_tag "prototype" %>
  </head>
  <body>
    <h1>Using Ajax</h1>
    <br>
    <%= link_to_remote("Click me to use Ajax",
```

```
    :update => "displayDiv",
    :url => {:action => :replacer }) %>
  <br>
  <div id = "displayDiv">The new text will appear here.</div>
</body>
</html>
```

This code makes use of an action named `replacer`, so you need to add that action to the code in the file ajax\app\controllers\look_controller.rb. This action reads the text to download, so you set the `:layout` symbol to `false` here, indicating that you don't want a page refresh:

```
class LookController < ApplicationController
  def at
  end

  def replacer
    render(:layout => false)
  end
end
```

Finally, create the view for the `replacer` action, ajax\app\views\look\replacer.rhtml, and place this code in it:

```
This text was downloaded using Ajax.
```

To test this application, you can run the Web server that comes with Rails. To do that, you enter this command in the ajax application's directory:

```
%ruby script/server
```

And this is what you see:

```
%ruby script/server
=> Booting WEBrick...
=> Rails application started on http://0.0.0.0:3000
=> Ctrl-C to shutdown server; call with --help for options
[2006-09-12 11:52:40] INFO  WEBrick 1.3.1
[2006-09-12 11:52:40] INFO  ruby 1.8.2 (2004-12-25) [i386-
mswin32]
[2006-09-12 11:52:40] INFO  WEBrick::HTTPServer#start: pid=2304
port=3000
```

That starts the Rails Web server; to see what this application looks like in action, navigate your browser to `http://localhost:3000/look/at`, as shown in Figure 7.22, and then click the link. You should see the downloaded text, as shown in Figure 7.23.

FIGURE 7.22

A Ruby on Rails Ajax application

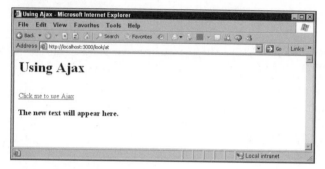

FIGURE 7.23

Downloading text with a Ruby on Rails Ajax application

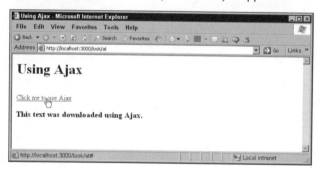

How does this application do what it does? Here, you used Ajax to fetch text and display that text in a `<div>` element. You started by including the Rails prototype.js JavaScript library in the view where you want to use Ajax:

```
<html>
  <head>
    <title>Using Ajax</title>
    <%= javascript_include_tag "prototype" %>
  </head>
  <body>
    <h1>Using Ajax</h1>
    <br>
    <%= link_to_remote("Click me to use Ajax",
      :update => "displayDiv",
      :url => {:action => :replacer }) %>
    <br>
```

```
  <div id = "displayDiv">The new text will appear here.</div>
  </body>
</html>
```

Now you can use link_to_remote to create a hyperlink that will fetch the results of an action and display them in a <div> element. To set up a hyperlink that displays the text Click me to use Ajax, updates the <div> element named displayDiv with the fetched data, and fetches the text to display from the replacer action, you call link_to_remote:

```
<html>
  <head>
    <title>Using Ajax</title>
    <%= javascript_include_tag "prototype" %>
  </head>
  <body>
    <h1>Using Ajax</h1>
    <br>
    <%= link_to_remote("Click me to use Ajax",
      :update => "displayDiv",
      :url => {:action => :replacer }) %>
    <br>
    <div id = "displayDiv">The new text will appear here.</div>
  </body>
</html>
```

In HTML, this creates a call to the Rails prototype.js library function Ajax.Updater in the HTML code created after Rails processes the at.rhtml document:

```
<html>
  <head>
    <title>Using Ajax</title>
    <script
     src="/javascripts/prototype.js?1151422045"
     type="text/javascript"></script>
  </head>
  <body>
    <h1>Using Ajax</h1>
    <br>
    <a href="#" onclick="new Ajax.Updater('displayDiv',
    '/look/replacer', {asynchronous:true, evalScripts:true});
      return
    false;">Click me to use Ajax</a>
    <br>
    <br>
    <h3><div id = "displayDiv">The new text will appear
      here.</div></h3>
  </body>
</html>
```

The `replacer` action simply renders its output without including any layout, which means it just shows the text in the `replacer` action's view, which is replacer.rhtml. Here's what the `replacer` action looks like:

```
class LookController < ApplicationController
  def at
  end

  def replacer
    render(:layout => false)
  end
end
```

And here's the text that the replacer view returns, ajax\app\views\look\replacer.rhtml:

```
This text was downloaded using Ajax.
```

This is the text that will be displayed in the `displayDiv` `<div>` element. Here's what the text in that `<div>` element starts off as:

```
<html>
  <head>
    <title>Using Ajax</title>
    <%= javascript_include_tag "prototype" %>
  </head>
  <body>
    <h1>Using Ajax</h1>
    <br>
    <%= link_to_remote("Click me to use Ajax", :update =>
      "displayDiv",
      :url => {:action => :replacer }) %>
    <br>
    <h3><div id = "displayDiv">The new text will appear
      here.</div></h3>
  </body>
</html>
```

Here's what this page looks like in the browser after you've downloaded the text using Ajax:

```
<html>
  <head>
    <title>Using Ajax</title>
    <script src="/javascripts/prototype.js?1151422045"
      type="text/javascript"></script>
  </head>
  <body>
    <h1>Using Ajax</h1>
    <br>
    <a href="#" onclick="new Ajax.Updater('displayDiv',
```

```
              '/look/replacer', {asynchronous:true, evalScripts:true});
              return false;">Click me to use Ajax</a>
          <br>
          <br>
          <h3><div id = "displayDiv">This text was downloaded
            using Ajax.</div></h3>
        </body>
      </html>
```

That's a good start with Ajax and Ruby on Rails, but it's only a start. Here, Rails handled the details for you, placing the downloaded text into the `<div>` element itself. But what if you want access to the Ajax data yourself? That's coming up next.

Accessing downloaded data in code

You can configure `link_to_remote` to call a JavaScript function when your Ajax data is downloaded, which is more in line with the other Ajax frameworks described in this chapter. Here are the possible parameters to pass to `link_to_remote` to specify when you want your JavaScript function called:

- `:loading` — The data is being loaded by the browser.

- `:loaded` — The browser has finished getting the data.

- `:interactive` — The user can interact with the data, even if it has not finished loading.

- `:success` — The Ajax download is completed successfully.

- `:failure` — The Ajax download failed.

- `:complete` — The Ajax request is complete (whether it was successful or failed).

This next example uses the `:success` parameter to have a JavaScript function called with the downloaded data so you can handle that data in code. To start this new application, `ajaxdata`, create it this way:

```
%rails ajaxdata
      create
      create  app/controllers
      create  app/helpers
      create  app/models
      create  app/views/layouts
      create  config/environments
      create  components
      create  db
      create  doc
      create  lib
         .
         .
         .
      create  public/javascripts/prototype.js
```

```
create  public/javascripts/effects.js
create  public/javascripts/dragdrop.js
create  public/javascripts/controls.js
create  public/javascripts/application.js
create  doc/README_FOR_APP
create  log/server.log
create  log/production.log
create  log/development.log
create  log/test.log
```

then change directories to the `ajaxdata` directory:

```
%cd ajaxdata
```

and create a controller named `Look` for the `ajaxdata` application:

```
%ruby script/generate controller Look
    exists  app/controllers/
    exists  app/helpers/
    create  app/views/look
    exists  test/functional/
    create  app/controllers/look_controller.rb
    create  test/functional/look_controller_test.rb
    create  app/helpers/look_helper.rb
```

Now edit ajaxdata\app\controllers\look_controller.rb, adding this code to create an action named `at`:

```
class LookController < ApplicationController

  def at
  end

end
```

Next, create the file ajaxdata\app\views\look\at.rhtml, and place this code in it, including a JavaScript function that will display the downloaded text in the `<div>` element in this Web page:

```
<html>
  <head>
    <title>Handling Ajax Data</title>
    <%= javascript_include_tag "prototype" %>

    <script language="JavaScript">
      function handleData(request)
      {
          var displayDiv = document.getElementById("displayDiv");
          displayDiv.innerHTML = request.responseText;
      }
    </script>

  </head>
```

```
<body>
  <h1>Handling Ajax Data</h1>
  <br>
  <%= link_to_remote("Click me to handle Ajax data", :success =>
    "handleData(request)", :url => {:action => :getter }) %>
  <br>
  <br>
  <h3><div id = "displayDiv">The new text will appear
   here.</div></h3>
</body>
</html>
```

then edit ajaxdata\app\controllers\look_controller.rb, adding this code to create the `getter` action:

```
class LookController < ApplicationController
  def at
  end

  def getter
    render(:layout => false)
  end
end
```

Finally, create ajaxdata\app\views\look\getter.rhtml, and place this code in it:

```
This text was downloaded using Ajax.
```

Okay, that's it; start the Rails Web server:

```
%ruby script/server
=> Booting WEBrick...
=> Rails application started on http://0.0.0.0:3000
=> Ctrl-C to shutdown server; call with --help for options
[2006-09-12 11:52:40] INFO  WEBrick 1.3.1
[2006-09-12 11:52:40] INFO  ruby 1.8.2 (2004-12-25) [i386-
  mswin32]
[2006-09-12 11:52:40] INFO  WEBrick::HTTPServer#start: pid=2304
port=3000
```

Open your browser and navigate to `http://localhost:3000/look/at`, as shown in Figure 7.24.

FIGURE 7.24

A Ruby on Rails Ajax application that lets you handle data

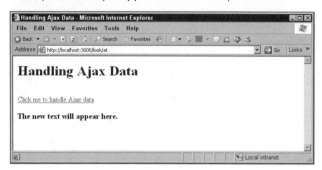

Then click the link; you should see the downloaded text, as shown in Figure 7.25.

FIGURE 7.25

A data-handling Ruby on Rails Ajax application

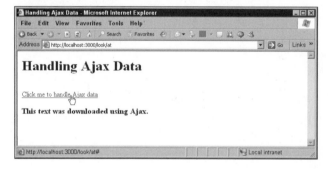

This Ruby on Rails example lets you set up a callback function to handle the downloaded data. The application starts by including the Rails prototype.js Ajax library in the view file, at.rhtml:

```
<html>
  <head>
    <title>Handling Ajax Data</title>
    <%= javascript_include_tag "prototype" %>

    <script language="JavaScript">
      function handleData(request)
      {
          var displayDiv = document.getElementById("displayDiv");
          displayDiv.innerHTML = request.responseText;
```

291

```
      }
    </script>

  </head>
  <body>
    <h1>Handling Ajax Data</h1>
    <br>
    <%= link_to_remote("Click me to handle Ajax data", :success
      => "handleData(request)", :url => {:action => :getter }) %>
    <br>
    <br>
    <h3><div id = "displayDiv">The new text will appear
      here.</div></h3>
  </body>
</html>
```

In this example, you connected a successful download from an action named `getter` to a JavaScript function, `handleData`, which is passed the data sent to the browser from the `getter` action:

```
<html>
  <head>
    <title>Handling Ajax Data</title>
    <%= javascript_include_tag "prototype" %>

    <script language="JavaScript">
      function handleData(request)
      {
          var displayDiv = document.getElementById("displayDiv");
          displayDiv.innerHTML = request.responseText;
      }
    </script>

  </head>
  <body>
    <h1>Handling Ajax Data</h1>
    <br>
    <%= link_to_remote("Click me to handle Ajax data", :success
      => "handleData(request)", :url => {:action => :getter }) %>
    <br>
    <br>
    <h3><div id = "displayDiv">The new text will appear
here.</div></h3>
  </body>
</html>
```

In code, the `getter` action renders its view, without a layout:

```
class LookController < ApplicationController
  def at
  end

  def getter
    render(:layout => false)
  end
end
```

The getter view passes this text data back to the browser:

```
This text was downloaded using Ajax.
```

In the browser, that text is stored in the XMLHttpRequest object's responseText property, and that object is passed to the JavaScript handleData function like this, as the request parameter:

```
<html>
  <head>
    <title>Handling Ajax Data</title>
    <%= javascript_include_tag "prototype" %>

    <script language="JavaScript">
      function handleData(request)
      {
          .
          .
          .
      }
    </script>

  </head>
  <body>
    <h1>Handling Ajax Data</h1>
    <br>
    <%= link_to_remote("Click me to handle Ajax data", :success
      => "handleData(request)", :url => {:action => :getter }) %>
    <br>
    <br>
    <h3><div id = "displayDiv">The new text will appear
      here.</div></h3>
  </body>
</html>
```

You can display the text in a <div> element using code in the JavaScript handleData function:

```
<script language="JavaScript">
  function handleData(request)
```

```
        {
            var displayDiv = document.getElementById("displayDiv");
            displayDiv.innerHTML = request.responseText;
        }
    </script>
```

What does this action look like in HTML in the browser? Here it is:

```
<html>
  <head>
    <title>Handling Ajax Data</title>
    <script src="/javascripts/prototype.js?1151428997"
      type="text/javascript"></script>

    <script language="JavaScript">
      function handleData(request)
      {
          var displayDiv = document.getElementById("displayDiv");
          displayDiv.innerHTML = request.responseText;
      }
    </script>

  </head>
  <body>
    <h1>Handling Ajax Data</h1>
    <br>
    <a href="#" onclick="new Ajax.Request('/look/getter',
{asynchronous:true, evalScripts:true,
onSuccess:function(request){handleData(request)}}); return
false;">Click me to handle Ajax data</a>
    <br>
    <br>
    <h3><div id = "displayDiv">The new text will appear
here.</div></h3>
  </body>
</html>
```

This is what gives you the result you see in Figures 7.24 and 7.25.

Summary

This chapter covered some of the server-side Ajax frameworks available. As you can see, there is a considerable range of server-side frameworks, and which one you select depends on the language you use on your server, PHP, Java, Ruby, and so on. For each language, there are multiple frameworks available. Try them out and choose the one you like best.

Part III

Ajax and the DOM, XML, CSS, and Dynamic HTML

Chapter 8

The DOM and Event Handling

This chapter is all about working in-depth in Ajax applications. In this chapter the Document Object Model (DOM) and handling events are described. A huge part of Ajax programming involves working in the Web page, of course, and the DOM lets you do that kind of work. Using the DOM, you can append elements to what's already there, replace elements, search for and find elements, and so on. Event handling is also important when you're working with Ajax, and in this chapter you're going to see how to handle events to create a drag-and-drop, Ajax-enabled shopping cart.

This chapter starts with an introduction to the DOM, which gives you access to all the parts of a Web page in JavaScript code.

Introducing the DOM

Your Web browser sees an HTML document as a tree of nodes that support properties and methods you can use to navigate or edit that page in real time. Those properties and methods are specified in the HTML Document Object Model, or DOM.

> **NOTE** The DOM is the creation of the World Wide Web Consortium (W3C). For the rigorous DOM details, take a look at http://www.w3.org/DOM/.

For example, here's the code for an innocent-looking Web page:

```
<html>
  <head>
    <title>
      Hello from HTML
```

```
        </title>
      </head>

      <body>
        <h1>
            Hello from HTML!
        </h1>
      </body>
    <html>
```

Here, everything is a node — from the elements you see to the text (which is stored in text nodes).
Following is the tree of nodes corresponding to this Web page that your browser sees:

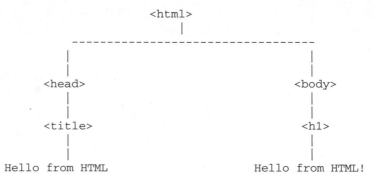

JavaScript has built-in properties you can use to work with the nodes in Web documents like this
one. They are

- `attributes`: Attributes by this node
- `childNodes`: Array of child nodes
- `documentElement`: The document element
- `firstChild`: First child node
- `lastChild`: Last child node
- `localName`: Local name of the node
- `name`: Name of the node, with namespace
- `nextSibling`: Next sibling node
- `nodeName`: Name of the node
- `nodeType`: Node type
- `nodeValue`: Value of the node
- `previousSibling`: Previous sibling node

You'll see how to use these properties in JavaScript later in this chapter and in Chapter 9. Note in
particular that the `nodeType` property holds the type of a node, which is given by number in
HTML documents:

- 1 Element
- 2 Attribute
- 3 Text node

Here are the various node types in the HTML document you saw earlier:

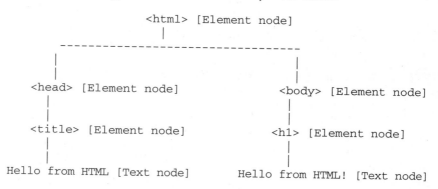

```
                    <html> [Element node]
                      |
        -------------------------------------------
        |                                       |
        |                                       |
     <head> [Element node]              <body> [Element node]
        |                                       |
        |                                       |
     <title> [Element node]              <h1> [Element node]
        |                                       |
        |                                       |
   Hello from HTML [Text node]      Hello from HTML! [Text node]
```

Besides these properties, nodes support the following methods:

- `replaceNode(a, b)`: Replaces node b with node a
- `insertBefore(a, b)`: Inserts node a before node b
- `appendChild(a)`: Appends a child, a, to the node that you call this method on.

How do you get a node to work with JavaScript? You can use the `documentElement` property, which returns the node corresponding to the <html> element, and use properties such as `nextSibling`, `lastChild`, `firstChild`, and so on to navigate to the node you want. Or you can use a method such as `document.getElementById` to create a node object by accessing elements by ID value.

Now, how about putting this discussion to work in an Ajax example?

Appending Elements Using the DOM

Here's an example putting the DOM to work for you. Up to this point, the text you've downloaded from the server using Ajax has been displayed in a <div> element using the <div> element's innerHTML property, like this:

```
function getData(dataSource, divID)
{
  if(XMLHttpRequestObject) {
    var obj = document.getElementById(divID);
    XMLHttpRequestObject.open("GET", dataSource);

    XMLHttpRequestObject.onreadystatechange = function()
```

```
                    {
                      if (XMLHttpRequestObject.readyState == 4 &&
                        XMLHttpRequestObject.status == 200) {
                          obj.innerHTML =
                            XMLHttpRequestObject.responseText;
                      }
                    }
```

That works, but strictly speaking, innerHTML is not a property of the DOM. How about creating an example to display downloaded text using strict DOM techniques?

> **NOTE** Even though innerHTML isn't a property of the DOM, this may change. innerHTML was introduced by Microsoft in Internet Explorer, and there's a good chance it'll be added to the DOM at some point.

The first way you'll see this work is in an example named appender.html, which uses the DOM appendChild method to display downloaded text. You can see appender.html ready to go to work in Figure 8.1.

FIGURE 8.1

Using appender.html

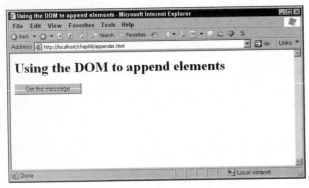

The page you see in Figure 8.1 includes an empty <div> element. When you click the button, the application downloads text and appends that text to the <div> element using DOM techniques, as you see in Figure 8.2.

FIGURE 8.2

Using appender.html to download text

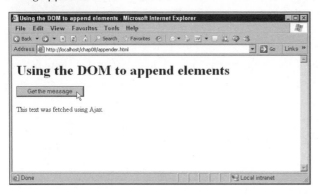

When you click the button again, the text is downloaded and appended to the text already displayed, as shown in Figure 8.3.

FIGURE 8.3

Using appender.html to append downloaded text

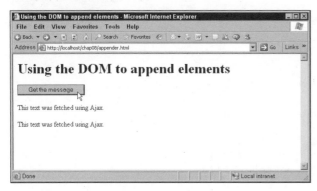

So how does this example work in code? It starts with the button you see in the Web page, which is connected to a function named `getData`:

```
<body>

    <h1>Using the DOM to append elements</h1>

    <form>
```

```
        <input type = "button" value = "Get the message"
          onclick = "getData()">
      </form>
            .
            .
            .
```

You also need to create the <div> element to which you can append downloaded text (note that it starts off with an empty <p> element):

```
<body>

  <h1>Using the DOM to append elements</h1>

  <form>
    <input type = "button" value = "Get the message"
      onclick = "getData()">
  </form>

  <div id="targetDiv" width =100 height=100>
    <p id="text"></p>
  </div>
        .
        .
        .
```

In the getData function, create an XMLHttpRequest object as usual:

```
<html>
  <head>

    <title>Using the DOM to append elements</title>

    <script language = "javascript">

      function getData()
      {
        var XMLHttpRequestObject = false;

        if (window.XMLHttpRequest) {
          XMLHttpRequestObject = new XMLHttpRequest();
        } else if (window.ActiveXObject) {
          XMLHttpRequestObject = new
            ActiveXObject("Microsoft.XMLHTTP");
        }
            .
            .
            .
```

then download the text as usual:

```
<html>
  <head>

    <title>Using the DOM to append elements</title>

    <script language = "javascript">

      function getData()
      {
        .
        .
        .
        if(XMLHttpRequestObject) {

          XMLHttpRequestObject.open("GET", "data1.txt");

          XMLHttpRequestObject.onreadystatechange = function()
          {
            if (XMLHttpRequestObject.readyState == 4 &&
              XMLHttpRequestObject.status == 200) {
              .
              .
              .
            }
          }
          .
          .
          .
  </head>
```

Now that you've downloaded the text, how do you append that text to the targetDiv <div> element? To start, you can enclose the downloaded text in a <p> element, and then append that <p> element to the <div> element.

To create a new <p> element, use the document object's DOM method createElement:

```
          XMLHttpRequestObject.onreadystatechange = function()
          {
            if (XMLHttpRequestObject.readyState == 4 &&
              XMLHttpRequestObject.status == 200) {
              var newP = document.createElement("p");
              .
              .
              .
            }
          }
```

To enclose a text node with the downloaded text in the new <p> element, create a new text node holding the downloaded text using the document object's `createTextNode` method:

```
XMLHttpRequestObject.onreadystatechange = function()
{
  if (XMLHttpRequestObject.readyState == 4 &&
    XMLHttpRequestObject.status == 200) {
    var newP = document.createElement("p");
    var newText =
      document
      .createTextNode(XMLHttpRequestObject.responseText);
        .
        .
        .
  }
}
```

To make the text node a child of the <p> element, append the text node to the <p> element:

```
XMLHttpRequestObject.onreadystatechange = function()
{
  if (XMLHttpRequestObject.readyState == 4 &&
    XMLHttpRequestObject.status == 200) {
    var newP = document.createElement("p");
    var newText =
      document
      .createTextNode(XMLHttpRequestObject.responseText);
    newP.appendChild(newText);
        .
        .
        .
  }
}
```

then you can append the new <p> element to the `targetDiv` element in the Web page. Here's what that looks like:

```
XMLHttpRequestObject.onreadystatechange = function()
{
  if (XMLHttpRequestObject.readyState == 4 &&
    XMLHttpRequestObject.status == 200) {
    var newP = document.createElement("p");
    var newText =
      document
      .createTextNode(XMLHttpRequestObject.responseText);
    newP.appendChild(newText);
    var div = document.getElementById("targetDiv");
```

```
        div.appendChild(newP);
    }
}
```

And there you have it. This example lets you append downloaded text to previously downloaded text.

Replacing Elements Using the DOM

What if you didn't want to append the new text to the text already displayed, but wanted to replace what's already there with the newly downloaded text? Take a look at replacer.html, which is shown in Figure 8.4.

When you click the first button, a message is downloaded and displayed, as you see in Figure 8.5.

FIGURE 8.4

Using replacer.html

FIGURE 8.5

Using replacer.html to download text

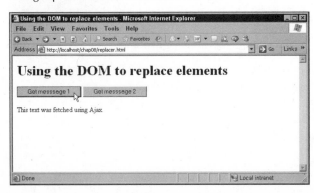

Clicking the second button replaces the current text with the newly downloaded text, as you see in Figure 8.6.

Using replacer.html to replace existing text with downloaded text

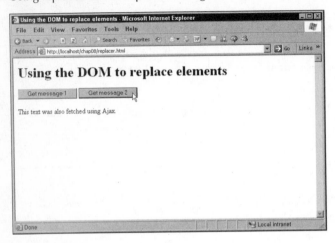

How does this work in code? You're going to need two buttons for the two messages:

```
<body>

    <h1>Using the DOM to replace elements</h1>

    <form>
      <input type = "button" value = "Get message 1"
        onclick = "getData('1')">
      <input type = "button" value = "Get message 2"
        onclick = "getData('2')">
    </form>
         .
         .
         .
</body>
```

This example uses a `<p>` element with the ID `text`, contained in a `<div>` element with the ID `targetDiv` to display the downloaded text:

```
<body>

    <h1>Using the DOM to replace elements</h1>

    <form>
```

```
      <input type = "button" value = "Get message 1"
        onclick = "getData('1')">
      <input type = "button" value = "Get message 2"
        onclick = "getData('2')">
    </form>

    <div id="targetDiv" width =100 height=100>
      <p id="text">The fetched text will appear here.</p>
    </div>

  </body>
```

In the getData function, create an XMLHttpRequest object in preparation for downloading one or the other text file on the server that this examples uses, data1.txt or data2.txt:

```
      function getData(number)
      {
        var XMLHttpRequestObject = false;

        if (window.XMLHttpRequest) {
          XMLHttpRequestObject = new XMLHttpRequest();
        } else if (window.ActiveXObject) {
          XMLHttpRequestObject = new
            ActiveXObject("Microsoft.XMLHTTP");
        }
        .
        .
        .
```

then call the XMLHttpRequest object's open method, configuring that object to download data1.txt or data2.txt, depending on which button was clicked:

```
      function getData(number)
      {
        var XMLHttpRequestObject = false;

        if (window.XMLHttpRequest) {
          XMLHttpRequestObject = new XMLHttpRequest();
        } else if (window.ActiveXObject) {
          XMLHttpRequestObject = new
            ActiveXObject("Microsoft.XMLHTTP");
        }

        if(XMLHttpRequestObject) {

          XMLHttpRequestObject.open("GET", "data" + number +
            ".txt");
          .
          .
          .
```

Finally, add code to handle the downloaded text:

```html
<html>
  <head>

    <title>Using the DOM to replace elements</title>

    <script language = "javascript">
        .
        .
        .
        if(XMLHttpRequestObject) {

          XMLHttpRequestObject.open("GET", "data" + number +
            ".txt");

          XMLHttpRequestObject.onreadystatechange = function()
          {
            if (XMLHttpRequestObject.readyState == 4 &&
              XMLHttpRequestObject.status == 200) {
              .
              .
              .
            }
          }
```

To replace the current text in the <p> element with the ID text in the Web page with the newly downloaded text, start by creating a new <p> element, also with the ID text (so it can be replaced the next time the user clicks a button). To create that <p> element, use the document object's createElement method. To add the ID attribute to the <p> element, use that element's setAttribute method:

```
XMLHttpRequestObject.onreadystatechange = function()
{
  if (XMLHttpRequestObject.readyState == 4 &&
    XMLHttpRequestObject.status == 200) {
    var newP = document.createElement("p");
    newP.setAttribute("id", "text");
    .
    .
    .
  }
}
```

then you can create the text node that will hold the newly downloaded text inside the <p> element:

```
XMLHttpRequestObject.onreadystatechange = function()
{
  if (XMLHttpRequestObject.readyState == 4 &&
    XMLHttpRequestObject.status == 200) {
    var newP = document.createElement("p");
```

```
        newP.setAttribute("id", "text");
        var newText =
        document
        .createTextNode(XMLHttpRequestObject.responseText);
          .
            .
              .
        }
    }
```

and then append that text node to the new <p> element:

```
XMLHttpRequestObject.onreadystatechange = function()
{
    if (XMLHttpRequestObject.readyState == 4 &&
        XMLHttpRequestObject.status == 200) {
        var newP = document.createElement("p");
        newP.setAttribute("id", "text");
        var newText =
        document
        .createTextNode(XMLHttpRequestObject.responseText);
        newP.appendChild(newText);
          .
            .
              .
        }
    }
```

The goal now is to replace the text in the current <p> element with the text in the new <p> element, which you can do using the enclosing <div> element's replaceChild method:

```
XMLHttpRequestObject.onreadystatechange = function()
{
    if (XMLHttpRequestObject.readyState == 4 &&
        XMLHttpRequestObject.status == 200) {
        var newP = document.createElement("p");
        newP.setAttribute("id", "text");
        var newText =
        document
        .createTextNode(XMLHttpRequestObject.responseText);
        newP.appendChild(newText);
        var div = document.getElementById("targetDiv");
        var oldP = document.getElementById("text");
          .
            .
              .
        }
    }
```

Now you can replace the old <p> element with the new <p> element, like this:

```
XMLHttpRequestObject.onreadystatechange = function()
{
  if (XMLHttpRequestObject.readyState == 4 &&
    XMLHttpRequestObject.status == 200) {
    var newP = document.createElement("p");
    newP.setAttribute("id", "text");
    var newText =
    document
    .createTextNode(XMLHttpRequestObject.responseText);
    newP.appendChild(newText);
    var div = document.getElementById("targetDiv");
    var oldP = document.getElementById("text");
    div.replaceChild(newP, oldP);
  }
}
```

And you're done! That completes the code for replacer.html.

Creating an Ajax-Enabled Shopping Cart

Ajax is often used with applications that support drag and drop using the mouse. For example, one application that seems tailor-made for Ajax is a drag-and-drop shopping cart application. Currently on most Internet commerce sites, when you use a shopping cart in online applications, you have to click an Add to Cart button, which takes you to a new page, and you have to get back to the shopping section from there.

Ajax can improve this situation dramatically. With Ajax, all you have to do is to drag the item(s) you want to a shopping cart on the same page. Behind the scenes, the page can send data to the server and get a confirming response back. For example, you might drag a DVD player to a shopping cart icon, and when you drop that item in the cart, your purchase is registered on the server — without a page refresh.

For example, take a look at the Ajax-enabled shopping cart example shown in Figure 8.7.

FIGURE 8.7

An Ajax-enabled shopping cart example

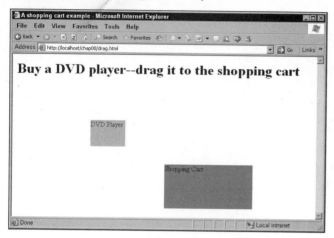

In this example, you can drag the DVD player using the mouse, as you see in Figure 8.8.

FIGURE 8.8

Dragging a DVD player

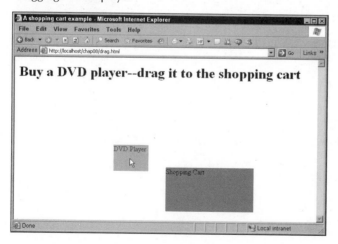

When you drop the DVD player in the shopping cart, the server sends back the message "Congratulations, you just bought a fine DVD player," as you can see in Figure 8.9.

FIGURE 8.9

Buying a DVD player

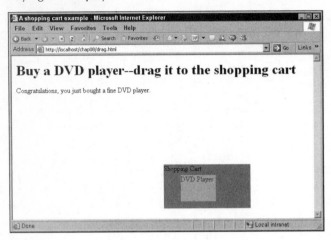

This example shows you how to handle drag-and-drop operations (including working with mouse events) and Ajax. It starts by creating a `<div>` element for the DVD player. The text you see in Figure 8.7 for the DVD player is simply enclosed in the `<div>` element:

```
<body>
  <h1>Buy a DVD player--drag it to the shopping cart</h1>

    <div id="dvdplayer"
      style="left:180px; top:150px; width:80px; height:60px;">
      DVD Player</div>
      .
      .
      .
</body>
```

You can also add additional styles for the cart in a `<style>` element in the page's `<head>` element:

```
<style type="text/css">
  #dvdplayer {
    .
    .
    .
  }
</style>
```

For example, you should set the `position` style of the DVD player `<div>` element to `absolute`, which means you can position this `<div>` element using the mouse:

```
<style type="text/css">
  #dvdplayer {
    position:absolute;
       .
       .
       .
  }
</style>
```

And you should give the DVD player a high value for its `z-index` property. This property sets the "stacking order" of the `<div>` with respect to other items in the page. You want to give the DVD player `<div>` element a high stacking order value so that it rides above other items on the page — in particular, so that the user can drag it on top of the cart `<div>` element. Here's how you set the `z-index` property in this example:

```
<style type="text/css">
  #dvdplayer {
    position:absolute;
    z-index:200;
       .
       .
       .
  }
</style>
```

You can also set the color of the background as well as the color of text of the DVD player `<div>` element:

```
<style type="text/css">
  #dvdplayer {
    position:absolute;
    z-index:200;
    background: #eecc00;
    color:#0000FF;
  }
</style>
```

That completes the `<div>` element for the DVD player. You also need a `<div>` element for the shopping cart:

```
<body>
  <h1>Buy a DVD player--drag it to the shopping cart</h1>

    <div id="dvdplayer"
      style="left:180px; top:150px; width:80px; height:60px;">
      DVD Player</div>

    <div id="cart"
      style="left:350px; top:250px; width:200px; height:100px;">
```

```
      Shopping Cart</div>

   </body>
```

And you can set additional properties for the cart in the `<style>` element in the page's `<head>` element. For example, to position the cart where you want it, you have to set its `position` property to `absolute`:

```
      <style type="text/css">
        #dvdplayer {
          position:absolute;
          z-index:200;
          background: #eecc00;
          color:#0000FF;
        }

        #cart {
          position:absolute;
          .
          .
          .
        }
      </style>
```

You can set its color and background color here as well:

```
      <style type="text/css">
        #dvdplayer {
          position:absolute;
          z-index:200;
          background: #eecc00;
          color:#0000FF;
        }

        #cart {
          position:absolute;
          background: #00ff00;
          color:#000000;
        }
      </style>
```

That's it for the cart `<div>` element. Note that you also need a `<div>` element in which to display the server's acknowledgement of your purchase, `targetDiv`, which looks like this:

```
      <body>
        <h1>Buy a DVD player--drag it to the shopping cart</h1>
          <div id="targetDiv"></div>

          <div id="dvdplayer"
```

```
            style="left:180px; top:150px; width:80px; height:60px;">
            DVD Player</div>

        <div id="cart"
            style="left:350px; top:250px; width:200px;
    height:100px;">
            Shopping Cart</div>

    </body>
```

That sets up the `<div>` elements for the cart, DVD player, and the server's notification. Now you can start working with the mouse. That all starts with the DVD player `<div>` element, for which you have to enable dragging and dropping. The process begins when you connect a JavaScript function to the onmousedown event of the DVD player `<div>` element like this:

```
    <body>
      <h1>Buy a DVD player--drag it to the shopping cart</h1>
        <div id="targetDiv"></div>

        <div id="dvdplayer"
          style="left:180px; top:150px; width:80px; height:60px;"
          onmousedown="processMouseDown(event);">DVD Player</div>

        <div id="cart"
          style="left:350px; top:250px; width:200px;
            height:100px;">
          Shopping Cart</div>

    </body>
```

The whole process of dragging and dropping starts when the user presses the mouse button on the DVD player, and the onmousedown event connects the mouse press to a JavaScript function named processMouseDown. That begins the mouse handling for this example.

Creating a cross-browser mouse event object

When the user presses the mouse button, the processMouseDown function is called; that function begins by creating a new MouseEvent object:

```
        function processMouseDown(e)
        {
          var e = new MouseEvent(e);
            .
            .
            .
        }
```

What's that all about? It turns out that working with the mouse differs radically between browsers, so this example starts its mouse work by creating a mouse object that has the same properties, no matter what browser the user has. All the mouse handler functions in this example use this cross-browser mouse object.

In fact, working with the mouse differs from the very start, as soon as the mouse button goes down. The onmousedown event is connected to the processMouseDown function, and passes the current event object to that function:

```
<body>
  <h1>Buy a DVD player--drag it to the shopping cart</h1>
    <div id="targetDiv"></div>

    <div id="dvdplayer"
       style="left:180px; top:150px; width:80px; height:60px;"
       onmousedown="processMouseDown(event);">DVD Player</div>

    <div id="cart"
       style="left:350px; top:250px; width:200px;
height:100px;">
       Shopping Cart</div>

  </body>
```

This event object actually only gets passed to the processMouseDown function in the Mozilla/Netscape/Firefox-type browsers. In Internet Explorer, this event object is simply null — you use the window.event object instead.

So the MouseEvent function first tests the event object passed to it; if it exists, it's stored as a property of the new MouseEvent object with the syntax this.e ("this" refers to the current object):

```
function MouseEvent(e)
{
  if(e) {
    this.e = e;
  }
  .
  .
  .
}
```

If the event object is null, on the other hand, then you should use the window.event object as the event object, which looks like this:

```
function MouseEvent(e)
{
  if(e) {
    this.e = e;
  } else {
```

```
    this.e = window.event;
  }
    .
    .
    .
}
```

That stores the `event` object in the `MouseEvent` object's e property. Now it's time to determine where the mouse event occurred in the Web page. Coordinates in a Web page start in the upper left of the client area. Positive X is to the right, and positive Y is downward.

NOTE The *client area* is the area where content is displayed, excluding toolbars, menu bars, and so on.

In Mozilla/Netscape/Firefox-type browsers, you use the `event` object's `pageX` property to get the mouse event's X coordinate. You can test whether that property exists, and if so, store it as the `MouseEvent` object's x property like this:

```
function MouseEvent(e)
{
  if(e) {
    this.e = e;
  } else {
    this.e = window.event;
  }

  if(e.pageX) {
    this.x = e.pageX;
  }
```

On the other hand, if the `pageX` property doesn't exist, you should use Internet Explorer's X coordinate property, `clientX`:

```
function MouseEvent(e)
{
  if(e) {
    this.e = e;
  } else {
    this.e = window.event;
  }

  if(e.pageX) {
    this.x = e.pageX;
  } else {
    this.x = e.clientX;
  }
    .
    .
    .
}
```

Similarly, when you create the Y coordinate of the mouse location, stored in the `MouseEvent` object's y property, first check for the `pageY` of the Mozilla/Netscape/Firefox browsers:

```
function MouseEvent(e)
{
  if(e) {
    this.e = e;
  } else {
    this.e = window.event;
  }

  if(e.pageX) {
    this.x = e.pageX;
  } else {
    this.x = e.clientX;
  }

  if(e.pageY) {
    this.y = e.pageY;
  }
    .
    .
    .

}
```

If the `pageY` property doesn't exist, you should use Internet Explorer's `clientY` property instead:

```
function MouseEvent(e)
{
  if(e) {
    this.e = e;
  } else {
    this.e = window.event;
  }

  if(e.pageX) {
    this.x = e.pageX;
  } else {
    this.x = e.clientX;
  }

  if(e.pageY) {
    this.y = e.pageY;
  } else {
    this.y = e.clientY;
  }
    .
    .
    .

}
```

That creates the e (holding the original event object), x, and y properties of the MouseEvent object.

There's one more property this object supports: the target property, which holds the element inside of which the mouse event occurred. If you're dealing with a Mozilla/Netscape/Firefox-type browser, the target element is stored as the event object's target property:

```
function MouseEvent(e)
{
  if(e) {
    this.e = e;
  } else {
    this.e = window.event;
  }

  if(e.pageX) {
    this.x = e.pageX;
  } else {
    this.x = e.clientX;
  }

  if(e.pageY) {
    this.y = e.pageY;
  } else {
    this.y = e.clientY;
  }

  if(e.target) {
    this.target = e.target;
  }
    .
    .
    .
}
```

If the target property doesn't exist, you should use Internet Explorer's srcElement property:

```
function MouseEvent(e)
{
  if(e) {
    this.e = e;
  } else {
    this.e = window.event;
  }

  if(e.pageX) {
    this.x = e.pageX;
  } else {
    this.x = e.clientX;
```

```
        }

        if(e.pageY) {
          this.y = e.pageY;
        } else {
          this.y = e.clientY;
        }

        if(e.target) {
          this.target = e.target;
        } else {
          this.target = e.srcElement;
        }
      }
```

As you can see, the cross-browser MouseEvent object has taken the whirl of individual browser properties — srcElement, clientX, pageY, and so on — and created a set of properties that are easy to work with in your code, no matter which browser you have:

- e: The original event object, as created by the browser
- x: The x coordinate of the mouse
- y: The y coordinate of the mouse
- target: The target element, where the mouse event took place

Now instead of worrying about using pageX, clientX, target, or srcElement in your code, all you have to do is to create a new MouseEvent object and use the four cross-browser properties described.

Handling mouse down events

When the mouse button is pressed in the browser, the processMouseDown function is called:

```
<body>
  <h1>Buy a DVD player--drag it to the shopping cart</h1>
    <div id="targetDiv"></div>

    <div id="dvdplayer"
      style="left:180px; top:150px; width:80px; height:60px;"
      onmousedown="processMouseDown(event);">DVD Player</div>

    <div id="cart"
      style="left:350px; top:250px; width:200px;
height:100px;">
      Shopping Cart</div>

  </body>
```

The code in that function starts by creating a new cross-browser mouse event object:

```
function processMouseDown(e)
{
  var e = new MouseEvent(e);
      .
      .
      .
}
```

Then the code in `processMouseDown` starts the dragging process by connecting mouse "listener" functions to the mouse move event (the event that occurs when the user drags the DVD player) and the mouse up event (the event that occurs when the DVD player is dropped). The function that tracks mouse movements is `processMouseMove`, and the function that tracks mouse up events is `processMouseUp`. You start the dragging-and-dropping process by connecting functions that will catch mouse move and mouse up events:

```
function processMouseDown(e)
{
  var e = new MouseEvent(e);
  addListener("mousemove", processMouseMove);
  addListener("mouseup", processMouseUp);
      .
      .
      .
}
```

What is the `addListener` function? Is it built into all browsers in an (amazing) display of cross-browser programming? No, it's a function this example creates itself, because the way you connect events to functions varies by browser. The `addListener` function is passed the type of event you want to track and the callback function that should be called when that event occurs:

```
function addListener(type, callback)
{
      .
      .
      .
}
```

If the browser's `document` object supports the `addEventListener` method, you can use that method to connect a `callback` function to an event like this:

```
function addListener(type, callback)
{
  if (document.addEventListener) {
    document.addEventListener(type, callback, false);
  }
      .
      .
      .
}
```

On the other hand, if the browser's document object supports the attachEvent method, you can use that to connect a callback function to an event:

```
function addListener(type, callback)
{
  if (document.addEventListener) {
    document.addEventListener(type, callback, false);
  } else if (document.attachEvent) {
    document.attachEvent("on" + type, callback, false);
  }
}
```

That's the function you use in processMouseDown to connect the mouse move and mouse up events to the processMouseMove and processMouseUp functions.

Now that you're tracking those events, what's next?

When users move the mouse, you have to move the HTML element they're dragging yourself. To do that, you should record the location at which the mouse was pressed inside that element. To move an element using dynamic styles, you can position its top left corner to match the new mouse location, but if the user pressed the mouse somewhere inside the element, you have to keep in mind that the upper left corner doesn't necessarily correspond to the mouse location in the element. To account for that, you can store the X and Y offsets of the mouse with respect to the upper-left corner of the dragged element. For example, here's how you store the X offset in processMouseDown, as offsetX:

```
var offsetX;

function processMouseDown(e)
{
  var e = new MouseEvent(e);
  addListener("mousemove", processMouseMove);
  addListener("mouseup", processMouseUp);
  offsetX = e.x - parseInt(e.target.style.left);
    .
    .
    .
}
```

Here's what's happening: the offset is the position of the mouse inside the dragged element, and in the X direction, that's equal to the x location of the mouse — e.x — minus the left position of the dragged element. To find the left position of the dragged element, you can use the element's left style property. The dragged element is accessible as e.target, and its style properties are accessible through the style object, e.target.style. The left-hand edge of the element is at position e.target.style.left, but that property is stored as text. To convert from text to a number, you can use the JavaScript parseInt function, so you get offsetX = e.x - parseInt(e.target.style.left);.

Similarly, here's how you can calculate the Y offset of the mouse inside the dragged element:

```
var offsetX, offsetY;

function processMouseDown(e)
{
  var e = new MouseEvent(e);
  addListener("mousemove", processMouseMove);
  addListener("mouseup", processMouseUp);
  offsetX = e.x - parseInt(e.target.style.left);
  offsetY = e.y - parseInt(e.target.style.top);
  .
  .
  .
}
```

You'll use `offsetX` and `offsetY` when positioning the dragged element later in this chapter.

Finally, now that the mouse button was pressed, starting a new drag-and-drop process, you can erase any text in the `targetDiv` <div> element, which will display text from the server:

```
function processMouseDown(e)
{
  var e = new MouseEvent(e);
  addListener("mousemove", processMouseMove);
  addListener("mouseup", processMouseUp);
  offsetX = e.x - parseInt(e.target.style.left);
  offsetY = e.y - parseInt(e.target.style.top);
  document.getElementById("targetDiv").innerHTML = "";
}
```

That's the `processMouseDown` function: it connects functions to the mouse move and mouse up events, and calculates the offset of the mouse location in the dragged element.

The next step happens when the user starts dragging the mouse.

Handling mouse move events

After starting the dragging operations by pressing the mouse button in a draggable HTML element, the user moves the mouse. Your goal is to make sure the draggable element follows that mouse movement. When the user pressed the mouse button in the DVD player <div> element, the `onmousemove` event was connected to the `processMouseMove` function, which looks like this in the code:

```
function processMouseMove(e)
{
  .
  .
  .
}
```

The first step is to convert the mouse event to a cross-browser `MouseEvent` event object:

```
function processMouseMove(e)
{
  var e = new MouseEvent(e);
     .
     .
     .
}
```

Then you need the new position of the dragged element. You can find the new x position of the element like this:

```
function processMouseMove(e)
{
  var e = new MouseEvent(e);
  var x = e.x - offsetX;
     .
     .
     .
}
```

> **NOTE** This action subtracts the x offset of the actual mouse location inside the dragged element in order to find the real new position of the left edge.

then you can set the location of the left-hand edge of the dragged element like this:

```
function processMouseMove(e)
{
  var e = new MouseEvent(e);
  var x = e.x - offsetX;
  e.target.style.left = x + "px";
     .
     .
     .
}
```

Similarly, you can position the top of the dragged element using the new y position of the mouse:

```
function processMouseMove(e)
{
  var e = new MouseEvent(e);
  var x = e.x - offsetX;
  e.target.style.left = x + "px";
  var y = e.y - offsetY;
  e.target.style.top = y + "px";
}
```

That moves the dragged element to the new location of the mouse. But what about when the user drops the element?

Handling mouse up events

When the user releases the mouse button, that action causes a mouse up event, which means that if the user drags an element, that element is dropped. For example, if the user drags the DVD player <div> element, the drop event is tied to the function processMouseUp:

```
function processMouseUp(e)
{
  .
  .
  .
}
```

The code in processMouseUp starts by creating a cross-browser event object:

```
function processMouseUp(e)
{
  var e = new MouseEvent(e);
  .
  .
  .
}
```

then the code removes the mouse move and mouse up event handlers, using a function named removeListener:

```
function processMouseUp(e)
{
  var e = new MouseEvent(e);
  removeListener("mousemove", processMouseMove);
  removeListener("mouseup", processMouseUp);
  .
  .
  .
}
```

The removeListener function removes a callback function from an event, if the document object supports the removeEventListener method:

```
function removeListener (type, callback)
{
  if (document.removeEventListener) {
    document.removeEventListener(type, callback, false);
  }
  .
  .
  .
}
```

In other browsers, you can use the detachEvent method to do the same thing:

```
function removeListener (type, callback)
{
  if (document.removeEventListener) {
    document.removeEventListener(type, callback, false);
  } else if (document.detachEvent) {
    document.detachEvent("on" + type, callback, false);
  }
}
```

After the mouse up and mouse move listener functions have been removed, you have to determine whether the dragged element was dropped inside the cart <div> element. Start by getting an object corresponding to the cart:

```
function processMouseUp(e)
{
  var e = new MouseEvent(e);
  removeListener("mousemove", processMouseMove);
  removeListener("mouseup", processMouseUp);

  var cart = document.getElementById("cart");
    .
    .
    .
}
```

Get the position of the cart, as well as its width and height:

```
function processMouseUp(e)
{
  var e = new MouseEvent(e);
  removeListener("mousemove", processMouseMove);
  removeListener("mouseup", processMouseUp);

  var cart = document.getElementById("cart");
  var x = parseInt(cart.style.left);
  var y = parseInt(cart.style.top);
  var width = parseInt(cart.style.width);
  var height = parseInt(cart.style.height);
    .
    .
    .
}
```

then test to make sure the dragged element was dropped inside the cart:

```
function processMouseUp(e)
{
  var e = new MouseEvent(e);
```

```
        removeListener("mousemove", processMouseMove);
        removeListener("mouseup", processMouseUp);

        var cart = document.getElementById("cart");
        var x = parseInt(cart.style.left);
        var y = parseInt(cart.style.top);
        var width = parseInt(cart.style.width);
        var height = parseInt(cart.style.height);

        if(e.x > x && e.x < x + width &&
          e.y > y && e.y < y + height){
          .
          .
          .
        }
    }
```

At this point, you've determined that the user dropped the DVD player inside the cart. It's time to fetch the message from the server, which is stored in a file named buy.txt. You can do that by creating a new XMLHttpRequest object and configuring it to download buy.txt:

```
    function processMouseUp(e)
    {
      var e = new MouseEvent(e);
        .
        .
        .
      if(e.x > x && e.x < x + width &&
        e.y > y && e.y < y + height){
        var XMLHttpRequestObject = false;

        if (window.XMLHttpRequest) {
          XMLHttpRequestObject = new XMLHttpRequest();
        } else if (window.ActiveXObject) {
          XMLHttpRequestObject = new
          ActiveXObject("Microsoft.XMLHTTP");
        }

        if(XMLHttpRequestObject) {
          XMLHttpRequestObject.open("GET", "buy.txt");
            .
            .
            .
        }
      }
    }
```

Finally, you can handle the download and display the "Congratulations, you just bought a fine DVD player" text from buy.txt in the targetDiv element in the Web page:

```
function processMouseUp(e)
{
  var e = new MouseEvent(e);
        .
        .
        .
    if (window.XMLHttpRequest) {
      XMLHttpRequestObject = new XMLHttpRequest();
    } else if (window.ActiveXObject) {
      XMLHttpRequestObject = new
      ActiveXObject("Microsoft.XMLHTTP");
    }

    if(XMLHttpRequestObject) {
      XMLHttpRequestObject.open("GET", "buy.txt");

      XMLHttpRequestObject.onreadystatechange = function()
      {
        if (XMLHttpRequestObject.readyState == 4 &&
          XMLHttpRequestObject.status == 200) {
            document.getElementById("targetDiv").innerHTML =
              XMLHttpRequestObject.responseText;
            delete XMLHttpRequestObject;
            XMLHttpRequestObject = null;
        }
      }

      XMLHttpRequestObject.send(null);
    }
  }
}
```

That completes the shopping cart example, which put dragging and dropping and Ajax to work.

Downloading Images with Ajax

How about downloading images using Ajax? How's that, you might ask? Downloading *images*? Can't you just download text-based data using Ajax?

That's correct, but with a little assist from dynamic HTML, you can download images using Ajax as well. Here's the trick: you download the name of the image file and then use an <img> element to make the browser download the image. For example, take a look at Figure 8.10, the image.html application.

FIGURE 8.10

The Ajax image application

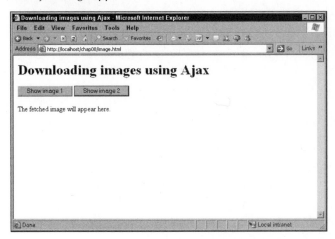

When you click the first button, image number 1 is downloaded, as you see in Figure 8.11. When you click the second button, image number 2 is downloaded, as shown in Figure 8.12.

FIGURE 8.11

Downloading the first image

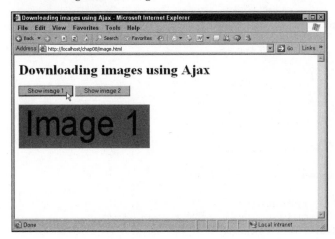

FIGURE 8.12

Downloading the second image

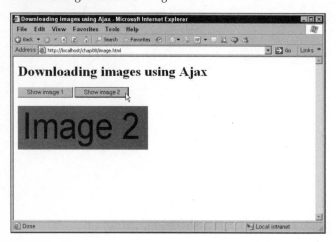

Here's how this works. The buttons are connected to a function named, for example, `getData`. That function then passes the name of a text file containing an image name and a callback function. Also added is a `<div>` element in which to display the downloaded image:

```
<form>
  <input type = "button" value = "Show image 1"
    onclick = "getData('imageName1.txt', callback)">
  <input type = "button" value = "Show image 2"
    onclick = "getData('imageName2.txt', callback)">
</form>

<div id="targetDiv">
  <p>The fetched image will appear here.</p>
</div>
```

In the `getData` function, you can create a new `XMLHttpRequest` object this way:

```
function getData(dataSource, callback)
{
  var XMLHttpRequestObject = false;

  if (window.XMLHttpRequest) {
    XMLHttpRequestObject = new XMLHttpRequest();
  } else if (window.ActiveXObject) {
    XMLHttpRequestObject = new
      ActiveXObject("Microsoft.XMLHTTP");
  }
```

```
            .
            .
            .
        }
```

If the `XMLHttpRequest` object was created, you can connect to the server and download the requested image's name:

```
        function getData(dataSource, callback)
        {
          var XMLHttpRequestObject = false;

          if (window.XMLHttpRequest) {
            XMLHttpRequestObject = new XMLHttpRequest();
          } else if (window.ActiveXObject) {
            XMLHttpRequestObject = new
              ActiveXObject("Microsoft.XMLHTTP");
          }

          if(XMLHttpRequestObject) {
            XMLHttpRequestObject.open("GET", dataSource);

            XMLHttpRequestObject.onreadystatechange = function()
            {
              if (XMLHttpRequestObject.readyState == 4 &&
                XMLHttpRequestObject.status == 200) {
                .
                .
                .
              }
            }

          }
        }
```

And you can call the `callback` function with that image name:

```
        function getData(dataSource, callback)
        {
          var XMLHttpRequestObject = false;

          if (window.XMLHttpRequest) {
            XMLHttpRequestObject = new XMLHttpRequest();
          } else if (window.ActiveXObject) {
            XMLHttpRequestObject = new
              ActiveXObject("Microsoft.XMLHTTP");
          }

          if(XMLHttpRequestObject) {
```

```
XMLHttpRequestObject.open("GET", dataSource);

XMLHttpRequestObject.onreadystatechange = function()
{
  if (XMLHttpRequestObject.readyState == 4 &&
    XMLHttpRequestObject.status == 200) {
      callback(XMLHttpRequestObject.responseText);
      .
      .
      .

  }
}

XMLHttpRequestObject.send(null);
  }
}
```

Finally, in the getData function, delete the XMLHttpRequest object when it's served its purpose, and get the data from the server:

```
function getData(dataSource, callback)
{
  .
  .
  .

  XMLHttpRequestObject.onreadystatechange = function()
  {
    if (XMLHttpRequestObject.readyState == 4 &&
      XMLHttpRequestObject.status == 200) {
        callback(XMLHttpRequestObject.responseText);
        delete XMLHttpRequestObject;
        XMLHttpRequestObject = null;
    }
  }

  XMLHttpRequestObject.send(null);
  }
}
```

The dynamic HTML magic happens in the callback function:

```
function callback(text)
{
  .
  .
  .

}
```

This is the function that is passed the name of the image file to download. All it has to do is to create an `<img>` element using that name, and store that `<img>` element in the target `<div>` element:

```
function callback(text)
{
    document.getElementById("targetDiv").innerHTML =
        "<img src= " + text + ">";
}
```

And that's all there is to it! Now you're downloading images using Ajax.

Handling Ajax Timeouts

One issue of concern in Ajax is whether or not the server access times out. In other words, what if the server doesn't answer back? You don't want your Ajax application to wait forever.

You can handle timeouts using a little JavaScript. Take a look at timeout.html in Figure 8.13.

FIGURE 8.13

Handling timeouts

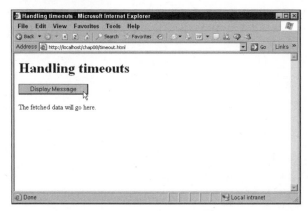

When you click the button, the application tries to download a nonexistent file, data.txt, and it times out, as you see in Figure 8.14.

FIGURE 8.14

The application timed out

So how do you write this application? As usual, start with a button that downloads data.txt using a function named `getData`, and a `<div>` element in which to display the downloaded data:

```
<body>

  <H1>Handling timeouts</H1>

  <form>
    <input type = "button" value = "Display Message"
      onclick = "getData('data.txt', 'targetDiv')">
  </form>

  <div id="targetDiv">
    <p>The fetched data will go here.</p>
  </div>

</body>
```

Start the getData function by creating an XMLHttpRequest object and configuring it:

```
function getData(dataSource, divID)
{
  var XMLHttpRequestObject = false;

  if (window.XMLHttpRequest) {
    XMLHttpRequestObject = new XMLHttpRequest();
  } else if (window.ActiveXObject) {
    XMLHttpRequestObject = new
      ActiveXObject("Microsoft.XMLHTTP");
  }

  if(XMLHttpRequestObject) {
    var obj = document.getElementById(divID);
    XMLHttpRequestObject.open("GET", dataSource);
      .
      .
      .
}
```

Then you'll need two variables, timeoutSet and downloadOK, both of which start off as false:

```
function getData(dataSource, divID)
{
  var XMLHttpRequestObject = false;

  if (window.XMLHttpRequest) {
    XMLHttpRequestObject = new XMLHttpRequest();
  } else if (window.ActiveXObject) {
    XMLHttpRequestObject = new
      ActiveXObject("Microsoft.XMLHTTP");
  }

  if(XMLHttpRequestObject) {
    var obj = document.getElementById(divID);
    XMLHttpRequestObject.open("GET", dataSource);

    var timeoutSet = false;
    var downloadOK = false;
    .
    .
    .
}
```

When the connection is made to the server (the XMLHttpRequest object's readyState property will hold 1), you can request that a JavaScript function be called in a specific time you request. This example uses 1000 milliseconds (one second):

```
function getData(dataSource, divID)
{
  var XMLHttpRequestObject = false;

  if (window.XMLHttpRequest) {
    XMLHttpRequestObject = new XMLHttpRequest();
  } else if (window.ActiveXObject) {
    XMLHttpRequestObject = new
      ActiveXObject("Microsoft.XMLHTTP");
  }

  if(XMLHttpRequestObject) {
    var obj = document.getElementById(divID);
    XMLHttpRequestObject.open("GET", dataSource);

    var timeoutSet = false;
    var downloadOK = false;

    XMLHttpRequestObject.onreadystatechange = function()
    {
```

```
        if (XMLHttpRequestObject.readyState == 1) {
          if(!timeoutSet){
            window.setTimeout(function(){
                  .

                  .

                  .
                }
            },
            1000);
            timeoutSet = true;
          }
        }
            .

            .

            .


    }
}
```

This timeout function should check the downloadOK variable. If it's still false, the download did not yet happen, so the timeout function should display an alert box saying the operation timed out, and abort the XMLHttpRequest object's connection with the server:

```
function getData(dataSource, divID)
{
  var XMLHttpRequestObject = false;
        .

        .

        .
  XMLHttpRequestObject.onreadystatechange = function()
  {
    if (XMLHttpRequestObject.readyState == 1) {
      if(!timeoutSet){
        window.setTimeout(function(){
          if(!downloadOK){
            alert("Sorry, timed out.");
            XMLHttpRequestObject.abort();
          }
        },
        1000);
        timeoutSet = true;
      }
    }
        .

        .

        .


  }
}
```

If, on the other hand, the download did happen before the operation timed out, the code should set the `downloadOK` variable to make sure the timeout alert box isn't shown:

```
function getData(dataSource, divID)
{
  var XMLHttpRequestObject = false;
    .
    .
    .
  XMLHttpRequestObject.onreadystatechange = function()
  {
    if (XMLHttpRequestObject.readyState == 1) {
      if(!timeoutSet){
        window.setTimeout(function(){
          if(!downloadOK){
            alert("Sorry, timed out.");
            XMLHttpRequestObject.abort();
          }
        },
        1000);
        timeoutSet = true;
      }
    }

    if (XMLHttpRequestObject.readyState == 4 &&
      XMLHttpRequestObject.status == 200) {
      downloadOK = true;
      obj.innerHTML =
        XMLHttpRequestObject.responseText;
    }
  }

  XMLHttpRequestObject.send(null);
  }
}
```

And that completes this example. Now you can handle the case where Ajax operations time out.

Summary

You were introduced to the HTML DOM in this chapter, including various techniques for working with the DOM. Ajax applications frequently put the DOM to work when handling downloaded data. In addition, you saw an extensive shopping cart example that put dragging and dropping to work in Ajax applications. You also saw how to handle timeouts in Ajax and how to download images.

Chapter 9

XML and Ajax

A s you may remember from Chapter 1, Ajax stands for *Asynchronous JavaScript and XML.* This chapter is on the *XML* part of Ajax. Handling XML in a browser using JavaScript is far from intuitive, and this chapter covers the details — which you're going to need to know if you download XML from the server.

JavaScript has some great XML-handling functions built in, but they're not much use unless you know how to use them, and how XML is treated in the browser. But don't worry: you'll get the expertise you need here.

Creating XML

The name of the game in XML is data storage, and that's what XML excels at. XML got to be so popular because it's a text-based way of storing your data, and the Internet is based on text transfer. So XML became the Internet's way of slinging data around, as you already know now that you're an Ajax developer.

When you create an XML document, you also create the tags that go into that document. Unlike HTML, XML has no set element tag names that you have to work with; you're free to create your own tags and structure your data as you like. However, there are a number of rules to creating XML, and you'll see the most important ones here.

> **TIP** For the full XML story, take a look at the XML specification published by the World Wide Web Consortium, the people responsible for the XML specs, at `www.w3.org/TR/REC-xml`.

To start an XML document, you need to use an *XML declaration*, which indicates which version of XML you're using. Currently, only two versions are possible: version 1.0, the most common, and version 1.1. Version 1.1 is different from version 1.0 largely in the number of Unicode characters that are legal, but that doesn't concern this discussion very much.

Here's what an XML declaration looks like (bear in mind that every XML document must begin with an XML declaration):

```
<? xml version = "1.0" ?>
          .
          .
          .
```

In addition, every XML document must contain a document element, that is, a single element that contains all the other elements in the XML document:

```
<? xml version = "1.0" ?>
<party>
     .
     .
     .
</party>
```

Every other element inside the document must be enclosed inside the document element:

```
<? xml version = "1.0" ?>
<party>
  <frank>
     .
     .
     .
  </frank>
  <mary>
     .
     .
     .
  </mary>
  <tom>
     .
     .
     .
  </tom>
</party>
```

Each XML document starts with a start tag and ends with an end tag:

```
<tom>
   .
   .
   .
</tom>
```

and can contain other elements:

```
<tom>
  <address>
    .
    .
    .
  </address>
  <phone>
    .
    .
    .
  </phone>
</tom>
```

and/or text:

```
<tom>
  Tom is a pretty good guy.
</tom>
```

unless the element is an empty element, in which case it can't contain any content — other elements or text. In XML, the shortcut for an empty element is this:

```
<tom />
```

 See the **/>** at the end of the element? You use this to avoid having to use both a start tag and an end tag for empty elements.

You create your own tag names in XML, but there are some rules about what tag names are legal. Tag names can't start with a number, can't contain spaces, and can't contain a few other illegal characters, such as quotation marks. Here are some illegal tag names:

```
<12steps>
<big dog>
<"ok">
```

Elements can also contain attributes, just as in HTML, which you use to give more information about the element. You give the attributes in the start tag of an element. Here are some examples:

```
<wife name = "Sally Rogers">
<movie title = "Withnail and I">
<dinner type = "turkey" side = "potatoes">
```

Empty elements can also have attributes:

```
<tom phone = "555-1212"/>
```

Note the syntax here. If you use an attribute, you always have to assign a value to that attribute (unlike in HTML), and that value has to be quoted (also unlike HTML, where browsers are very tolerant of unquoted values). So in XML, attributes have to be attribute name/value pairs, used like this:

```
type = "Swedish"
```

In addition, each XML element has to be *nested* properly. For example, you can't mix start and end tags for different elements, like this:

```
<? xml version = "1.0" ?>
<party>
  <frank>

     .

     .

     .

  <mary>
  </frank>

     .

     .

     .

  </mary>
  <tom>

     .

     .

     .

  </tom>
</party>
```

Here's an example, event.xml, of a well-nested XML document:

```
<?xml version="1.0"?>
<events>
    <event type="fundraising">
        <event_title>National Awards</event_title>
        <event_number>3</event_number>
        <subject>Pet Awards</subject>
        <date>5/5/2007</date>
        <people>
            <person attendance="present">
                <first_name>June</first_name>
                <last_name>Allyson</last_name>
            </person>
            <person attendance="absent">
                <first_name>Virginia</first_name>
                <last_name>Mayo</last_name>
            </person>
            <person attendance="present">
                <first_name>Jimmy</first_name>
                <last_name>Stewart</last_name>
            </person>
        </people>
    </event>
</events>
```

There are two primary correctness criteria for XML documents: *well-formedness* and *validity*. The XML specification contains the rules for well-formedness, and the primary one is that elements must be nested properly.

When you create an XML document, you can specify its syntax rules (for example, which elements are allowed to nest inside which others, and in which sequence), and a document that adheres to the syntax rules you specify for it is called valid. There are two ways of specifying the syntax rules of a document: you can use a document type definition or an XML schema.

ON the WEB For more information on DTD, see www.w3.org/TR/REC-xml. For more information on XML schema, see www.w3.org/XML/Schema.

How you create DTDs and schema is beyond the scope of this book, but some browsers, like Internet Explorer, let you validate XML if you supply a DTD or a schema. Following is an example that illustrates what a DTD would look like for event.xml:

```xml
<?xml version="1.0"?>
<!DOCTYPE events [
<!ELEMENT events (event*)>
<!ELEMENT event (event_title, event_number, subject, date,
   people*)>
<!ELEMENT event_title (#PCDATA)>
<!ELEMENT event_number (#PCDATA)>
<!ELEMENT subject (#PCDATA)>
<!ELEMENT date (#PCDATA)>
<!ELEMENT first_name (#PCDATA)>
<!ELEMENT last_name (#PCDATA)>
<!ELEMENT people (person*)>
<!ELEMENT person (first_name,last_name)>
<!ATTLIST event
    type CDATA #IMPLIED>
<!ATTLIST person
    attendance CDATA #IMPLIED>
]>
<events>
    <event type="fundraising">
        <event_title>National Awards</event_title>
        <event_number>3</event_number>
        <subject>Pet Awards</subject>
        <date>5/5/2007</date>
        <people>
            <person attendance="present">
                <first_name>June</first_name>
                <last_name>Allyson</last_name>
            </person>
            <person attendance="absent">
                <first_name>Virginia</first_name>
                <last_name>Mayo</last_name>
            </person>
```

```
        <person attendance="present">
            <first_name>Jimmy</first_name>
            <last_name>Stewart</last_name>
        </person>
    </people>
  </event>
</events>
```

Handling XML with JavaScript

As discussed in Chapter 8, a browser sees an XML document as a tree of nodes, and that's important to understand if you want to work with XML in Javascript. For example, take a look at this simple XML document:

```
<?xml version="1.0" ?>
<document>
    <greeting>
        Welcome to XML
    </greeting>
    <info>
        This is an XML document.
    </info>
</document>
```

In this case, the <document> node has two child nodes, the <greeting> and <info> nodes. These nodes are child nodes of the <document> node, and sibling nodes of each other. Both the <greeting> and <info> elements themselves have one child node: a text node that holds character data. In terms of a tree of nodes, this is what this document looks like:

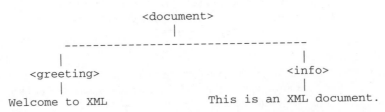

JavaScript has built-in properties you can use to work with the nodes in XML documents like the one that's returned in the XMLHTTPRequest object's responseXML property. JavaScript's built-in properties are listed in Chapter 8, but to refresh your memory, they are

- attributes: Attributes by this node
- childNodes: Array of child nodes
- documentElement: The document element

- `firstChild`: First child node
- `lastChild`: Last child node
- `localName`: Local name of the node (without namespaces)
- `name`: Name of the node
- `nextSibling`: Next sibling node
- `nodeName`: Name of the node
- `nodeType`: Node type
- `nodeValue`: Value of the node
- `previousSibling`: Previous sibling node

You'll see how to use these properties in JavaScript later in this chapter. Note in particular that the `nodeType` property holds the type of a node, which can be any of the following:

- 1 Element
- 2 Attribute
- 3 Text node
- 4 CDATA (XML character data) section
- 5 XML entity reference
- 6 XML entity node
- 7 XML processing instruction
- 8 XML comment
- 9 XML document node
- 10 XML Document Type Definition (DTD)
- 11 XML document fragment
- 12 XML Notation

It's time to start working with some code. Say, for example, that you wanted to start by loading an XML document into a JavaScript object, creating an object corresponding to the document element of the XML document. All the data in the XML document is accessible from the document element, because the document element contains all the data in the document (you can use the `firstChild`, `childNodes`, `lastChild`, and other properties on the document element to access the data in the document).

So how do you load an XML document into JavaScript and get an object for the document element? Take a look at documentElement.html, which appears in Figure 9.1.

FIGURE 9.1

The documentElement.html application

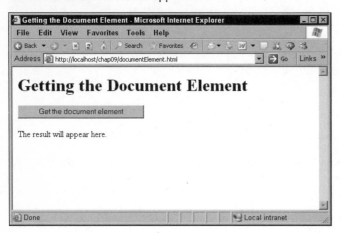

This application reads in event.xml and creates an object corresponding to event.xml's document element when you click the button, as shown in Figure 9.2.

FIGURE 9.2

The documentElement.html application at work

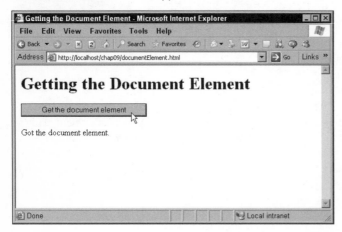

This application gives you your formal start in handling XML with Ajax. Start by creating the button you see in Figure 9.1, and the `<div>` element in which to display the results:

```
<body>

  <h1>Getting the Document Element</h1>

  <form>
    <input type = "button" value = "Get the document element"
      onclick = "getDocumentElement()">
  </form>

  <div id="targetDiv" width =100 height=100>
    The result will appear here.
  </div>

</body>
```

The button is tied to a JavaScript function named `getDocumentElement`, which starts by creating an `XMLHttpRequest` object:

```
function getDocumentElement()
{
  var XMLHttpRequestObject = false;

  if (window.XMLHttpRequest) {
    XMLHttpRequestObject = new XMLHttpRequest();
  } else if (window.ActiveXObject) {
    XMLHttpRequestObject = new
      ActiveXObject("Microsoft.XMLHTTP");
  }
      .
      .
      .
}
```

If the `XMLHttpRequest` object was created, you can download event.xml and get its XML from the `XMLHttpRequest` object's `responseXML` property as an XML document object:

```
function getDocumentElement()
{
  var XMLHttpRequestObject = false;

  if (window.XMLHttpRequest) {
    XMLHttpRequestObject = new XMLHttpRequest();
  } else if (window.ActiveXObject) {
    XMLHttpRequestObject = new
      ActiveXObject("Microsoft.XMLHTTP");
  }
```

```
if(XMLHttpRequestObject) {
  XMLHttpRequestObject.open("GET", "event.xml", true);

  XMLHttpRequestObject.onreadystatechange = function()
  {
    if (XMLHttpRequestObject.readyState == 4 &&
      XMLHttpRequestObject.status == 200) {
      var xmlDocument = XMLHttpRequestObject.responseXML;
        .
        .
        .
    }
  }
}
}
```

To get the document element object, use the document object's documentElement property:

```
function getDocumentElement()
{
  var XMLHttpRequestObject = false;

  if (window.XMLHttpRequest) {
    XMLHttpRequestObject = new XMLHttpRequest();
  } else if (window.ActiveXObject) {
    XMLHttpRequestObject = new
      ActiveXObject("Microsoft.XMLHTTP");
  }

  if(XMLHttpRequestObject) {
    XMLHttpRequestObject.open("GET", "event.xml", true);

    XMLHttpRequestObject.onreadystatechange = function()
    {
      if (XMLHttpRequestObject.readyState == 4 &&
        XMLHttpRequestObject.status == 200) {
        var xmlDocument = XMLHttpRequestObject.responseXML;
        var documentElement = xmlDocument.documentElement;
          .
          .
          .
      }
    }
  }
}
```

If the document element object was created, you can notify the user of that fact:

```
function getDocumentElement()
{
  var XMLHttpRequestObject = false;

  if (window.XMLHttpRequest) {
    XMLHttpRequestObject = new XMLHttpRequest();
  } else if (window.ActiveXObject) {
    XMLHttpRequestObject = new
      ActiveXObject("Microsoft.XMLHTTP");
  }

  if(XMLHttpRequestObject) {
    XMLHttpRequestObject.open("GET", "event.xml", true);

    XMLHttpRequestObject.onreadystatechange = function()
    {
      if (XMLHttpRequestObject.readyState == 4 &&
        XMLHttpRequestObject.status == 200) {
        var xmlDocument = XMLHttpRequestObject.responseXML;
        var documentElement = xmlDocument.documentElement;
        if(documentElement){
          document.getElementById("targetDiv").innerHTML =
            "Got the document element.";
        }
      }
    }

    XMLHttpRequestObject.send(null);
  }
}
```

And that completes the example—you've grabbed the document element. Now how about actually doing something with that element?

Retrieving Data from an XML Document

Take a look at event.html, which is shown in Figure 9.3.

FIGURE 9.3

The event.html application at work

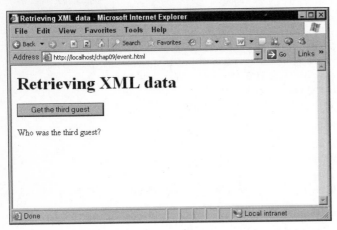

This application reads in event.xml and retrieves the name of the third guest from the guest list in that XML document:

```
<?xml version="1.0"?>
<events>
    <event type="fundraising">
        <event_title>National Awards</event_title>
        <event_number>3</event_number>
        <subject>Pet Awards</subject>
        <date>5/5/2007</date>
        <people>
            <person attendance="present">
                <first_name>June</first_name>
                <last_name>Allyson</last_name>
            </person>
            <person attendance="absent">
                <first_name>Virginia</first_name>
                <last_name>Mayo</last_name>
            </person>
            <person attendance="present">
                <first_name>Jimmy</first_name>
                <last_name>Stewart</last_name>
            </person>
        </people>
    </event>
</events>
```

You can see how this works in Figure 9.4, in which the application displays the name of the third guest, Jimmy Stewart.

Accessing the third guest

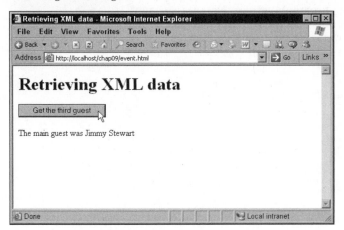

How does this work in code? You start with the button, which is connected to a function named getData here, and the <div> element in which to display the results:

```
<body>

    <h1>Retrieving XML data</h1>

    <form>
      <input type = "button" value = "Get the third guest"
        onclick = "getData()" />
    </form>

    <div id="targetDiv" width =100 height=100>
      Who was the third guest?
    </div>

</body>
```

In the getData function, you download event.xml and pass the XML document object to a new function, displayThirdGuest, like this:

```
        function getData()
        {
          .
          .
          .
          if(XMLHttpRequestObject) {
            XMLHttpRequestObject.open("GET", "event.xml", true);
```

```
        XMLHttpRequestObject.onreadystatechange = function()
        {
          if (XMLHttpRequestObject.readyState == 4 &&
            XMLHttpRequestObject.status == 200) {
          var xmlDocument = XMLHttpRequestObject.responseXML;
          displayThirdGuest(xmlDocument);
          }
        }

        XMLHttpRequestObject.send(null);
      }
    }
```

In the `displayThirdGuest` function, you want to display the name of the third guest, Jimmy Stewart. Start by getting an object corresponding to the document element, <events>:

```
<?xml version="1.0"?>
<events>
    <event type="fundraising">
        <event_title>National Awards</event_title>
        <event_number>3</event_number>
        <subject>Pet Awards</subject>
        <date>5/5/2007</date>
        <people>
          .

          .

            <person attendance="present">
                <first_name>Jimmy</first_name>
                <last_name>Stewart</last_name>
            </person>
        </people>
    </event>
</events>
```

The `displayThirdGuest` function is passed an XML document object, so you can get an object corresponding to the <events> node like this:

```
        function displayThirdGuest (xmldoc)
        {
          var eventsNode;

          eventsNode = xmldoc.documentElement;
          .
          .
          .
        }
```

Next, you want to get an object corresponding to the <event> element:

```
<?xml version="1.0"?>
<events>
    <event type="fundraising">
           .
             .
               .
               <person attendance="present">
                   <first_name>Jimmy</first_name>
                   <last_name>Stewart</last_name>
               </person>
           </people>
      </event>
</events>
```

To do that, use the document element's firstChild property this way in the displayThirdGuest function:

```
function displayThirdGuest (xmldoc)
{
  var eventsNode, eventNode;

  eventsNode = xmldoc.documentElement;
  eventNode = eventsNode.firstChild;
     .
       .
         .
}
```

To get an object corresponding to the <people> element, use the <event> element's lastChild property:

```
<?xml version="1.0"?>
<events>
    <event type="fundraising">
        <event_title>National Awards</event_title>
        <event_number>3</event_number>
        <subject>Pet Awards</subject>
        <date>5/5/2007</date>
        <people>
            <person attendance="present">
                <first_name>June</first_name>
                <last_name>Allyson</last_name>
            </person>
            <person attendance="absent">
                <first_name>Virginia</first_name>
                <last_name>Mayo</last_name>
            </person>
```

```
            <person attendance="present">
                <first_name>Jimmy</first_name>
                <last_name>Stewart</last_name>
            </person>
        </people>
    </event>
</events>
```

Here's what it looks like in code:

```
function displayThirdGuest (xmldoc)
{
  var eventsNode, eventNode, peopleNode;

  eventsNode = xmldoc.documentElement;
  eventNode = eventsNode.firstChild;
  peopleNode = eventNode.lastChild;
  .
  .
  .
}
```

Next, get an object corresponding to the third person:

```
<?xml version="1.0"?>
<events>

        .
        .
        .

    <people>
        <person attendance="present">
            <first_name>June</first_name>
            <last_name>Allyson</last_name>
        </person>
        <person attendance="absent">
            <first_name>Virginia</first_name>
            <last_name>Mayo</last_name>
        </person>
        <person attendance="present">
            <first_name>Jimmy</first_name>
            <last_name>Stewart</last_name>
        </person>
    </people>
  </event>
</events>
```

To do that, use the <people> element object's lastChild property:

```
function displayThirdGuest (xmldoc)
{
  var eventsNode, eventNode, peopleNode;
  var personNode;

  eventsNode = xmldoc.documentElement;
  eventNode = eventsNode.firstChild;
  peopleNode = eventNode.lastChild;
  personNode = peopleNode.lastChild;
    .
    .
    .
}
```

Next, grab the third guest's <first_name> element:

```
<?xml version="1.0"?>
<events>
    <event type="fundraising">
        .
        .
        .
      <people>
          <person attendance="present">
              <first_name>June</first_name>
              <last_name>Allyson</last_name>
          </person>
          <person attendance="absent">
              <first_name>Virginia</first_name>
              <last_name>Mayo</last_name>
          </person>
          <person attendance="present">
              <first_name>Jimmy</first_name>
              <last_name>Stewart</last_name>
          </person>
      </people>
    </event>
</events>
```

To get the <first_name> element, use the <person> element node's firstChild property:

```
function displayThirdGuest (xmldoc)
{
  var eventsNode, eventNode, peopleNode;
  var personNode, firstNameNode, lastNameNode, displayText;

  eventsNode = xmldoc.documentElement;
  eventNode = eventsNode.firstChild;
```

```
      peopleNode = eventNode.lastChild;
      personNode = peopleNode.lastChild;
      firstNameNode = personNode.firstChild;
            .
            .
            .
   }
```

And you also need the last name of the third guest:

```
<?xml version="1.0"?>
<events>
   <event type="fundraising">
         .
         .
         .
      <people>
         <person attendance="present">
            <first_name>June</first_name>
            <last_name>Allyson</last_name>
         </person>
         <person attendance="absent">
            <first_name>Virginia</first_name>
            <last_name>Mayo</last_name>
         </person>
         <person attendance="present">
            <first_name>Jimmy</first_name>
            <last_name>Stewart</last_name>
         </person>
      </people>
   </event>
</events>
```

Here's what that looks like in code:

```
   function displayThirdGuest (xmldoc)
   {
     var eventsNode, eventNode, peopleNode;
     var personNode, firstNameNode, lastNameNode, displayText;

     eventsNode = xmldoc.documentElement;
     eventNode = eventsNode.firstChild;
     peopleNode = eventNode.lastChild;
     personNode = peopleNode.lastChild;
     firstNameNode = personNode.firstChild;
     lastNameNode = firstNameNode.nextSibling;
           .
           .
           .
   }
```

Now that you have a node object corresponding to the <first_name> and <last_name> elements of the third guest, how do you retrieve the person's actual name? The first and last names are embedded in the <first_name> and <last_name> elements:

```
<person attendance="present">
    <first_name>Jimmy</first_name>
    <last_name>Stewart</last_name>
</person>
```

In fact, the first and last names are text nodes inside the <first_name> and <last_name> element nodes, so you can start by assembling a text string that will display the name of the third guest:

```
function displayThirdGuest (xmldoc)
{
  var eventsNode, eventNode, peopleNode;
  var personNode, firstNameNode, lastNameNode, displayText;

  eventsNode = xmldoc.documentElement;
  eventNode = eventsNode.firstChild;
  peopleNode = eventNode.lastChild;
  personNode = peopleNode.lastChild;
  firstNameNode = personNode.firstChild;
  lastNameNode = firstNameNode.nextSibling;

  displayText = "The third guest was " +
     .
     .
     .
}
```

To refer to the text node of the person's first name, you use the expression firstNameNode.firstChild. To extract the text from that text node, you use the nodeValue property, so here's how you recover the person's first name:

```
function displayThirdGuest (xmldoc)
{
  var eventsNode, eventNode, peopleNode;
  var personNode, firstNameNode, lastNameNode, displayText;

  eventsNode = xmldoc.documentElement;
  eventNode = eventsNode.firstChild;
  peopleNode = eventNode.lastChild;
  personNode = peopleNode.lastChild;
  firstNameNode = personNode.firstChild;
  lastNameNode = firstNameNode.nextSibling;

  displayText = "The third guest was " +
```

```
    firstNameNode.firstChild.nodeValue + ' '
      .
      .
      .
}
```

Similarly, here's how you recover the person's last name:

```
function displayThirdGuest (xmldoc)
{
  var eventsNode, eventNode, peopleNode;
  var personNode, firstNameNode, lastNameNode, displayText;

  eventsNode = xmldoc.documentElement;
  eventNode = eventsNode.firstChild;
  peopleNode = eventNode.lastChild;
  personNode = peopleNode.lastChild;
  firstNameNode = personNode.firstChild;
  lastNameNode = firstNameNode.nextSibling;

  displayText = "The third guest was " +
    firstNameNode.firstChild.nodeValue + ' '
    + lastNameNode.firstChild.nodeValue;
      .
      .
      .
}
```

All that's left is to display the person's name, using the `displayText` string:

```
function displayThirdGuest (xmldoc)
{
  var eventsNode, eventNode, peopleNode;
  var personNode, firstNameNode, lastNameNode, displayText;

  eventsNode = xmldoc.documentElement;
  eventNode = eventsNode.firstChild;
  peopleNode = eventNode.lastChild;
  personNode = peopleNode.lastChild;
  firstNameNode = personNode.firstChild;
  lastNameNode = firstNameNode.nextSibling;

  displayText = "The third guest was " +
    firstNameNode.firstChild.nodeValue + ' '
    + lastNameNode.firstChild.nodeValue;

  var target = document.getElementById("targetDiv");
  target.innerHTML=displayText;
}
```

And that completes event.html, which recovers the third person's name and displays it. However, as written, this example only works in Internet Explorer. Why won't it work in the Mozilla, Netscape, and Firefox Web browsers?

Handling White Space in the Mozilla, Netscape, and Firefox Web Browsers

By default, the Mozilla, Netscape, and Firefox browsers don't omit the white space used for indentation of an XML document. Take a look at event.xml, which is full of indentation white space:

```xml
<?xml version="1.0"?>
<events>
    <event type="fundraising">
        <event_title>National Awards</event_title>
        <event_number>3</event_number>
        <subject>Pet Awards</subject>
        <date>5/5/2007</date>
        <people>
            <person attendance="present">
                <first_name>June</first_name>
                <last_name>Allyson</last_name>
            </person>
               .
               .
               .
        </people>
    </event>
</events>
```

To navigate from the `<events>` node to the `<event>` node, you have to navigate over the white space text node, which is the first child of the `<events>` node (marked with **xxxx** here):

```xml
<?xml version="1.0"?>
<events>
xxxx<event type="fundraising">
       .
       .
       .
```

That means you'd have to use this code to get to the `<event>` element node (note the use of the `nextSibling` property to get past the indentation white space text node):

```
eventsNode = xmldoc.documentElement;
eventNode = eventsNode.firstChild.nextSibling;
   .
   .
   .
```

Similarly, you can navigate over white space text nodes to reach the `<people>` element:

```xml
<?xml version="1.0"?>
<events>
    <event type="fundraising">
        <event_title>National Awards</event_title>
        <event_number>3</event_number>
        <subject>Pet Awards</subject>
        <date>5/5/2007</date>
        <people>
            <person attendance="present">
                <first_name>June</first_name>
                <last_name>Allyson</last_name>
            </person>
            .
            .
            .
        </people>
    </event>
</events>
```

In this case, the last child of the `<event>` element is not the `<people>` element, but the white space text node that follows the `</people>` tag. To take that white space node into account, you can use this expression to get a node corresponding to the `<people>` element:

```
eventsNode = xmldoc.documentElement;
eventNode = eventsNode.firstChild.nextSibling;
peopleNode = eventNode.lastChild.previousSibling;
    .
    .
    .
```

Here's how to rewrite the `displayThirdGuest` function to take into account the default white space handling in Mozilla, Netscape, and Firefox:

```
function displayThirdGuest(xmldoc)
{
    var eventsNode, eventNode, peopleNode;
    var personNode, firstNameNode, lastNameNode, displayText;

    eventsNode = xmldoc.documentElement;
    eventNode = eventsNode.firstChild.nextSibling;
    peopleNode = eventNode.lastChild.previousSibling;
    personNode = peopleNode.firstChild.nextSibling
        .nextSibling.nextSibling.nextSibling.nextSibling;
    firstNameNode = personNode.firstChild.nextSibling;
    lastNameNode = firstNameNode.nextSibling.nextSibling;

    displayText = "The third guest is: " +
        firstNameNode.firstChild.nodeValue + ' '
```

```
                   + lastNameNode.firstChild.nodeValue;

        var target = document.getElementById("targetDiv");
            target.innerHTML=displayText;
    }
```

You can see the results on Figure 9.5.

FIGURE 9.5

Accessing the third guest in Firefox

The different ways of handling white space nodes in Internet Explorer and the Mozilla, Netscape, and Firefox browsers is troublesome. Isn't there some way to use the same Ajax application to handle both types of browsers? There is: you can strip the white space out of the XML document before working with it.

Handling White Space in a Cross-Browser Way

You can write a function to strip white space from XML before working with that XML, which means your code will work with Internet Explorer as well as the Mozilla, Netscape, and Firefox browsers. To do that, you might create a function named removeWhitespace:

```
function removeWhitespace(xml)
{
    .
    .
    .
}
```

You can then loop over all nodes in the XML object passed to this function:

```
function removeWhitespace(xml)
{
  var loopIndex;

  for (loopIndex = 0; loopIndex < xml.childNodes.length;
    loopIndex++) {
    .
    .
    .
  }
}
```

Then you get an object corresponding to the current node in the loop:

```
function removeWhitespace(xml)
{
  var loopIndex;

  for (loopIndex = 0; loopIndex < xml.childNodes.length;
    loopIndex++) {

    var currentNode = xml.childNodes[loopIndex];
    .
    .
    .
}
```

If that current node is an element node (nodeType = 1), you should loop over all the children of the element, checking for white space nodes, which you can do by calling removeWhitespace again:

```
function removeWhitespace(xml)
{
  var loopIndex;

  for (loopIndex = 0; loopIndex < xml.childNodes.length;
    loopIndex++) {

    var currentNode = xml.childNodes[loopIndex];

    if (currentNode.nodeType == 1) {
      removeWhitespace(currentNode);
    }
    .
    .
    .
  }
}
```

If, on the other hand, you're dealing with a text node (nodeType = 3), you have to check whether it's a pure white space node. To do that, this code uses a regular expression to check whether the text node contains only spaces:

```
function removeWhitespace(xml)
{
  var loopIndex;

  for (loopIndex = 0; loopIndex < xml.childNodes.length;
    loopIndex++) {

    var currentNode = xml.childNodes[loopIndex];

    if (currentNode.nodeType == 1) {
      removeWhitespace(currentNode);
    }

    if (((/^\s+$/.test(currentNode.nodeValue))) &&
      (currentNode.nodeType == 3)) {

        .
        .
        .

    }
  }
}
```

NOTE A full discussion on regular expressions is beyond the scope of this book. If you want all the details, take a look at `http://perldoc.perl.org/perlre.html`.

If you have found a pure white space node, you can remove it from the XML object with the `removeChild` method and decrement the loop index like this:

```
function removeWhitespace(xml)
{
  var loopIndex;

  for (loopIndex = 0; loopIndex < xml.childNodes.length;
    loopIndex++) {

    var currentNode = xml.childNodes[loopIndex];

    if (currentNode.nodeType == 1) {
      removeWhitespace(currentNode);
    }

    if (((/^\s+$/.test(currentNode.nodeValue))) &&
      (currentNode.nodeType == 3)) {
```

```
              xml.removeChild(xml.childNodes[loopIndex--]);
          }
        }
      }
```

That completes the removeWhitespace function. Now you have to pass the XML you got from the server to that function if you're dealing with a Mozilla/Netscape/Firefox-type browser. To check whether you are dealing with that type of browser, you can set up a true/false variable named mozillaFlag in event.html:

```
<html>
  <head>

    <title>Retrieving XML data</title>

    <script language = "javascript">

      function getData()
      {
        var mozillaFlag = false;
        var XMLHttpRequestObject = false;
          .
          .
          .
```

You can set the mozillaFlag variable to true if you're dealing with a Mozilla/Netscape/Firefox-type browser, which you can check when you determine how to create the XMLHttpRequest object:

```
<html>
  <head>

    <title>Retrieving XML data</title>

    <script language = "javascript">

      function getData()
      {
        var mozillaFlag = false;
        var XMLHttpRequestObject = false;

        if (window.XMLHttpRequest) {
          XMLHttpRequestObject = new XMLHttpRequest();
          mozillaFlag = true;
        } else if (window.ActiveXObject) {
          XMLHttpRequestObject = new
            ActiveXObject("Microsoft.XMLHTTP");
        }
          .
          .
          .
```

And if you are working with a browser that needs to have white space removed from its XML documents, you can call the `removeWhitespace` function before going after the third guest:

```html
<html>
  <head>

    <title>Retrieving XML data</title>

    <script language = "javascript">

      function getData()
      {
        var mozillaFlag = false;
        var XMLHttpRequestObject = false;
        .

        .

        .
        if(XMLHttpRequestObject) {
          XMLHttpRequestObject.open("GET", "event.xml", true);

          XMLHttpRequestObject.onreadystatechange = function()
          {
            if (XMLHttpRequestObject.readyState == 4 &&
              XMLHttpRequestObject.status == 200) {
            var xmlDocument = XMLHttpRequestObject.responseXML;
            if(mozillaFlag){
              removeWhitespace(xmlDocument);
            }
            displayThirdGuest(xmlDocument);
            }
          }

          XMLHttpRequestObject.send(null);
        }
      }
```

That lets you handle the white space issue in a cross-browser manner.

Accessing XML Data Directly

There's a more direct way of accessing XML data if you want simply to grab data from a specific XML element: You can search for that XML element using the `getElementsByTagName` method. This method returns an array of elements, which makes navigating through an XML document very easy. You can see an example, event2.html, in Figure 9.6.

FIGURE 9.6

An example that accesses the third guest directly

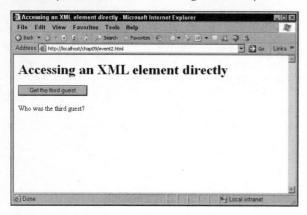

When you click the button in this example, the third guest is fetched from event.xml and displayed, just as before, which you can see in Figure 9.7.

FIGURE 9.7

Accessing the third guest directly

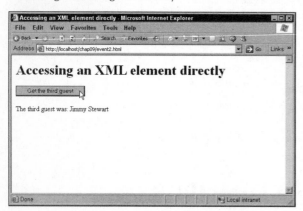

Here's how event2.html works. It starts by creating the button you see in Figure 9.6, and connecting that button to a function named getData:

```html
<body>

  <h1>Accessing an XML element directly</h1>

  <form>
    <input type = "button" value = "Get the third guest"
      onclick = "getData()">
  </form>

  <div id="targetDiv" width =100 height=100>
    Who was the third guest?
  </div>

</body>
```

Next, in the getData function, the code creates an XMLHttpRequest object:

```javascript
function getData()
{
  var XMLHttpRequestObject = false;

  if (window.XMLHttpRequest) {
    XMLHttpRequestObject = new XMLHttpRequest();
  } else if (window.ActiveXObject) {
    XMLHttpRequestObject = new
      ActiveXObject("Microsoft.XMLHTTP");
  }
  .
  .
  .
}
```

If that object was created successfully, the code downloads the XML data, passing it to a function named displayThirdGuest:

```javascript
function getData()
{
  var XMLHttpRequestObject = false;

  if (window.XMLHttpRequest) {
    XMLHttpRequestObject = new XMLHttpRequest();
  } else if (window.ActiveXObject) {
    XMLHttpRequestObject = new
      ActiveXObject("Microsoft.XMLHTTP");
  }
```

```
if(XMLHttpRequestObject) {
  XMLHttpRequestObject.open("GET", "event.xml", true);

  XMLHttpRequestObject.onreadystatechange = function()
  {
    if (XMLHttpRequestObject.readyState == 4 &&
      XMLHttpRequestObject.status == 200) {
    var xmlDocument = XMLHttpRequestObject.responseXML;
    displayThirdGuest(xmlDocument);
    }
  }

  XMLHttpRequestObject.send(null);
}
}
```

Now it's up to the `displayThirdGuest` function to handle the XML document:

```
function displayThirdGuest (xmldoc)
{
    .
    .
    .
}
```

The code here starts by using the `getElementsByTagName` method to get an array of `<first_name>` elements:

```
function displayThirdGuest (xmldoc)
{
  firstnamenodes =
    xmldoc.getElementsByTagName("first_name");
    .
    .
    .
}
```

That's how you access elements using `getElementsByTagName`: you pass this method the name of the element you're interested in, and it returns an array of elements matching the name you supply, or null if no elements matched what you're looking for.

You can also get an array of `<last_name>` elements:

```
function displayThirdGuest (xmldoc)
{
  firstnamenodes =
    xmldoc.getElementsByTagName("first_name");
```

```
lastnamenodes = xmldoc.getElementsByTagName("last_name");
        .
        .
        .
    }
```

To get the first name of the third guest, you can access `firstnamenodes[2]`:

```
function displayThirdGuest (xmldoc)
{
  firstnamenodes =
    xmldoc.getElementsByTagName("first_name");
  lastnamenodes = xmldoc.getElementsByTagName("last_name");

  var displayText = "The third guest was: " +
    firstnamenodes[2]...
        .
        .
        .
    }
```

Accessing `firstnamenodes[2]` gives you the `<first_name>` node, and you need the value of the text node inside that element:

```
<?xml version="1.0"?>
<events>
        .
        .
        .
    <people>
        <person attendance="present">
            <first_name>June</first_name>
            <last_name>Allyson</last_name>
        </person>
        <person attendance="absent">
            <first_name>Virginia</first_name>
            <last_name>Mayo</last_name>
        </person>
        <person attendance="present">
            <first_name>Jimmy</first_name>
            <last_name>Stewart</last_name>
        </person>
    </people>
  </event>
</events>
```

You reach that text node as the first child of the `<first_name>` element, and get the contents of that text node with the `nodeValue` property:

```
function displayThirdGuest (xmldoc)
{
  firstnamenodes =
    xmldoc.getElementsByTagName("first_name");
  lastnamenodes = xmldoc.getElementsByTagName("last_name");

  var displayText = "The third guest was: " +
    firstnamenodes[2].firstChild.nodeValue + ' '
    .
    .
    .
}
```

Similarly, you can get access to the third guest's last name:

```
function displayThirdGuest (xmldoc)
{
  firstnamenodes =
    xmldoc.getElementsByTagName("first_name");
  lastnamenodes = xmldoc.getElementsByTagName("last_name");

  var displayText = "The third guest was: " +
    firstnamenodes[2].firstChild.nodeValue + ' '
    + lastnamenodes[2].firstChild.nodeValue;
    .
    .
    .
}
```

All that's left is to display the third guest's name:

```
function displayThirdGuest (xmldoc)
{
  firstnamenodes =
    xmldoc.getElementsByTagName("first_name");
  lastnamenodes = xmldoc.getElementsByTagName("last_name");

  var displayText = "The third guest was: " +
    firstnamenodes[2].firstChild.nodeValue + ' '
    + lastnamenodes[2].firstChild.nodeValue;

  var target = document.getElementById("targetDiv");
  target.innerHTML=displayText;
}
```

That's it; you've accessed the third guest with remarkably little code. All you had to do was use the handy getElementsByTagName method, which saved you the trouble of navigating through the entire document. As you can see, the getElementsByTagName method is a very handy one, and saves you from having to know the detailed structure of the document beforehand.

Accessing XML Attribute Values

The event.xml document's <person> elements contain an attendance attribute, which is set to present or absent:

```xml
<?xml version="1.0"?>
<events>
       .
       .
       .
    <people>
        <person attendance="present">
            <first_name>June</first_name>
            <last_name>Allyson</last_name>
        </person>
        <person attendance="absent">
            <first_name>Virginia</first_name>
            <last_name>Mayo</last_name>
        </person>
        <person attendance="present">
            <first_name>Jimmy</first_name>
            <last_name>Stewart</last_name>
        </person>
    </people>
 </event>
</events>
```

How can you recover the value of, for example, the third guest's attendance? Take a look at the attributes.html application, which you can see in Figure 9.8. To determine whether the third guest was present, all you have to do is click the button, as you see in the figure, where Jimmy Stewart is listed as being present.

Accessing the third guest's attendance attribute

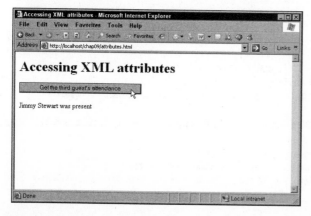

This application starts by connecting its button to a getData function:

```
<body>

  <h1>Accessing XML attributes</h1>

  <form>
    <input type = "button" value = "Get the third
      guest's attendance"
      onclick = "getData()">
  </form>

  <div id="targetDiv" width =100 height=100>
    Was the third guest present?
  </div>

</body>
```

In getData, the code creates an XMLHttpRequest object and sets the mozillaFlag variable in case you need to remove white space. Then you can read in the XML, remove white space if needed, and pass the XML data to another function, displayThirdGuest:

```
<html>
  <head>

    <title>Accessing XML attributes</title>

    <script language = "javascript">

      function getData()
      {
        var mozillaFlag = false;
        var XMLHttpRequestObject = false;

        if (window.XMLHttpRequest) {
          XMLHttpRequestObject = new XMLHttpRequest();
          mozillaFlag = true;
        } else if (window.ActiveXObject) {
          XMLHttpRequestObject = new
            ActiveXObject("Microsoft.XMLHTTP");
        }

        if(XMLHttpRequestObject) {
          XMLHttpRequestObject.open("GET", "event.xml", true);

          XMLHttpRequestObject.onreadystatechange = function()
          {
            if (XMLHttpRequestObject.readyState == 4 &&
              XMLHttpRequestObject.status == 200) {
            var xmlDocument = XMLHttpRequestObject.responseXML;
```

```
             if(mozillaFlag){
               removeWhitespace(xmlDocument);
             }
             displayThirdGuest(xmlDocument);
             }
          }

          XMLHttpRequestObject.send(null);
       }
    }
```

In the `displayThirdGuest` function, you access the third guest's `<first_name>` and `<last_name>` nodes this way:

```
function displayThirdGuest (xmldoc)
{
  var eventsNode, eventNode, peopleNode;
  var firstNameNode, lastNameNode, displayText;

  eventsNode = xmldoc.documentElement;
  eventNode = eventsNode.firstChild;
  peopleNode = eventNode.lastChild;
  personNode = peopleNode.lastChild;
  firstNameNode = personNode.firstChild;
  lastNameNode = firstNameNode.nextSibling;
  .
  .
  .
}
```

In addition, you want the value of the third guest's `attendance` attribute, which is an attribute of the `<person>` element. You can get a `NamedNodeList` object holding the `attendance` attribute with the `personNode` object's `attributes` property:

```
function displayThirdGuest (xmldoc)
{
  var eventsNode, eventNode, peopleNode;
  var firstNameNode, lastNameNode, displayText;

  eventsNode = xmldoc.documentElement;
  eventNode = eventsNode.firstChild;
  peopleNode = eventNode.lastChild;
  personNode = peopleNode.lastChild;
  firstNameNode = personNode.firstChild;
  lastNameNode = firstNameNode.nextSibling;
  attributes = personNode.attributes
  .
  .
  .
}
```

To recover the value of the `attendance` attribute, you can use the `NamedNodeList` `getNamedItem` method like this:

```
function displayThirdGuest (xmldoc)
{
  var eventsNode, eventNode, peopleNode;
  var firstNameNode, lastNameNode, displayText;

  eventsNode = xmldoc.documentElement;
  eventNode = eventsNode.firstChild;
  peopleNode = eventNode.lastChild;
  personNode = peopleNode.lastChild;
  firstNameNode = personNode.firstChild;
  lastNameNode = firstNameNode.nextSibling;
  attributes = personNode.attributes
  attendancePerson = attributes.getNamedItem("attendance");
    .
    .
    .
}
```

Now all you have to do is display the value of the `attendance` attribute:

```
function displayThirdGuest (xmldoc)
{
  var eventsNode, eventNode, peopleNode;
  var firstNameNode, lastNameNode, displayText;

  eventsNode = xmldoc.documentElement;
  eventNode = eventsNode.firstChild;
  peopleNode = eventNode.lastChild;
  personNode = peopleNode.lastChild;
  firstNameNode = personNode.firstChild;
  lastNameNode = firstNameNode.nextSibling;
  attributes = personNode.attributes
  attendancePerson = attributes.getNamedItem("attendance");

  var displayText = firstNameNode.firstChild.nodeValue
     + ' ' + lastNameNode.firstChild.nodeValue
     + " was " + attendancePerson.nodeValue;


  var target = document.getElementById("targetDiv");
  target.innerHTML=displayText;
}
```

Now you can retrieve the values of attributes from XML data.

Validating Your XML

You can validate your XML data after it's been downloaded if you use a browser like Internet Explorer. For example, say that you add a document type definition (DTD) to event.xml, creating eventdtd.xml:

```
<?xml version="1.0"?>
<!DOCTYPE events [
<!ELEMENT events (event*)>
<!ELEMENT event (event_title, event_number, subject, date,
people*)>
<!ELEMENT event_title (#PCDATA)>
<!ELEMENT event_number (#PCDATA)>
<!ELEMENT subject (#PCDATA)>
<!ELEMENT date (#PCDATA)>
<!ELEMENT first_name (#PCDATA)>
<!ELEMENT last_name (#PCDATA)>
<!ELEMENT people (person*)>
<!ELEMENT person (first_name,last_name)>
<!ATTLIST event
    type CDATA #IMPLIED>
<!ATTLIST person
    attendance CDATA #IMPLIED>
]>
<events>
    <event type="informal">
        <event_title>National Awards</event_title>
        <event_number>3</event_number>
        <subject>Pet Awards</subject>
        <date>5/5/2007</date>
        <peoples>
            <person attendance="present">
                <first_name>June</first_name>
                <last_name>Allyson</last_name>
            </person>
            <person attendance="absent">
                <first_name>Virginia</first_name>
                <last_name>Mayo</last_name>
            </person>
            <person attendance="present">
                <first_name>Jimmy</first_name>
                <last_name>Stewart</last_name>
            </person>
        </peoples>
    </event>
</events>
```

That DTD lets you check the syntax of your XML document, which is a good thing because there's an error in this document: the `<peoples>` element has replaced `<people>`. But as you can see in Figure 9.9, you can catch this kind of validation error in Ajax applications.

FIGURE 9.9

Validating an XML document

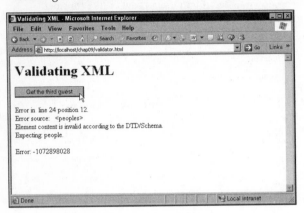

Here's how it works. After downloading the XML data in Internet Explorer, you can create an MSXML2.DOMDocument object that will parse your downloaded XML:

```
function getData()
{
  var XMLHttpRequestObject = false;

  XMLHttpRequestObject = new
    ActiveXObject("Microsoft.XMLHTTP");

  if(XMLHttpRequestObject) {
    XMLHttpRequestObject.open("GET", "eventdtd.xml?k=4",
true);

    XMLHttpRequestObject.onreadystatechange = function()
    {
      if (XMLHttpRequestObject.readyState == 4 &&
        XMLHttpRequestObject.status == 200) {
        var xmlDocument = XMLHttpRequestObject.responseXML;

        var parser = new
          ActiveXObject("MSXML2.DOMDocument");
          .
          .
          .
      }
    }
```

then you set the `parser` object's `validateOnParse` property to `true`, and load the XML you've already downloaded:

```
function getData()
{
  var XMLHttpRequestObject = false;

  XMLHttpRequestObject = new
    ActiveXObject("Microsoft.XMLHTTP");

  if(XMLHttpRequestObject) {
    XMLHttpRequestObject.open("GET", "eventdtd.xml?k=4",
      true);

    XMLHttpRequestObject.onreadystatechange = function()
    {
      if (XMLHttpRequestObject.readyState == 4 &&
        XMLHttpRequestObject.status == 200) {
        var xmlDocument = XMLHttpRequestObject.responseXML;

        var parser = new
          ActiveXObject("MSXML2.DOMDocument");
        parser.validateOnParse = true;
        parser.load(XMLHttpRequestObject.responseXML);
        .
        .
        .
  }
}
```

After having parsed the XML, you can check the `parser.parseError.errorCode` property, and if it's not `0`, there was an error. You can get more data about the error with the `parseError` properties such as `line`, `url`, `errorCode`, and `srcText`:

```
function getData()
{
  var XMLHttpRequestObject = false;

  XMLHttpRequestObject = new
    ActiveXObject("Microsoft.XMLHTTP");

  if(XMLHttpRequestObject) {
    XMLHttpRequestObject.open("GET", "eventdtd.xml?k=4",
      true);

    XMLHttpRequestObject.onreadystatechange = function()
    {
      if (XMLHttpRequestObject.readyState == 4 &&
        XMLHttpRequestObject.status == 200) {
        var xmlDocument = XMLHttpRequestObject.responseXML;
```

```
                  var parser = new
    ActiveXObject("MSXML2.DOMDocument");
                  parser.validateOnParse = true;
                  parser.load(XMLHttpRequestObject.responseXML);
                  var target = document.getElementById("targetDiv");

                  if (parser.parseError.errorCode != 0) {
                    target.innerText = "Error in " +
                      parser.parseError.url +
                      " line " + parser.parseError.line +
                      " position " + parser.parseError.linepos +
                      ".\nError source: " + parser.parseError.srcText +
                      "\n" + parser.parseError.reason +
                      "\n" +   "Error: " +
                      parser.parseError.errorCode;
                  }
                  else {

                  displayThirdGuest(xmlDocument);
                  }
                }
              }

          XMLHttpRequestObject.send(null);
        }
      }
```

Handling XML documents like this lets you check their validity.

Summary

In this chapter, you were introduced to working with XML in Ajax, in particular, how to handle XML in JavaScript. You saw how to download XML and how to navigate through it in a number of ways to recover the data you want, using methods like nextSibling, previousSibling, and so on. You also saw how to handle whitespace and how to validate XML documents.

Chapter 10

Cascading Style Sheets and Ajax

When you work with Ajax, you're often going to be updating Web pages on the fly, and one of the best ways to do that is by using *cascading style sheets* (CSS). CSS is one of the more important Ajax-related topics, in fact, simply because updating Web pages is so important in Ajax.

ON the WEB You're going to see Ajax at work with CSS in this chapter; for the full, formal details on CSS, see the CSS specification at `www.w3.org/TR/CSS21/`.

CSS is great at positioning elements in a Web page and letting you work with those elements (as by using the mouse, for example). And this chapter starts with just such an example: an Ajax-enabled menu system that uses CSS to display drop-down menus and handle mouse events in them. Although this example uses a menu system, the techniques here show you how to create general popups in a Web page, which let you place text or other elements anywhere you want them.

Ajax-Enabled Menus

Take a look at the Ajax-enabled menu system you see in Figure 10.1, with two menus, Fruits and Vegetables.

FIGURE 10.1

FIGURE 10.1

The Ajax-enabled menu application

When the user positions the mouse over one of those menus, the items in a drop-down menu are downloaded using Ajax and displayed, as shown in Figure 10.2.

FIGURE 10.2

Displaying an Ajax-enabled menu

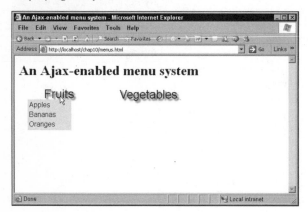

The user can select items from the menu, as you see in Figure 10.3. (Note that in Internet Explorer, the mouse cursor changes to a hand in the menu.) When the user does make a selection, that selection is displayed, as shown in Figure 10.4.

FIGURE 10.3

Selecting a menu item

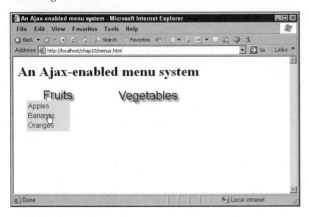

FIGURE 10.4

Displaying a menu selection

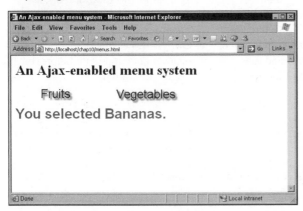

This application lets you download Ajax data and display that data using CSS, and it's a good example of CSS working with Ajax.

Creating the styles

You can use CSS styles in a number of ways, starting with inline styles using the HTML `style` attribute. For example, to position the first menu image, the "Fruits" menu, which is stored in the image file image1.jpg, you can use the `style` attribute of the HTML `<img>` element like this:

```
<body onclick = "hide()" onmousemove = "checkMenu(event)">

  <H1>An Ajax-enabled menu system</H1>

    <img id = "image1" src="image1.jpg"
      style="left:30; top:50; width:200; height:40;">
      .
      .
      .
    <div id = "targetDiv"></div>
</body>
```

NOTE   Note the addition of a `<div>` element, `targetDiv`, which is used to display the user's menu selection.

This sets the location and dimensions of the "Fruits" image, setting its upper left-hand corner to (30, 50) in the browser's client area (the client area is the area that you get to work with — it's the browser's display minus borders, menu bars, toolbars, and so on). That is, the x location of the image's upper left corner will be at 30 pixels, and the y location will be 50 pixels. In a browser, positive x is to the right (and x = 0 on the left-hand edge of the client area), and positive y is downward (and y = 0 on the top of the client area). That way of measuring — especially positive y going downward instead of upward — might seem odd to you if you've never encountered it before, but the idea is that it follows the way you read text on a page: to the right, and down.

The text you assign to the `style` attribute, `"left:30; top:50; width:200; height:40;"`, is made up of style *rules*, such as `left:30;`. Each rule is made up of a style property, such as `left`, which is assigned a value, such as `30`. That's the way you use CSS: you assign values to style properties, and the browser takes the new value and arranges things as you've directed.

Similarly, you can set the location of the second menu, the Vegetables menu:

```
<body onclick = "hide()" onmousemove = "checkMenu(event)">

  <H1>An Ajax-enabled menu system</H1>

    <img id = "image1" src="image1.jpg"
      style="left:30; top:50; width:200; height:40;">
    <img id = "image2" style="left:270; top:50; width:200;
      height:40;" src="image2.jpg">
      .
      .
      .
    <div id = "targetDiv"></div>
</body>
```

Besides the <img> elements, you're going to need some way of displaying the drop-down menus themselves. You can display the drop-down menus in <div> elements, menuDiv1 and menuDiv2.

Here's how to create those <div> elements:

```
<body onclick = "hide()" onmousemove = "checkMenu(event)">

   <H1>An Ajax-enabled menu system</H1>

     <img id = "image1" src="image1.jpg"
       style="left:30; top:50; width:200; height:40;">
     <div id = "menuDiv1" style="left:30; top:100; width:100;
       height: 70; visibility:hidden;"><div></div></div>
     <img id = "image2" style="left:270; top:50; width:200;
       height:40;" src="image2.jpg">
     <div id = "menuDiv2" style="left:270; top:100; width:100;
       height: 70; visibility:hidden;"><div></div></div>
     <div id = "targetDiv"></div>
   </body>
```

Note in particular the visibility style property here. This property lets you specify whether or not a Web page element appears in the browser or is invisible. You set it to hidden, as here, to make an element invisible, or to visible to make the element appear. In other words, the two <div> elements here start off as invisible.

Besides using inline styles with the style attribute, you can also assign styles using a <style> element, which is usually placed in the <head> section of a page. In this case, you specify the element you want to set up styles for, and enclose the style rules you want to use — separated by semicolons — inside curly braces.

Here's an example that sets the styles for the <body> element, setting the foreground (text) color, the background color, and the font to use:

```
<style>
  body {
    color: #000000;
    background-color: #FFFFFF;
    font-family: times;
  }
      .
      .
      .
</style>
```

NOTE You can specify colors using the same kind of hexadecimal color values that you use in HTML as color triplets like this: #rrggbb.

You can specify the type of the styles you're using with the `type` attribute, which you set to `text/css` for CSS styles — that's the default, however, so you can omit this attribute without problem:

```
<style type="text/css">
  body {
    color: #000000;
    background-color: #FFFFFF;
    font-family: times;
  }
     .
     .
     .
</style>
```

Some elements, like the `<a>` anchor element, let you style specific aspects of the element, such as the link color (you refer to links as `a:link`), the color of already visited links (`a:visited`), and the color that links display when clicked (`a:active`):

```
<style>
    body {background: white; color: black}
    a:link {color: red}
    a:visited {color: blue}
    a:active {color: green}
  .
  .
  .
</style>
```

You can also use the `<style>` element to set the styles for multiple elements of the same kind, such as `<div>` elements. But how can you tell two `<div>` elements apart in the `<style>` element? The present example, menus.html, contains a number of `<div>` elements that you can supply styles for in a `<style>` element:

```
<body onclick = "hide()" onmousemove = "checkMenu(event)">

  <H1>An Ajax-enabled menu system</H1>

    <img id = "image1" src="image1.jpg"
      style="left:30; top:50; width:200; height:40;">
    <div id = "menuDiv1" style="left:30; top:100; width:100;
      height: 70; visibility:hidden;"><div></div></div>
    <img id = "image2" style="left:270; top:50; width:200;
      height:40;" src="image2.jpg">
    <div id = "menuDiv2" style="left:270; top:100; width:100;
      height: 70; visibility:hidden;"><div></div></div>
    <div id = "targetDiv"></div>
</body>
```

Each such <div> element has a different ID value. To assign a style to a tag with a particular ID, you precede that ID with a pound sign (#) like this in the <style> element:

```
<style>
  #menuDiv1 {
      .
      .
      .
  }
      .
      .
      .
</style>
```

Then you can set style rules in menus.html for menuDiv1. For example, you can use the color style property to set the color of text in this menu <div> element, and the background-color property to set the background color:

```
<style>
  #menuDiv1 {
    color: #222222;
    background-color: #FFCCFF;
      .
      .
      .
  }
      .
      .
      .
</style>
```

You can specify more about the text in the <div> element with the font-weight and font-family properties. The font-weight property lets you specify that you want your text bold, for example, and the font-family property lets you specify the font face you want to use (more about these properties is coming up in this chapter):

```
<style>
  #menuDiv1 {
    color: #222222;
    background-color: #FFCCFF;
    font-weight: bold;
    font-family: arial;
      .
      .
      .
  }
      .
      .
      .
</style>
```

For pop-up elements like the menu <div> elements, you also need to set the position style property to absolute (you can do this in the <style> element or with the style HTML property) to allow you to position the <div> elements where you want:

```
<style>
  #menuDiv1 {
    color: #222222;
    background-color: #FFCCFF;
    font-weight: bold;
    font-family: arial;
    position: absolute;
       .
       .
       .
  }
       .
       .
       .
</style>
```

And you can also set the cursor style property to hand, which makes Internet Explorer (only) change the mouse cursor to a hand when the mouse is over the <div> element:

```
<style>
  #menuDiv1 {
    color: #222222;
    background-color: #FFCCFF;
    font-weight: bold;
    font-family: arial;
    position: absolute;
    visibility: hidden;
    cursor: hand;
  }
       .
       .
       .
</style>
```

Here's what the <style> element looks like in menus.html:

```
<style>
  #menuDiv1 {
    color: #222222;
    background-color: #FFCCFF;
    font-weight: bold;
    font-family: arial;
    position: absolute;
    visibility: hidden;
    cursor: hand;
  }
```

```
#menuDiv2 {
  color: #222222;
  background-color: #FFCCFF;
  font-weight: bold;
  font-family: arial;
  position: absolute;
  visibility: hidden;
  cursor: hand;
}

#targetDiv {
  color: #9900FF;
  font-size: 24pt;
  font-weight: bold;
  font-family: arial;
}

</style>
```

Another way of handling styles (which this example, menus.html, doesn't use) is to use an *external style sheet*. For example, you could put the previous style rules from the `<style>` element into an external file named, say, style.css, which would have these contents:

```
#menuDiv1 {
  color: #222222;
  background-color: #FFCCFF;
  font-weight: bold;
  font-family: arial;
  position: absolute;
  visibility: hidden;
  cursor: hand;
}

#menuDiv2 {
  color: #222222;
  background-color: #FFCCFF;
  font-weight: bold;
  font-family: arial;
  position: absolute;
  visibility: hidden;
  cursor: hand;
}

#targetDiv {
  color: #9900FF;
  font-size: 24pt;
  font-weight: bold;
  font-family: arial;
}
```

You connect an external style sheet to a Web page with the `<link>` element, setting the `rel` attribute to `stylesheet` and the `href` attribute to the URL of the style sheet, like this:

```
<html>
    <head>
        <title>
            Using An External Style Sheet
        </title>

        <link rel="stylesheet" href="style.css">

    </head>

    <body>

        <center>
            <h1>
                Using An External Style Sheet
            </h1>

            <P>
            This page uses an external style sheet.
        </center>

    </body>
</html>
```

That includes the new style sheet, style.css, in the page, and applies the styles defined in it as appropriate. That's how to set up an external style sheet (the current example, menus.html, sets up its styles using a `<style>` element and inline styles, not an external style sheet).

Now that the styles are set up and ready, how do you actually make something happen? You work with the mouse, which is described next.

Working with the mouse

Note the `onclick` and onmousemove attributes in this example's <body> element:

```
<body onclick = "hide()" onmousemove = "checkMenu(event)">

    <H1>An Ajax-enabled menu system</H1>

    <img id = "image1" src="image1.jpg"
      style="left:30; top:50; width:200; height:40;">
    <div id = "menuDiv1" style="left:30; top:100; width:100;
      height: 70; visibility:hidden;"><div></div></div>
    <img id = "image2" style="left:270; top:50; width:200;
      height:40;" src="image2.jpg">
```

```
        <div id = "menuDiv2" style="left:270; top:100; width:100;
          height: 70; visibility:hidden;"><div></div></div>
        <div id = "targetDiv"></div>
    </body>
```

The onclick attribute handles mouse clicks and connects to a JavaScript function named hide, which hides the menu after the user makes a selection, as will be discussed in a few pages. The onmousemove attribute is the one of interest here because when the user moves the mouse, you might need to display a menu.

For that reason, the onmousemove attribute is connected to a JavaScript function named checkMenu that checks whether you should display a menu. This function is passed a mouse event object (which, as usual, is null in Internet Explorer):

```
function checkMenu(evt)
{
    .
    .
    .

}
```

The first step in checkMenu is to get a cross-browser mouse event object, as you saw when creating the drag-and-drop shopping cart in Chapter 8. As with the shopping cart, you create this cross-browser mouse object by calling a function named MouseEvent:

```
function checkMenu(evt)
{
    var e = new MouseEvent(evt);
    .
    .
    .

}
```

The MouseEvent function creates a new object and stores the mouse event in the object's e member:

```
function MouseEvent(e)
{
    if(e) {
        this.e = e;
    } else {
        this.e = window.event;
    }
    .
    .
    .

}
```

It also creates an x member and a y member to hold the location at which the mouse event occurred:

```
function MouseEvent(e)
{
  if(e) {
    this.e = e;
  } else {
    this.e = window.event;
  }

  if(e.pageX) {
    this.x = e.pageX;
  } else {
    this.x = e.clientX;
  }

  if(e.pageY) {
    this.y = e.pageY;
  } else {
    this.y = e.clientY;
  }
    .
    .
    .
}
```

And finally, the mouse object stores the target element of the mouse event in the member named target:

```
function MouseEvent(e)
{
    .
    .
    .
  if(e.pageY) {
    this.y = e.pageY;
  } else {
    this.y = e.clientY;
  }

  if(e.target) {
    this.target = e.target;
  } else {
    this.target = e.srcElement;
  }
}
```

Now that you've created a cross-browser mouse event object, you can check where the mouse was. For example, if the mouse was moved so that it's now over the first image, you can call a function named getData to download and display the first menu by passing a value of 1 to getData:

```
function checkMenu(evt)
{
  var e = new MouseEvent(evt);
  var img;

  img = document.getElementById("image1");

  if(e.target == img){
    getData(1);
  }
  .
  .
  .
}
```

And if the mouse moved so that it's now over the second image, you can call getData with a value of 2 to download and display the second menu:

```
function checkMenu(evt)
{
  var e = new MouseEvent(evt);
  var img;

  img = document.getElementById("image1");

  if(e.target == img){
    getData(1);
  }

  img = document.getElementById("image2");

  if(e.target == img){
    getData(2);
  }
  .
  .
  .
}
```

Besides opening menus using the yet-to-be-written getData function, you also have to hide menus if the mouse moves away from a particular menu. You can do that if the menu is visible, which you check like this for the first menu:

```
function checkMenu(evt)
{
  var e = new MouseEvent(evt);
  var target = null;
  var img;

  img = document.getElementById("image1");

  if(e.target == img){
    getData(1);
  }

  img = document.getElementById("image2");

  if(e.target == img){
    getData(2);
  }

  target = document.getElementById("menuDiv1");

  if (target.style.visibility == "visible"){
    .
    .
    .
  }
    .
    .
    .
}
```

Then you can check whether the mouse is outside both the menu's image and the menu's <div>
element. To do that, you can check style properties such as target.style.left, which is the
left-hand side of the <div> element. Those style properties are stored as text, however, so you
have to convert them to numbers, which you can do with the JavaScript parseInt function. For
example, here's how you can check whether the mouse location is to the left of the <div> element:

```
function checkMenu(evt)
{
  var e = new MouseEvent(evt);
  var target = null;
    .
    .
    .
  target = document.getElementById("menuDiv1");

  if (target.style.visibility == "visible"){
    if(e.x < parseInt(target.style.left)
    .
    .
    .
```

```
        }
      }
      .
      .
      .
   }
```

You can add a check to determine whether the mouse is above the image's top this way:

```
function checkMenu(evt)
{
  var e = new MouseEvent(evt);
  var target = null;
  var img;
  .
  .
  .
  target = document.getElementById("menuDiv1");
  img = document.getElementById("image1");

  if (target.style.visibility == "visible"){
    if(e.x < parseInt(target.style.left)
      || e.y < parseInt(img.style.top)
      .
      .
      .
    }
  }
  .
  .
  .
}
```

If the mouse is outside the menu's <div> element and image, you can call a function named hide to hide the menu:

```
function checkMenu(evt)
{
  var e = new MouseEvent(evt);
  var target = null;
  var img;
  .
  .
  .
  target = document.getElementById("menuDiv1");
  img = document.getElementById("image1");

  if (target.style.visibility == "visible"){
    if(e.x < parseInt(target.style.left) || e.y <
      parseInt(img.style.top) ||
```

```
          e.x > (parseInt(img.style.left) +
          parseInt(img.style.width))
          || e.y > (parseInt(target.style.top) +
          parseInt(target.style.height))){
          hide();
       }
    }
    .
    .
    .

 }
```

And you can do the same for the second menu as well, calling the `hide` method if needed:

```
function checkMenu(evt)
{
  var e = new MouseEvent(evt);
  var target = null;
  var img;
  .
  .
  .

  target = document.getElementById("menuDiv1");
  img = document.getElementById("image1");

  if (target.style.visibility == "visible"){
    if(e.x < parseInt(target.style.left) || e.y <
      parseInt(img.style.top) ||
      e.x > (parseInt(img.style.left) +
      parseInt(img.style.width))
      || e.y > (parseInt(target.style.top) +
      parseInt(target.style.height))){
      hide();
    }
  }

  target = document.getElementById("menuDiv2");
  img = document.getElementById("image2");

  if (target.style.visibility == "visible"){
    if(e.x < parseInt(target.style.left) || e.y <
    parseInt(img.style.top) ||
    e.x > (parseInt(img.style.left) +
    parseInt(img.style.width))
    || e.y > (parseInt(target.style.top) +
    parseInt(target.style.height))){
      hide();
    }
  }
}
```

That completes the checkMenu function, which checks to see whether the mouse is inside or outside a menu and whether or not the menu should be shown or hidden. If the menu should be shown, checkMenu calls the getData function, which downloads the menu items.

Downloading the menu items

The getData function is responsible for downloading the menu items from the server, using Ajax. This function starts by getting an XMLHttpRequest object:

```
function getData(menu)
{
  var XMLHttpRequestObject = false;

  if (window.XMLHttpRequest) {
    XMLHttpRequestObject = new XMLHttpRequest();
  } else if (window.ActiveXObject) {
    XMLHttpRequestObject = new
      ActiveXObject("Microsoft.XMLHTTP");
  }
    .
    .
    .
```

You pass the menu number, 1 or 2, to the getData function, and the code in that function decides whether to download the items for menu 1, in items1.txt, or for menu 2, from items2.txt, using a JavaScript conditional operator:

```
function getData(menu)
{
  var XMLHttpRequestObject = false;

  if (window.XMLHttpRequest) {
    XMLHttpRequestObject = new XMLHttpRequest();
  } else if (window.ActiveXObject) {
    XMLHttpRequestObject = new
      ActiveXObject("Microsoft.XMLHTTP");
  }

  var dataSource = (menu == 1) ? "items1.txt" :
    "items2.txt";
    .
    .
    .
```

Then the getData function downloads the items for the requested menu, and passes those items to a function named show:

```
function getData(menu)
{
  var XMLHttpRequestObject = false;

  if (window.XMLHttpRequest) {
    XMLHttpRequestObject = new XMLHttpRequest();
  } else if (window.ActiveXObject) {
    XMLHttpRequestObject = new
      ActiveXObject("Microsoft.XMLHTTP");
  }

  var dataSource = (menu == 1) ? "items1.txt" :
    "items2.txt";

  if(XMLHttpRequestObject) {
    XMLHttpRequestObject.open("GET", dataSource);

    XMLHttpRequestObject.onreadystatechange = function()
    {
      if (XMLHttpRequestObject.readyState == 4 &&
        XMLHttpRequestObject.status == 200) {
          show(menu, XMLHttpRequestObject.responseText);
      }
    }

    XMLHttpRequestObject.send(null);
  }
}
```

Now that you've downloaded the menu items, all that's left is to show them.

Showing a menu

The show method is designed to display menus, and you pass it the number of the menu to show (1 or 2) and the menu items to show. The menu items are stored in a single string, separated by commas, like this for menu 1:

```
Apples, Bananas, Oranges
```

It's the job of the show function to separate those items and display them in a pop-up menu. Splitting the string "Apples, Bananas, Oranges" into separate items in an array turns out to be very easy: you only need to use the JavaScript split function, telling it that you want to split the text on the string ", " like this:

```
function show(menu, items)
{
  arrayItems = items.split(", ");
    .
    .
    .
}
```

Now you have the menu items in an array of strings. To display those items, you can use an HTML table. The HTML for that table can be stored in a string named, say, `data`, which starts like this:

```
function show(menu, items)
{
  var data = "<table width = '100%'>";
  arrayItems = items.split(", ");
    .
    .
    .
}
```

There's one more consideration here: you need to enable the user to click a displayed menu item and have something happen. To do that, you can connect each table <td> element's onclick event attribute to a new function, `display`, which will display text like `You selected Bananas`. Here, then, is how you assemble the HTML for the menu's table-based display:

```
function show(menu, items)
{
  var data = "<table width = '100%'>";
  var loopIndex;
  arrayItems = items.split(", ");

  if (arrayItems.length != 0) {
    for (var loopIndex = 0; loopIndex < arrayItems.length;
      loopIndex++) {
      var text = "display(" + loopIndex + ")";
      data += "<tr><td "
        + "onclick='" + text + "'>" +
        arrayItems[loopIndex] +
        "</td></tr>";
    }
  }

  data += "</table>";
    .
    .
    .
}
```

Now you have the HTML for the menu's table, stored in a string named `data`. All you have to do now is determine which menu should be displayed, and then display it. Here's what that looks like:

```
function show(menu, items)
{
  var data = "<table width = '100%'>";
  var loopIndex;
  arrayItems = items.split(", ");
  var target;

  if (arrayItems.length != 0) {
    for (var loopIndex = 0; loopIndex < arrayItems.length;
      loopIndex++) {
      var text = "display(" + loopIndex + ")";
      data += "<tr><td "
        + "onclick='" + text + "'>" +
        arrayItems[loopIndex] +
        "</td></tr>";
    }
  }

  data += "</table>";

  if(menu == "1"){
    target = document.getElementById("menuDiv1");
  }

  if(menu == "2"){
    target = document.getElementById("menuDiv2");
  }

  if(target.style.visibility == "hidden"){
    target.innerHTML = data;
    target.style.visibility = "visible";
  }
}
```

The next step is to handle the case where the user clicks an item in a menu.

Handling menu item clicks

When the user clicks a menu item, a function named `display` is called, and you can display the item the user selected (`You selected Bananas.`) in the `<div>` element named `targetDiv`. The `display` function is passed the index of the selected item in the array named `arrayItems`, which contains the text of the menu items, so all you need to do is recover the appropriate text from that array and display it.

First, you can get an object corresponding to the target <div> element in which to display text:

```
<script language = "javascript">
  var arrayItems;
     .
     .
     .
  function display(index)
  {
    var targetDiv = document.getElementById("targetDiv");
     .
     .
     .
  }
```

then you can display the selected item in the target <div> element like this:

```
<script language = "javascript">
  var arrayItems;
     .
     .
     .
  function display(index)
  {
    var targetDiv = document.getElementById("targetDiv");

    targetDiv.innerHTML = "You selected "
      + arrayItems[index] + ".";
  }
```

The target <div> element is styled like this in this application:

```
#targetDiv {
  color: #9900FF;
  font-size: 24pt;
  font-weight: bold;
  font-family: arial;
}
```

so text displayed in this <div> will appear large, as shown earlier in Figure 10.4.

That completes the display process. All that's left is to hide a menu when needed with the hide function.

Hiding a menu

In this application, the hide function is responsible for hiding the menus when needed:

```
function hide()
{
  .
  .
  .
}
```

Hiding a menu simply means hiding the <div> element it appears in, menuDiv1 or menuDiv2. Here's how that works for menu 1:

```
function hide()
{
  var menuDiv1 = document.getElementById("menuDiv1");

  if(menuDiv1.style.visibility == "visible"){
    menuDiv1.innerHTML = "<div></div>";
    menuDiv1.style.visibility = "hidden";
  }
  .
  .
  .
}
```

And here's menu 2:

```
function hide()
{
  var menuDiv1 = document.getElementById("menuDiv1");

  if(menuDiv1.style.visibility == "visible"){
    menuDiv1.innerHTML = "<div></div>";
    menuDiv1.style.visibility = "hidden";
  }

  var menuDiv2 = document.getElementById("menuDiv2");

  if(menuDiv2.style.visibility == "visible"){
    menuDiv2.innerHTML = "<div></div>";
    menuDiv2.style.visibility = "hidden";
  }
}
```

And that completes the menus.html application. Cool.

Getting Text Noticed in Ajax Applications

One of the problems with Ajax applications is that the new text you download and display has a good chance of not being noticed because there was no page refresh. CSS includes a variety of ways to get text noticed; for example, you can change the color of that text.

The example changeColor.html, which you can see at work in Figure 10.5, downloads text and displays it in red for half a second, after which it changes to black. It's hard not to notice that.

Changing the color of text to get it noticed

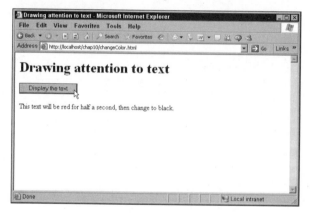

This application starts with the button and a `<div>` element to display text in:

```
<body>

  <H1>Drawing attention to text</H1>

  <form>
    <input type = "button" value = "Display the text"
      onclick = "getData('message.txt', 'targetDiv')">
  </form>

  <div id="targetDiv">
    <p>The fetched data will go here.</p>
  </div>

</body>
```

The button is connected to a function named `getData`, which starts by creating an `XMLHttpRequest` object:

```
function getData(dataSource, divID)
{
  var XMLHttpRequestObject = false;

  if (window.XMLHttpRequest) {
    XMLHttpRequestObject = new XMLHttpRequest();
  } else if (window.ActiveXObject) {
    XMLHttpRequestObject = new
      ActiveXObject("Microsoft.XMLHTTP");
  }
  .
  .
  .
}
```

If the `XMLHttpRequest` object creation was successful, the code continues on to download the file message.txt, which contains the text "This text will be red for half a second, then change to black.":

```
<html>
  <head>
    <title>Drawing attention to text</title>

  <script language = "javascript">
    function getData(dataSource, divID)
    {
      var XMLHttpRequestObject = false;

      if (window.XMLHttpRequest) {
        XMLHttpRequestObject = new XMLHttpRequest();
      } else if (window.ActiveXObject) {
        XMLHttpRequestObject = new
          ActiveXObject("Microsoft.XMLHTTP");
      }

      if(XMLHttpRequestObject) {
        var obj = document.getElementById("targetDiv");
        XMLHttpRequestObject.open("GET", dataSource);

        XMLHttpRequestObject.onreadystatechange = function()
        {
          if (XMLHttpRequestObject.readyState == 4 &&
            XMLHttpRequestObject.status == 200) {
              obj.style.color = "#FF0000";
```

```
                 obj.innerHTML =
                   XMLHttpRequestObject.responseText;
                   .
                   .
                   .
             }
           }

         XMLHttpRequestObject.send(null);
       }
       .
       .
       .
     }
```

Here's the key: at this point, the code calls a JavaScript function named setTimeout, which lets you execute code after a time interval has passed. In this case, you pass the name of a function you've written, named changer in this case, and the time interval that has to elapse before changer is called:

```html
<html>
  <head>
    <title>Drawing attention to text</title>

    <script language = "javascript">
      function getData(dataSource, divID)
      {
        var XMLHttpRequestObject = false;

        if (window.XMLHttpRequest) {
          XMLHttpRequestObject = new XMLHttpRequest();
        } else if (window.ActiveXObject) {
          XMLHttpRequestObject = new
            ActiveXObject("Microsoft.XMLHTTP");
        }

        if(XMLHttpRequestObject) {
          var obj = document.getElementById("targetDiv");
          XMLHttpRequestObject.open("GET", dataSource);

          XMLHttpRequestObject.onreadystatechange = function()
          {
            if (XMLHttpRequestObject.readyState == 4 &&
              XMLHttpRequestObject.status == 200) {
                obj.style.color = "#FF0000";
                obj.innerHTML =
                  XMLHttpRequestObject.responseText;
```

```
            setTimeout(changer, 500);
        }
    }

    XMLHttpRequestObject.send(null);
    }
}
```

The time interval is in milliseconds (thousandths of a second), so to be sure that
changer is called after half a second, you pass setTimeout a value of 500.

And you're nearly done. The changer function, which changes the color of the downloaded text
from red to black, is called half a second after the text has been downloaded and displayed. All
that's left is to write the changer function:

```
function changer()
{
    .
    .
    .
}
```

The changer function starts by getting an object corresponding to the target <div> element:

```
<body>

    <H1>Drawing attention to text</H1>

    <form>
      <input type = "button" value = "Display the text"
        onclick = "getData('message.txt', 'targetDiv')">
    </form>

    <div id="targetDiv">
      <p>The fetched data will go here.</p>
    </div>

</body>
```

Here's how that works in code:

```
function changer()
{
    var target = document.getElementById("targetDiv");
    .
    .
    .
}
```

Then you can use CSS to change the color of the text in the target `<div>` element to black, accessing that text color as `target.style.color`:

```
function changer()
{
    var target = document.getElementById("targetDiv");

    target.style.color = "#000000";
}
```

That's all you need.

This application points out a big use of CSS in Ajax applications: making sure the user sees the changes you've made in a Web page. That's an important point to bear in mind in Ajax applications, because without a page refresh, the user may not even notice that anything has changed.

Besides changing the color of downloaded text, you can also change its size. For example, if you had originally displayed text in 24-point font, you could change it back to 12 points in the `changer` function like this:

```
function changer()
{
    var target = document.getElementById("targetDiv");

    target.style.font-size = "12pt";
}
```

Another use for the `setTimeout` function is to display scrolling text, which is discussed in the next section.

Scrolling Text

Ever seen that scrolling text in the status bar at the bottom of a Web page? That's another technique to get text noticed, and it uses the `setTimeout` method. You can see an example, scroller.html, in Figure 10.6, which scrolls the text "Hello from JavaScript!" in the status bar at the bottom of the window.

FIGURE 10.6

Scrolling text to get it noticed

This example calls a function named `scroller` when the page loads:

```
<body onload="scroller()">
  <h1>
    Scrolling status bar text with JavaScript
  </h1>
</body>
```

In the `scroller` function, the code starts by storing the text "Hello from JavaScript! Hello from JavaScript!" in the status bar, using the `window.status` property like this:

```
<html>
  <head>
    <title>
      Scrolling with JavaScript
    </title>
    <script language="JavaScript">

        var text = "Hello from JavaScript! Hello from JavaScript! "

        function scroller()
        {
            window.status = text
            .
            .
            .
        }
    </script>

  </head>
```

Then the code shuffles the text so that it's "ello from JavaScript! Hello from JavaScript! H" using the JavaScript substring function:

```
<script language="JavaScript">

    var text = "Hello from JavaScript! Hello from JavaScript! "

    function scroller()
    {
        window.status = text
        text = text.substring(1, text.length) +
          text.substring(0, 1)
          .
          .
          .

    }
</script>
```

And then the code uses the setTimeout function to call scroller again in 150 milliseconds:

```
<script language="JavaScript">

    var text = "Hello from JavaScript! Hello from JavaScript! "

    function scroller()
    {
        window.status = text
        text = text.substring(1, text.length) +
          text.substring(0, 1)
        setTimeout("scroller()", 150)
    }
</script>
```

The next time scroller is called, it displays the current text, then shuffles that text and calls itself again to display the new text in another 150 milliseconds, giving the impression that the text in the status bar is indeed scrolling.

Styling Text Using CSS

CSS supports many different text styles that you can use to make newly downloaded text stand out. Following is a list of the most popular style properties and what they let you set:

- font-family: Specifies the actual font, like Arial or Helvetica. If you want to list alternative fonts in case the target computer is missing your first choice, specify them as a comma-separated list (like this: {font-family: Arial, Helvetica}).

- **font-style**: Specifies how the text is to be rendered. Set to `normal`, `italic`, or `oblique`.

- **font-weight**: Refers to the boldness or lightness of the glyphs used to render the text, relative to other fonts in the same font family. Set to `normal`, `bold`, `bolder`, `lighter`, `100`, `200`, `300`, `400`, `500`, `600`, `700`, `800`, or `900`.

- **line-height**: Indicates the height given to each line.

- **font-size**: Refers to the size of the font.

- **text-decoration**: Underlines text. Set to `none`, `underline`, `overline`, `line-through`, or `blink`.

- **text-align**: Centers text. Set to `left`, `right`, or `center`.

Following is an example, fontStyles.html, that puts these font properties to work. This example sets the styles for the <body> element in a <style> element:

```
<html>
    <head>
        <title>
            Setting fonts with CSS
        </title>
        <style type="text/css">
            body {
                .
                .
                .
            }
        </style>
    </head>

    <body>
        <h1>Setting fonts with CSS</h1>
        <br>
        This page displays a CSS example styling text.
    </body>
</html>
```

Here's how you can put the style properties to work:

```
<html>
    <head>
        <title>
            Setting fonts with CSS
        </title>
        <style type="text/css">
            body {font-style: italic; font-weight: bold;
                font-size: 16pt; line-height: 12pt;
                font-family: arial, helvetica; text-align: center}
        </style>
    </head>
```

```
<body>
    <h1>Setting fonts with CSS</h1>
    <br>
    This page displays a CSS example styling text.
</body>
</html>
```

Here are the CSS style settings for this example:

```
font-style: italic

font-weight: bold

font-size: 16pt

line-height: 12pt

font-family: arial, helvetica

text-align: center
```

Note in particular the `font-family` style property, which you can set to a comma-separated list of font names such as `arial`, `helvetica`, `times`, and so on. If the browser can't find the first font, it searches for the next, and so on down the line. You can see this page in Figure 10.7, where the styles have been applied to the text.

FIGURE 10.7

Styling fonts using CSS

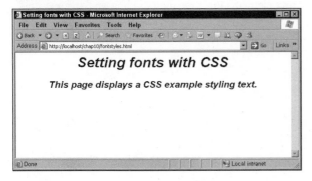

Another example, textStyles.html, also puts these styles to work:

- `font-style` to make text italic
- `font-weight` to make text bold
- `font-size` to set the font size
- `font-family` to set the font face

- `text-decoration` to underline the text
- `text-align` to center the text

The textStyles.html example styles the text in <p> elements in the page:

```
<html>
    <head>
        <title>
            Styling text using CSS
        </title>

        <style>
            p {font-size: 16pt; font-style: italic;
               text-align: center; font-family: Arial, Helvetica;}
        </style>
    </head>

    <body>
        <h1>
                Styling text using CSS
        </h1>
            .
            .
            .
    </body>
</html>
```

and it also uses the `style` attribute of <span> elements for some inline styling, making text bold and italic:

```
<html>
    <head>
        <title>
            Styling text using CSS
        </title>

        <style>
            p {font-size: 16pt; font-style: italic;
               text-align: center; font-family: Arial, Helvetica;}
        </style>
    </head>

    <body>
        <h1>
                Styling text using CSS
        </h1>
        <p>
            This text is styled in italics. Some of this text is
            <span style="font-weight: bold">bold</span>,
```

```
            and some of it is even
            <span style="text-decoration: underline">
            underlined</span>.
        </p>
    </body>
</html>
```

The results are shown in Figure 10.8.

FIGURE 10.8

Styling text using CSS

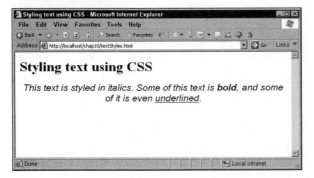

Styling Colors and Backgrounds Using CSS

As you'd expect, CSS supports many styles to set colors and backgrounds. Here's a list of the most popular color and background styles:

- `color`: Sets the foreground color (in hexadecimal format, like #FFFFFF), or names of colors.

- `background-color`: Sets the background color (in hexadecimal format, like #FFFFFF), or names of colors.

- `background-image`: Sets the background image (as a URL).

- `background-repeat`: Specifies whether the background image should be tiled, set to `repeat`, `repeat-x`, `repeat-y`, or `no-repeat`.

- `background-attachment`: Specifies whether the background scrolls with the rest of the document, set to `scroll` or `fixed`.

- `background-position`: Sets the initial position of the background, set to `top`, `center`, `bottom`, `left`, or `right`.

colorStyles.html is an example that puts these styles to work:

```html
<html>
    <head>
        <title>
            Styling foregrounds and backgrounds using CSS
        </title>
    </head>

    <body style="background-color: #55DDDD">

        <div align="left">
            CEO
            <br>
            Terrific HTML Designs, Inc.
            <br>
            New York
        </div>

        <p>
            Dear you:
            <div align="center"
              style="color: #FF0000; background-color: #FFFFFF;
              font-style: italic">
            <br>
                How's this for styling?
            <br>
            <br>
            </div>

            <div align="right">
                <p>
                CEO
                <br>
                Exceptional CSS Styles, Inc.
                <br>
                San Francisco
            </div>

        </body>
    </html>
```

You can see colorStyles.html at work in Figure 10.9.

FIGURE 10.9

Styling colors using CSS

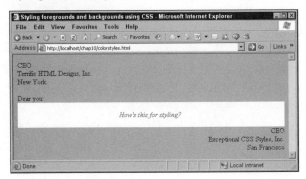

NOTE You can specify colors using the standard HTML color triplets like this: #rrggbb. In CSS, you can also specify colors using the **rgb** function, where you pass three color values to that function: red, green, and blue values, which range from 0 to 255.

Here's an example, colorTable.html, which displays colors in a table:

```
<html>
    <head>
        <title>
            Setting colors
        </title>
    </head>

    <body style="background-color: #55DDDD">

      <h1>Setting colors</h1>

      <table border="2" width="400" height="200"
        style="text-align:center">
          <tr>
              <th style="background-color: rgb(255, 0,
                0)">Now</th>
              <th style="background-color: rgb(255, 0,
                0)">is</th>
              <th style="background-color: rgb(0, 255,
                0)">the</th>
              <th style="background-color: rgb(255, 0,
                0)">time</th>
          </tr>
            .
            .
            .
```

In fact, you can set colors using names in CSS, like red, blue, orange, cyan, white, and so on. Here's how that works in colorTable.html:

```html
<html>
    <head>
        <title>
            Setting colors
        </title>
    </head>

    <body style="background-color: #55DDDD">

      <h1>Setting colors</h1>

      <table border="2" width="400" height="200"
        style="text-align:center">
          <tr>
              <th style="background-color: rgb(255, 0,
                0)">Now</th>
              <th style="background-color: rgb(255, 0,
                0)">is</th>
              <th style="background-color: rgb(0, 255,
                0)">the</th>
              <th style="background-color: rgb(255, 0,
                0)">time</th>
          </tr>
          <tr>
              <td style="background-color: rgb(0, 0,
                255)">Now</td>
              <td style="background-color: rgb(0, 0, 0); color:
                  rgb(255, 255, 255)">
                  is
              </td>
              <td style="background-color: rgb(0, 255,
                0)">the</td>
              <td style="background-color: green">time</td>
          </tr>
          <tr>
              <td style="background-color: rgb(0, 0, 0);
                  color: white">
                  Now
              </td>
              <td
                style="background-color: rgb(255, 255,
                  255)">is</td>
              <td style="background-color: rgb(0, 0, 0); color:
                  rgb(255, 255, 255)">
                  the
              </td>
```

```
        <td style=
          "background-color: rgb(255, 255, 255)">time</td>
    </tr>
    <tr>
        <td style="background-color: rgb(255, 255,
          0)">Now</td>
        <td style="background-color: rgb(0, 0, 0); color:
          rgb(255, 255, 255)">
          is
        </td>
        <td style="background-color: cyan">the</td>
        <td style="background-color: blue">time</td>
    </tr>
  </table>

  </body>
</html>
```

You can see colorTable.html at work (in black and white, anyway) in Figure 10.10.

Setting colors

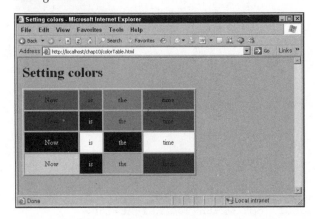

Besides standard colors like green, red, and so on, most modern browsers support a great number of color names like ivory, sand, viridian, and more. Give it a try!

Styling Locations in Web Pages

One of the most common uses of Ajax using CSS is setting absolute positions of the elements in a Web page, as when you create pop-up menus, dialog boxes, drop-down auto-complete list boxes, and so on. Here are the CSS styles you use when setting absolute positions:

- `position`: Set to `absolute` for absolute positioning.
- `top`: Offset of the top of the element on the screen.
- `bottom`: Offset of the bottom of the element in the browser's client area.
- `left`: Offset of the left edge of the element in the browser's client area.
- `right`: Offset of the right edge of the element in the browser's client area.

NOTE By default, the measurements of `top`, `bottom`, `left`, and `right` are taken to be in pixels. You can append **px** to the end of this value to make sure the browser interprets the measurement as pixels, as in **50px**.

- `z-order`: Sets the stacking order of the item with respect to other elements. Higher numbers stack to the front.

Here's an example, absolute.html, that positions images in <div> elements:

```
<html>

    <head>
        <title>
            Absolute Positioning
        </title>
    </head>

    <body>

        <h1 align="center">
            Absolute Positioning
        </h1>

        <div style="position:absolute; left:40; top:60;">
            <img src="image01.jpg" width=200 height=100>
            <br>
            Image 1
        </div>

        <div style="position:absolute; left:195; top:90;">
            <img src="image02.jpg" width=200 height=100>
            <br>
            Image 2
        </div>
```

```
<div style="position:absolute; left:350; top:120;">
    <img src="image03.jpg" width=200 height=100>
    <br>
    Image 3
</div>

</body>

</html>
```

You can see the results in Figure 10.11, where the images have been stacked.

FIGURE 10.11

Setting positions of Web page elements

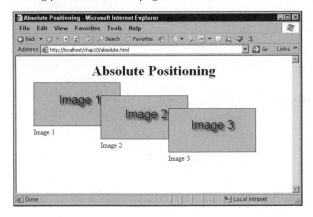

In fact, you can set the stacking order of Web page elements yourself with the `z-order` CSS property. For example, elements given a high `z-order` appear on top of other elements. Here's an example, which sets the `z-order` of the second image to 200 in absolute.html:

```
<html>
    .
    .
    .
    <div style="position:absolute; left:40; top:60;">
        <img src="image01.jpg" width=200 height=100>
        <br>
        Image 1
    </div>

    <div style="position:absolute; left:195; top:90;
        z-index:200">
```

```
            <img src="image02.jpg" width=200 height=100>
            <br>
            Image 2
        </div>

        <div style="position:absolute; left:350; top:120;">
            <img src="image03.jpg" width=200 height=100>
            <br>
            Image 3
        </div>

    </body>

</html>
```

You can see the results in Figure 10.12. As you can see in the figure, the second image has been moved on top of the others, which is because its z-order is higher than the others.

Setting the z-order of Web page elements

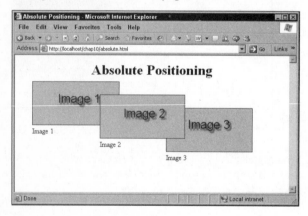

Summary

In this chapter, you saw how to use CSS to create an Ajax-enabled menu system. You also saw how to get text noticed in Ajax applications, as well as how to style colors and fonts. Finally, you saw how to set the absolute position of elements in Web pages.

Chapter 11

Dynamic HTML and Ajax

Working with Web pages on the fly is central to Ajax. Chapter 10 covered working with Web pages using cascading style sheets. This chapter discusses another way of working with Web pages on the fly: dynamic HTML.

Dynamic HTML is a powerhouse of options for the Ajax programmer, and you're going to see the best of it in this chapter.

Creating Mouseovers

This first dynamic HTML example demonstrates the use of dynamic styles by using the onmouseover attribute to handle mouse rollovers. In this example, positioning the mouse over some text changes the text's size, enlarging it. You can see this example, mouseOver.html, in Figure 11.1.

When you position the mouse over the text in this application, that text gets enlarged, as shown in Figure 11.2.

FIGURE 11.1

The mouseOver application

FIGURE 11.2

Enlarging text with dynamic styles

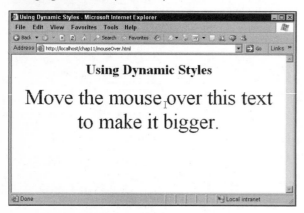

This example simply uses the `onmouseover` attribute of a `<span>` element to change the font size:

```html
<html>
    <head>
        <title>
            Using Dynamic Styles
        </title>
    </head>
```

```
<body>
    <center>
        <h1>
            Using Dynamic Styles
        </h1>
        <span onmouseover="this.style.fontSize = '48'">
            Move the mouse over this text to make it bigger.
        </span>
    </center>
</body>
</html>
```

If you want to change the font size (or style) back when the mouse leaves, use the onmouseout attribute. Here's an example where the text in an <h1> header turns red when the mouse is positioned over it, and goes back to black when the mouse leaves:

```
<html>

    <head>
        <title>
            Using Dynamic Styles
        </title>
    </head>

    <body>

        <center>
            <h1 onmouseover="this.style.color = 'red';"
                onmouseout="this.style.color = 'black';">
                Turn this text red with the mouse.
            </h1>
        </center>

    </body>

</html>
```

In fact, if you're only interested in creating mouseover effects, you can use the hover attribute, now supported in browsers such as Microsoft Internet Explorer and Mozilla Firefox. Here's an example, hover.html, that displays two hyperlinks whose styles change when the mouse rolls over them. You can see this application in Figure 11.3.

When you let the mouse roll over a hyperlink, that hyperlink's style changes, as shown in Figure 11.4.

FIGURE 11.3

The hover application

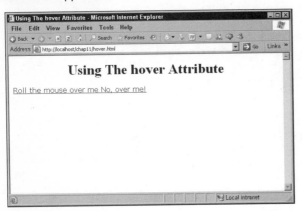

FIGURE 11.4

Using the mouse to set a new style

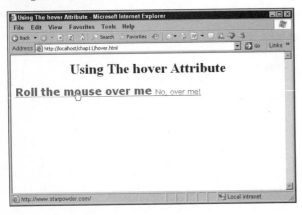

Here's how it works. This application starts by setting up various styles for the `<a>` element, including one for the `hover` attribute:

```
<html>
    <head>
        <title>
            Using The hover Attribute
        </title>
```

```
<style>
    a {font-family: verdana;
       font-weight: normal; color: blue}
    a:hover {font-weight: bold; color: red;
       font-size: 24}
    a:active {font-weight: bold; color: red;
    background-color: darkgray}
    a:visited {font-weight: bold; color: gray;
    background-color: darkgray}
</style>
</head>
    .
    .
    .
```

Then all you have to do is to create two new <a> elements and you're done:

```
<body>
    <center>
        <h1>
            Using The hover Attribute
        </h1>
    </center>

        <a href="http://www.ajaxsuperpower.com">
            Roll the mouse over me
        </a>
        <a href="http://www.ajaxsuperpower.com">
            No, over me!
        </a>
</body>
```

Using Dynamic Styles

With dynamic HTML, you can also set styles for the entire Web page as needed, which is great for getting text noticed. The following example, dynamicStyles.html, lets you toggle between two style sheets. The Web page example shown in Figure 11.5, demonstrates the normal style.

When you click the Dramatic Style button, the style sheet used in the application changes to the dramatic style shown in Figure 11.6.

FIGURE 11.5

The dynamicStyles application

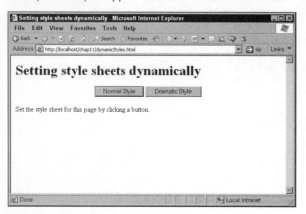

FIGURE 11.6

Setting a new style sheet

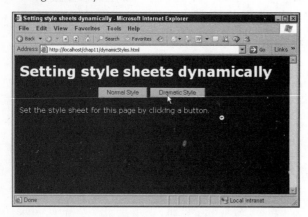

This example starts by creating a style sheet with the ID `dramatic` for a set of dramatic styles:

```
<html>
    <head>
        <title>
            Setting style sheets dynamically
        </title>
```

```
<style id="dramatic">
   body {font-family:
      verdana; color: white; background-color: black}
</style>
   .
   .
   .
```

and continues by creating a style sheet named `normal`, which starts off disabled:

```
<html>
   <head>
      <title>
         Setting style sheets dynamically
      </title>

      <style id="dramatic">
         body {font-family:
            verdana; color: white; background-color: black}
      </style>

      <style id="normal" disabled="true">
         body {font-family: 'times new roman'; color: black;
            background-color: white}
      </style>
         .
         .
         .
```

There are two buttons in this example, one to set the `normal` style, and one to set the `dramatic` style. Both buttons are connected to a JavaScript function named `setStyle`:

```
<body>
   <h1>
      Setting style sheets dynamically
   </h1>

   <center>
      <input type=button value="Normal Style"
         onclick="setStyle('normal')">
      <input type=button value="Dramatic Style"
         onclick="setStyle('dramatic')">
   </center>

   <p>
      Set the style sheet for this page by clicking a
         button.
   </p>
</body>
```

The `setStyle` function is passed the name of the style sheet to set:

```
<script language="javascript">

    function setStyle(styleName)
    {
        .
        .
        .
    }

</script>
```

You can access the style sheets in a document as `document.styleSheets`, which holds an array of named style sheets. To handle those style sheets, you can loop over that array:

```
<script language="javascript">
    function setStyle(styleName)
    {
        for (var loopIndex = 0; loopIndex <
            document.styleSheets.length; loopIndex++) {
            .
            .
            .
        }
    }
</script>
```

You can disable all style sheets as you loop over them:

```
<script language="javascript">
    function setStyle(styleName)
    {
        var sheet
        for (var loopIndex = 0; loopIndex <
            document.styleSheets.length; loopIndex++) {
            sheet = document.styleSheets[loopIndex]
            sheet.disabled = true
            .
            .
            .
        }
    }
</script>
```

and then enable only the style sheet that's been requested:

```
<script language="javascript">
    function setStyle(styleName)
    {
```

```
var sheet
for (var loopIndex = 0; loopIndex <
    document.styleSheets.length; loopIndex++) {
    sheet = document.styleSheets[loopIndex]
    sheet.disabled = true
    if (sheet.id == styleName) {
        sheet.disabled = false
    }
}
}
</script>
```

Using document.write

One of the mainstays of dynamic HTML is the `document.write` method, which lets you rewrite Web pages on the fly. You can use this method when a page loads, contacting the server using Ajax techniques for instructions on how to write the page. In this way, Web pages can become self-modifying.

Here's an example, selfModifying.html. This application can display one of two graphic images: a larger image or a smaller one. When opened, this page starts by asking users which image they want, as shown in Figure 11.7.

The selfModifying application

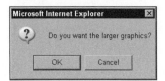

If the user clicks the OK button, the Web page is rewritten on the fly to display the larger image, as shown in Figure 11.8.

If the user clicks the other button, however, the Web page is rewritten to display the smaller image, as shown in Figure 11.9.

FIGURe 11.8

Displaying the larger image

FIGURE 11.9

Displaying the smaller image

This application uses a `<script>` element in the page's `<body>` element, not the page's `<head>` element, because when a script is executed in the `<head>` element, the `<body>` element has not been loaded, and so is not accessible. This example starts by displaying the confirmation box shown in Figure 11.7:

```
<html>
    <head>
        <title>
            A self-modifying Web page
        </title>
    </head>
```

```
<body>
    <center>
        <h1>
            A self-modifying Web page
        </h1>

        <script language="JavaScript">
            if(confirm("Do you want the larger graphics?")) {
                .
                .
                .
```

If the user clicks the OK button, the code uses document.write to write an <img> element to the page that uses the larger image in this example, image1.jpg:

```
<html>
    <head>
        <title>
            A self-modifying Web page
        </title>
    </head>

    <body>
        <center>
            <h1>
                A self-modifying Web page
            </h1>

            <script language="JavaScript">
                if(confirm("Do you want the larger graphics?")) {
                    document.write("<br><img "
                    + "src='image1.jpg'></IMG>")
                }
                .
                .
                .
```

If the user didn't click the OK button, on the other hand, the code writes an <img> element to the Web page that displays the smaller image, image1small.jpg:

```
<html>
    <head>
        <title>
            A self-modifying Web page
        </title>
    </head>

    <body>
        <center>
```

```
<h1>
    A self-modifying Web page
</h1>

<script language="JavaScript">
    if(confirm("Do you want the larger graphics?")) {
        document.write("<br><img "
        + "src='image1.jpg'></IMG>")
    }
    else {
        document.write("<br><img " +
        "src='image1small.jpg'></IMG>")
    }
</script>

</center>

</body>

</html>
```

You can also use `document.write` to rewrite an entire Web page, if you want. This is a perilous technique for the Ajax developer because it looks a lot like a page refresh, but it can be done. Take a look at the example application, rewrite.html, shown in Figure 11.10.

The rewrite application

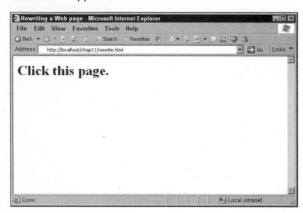

The page uses `document.write` to rewrite itself when you click it, as shown in Figure 11.11.

FIGURE 11.11

Rewriting a Web page on the fly

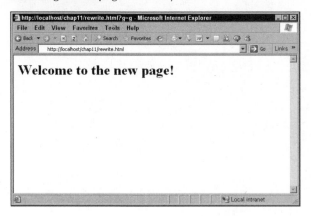

This application connects the page's onmousedown attribute to a function named `rewrite`:

```
<body onmousedown="rewrite()">

    <h1>
        Click this page.
    </h1>

</body>
```

and in the `rewrite` function, the code uses the `document.write` method to rewrite the entire page — you can't use `document.write` to write to just part of a page:

```
<html>

    <head>
        <title>
            Rewriting a Web page
        </title>

        <script>
            function rewrite()
            {
                document.write("<h1>Welcome to the new
                    page!</h1>")
            }
        </script>
    </head>
```

```
<body onmousedown="rewrite()">

    <h1>
        Click this page.
    </h1>

</body>

</html>
```

In fact, you can rewrite Web pages even based on the time of day. The example restaurant.html displays various menus — breakfast, lunch, or dinner — depending on the time of day using document.write:

```
<html>
    <head>

        <script language="JavaScript">
            var dateNow = new Date();
            var hourNow = dateNow.getHours();
            document.write( "<center>");
            document.write( "<h1>");
            document.write("Welcome to the Dynamic HTML
                Restaurant");
            document.write( "</h1>");
            document.write( "</center>");

            if (hourNow < 5 || hourNow > 23){
                document.write( "<center>");
                document.write( "<h1>");
                document.write( "Sorry, we're closed." );
                document.write( "</h1>");
                document.write( "</center>");
            }

            if (hourNow > 6 && hourNow < 12 ) {
                document.write( "<center>");
                document.write( "<table border>");
                document.write(
                    "<tr><th colspan = 2>Breakfast</th></tr>");
                document.write(
                    "<tr><td>Eggs</td><td>$2.50</td></tr>");
                document.write(
                    "<tr><td>Pancakes</td><td>$2.00</td></tr>");
                document.write(
                    "<tr><td>Oatmeal</td><td>$1.00</td></tr>");
                document.write(
                    "<tr><td>Waffles</td><td>$1.50</td></tr>");
                document.write( "</table>");
```

```
            document.write( "</center>");
            document.write( "</table>");
            document.write( "</center>");
      }

      if ( hourNow >= 12 && hourNow < 17 ) {
            document.write( "<center>");
            document.write( "<table border>");
            document.write(
                "<tr><th colspan = 2>Lunch</th></tr>");
            document.write(
                "<tr><td>Turkey
                   Sandwich</td><td>$3.50</td></tr>");
            document.write(
                "<tr><td>Chicken
                   Sandwich</td><td>$3.50</td></tr>");
            document.write(
                "<tr><td>Ham
                   Sandwich</td><td>$3.00</td></tr>");
            document.write(
                "<tr><td>Alligator
                   Nuggets</td><td>$5.00</td></tr>");
            document.write(
                "<tr><td>Ostrich</td><td>$4.50</td></tr>");
            document.write(
                "<tr><td>Chili</td><td>$2.00</td></tr>");
            document.write(
                "<tr><td>Crocodile
                   Soup</td><td>$1.50</td></tr>");
            document.write( "</table>");
            document.write( "</center>");
      }

      if ( hourNow >= 17 && hourNow < 22 ) {
            document.write( "<center>");
            document.write( "<table border>");
            document.write(
                "<tr><th colspan = 2>Dinner</th></tr>");
            document.write(
                "<tr><td>Lobster</td><td>$7.50</td></tr>");
            document.write(
                "<tr><td>Filet
                   Mignon</td><td>$8.00</td></tr>");
            document.write(
                "<tr><td>Flank
                   Steak</td><td>$7.00</td></tr>");
            document.write(
                "<tr><td>Tube
                   Steak</td><td>$3.50</td></tr>");
```

```
                        document.write(
                            "<tr><td>Salad</td><td>$2.50</td></tr>");
                        document.write(
                            "<tr><td>Potato</td><td>$1.50</td></tr>");
                        document.write(
                            "<tr><td>Eggplant</td><td>$1.50</td></tr>");
                        document.write( "</table>");
                        document.write( "</center>");
                    }

                </script>
            </head>

            <body>
            </body>

        </html>
```

You can see restaurant.html at work in Figure 11.12.

The restaurant.html application

That's fine, but sometimes, you may not want to rewrite the entire page.

Using Dynamic HTML Methods to Update Part of a Page

In Ajax, you frequently want to update just part of a Web page, not the whole page. Two methods enable you to do this: the `insertAdjacentHTML` method, which lets you insert HTML next to an element that already exists, and the `insertAdjacentText` method, which lets you insert text in the same way. You can determine where the new text or HTML will go with respect to the already existing element by passing the constants `BeforeBegin`, `AfterBegin`, `BeforeEnd`, or `AfterEnd` to `insertAdjacentHTML` and `insertAdjacentText`.

The example insertAdjacent.html uses the `insertAdjacentHTML` method. This page starts with just a button, as shown in Figure 11.13. When you click the button, the code inserts a new text field into the Web page, as shown in Figure 11.14.

FIGURE 11.13

The insertAdjacent.html application

FIGURE 11.14

Inserting a new text field into a page

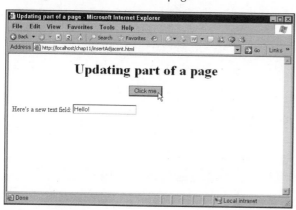

Here's how it works: the application contains a `<div>` element with the ID `div1`:

```
<body>

    <center>
        <h1>
            Updating part of a page
        </h1>
    </center>

    <div id="div1">
    .
    .
    .
    </div>

</body>
```

and that `<div>` element contains the button, which is connected to a JavaScript function named update:

```
<body>

    <center>
        <h1>
            Updating part of a page
        </h1>
    </center>

    <div id="div1">
        <input type=button value="Click Me!"
          onclick="update()">
    </div>

</body>
```

In the update function, you can call the `<div>` element's `insertAdjacentHTML` method to insert the text field next to the `<div>` element:

```
<head>
    <title>
        Updating part of a page
    </title>

    <script language="JavaScript">
        function update()
        {
            div1.insertAdjacentHTML(...);
        }
    </script>
</head>
```

Here's how you insert the new text field after the end of the <div> element:

```
<head>
    <title>
        Updating part of a page
    </title>

    <script language="JavaScript">
        function update()
        {
            div1.insertAdjacentHTML("AfterEnd",
            "<p>Here's A new text field: <input
                type=text value='Hello!'></p>");
        }
    </script>
</head>
```

Using `insertAdjacentHTML` and `insertAdjacentText`, you can insert HTML and text into a Web page, adjacent to another Web page item. In fact, there's another way to insert text and HTML into a Web page besides using these methods: you can use dynamic HTML properties, which gives you even finer control than the `insertAdjacentHTML` and `insertAdjacentText` methods.

Using Dynamic HTML Properties to Update Part of a Page

Each item in a Web page supports these dynamic HTML properties:

- `innerText`: Lets you change the text between the start and end tags of an element. (`innerText` is not supported by Mozilla, Netscape, or Firefox browsers.)
- `outerText`: Lets you change all the element's text, including the start and end tags. (`outerText` is not supported by Mozilla, Netscape, or Firefox browsers.)
- `innerHTML`: Changes contents of element between start and end tags and can include HTML.
- `outerHTML`: Changes contents of an element, including start and end tags, and treats text as HTML.

You've already seen `innerHTML` at work throughout the book, as you wrote applications that updated a <div> element with downloaded data:

```
<html>
  <head>
    <title>An Ajax demo</title>

    <script language = "javascript">
      var XMLHttpRequestObject = false;
```

```
      if (window.XMLHttpRequest) {
        XMLHttpRequestObject = new XMLHttpRequest();
      } else if (window.ActiveXObject) {
        XMLHttpRequestObject = new
          ActiveXObject("Microsoft.XMLHTTP");
      }

      function getData(dataSource, divID)
      {
        if(XMLHttpRequestObject) {
          var obj = document.getElementById(divID);
          XMLHttpRequestObject.open("GET", dataSource);

          XMLHttpRequestObject.onreadystatechange = function()
          {
            if (XMLHttpRequestObject.readyState == 4 &&
              XMLHttpRequestObject.status == 200) {
                obj.innerHTML =
                  XMLHttpRequestObject.responseText;
            }
          }

          XMLHttpRequestObject.send(null);
        }
      }
    </script>
  </head>

  <body>

    <H1>An Ajax demo</H1>

    <form>
      <input type = "button" value = "Fetch the message"
        onclick = "getData('data.txt', 'targetDiv')">
    </form>

    <div id="targetDiv">
      <p>The fetched message will appear here.</p>
    </div>

  </body>
</html>
```

You can also use the `innerText` property to set the inner text of an element, rather than rewrite it entirely. The example, innerText.html, lets you rewrite the text of an <h1> header element. You start with the header this way, giving it the ID `header` and connecting it to a function named `changeHeader`:

```
<body>

    <center>
        <h1 id = "header"
          onclick = "changeHeader()">
          Changing text on the fly
        </h1>

        Click the above header to make it change.
    </center>

</body>
```

Then, in the changeHeader function, you use the header's innerText property to change the text in the header, while leaving the header and <h1> header (that is, its HTML doesn't change):

```
<head>
    <title>
        Changing text on the fly
    </title>

    <script language = "JavaScript">
     function changeHeader()
     {
       var header = document.getElementById("header");
       header.innerText = "Here is the new text";
     }
    </script>

</head>
```

You can see the results in Figure 11.15, which is the innerText.html page.

FIGURE 11.15

The innerText.html application

When you click the header, its text changes, as shown in Figure 11.16.

Replacing text in the innerText.html application

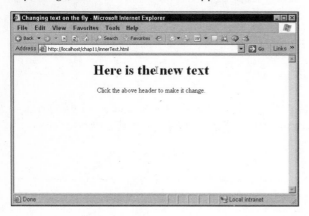

You could have used the `innerHTML` property instead to insert text that the browser will interpret as HTML. For example, you might use the (Internet Explorer–only) `<marquee>` element to display the new text in the header in a horizontally scrolling marquee:

```html
<html>

    <head>
        <title>
            Changing text on the fly
        </title>

        <script language = "JavaScript">
         function changeHeader()
         {
           var header = document.getElementById("header");
           header.innerHTML =
           "<marquee>This is a new marquee</marquee>"
         }
        </script>

    </head>

    <body>
```

```
<center>
    <h1 id = header
        onclick = "changeHeader()">
        Changing text on the fly
    </h1>

    Click the above header to make it change.
</center>

</body>

</html>
```

You can see the results in Figure 11.17, the innerHTML.html page, where the new text is scrolling in a horizontal marquee.

The innerHTML.html application

If you wanted to, you could replace the <h1> header entirely with the outerHTML property. Here's an example, outerHTML.html, which replaces the <h1> header with an <h3> header:

```
<html>

    <head>
        <title>
            Changing text on the fly
        </title>
```

```
<script language = "JavaScript">
 function changeHeader()
 {
   var header = document.getElementById("header");
   header.outerHTML =
   "<h3>This is the new header</h3>"
 }
</script>

</head>

<body>

   <center>
      <h1 id = header
         onclick = "changeHeader()">
         Changing text on the fly
      </h1>

      Click the above header to make it change.
   </center>

</body>

</html>
```

You can see the results in Figure 11.18, the outerHTML.html page.

FIGURE 11.18

The outerHTML.html application

When you click the header, it is rewritten as an <h3> header, as shown in Figure 11.19.

FIGURE 11.19

Replacing text in the outerHTML.html application

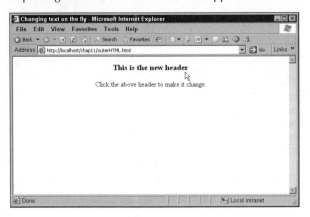

Another way to update part of a page in Internet Explorer is through the use of *text ranges*, which is discussed in the next section.

Using Text Ranges to Update Part of a Page

Internet Explorer supports text ranges, which you can use to replace text in Web pages. A full discussion of text ranges is beyond the scope this book, but here's a starter example, textranges.html, which appears in Figure 11.20.

FIGURE 11.20

The textranges.html application

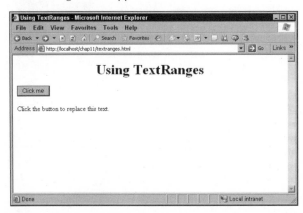

When you click the button, the text in the page is selected and rewritten, as shown in Figure 11.21.

FIGURE 11.21

Replacing text in the textranges.html application

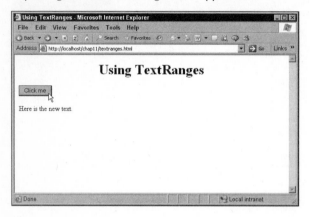

This example starts with a button connected to a function named `replaceText`:

```
<body>
    <center>
        <h1>
            Using TextRanges
        </h1>
    </center>

    <input type="button" value="Click me"
      onclick="replaceText()">

    <br>
    <br>
    .
    .
    .
</body>
```

and you can also add a `<div>` element with the ID `div1`:

```
<body>
    <center>
        <h1>
            Using TextRanges
        </h1>
    </center>
```

```
<input type="button" value="Click me"
  onclick="replaceText()">

<br>
<br>

<div id="div1">
    Click the button to replace this text.
</div>

</body>
```

When the user clicks the button, the replaceText function is called, which starts by creating a text range that can select text:

```
<head>
    <title>
        Using TextRanges
    </title>

    <script language="JavaScript">
        function replaceText()
        {
            var range = document.body.createTextRange();
            .
            .
            .
        }
    </script>
</head>
```

Next, you create an object corresponding to the <div> element:

```
<head>
    <title>
        Using TextRanges
    </title>

    <script language="JavaScript">
        function replaceText()
        {
            var range = document.body.createTextRange();
            var div = document.getElementById("div1");
            .
            .
            .
        }
    </script>
</head>
```

and then you can move your text range to encompass the <div> element with the range's
moveToElementText method:

```
<head>
    <title>
        Using TextRanges
    </title>

    <script language="JavaScript">
        function replaceText()
        {
            var range = document.body.createTextRange();
            var div = document.getElementById("div1");
            range.moveToElementText(div);
                 .
                 .
                 .
        }
    </script>
</head>
```

Now that you've enclosed the <div> element inside a text range, you can use the range's
pasteHTML method to overwrite the <div> element's HTML like this:

```
<head>
    <title>
        Using TextRanges
    </title>

    <script language="JavaScript">
        function replaceText()
        {
            var range = document.body.createTextRange();
            var div = document.getElementById("div1");
            range.moveToElementText(div);
            range.pasteHTML("Here is the new text.");
        }
    </script>
</head>
```

Besides pasting HTML into a text range, you can also move them around a Web page. The major
drawback, of course, is that text ranges are supported in Internet Explorer only.

Using createElement to Create New Elements on the Fly

There are even more ways to change Web pages on the fly with dynamic HTML. For example, you can use the `createElement` method to create entirely new elements. Take a look at the createElement.html application, which appears in Figure 11.22.

FIGURE 11.22

The createElement.html application

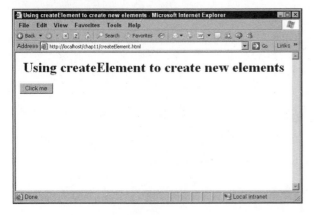

When you click the button, a new `<div>` element containing text, as well as a new text field, are created using the `createElement` method, as shown in Figure 11.23.

FIGURE 11.23

Creating new elements in the createElement.html application

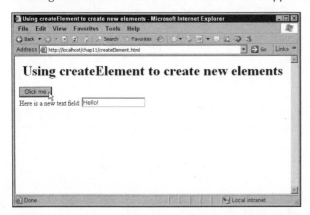

When you click the button again, another new `<div>` element and text field are created, as shown in Figure 11.24.

FIGURE 11.24

Creating more new elements in the createElement.html application

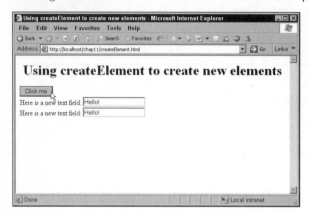

In this application the button is connected to a function named `create`:

```
<body>
  <center>
    <h1>
      Using createElement to create new elements
    </h1>
  </center>

  <div id="InitialDIV">
    <input type="button" value="Click me" onclick="create()">
  </div>

</body>
```

The `create` function starts by creating a new `<div>` element using the document's `createElement` method:

```
<head>
  <title>
    Using createElement to create new elements
  </title>

  <script language="JavaScript">
    function create()
    {
      var newDiv;
```

```
        newDiv = document.createElement("div");
        newDiv.id = "NewDIV";
          .
          .
          .
      }
    </script>
  </head>
```

then the code creates a new <input> element for the text field:

```
  <head>
    <title>
      Using createElement to create new elements
    </title>

    <script language="JavaScript">
      function create()
      {
        var newDiv, newTextfield;

        newDiv = document.createElement("div");
        newDiv.id = "NewDIV";

        newTextfield = document.createElement("input");
          .
          .
          .
      }
    </script>
  </head>
```

You can configure the attributes of new elements as properties of their objects. For example, here's how you set the type and value attributes of the new text field:

```
  <head>
    <title>
      Using createElement to create new elements
    </title>

    <script language="JavaScript">
      function create()
      {
        var newDiv, newTextfield, newText;

        newDiv = document.createElement("div");
        newDiv.id = "NewDIV";

        newTextfield = document.createElement("input");
        newTextfield.type = "text";
        newTextfield.value = "Hello!"
```

```
                .
                .
                .
      }
    </script>
  </head>
```

To insert some text into the `<div>` element, you need to create a new text node, which you can do with the document element's `createTextNode` method. This new text node contains the text "Here is a new text field:":

```
<head>
  <title>
    Using createElement to create new elements
  </title>

  <script language="JavaScript">
    function create()
    {
      var newDiv, newTextfield, newText;

      newDiv = document.createElement("div");
      newDiv.id = "NewDIV";

      newTextfield = document.createElement("input");
      newTextfield.type = "text";
      newTextfield.value = "Hello!"

      newText =
        document.createTextNode("Here is a new text field: ");
                .
                .
                .
    }
  </script>
</head>
```

Then you can insert the text node before the `<div>` element in the Web page using the `insertBefore` method:

```
<head>
  <title>
    Using createElement to create new elements
  </title>

  <script language="JavaScript">
    function create()
    {
      var newDiv, newTextfield, newText;
```

```
            newDiv = document.createElement("div");
            newDiv.id = "NewDIV";

            newTextfield = document.createElement("input");
            newTextfield.type = "text";
            newTextfield.value = "Hello!"

            newText =
              document.createTextNode("Here is a new text field: ");

            newDiv.insertBefore(newText, null);
            .
            .
            .
          }
        </script>
    </head>
```

and you can also insert the text field before the <div> element:

```
<head>
    <title>
      Using createElement to create new elements
    </title>

    <script language="JavaScript">
      function create()
      {
        var newDiv, newTextfield, newText;

        newDiv = document.createElement("div");
        newDiv.id = "NewDIV";

        newTextfield = document.createElement("input");
        newTextfield.type = "text";
        newTextfield.value = "Hello!"

        newText =
          document.createTextNode("Here is a new text field: ");

        newDiv.insertBefore(newText, null);
        newDiv.insertBefore(newTextfield, null);
        .
        .
        .
      }
    </script>
</head>
```

Then you insert the new `<div>` element:

```
<head>
    <title>
        Using createElement to create new elements
    </title>

    <script language="JavaScript">
        function create()
        {
            var newDiv, newTextfield, newText;

            newDiv = document.createElement("div");
            newDiv.id = "NewDIV";

            newTextfield = document.createElement("input");
            newTextfield.type = "text";
            newTextfield.value = "Hello!"

            newText =
                document.createTextNode("Here is a new text field: ");

            newDiv.insertBefore(newText, null);
            newDiv.insertBefore(newTextfield, null);

            document.body.insertBefore(newDiv, null);
        }
    </script>
</head>
```

And there you have it. Now you're creating new elements, a useful skill for Ajax programmers. When you need to download and display new data, you can create new elements, such as list controls, in which to display that data. In fact, you can even create dynamic tables.

Creating Dynamic Tables

Some Ajax applications display data in HTML tables. One way of updating an HTML table is to rewrite its HTML entirely, but that will make it flicker on screen. Instead, a set of methods enable you to update a table in browsers such as Internet Explorer, Mozilla, Netscape, and Firefox. Here are the built-in methods for the `<table>` element:

- `object.rows(index)`: Returns a collection (array) of the rows in the table.

- `object.insertRow(index)`: Inserts a new row. Returns the inserted `<tr>` element (which will be empty), or null for failure. If `index` isn't supplied, the `<tr>` element will be inserted at the end of the table.

- `object.deleteRow(index)`: Deletes a row. The `index` value indicates the row index of the row to delete.

And here are the methods for `<tr>` elements:

- `object.cells(index)`: Returns a collection (array) of the cells in the row.
- `object.rowIndex`: Returns the row index of the row. Useful for inserting and deleting rows.
- `object.insertCell(index)`: Inserts a new cell and returns the inserted `<td>` element (which will be empty), or null for failure. If `index` isn't supplied, the `<td>` element will be inserted at the end of the row.
- `object.deleteCell(index)`: Deletes a cell. The `index` value indicates the position in the cell collection to delete.

Here's an example showing how to create a dynamic table. This example inserts a new row in a table using the `insertRow` method, inserts three cells into the new row with the `insertCell` method, and sets the contents of the cell with the `innerText` property. You can see this example, dynamicTable.html, in Figure 11.25.

FIGURE 11.25

The dynamicTable.html application

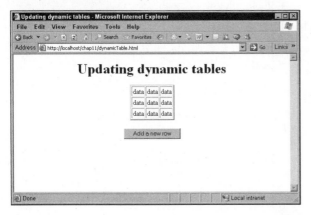

When you click the button, a new table row appears, as shown in Figure 11.26. When you click the button again, another new table row is created, as shown in Figure 11.27.

FIGURE 11.26

Creating a new table row in the dynamicTable.html application

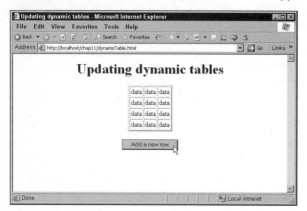

FIGURE 11.27

Creating another new table row in the dynamicTable.html application

This example starts by creating the HTML table shown in Figure 11.25:

```
<body>
    <center>
        <h1>
            Updating dynamic tables
        </h1>
```

```
            <table id="table1" border="2">
                <tr>
                    <td>data</td>
                    <td>data</td>
                    <td>data</td>
                </tr>
                <tr>
                    <td>data</td>
                    <td>data</td>
                    <td>data</td>
                </tr>
                <tr>
                    <td>data</td>
                    <td>data</td>
                    <td>data</td>
                </tr>
            </table>
            .
            .
            .

        </center>
    </body>
```

There's also a button, tied to a JavaScript function named addRow:

```
<body>
    <center>
        <h1>
            Updating dynamic tables
        </h1>

            <table id="table1" border="2">
                <tr>
                    <td>data</td>
                    <td>data</td>
                    <td>data</td>
                </tr>
                <tr>
                    <td>data</td>
                    <td>data</td>
                    <td>data</td>
                </tr>
                <tr>
                    <td>data</td>
                    <td>data</td>
                    <td>data</td>
                </tr>
            </table>
```

```
        <br>

        <input type="button" value="Add a new row"
          onclick="addRow()">

      </center>
    </body>
```

In the `addRow` function, you start by getting an object corresponding to the table:

```
        <script language="javascript">
            function addRow()
            {
                var table1 = document.getElementById("table1");
                    .
                    .
                    .

            }
        </script>
```

then you insert a new row at the end of the table with the table's `insertRow` method, passing that method a value of 3 to indicate you want to add a row after the current last row (which is row 2):

```
        <script language="javascript">
            function addRow()
            {
                var table1 = document.getElementById("table1");
                var newRow = table1.insertRow(3);
                    .
                    .
                    .

            }
        </script>
```

Next you have to create the cells in the new row, which you can do with the row's `insertCell` method. Here's how you create the first cell:

```
        <script language="javascript">
            function addRow()
            {
                var table1 = document.getElementById("table1");
                var newRow = table1.insertRow(3);
                var newCell = newRow.insertCell(0);
                    .
                    .
                    .

            }
        </script>
```

You can write your data to the new cell using its `innerHTML` property:

```
<script language="javascript">
    function addRow()
    {
        var table1 = document.getElementById("table1");
        var newRow = table1.insertRow(3);
        var newCell = newRow.insertCell(0);
        newCell.innerHTML = "data";
            .
            .
            .

    }
</script>
```

You can also create the other two cells and insert them into the row like this:

```
<script language="javascript">
    function addRow()
    {
        var table1 = document.getElementById("table1");
        var newRow = table1.insertRow(3);
        var newCell = newRow.insertCell(0);
        newCell.innerHTML = "data";
        newCell = newRow.insertCell(1);
        newCell.innerHTML = "data";
        newCell = newRow.insertCell(2);
        newCell.innerHTML = "data";
    }
</script>
```

And that completes this example. As you can see, it's easy enough to create, delete (using `deleteRow` and `deleteCell`), and edit (using the `innerHTML` property of cells) data in a table.

Catching the User's Attention with Animation

One sure way of catching the user's attention in Ajax applications is through animation, and using dynamic HTML, you can animate Web elements, moving them around at will. It does take a little effort to make sure you're cross-browser compliant, however.

Take a look at the example, animation.html, in Figure 11.28. There are three colored <div> elements in that page, and they move from side to side at different speeds.

FIGURE 11.28

Creating animation in the animation.html application

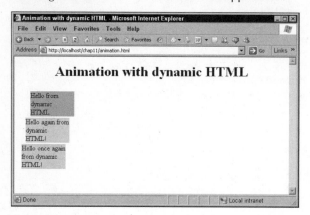

This example starts by creating three colored `<div>` elements, `div1`, `div2`, and `div3`, that can be moved around the Web page:

```
<body>
    <center>
        <h1>
            Animation with dynamic HTML
        </h1>
    </center>

    <div id="div1" style="position: absolute; top: 80; left:
      0;
        width: 100; background: cyan; font-size: 16">
        Hello from dynamic HTML.
    </div>

    <div id="div2" STYLE="position: absolute; top: 140; left:
        expression(div1.style.posLeft * 0.75);
        width: 100; background: pink; font-size: 16">
        Hello again from dynamic HTML!
    </div>

    <div id="div3" STYLE="position: absolute; top: 200; left:
        expression(div1.style.posLeft * 0.5);
        width: 100; background: yellow; font-size: 16">
        Hello once again from dynamic HTML!
    </div>

</body>
```

You can start the animation when the page loads by calling a JavaScript function named setPosition:

```
<body onload="setPosition()">
    <center>
        <h1>
            Animation with dynamic HTML
        </h1>
    </center>

    <div id="div1" style="position: absolute; top: 80; left:
      0;
        width: 100; background: cyan; font-size: 16">
        Hello from dynamic HTML.
    </div>
        .
        .
        .
    <div id="div3" STYLE="position: absolute; top: 200; left:
        expression(div1.style.posLeft * 0.5);
        width: 100; background: yellow; font-size: 16">
        Hello once again from dynamic HTML!
    </div>

</body>
```

The setPosition function starts by creating an object corresponding to each <div> element:

```
<script language="JavaScript">

    function setPosition()
    {
        var div1 = document.getElementById("div1");
        var div2 = document.getElementById("div2");
        var div3 = document.getElementById("div3");
            .
            .
            .
    }
</script>
```

You're going to need to set an increment that will be added to the <div> elements' horizontal positions each time the setPosition function is called, and in this example, that increment is 1 pixel:

```
<script language="JavaScript">

    var increment = 1;
```

```
function setPosition()
{
    var div1 = document.getElementById("div1");
    var div2 = document.getElementById("div2");
    var div3 = document.getElementById("div3");
          .
          .
          .
}
</script>
```

Here's the tricky part: Internet Explorer supports a style property named `posLeft`, which holds the left position of a Web page element as a number (and it also supports `posTop` for the top location). Unfortunately, the Mozilla brand of browsers, including Firefox, don't support `posLeft`, so you have to use the `left` style property in order to move an item from JavaScript.

That's a little awkward, because the `left` style property is stored as text, complete with the ending text px for pixels. Converting that text to a number is a little involved; if you were just dealing with Internet Explorer, you could use the `parseInt` function (actually, there'd be no need to do even that, because you could use the `posLeft` property, which holds the left position as a number) to convert the `left` property's value to a number; but the Mozilla, Netscape, and Firefox browsers don't support `parseInt`. So when you want to increment the `left` style property, you're stuck extracting the left position of a `<div>` element, minus the px at the end like this:

```
div1.style.left = div1.style.left.substring(0,
    div1.style.left.indexOf('px'))....
```

You multiply by a number to convert the text string to a number. Here, you can just multiply by 1:

```
div1.style.left = div1.style.left.substring(0,
    div1.style.left.indexOf('px')) * 1...
```

You add the increment to move the `<div>` element over one pixel:

```
div1.style.left = div1.style.left.substring(0,
    div1.style.left.indexOf('px')) * 1 + increment...
```

and then you append px to the end, converting the new `left` property to a string that ends with px like this:

```
div1.style.left = div1.style.left.substring(0,
    div1.style.left.indexOf('px')) * 1 + increment +
    'px';
```

That's how you move the first `<div>` element each time the `setPosition` function is called. The second `<div>` element moves at 3/4 the speed of the first, so you only need to multiply by 0.75 instead of 1:

```
    div2.style.left = div1.style.left.substring(0,
      div1.style.left.indexOf('px')) * .75 + increment
      + 'px';
```

The third <div> element moves at half the speed of the first <div> element, so you multiply by 0.5 there. Here's how moving all three <div> elements looks in the setPosition function:

```
<script language="JavaScript">

    var increment = 1;

    function setPosition()
    {
        var div1 = document.getElementById("div1");
        var div2 = document.getElementById("div2");
        var div3 = document.getElementById("div3");

        div1.style.left = div1.style.left.substring(0,
          div1.style.left.indexOf('px')) * 1 + increment
            + 'px';

        div2.style.left = div1.style.left.substring(0,
          div1.style.left.indexOf('px')) * .75 +
            increment + 'px';

        div3.style.left = div1.style.left.substring(0,
          div1.style.left.indexOf('px')) * .5 + increment
            + 'px';
              .
              .
              .
    }
</script>
```

You don't want the animated <div> elements to scroll off the screen entirely, so you might make them oscillate between 0 and 600 pixels. To do that, check to see whether the top <div> has moved past 600 pixels in the browser's client area:

```
<script language="JavaScript">

    var increment = 1;

    function setPosition()
    {
        var div1 = document.getElementById("div1");
        var div2 = document.getElementById("div2");
        var div3 = document.getElementById("div3");
```

```
            div1.style.left = div1.style.left.substring(0,
              div1.style.left.indexOf('px')) * 1 + increment
                + 'px';

            div2.style.left = div1.style.left.substring(0,
              div1.style.left.indexOf('px')) * .75 +
                increment + 'px';

            div3.style.left = div1.style.left.substring(0,
              div1.style.left.indexOf('px')) * .5 + increment
                + 'px';

            if (div1.style.left.substring(0,
              div1.style.left.indexOf('px')) * 1 >= 600
                .
                .
                .

        }
    </script>
```

or whether it's moved to a negative position — and if the top <div> has moved out of bounds, reverse the sign of the increment to make the <div> element start moving the other way:

```
        <script language="JavaScript">

            var increment = 1;

            function setPosition()
            {
                var div1 = document.getElementById("div1");
                var div2 = document.getElementById("div2");
                var div3 = document.getElementById("div3");

                div1.style.left = div1.style.left.substring(0,
                  div1.style.left.indexOf('px')) * 1 + increment
                    + 'px';

                div2.style.left = div1.style.left.substring(0,
                  div1.style.left.indexOf('px')) * .75 +
                    increment + 'px';

                div3.style.left = div1.style.left.substring(0,
                  div1.style.left.indexOf('px')) * .5 + increment
                    + 'px';
```

```
            if (div1.style.left.substring(0,
              div1.style.left.indexOf('px')) * 1 >= 600
              || div1.style.left.substring(0,
              div1.style.left.indexOf('px')) * 1 < 0) {
                increment = -1 * increment;
            }
            .
            .
            .
        }
    </script>
```

All that's left to do is to call the JavaScript `setTimeout` function to make sure the `setPosition` function is called after a short interval, for example, 50 milliseconds, like this:

```
    <script language="JavaScript">

        var increment = 1;

        function setPosition()
        {
            var div1 = document.getElementById("div1");
            var div2 = document.getElementById("div2");
            var div3 = document.getElementById("div3");

            div1.style.left = div1.style.left.substring(0,
              div1.style.left.indexOf('px')) * 1 + increment
                + 'px';
            .
            .
            .

            if (div1.style.left.substring(0,
              div1.style.left.indexOf('px')) * 1 >= 600 ||
              div1.style.left.substring(0,
              div1.style.left.indexOf('px')) * 1 < 0) {
                increment = -1 * increment;
            }

            setTimeout("setPosition()", 50)
        }
    </script>
```

That completes this example. Animation is a powerful tool in the hands of the Ajax programmer. It's a great way of getting changes to a Web page noticed.

Summary

In this chapter you took a look at dynamic HTML and allied techniques as they pertained to Ajax. You saw how to create dynamic mouseovers and dynamic style sheets. You saw how to write documents to the browser and how to update only part of a page using dynamic HTML techniques. You also saw how to create elements on the fly, and how to update tables with data.

Part IV

Advanced Ajax

Chapter 12

Introducing Ajax
and PHP

Ajax developers work on the server as well as in the browser, of course, and the most common server-side language used with Ajax these days is PHP. Accordingly, this chapter and Chapter 13 give you an introduction to using PHP with Ajax.

Getting Started with PHP

You can embed your PHP scripts inside HTML pages if you enclose the scripts in special markup. In code, you should enclose your PHP scripts (which are stored in files with the extension .php) inside the markup `<?php` and `?>` like this:

```
<?php
    .
    .
    .
    PHP goes here
    .
    .
    .
?>
```

However, in practice, you can use <? and ?>, and the server will still understand:

```
<?
    .
    .
    .
    PHP goes here
    .
    .
    .
?>
```

A PHP-enabled server will execute the PHP code inside the <?...?> markup. Here's an example that runs the built-in PHP function phpinfo, phpinfo.php, which creates an HTML table that tells you about your PHP installation.

> **NOTE**   Note in particular how the HTML and PHP are interspersed in this example, phpinfo.php. Also note that as in JavaScript, you end each PHP statement with a semicolon (;).

```
<html>
    <head>
        <title>
            A first PHP example
        </title>
    </head>

    <body>
        <h1>
            A first PHP example
        </h1>
        <?
            phpinfo();
        ?>
    </body>
</html>
```

What does this look like in a browser? You can see the results in Figure 12.1. The details will be different depending on your PHP installation, but the idea is the same: the phpinfo function displays the table you see in the figure.

That gets the ball rolling with PHP. How about sending some text of your own choosing back to the browser?

FIGURE 12.1

The phpinfo.php application

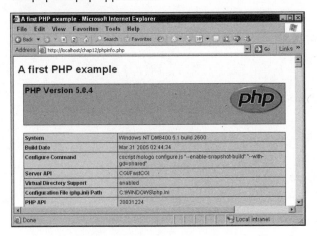

Sending text back to the browser

To send text back to the browser, use the PHP echo statement, which involves passing to the echo statement the text you want to send back to the browser.

Here's an example, echo.php. Start by including a PHP section among the HTML of a Web page like this:

```
<html>
    <head>
        <title>
            Using the echo statement
        </title>
    </head>

    <body>
        <h1>
            Using the echo statement
        </h1>

        <?
        .
        .
        .
        ?>
    </body>
</html>
```

Use the PHP echo statement to display some custom text:

```
<html>
    <head>
        <title>
            Using the echo statement
        </title>
    </head>

    <body>
        <h1>
            Using the echo statement
        </h1>

        <?
            echo "Greetings from PHP.";
        ?>
    </body>
</html>
```

You can see echo.php at work in Figure 12.2, which shows the echo statement sending text back to the browser.

Echoing text back to the browser

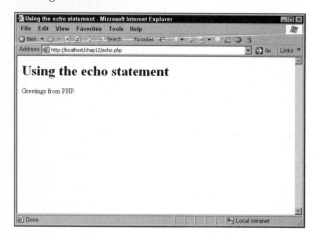

That sends text to the browser; how about sending XML data back to the browser?

Sending XML back to the browser

The echo statement sends text back to the browser, but sometimes in Ajax you don't just want to send text — you want to send XML data. After all, Ajax means *Asynchronous JavaScript and XML*. How can you send XML back to the browser?

This example sends the following XML data back to the browser:

```
<?xml version="1.0" ?>

<document>

  <data>Here</data>

  <data>is</data>

  <data>some</data>

  <data>XML.</data>

</document>
```

To be sure that the text sent back to the browser is interpreted as XML by the browser, you should use the PHP header function to set the HTTP Content-Type header to text/xml.

Here's an example, xml.php. Start off with the PHP <?...?> markup and the header function:

```
<?
header('Content-Type: text/xml');
        .
        .
        .
?>
```

then echo the XML declaration, which is needed at the start of every XML document:

```
<?
header('Content-Type: text/xml');

echo '<?xml version="1.0" ?>';
        .
        .
        .
?>
```

and then start the document element, which is just <document> here, by simply echoing <document> to the browser:

```
<?
header('Content-Type: text/xml');
echo '<?xml version="1.0" ?>';

echo '<document>';
        .
        .
        .
?>
```

Next, echo the <data> elements to the browser:

```
<?
header('Content-Type: text/xml');
echo '<?xml version="1.0" ?>';

echo '<document>';

echo '<data>';
echo 'Here';
echo '</data>';

echo '<data>';
echo 'is';
echo '</data>';

echo '<data>';
echo 'some';
echo '</data>';

echo '<data>';
echo 'XML.';
echo '</data>';
        .
        .
        .
?>
```

Finally, end the example by closing the <document> element:

```
<?
header('Content-Type: text/xml');
echo '<?xml version="1.0" ?>';

echo '<document>';
```

```
echo '<data>';
echo 'Here';
echo '</data>';

echo '<data>';
echo 'is';
echo '</data>';

echo '<data>';
echo 'some';
echo '</data>';

echo '<data>';
echo 'XML.';
echo '</data>';

echo '</document>';
?>
```

So what does this look like in a browser? You can see this example, xml.php, in Figure 12.3, where the XML it sends back to the browser is displayed. (Note that Internet Explorer is treating the output of xml.php as true XML, as it should.)

This gives you basics of echoing text and XML back to the browser using PHP. Now it's time to take a look at the kind of PHP programming you can do. We'll start with something simple: commenting your code.

FIGURE 12.3

Echoing XML back to the browser

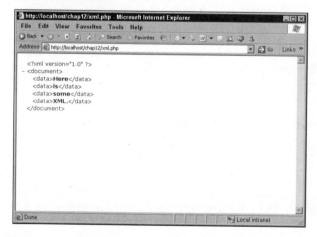

Commenting Your PHP

There are three types of comments in PHP. The first kind is similar to the one-line comments found in JavaScript, and starts with //:

```
<html>
    <head>
        <title>
            Using the echo statement
        </title>
    </head>

    <body>
        <h1>
            Using the echo statement
        </h1>

        <?
            //Send text back to the browser.
            echo "Greetings from PHP.";
        ?>
    </body>
</html>
```

In PHP, you can also use the # symbol in place of //:

```
<html>
    <head>
        <title>
            Using the echo statement
        </title>
    </head>

    <body>
        <h1>
            Using the echo statement
        </h1>

        <?
            #Send text back to the browser.
            echo "Greetings from PHP.";
        ?>
    </body>
</html>
```

You can also use multi-line comments as well. Multi-line comments start with /* and continue until a */ is encountered. Here's an example:

```
<html>
    <head>
        <title>
            Using the echo statement
        </title>
    </head>

    <body>
        <h1>
            Using the echo statement
        </h1>

        <?
            /* This code sends the text
               "Greetings from PHP."
               back to the browser.
            */
            echo "Greetings from PHP.";
        ?>
    </body>
</html>
```

Now it's time to start looking at how to work with variables in PHP.

Working with Variables

Using variables in PHP is nearly as easy as using them in JavaScript. In PHP, variables can store numbers, strings, or objects, just as they can in JavaScript. Unlike JavaScript, however, variables names start with $ in PHP, and you don't need to declare them, as with the var statement in JavaScript.

For example, here is how you set the variable named $sandwiches to 1:

```
$sandwiches = 1;
```

And here is how you can display the value in this variable with the echo statement:

```
echo "Number of sandwiches: ", $sandwiches, "<br>";
```

> **NOTE** You can pass multiple items to the echo statement if you separate them with commas. Also, you're echoing HTML to the browser here, so that can include HTML elements like <br>.

Here's an example, variables.php, that puts variables to work. This example starts by assigning the variable $sandwiches a value of 2:

```
<html>
    <head>
        <title>
            Using variables
        </title>
    </head>

    <body>
        <h1>
            Using variables
        </h1>

        <?
            echo "Setting number of sandwiches to 2.<br>";

            $sandwiches = 2;
                .
                .
                .
        ?>

    </body>

</html>
```

and it echoes the number of sandwiches to the browser:

```
<html>
            .
            .
            .
        <?
            echo "Setting number of sandwiches to 2.<br>";

            $sandwiches = 2;

            echo "Number of sandwiches: ", $sandwiches, "<br>";
                .
                .
                .
        ?>

    </body>

</html>
```

Then the code adds two more sandwiches to the total, using the PHP + operator, which acts just like the JavaScript + operator:

```
<html>
        .
        .
        .
    <?
            echo "Setting number of sandwiches to 2.<br>";

            $sandwiches = 2;

            echo "Number of sandwiches: ", $sandwiches, "<br>";

            echo "Adding 2 more sandwiches.<BR>";

            $sandwiches = $sandwiches + 2;
            .
            .
            .
    ?>

    </body>

</html>
```

and then the code displays the new number of sandwiches:

```
<html>
        .
        .
        .
    <?
            echo "Setting number of sandwiches to 2.<br>";

            $sandwiches = 2;

            echo "Number of sandwiches: ", $sandwiches, "<br>";

            echo "Adding 2 more sandwiches.<BR>";

            $sandwiches = $sandwiches + 2;

            echo "Number of sandwiches now: ", $sandwiches,
    "<br>";
            ?>

    </body>

</html>
```

You can see the results in Figure 12.4.

FIGURE 12.4

Using variables

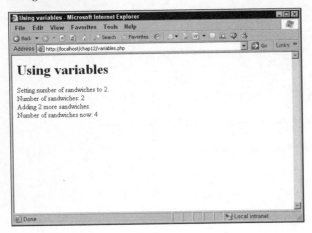

In addition to assigning numbers to variables, you can also assign text strings, as shown here:

```
$string = "Hello from PHP.";
```

In JavaScript, you join strings with the + operator, but in PHP, you use the dot (.) operator instead:

```
$string = "Hello " . "from " . "PHP.";
```

For more string power, PHP comes with many string functions built in:

- The `trim` function trims spaces from the beginning and end of a string.
- The `substr` function extracts substrings from a string.
- The `strpos` function finds the location of a substring in a string.
- The `substr_replace` function replaces text in a string.
- The `strtoupper` function converts a whole string to uppercase.

The example, string.php, puts these string functions to work. It starts by trimming the extra white space off the string " I like PHP. " with the `trim` function:

```
<html>
    <head>
        <title>
            Using strings
        </title>
    </head>
```

```
<body>
    <h1>
        Using strings
    </h1>

    <?
        echo trim("    I like PHP."), "<br>";
        .
        .
        .
    ?>

</body>

</html>
```

then it uses the substr function to extract the text PHP from the string "I like PHP.":

```
<html>
    <head>
        <title>
            Using strings
        </title>
    </head>

    <body>
        <h1>
            Using strings
        </h1>

        <?
            echo trim("    I like PHP."), "<br>";

            echo substr("I like PHP.", 7, 3), "<br>";
            .
            .
            .
        ?>

    </body>

</html>
```

The code then uses the strpos function to locate the first occurrence of PHP in the text "I like PHP." like this:

```
<html>
        .
        .
        .
    <?
       echo trim("    I like PHP."), "<br>";

       echo substr("I like PHP.", 7, 3), "<br>";

       echo "'PHP' starts at position ", strpos("I like PHP.",
          "PHP"), "<br>";
        .
        .
        .
    ?>

  </body>

</html>
```

and then the code determines how long the string "I like PHP." is:

```
<html>
        .
        .
        .
    <?
       echo trim("    I like PHP."), "<br>";

       echo substr("I like PHP.", 7, 3), "<br>";

       echo "'PHP' starts at position ", strpos("I like PHP.",
          "PHP"), "<br>";

       echo "'I like PHP.' is ", strlen("I like PHP."),
          " characters long.<br>";
        .
        .
        .
    ?>

  </body>

</html>
```

This example also replaces like in "I like PHP." with love using substr_replace:

```
<html>
        .
        .
        .
    <?
      echo trim("     I like PHP."), "<br>";

      echo substr("I like PHP.", 7, 3), "<br>";

      echo "'PHP' starts at position ", strpos("I like PHP.",
        "PHP"), "<br>";

      echo "'I like PHP.' is ", strlen("I like PHP."),
        " characters long.<br>";

      echo substr_replace("I like PHP.", "love", 2, 4),
        "<br>";
        .
        .
        .
    ?>

    </body>

</html>
```

and the example winds down by converting "I like PHP." to uppercase with strtoupper:

```
<html>
        .
        .
        .
    <?
      echo trim("     I like PHP."), "<br>";

      echo substr("I like PHP.", 7, 3), "<br>";

      echo "'PHP' starts at position ", strpos("I like PHP.",
        "PHP"), "<br>";

      echo "'I like PHP.' is ", strlen("I like PHP."),
        " characters long.<br>";

      echo substr_replace("I like PHP.", "love", 2, 4),
        "<br>";
```

```
            echo strtoupper("I like PHP."), "<br>";
        ?>

    </body>

</html>
```

You can see the results in Figure 12.5.

Using string functions

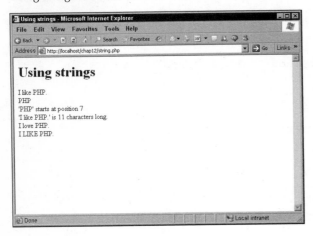

Table 12.1 lists all the PHP string functions and what they do.

The String Functions

Function	Does This
addslashes	Quotes a string with slashes
bin2hex	Converts binary data into hexadecimal representation
chop	Alias of the trim function
chr	Returns a specific character given its ASCII code
chunk_split	Splits a string into smaller chunks
convert_cyr_string	Converts from one Cyrillic character set to another

Function	Does This
count_chars	Returns information about characters in a string
crc32	Calculates the crc32 polynomial of a string
crypt	Supports one-way string encryption (hashing)
echo	Displays one or more strings
explode	Splits a string on a substring
fprintf	Writes a formatted string to a stream
get_html_translation_table	Returns the translation table
hebrev	Converts Hebrew text to visual text
hebrevc	Converts logical Hebrew text to visual text
html_entity_decode	Converts all HTML entities to their applicable characters
htmlentities	Converts all applicable characters to HTML entities
htmlspecialchars	Converts special characters to HTML entities
implode	Joins array elements with a string
join	Alias of the implode function
levenshtein	Calculates the Levenshtein distance between two strings
localeconv	Gets the numeric formatting information
ltrim	Strips white space from the beginning of a string
md5_file	Calculates the md5 hash of a given filename
md5	Calculates the md5 hash of a string
metaphone	Calculates the metaphone key of a string
money_format	Formats a number as a currency string
nl_langinfo	Queries language and locale information
nl2br	Inserts HTML line breaks before all new lines in a string
number_format	Formats a number with grouped thousand separators
ord	Returns the ASCII value of character
parse_str	Parses the string into variables
print	Displays a string
printf	Displays a formatted string
quoted_printable_decode	Converts a quoted-printable string to an 8-bit string
quotemeta	Quotes meta characters
rtrim	Strips white space from the end of a string
setlocale	Sets locale information

continued

TABLE 12.1 (continued)	
Function	**Does This**
sha1_file	Calculates the sha1 hash of a file
sha1	Calculates the sha1 hash of a string
similar_text	Calculates the similarity between two strings
soundex	Calculates the soundex key of a string
sprintf	Returns a formatted string
sscanf	Parses input from a string according to a format
str_ireplace	Case-insensitive version of the str_replace function
str_pad	Pads a string with another string
str_repeat	Repeats a string
str_replace	Replaces all occurrences of the search string with the replacement string
str_rot13	Performs the rot13 transform on a string
str_shuffle	Shuffles a string randomly
str_split	Converts a string to an array
str_word_count	Returns information about words used in a string
strcasecmp	Binary case-insensitive string comparison
strchr	Alias of the strstr function
strcmp	Binary-safe string comparison
strcoll	Locale-based string comparison
strcspn	Finds the length of the initial segment not matching a mask
strip_tags	Strips HTML and PHP tags from a string
stripcslashes	Un-quotes string quoted with addcslashes()
stripos	Finds position of first occurrence of a case-insensitive string
stripslashes	Un-quotes string quoted with addslashes()
stristr	Case-insensitive version of the strstr function
strlen	Gets a string's length
strnatcasecmp	Case-insensitive string comparisons
strnatcmp	String comparisons using a "natural order" algorithm
strncasecmp	Binary case-insensitive string comparison of the first n characters
strncmp	Binary safe string comparison of the first n characters
strpos	Finds position of first occurrence of a string
strrchr	Finds the last occurrence of a character in a string

Function	Does This
strrev	Reverses a string
strripos	Finds the position of last occurrence of a case-insensitive string
strrpos	Finds the position of last occurrence of a char in a string
strspn	Finds the length of initial segment matching mask
strstr	Finds the first occurrence of a string
strtok	Tokenizes a string
strtolower	Converts a string to lowercase
strtoupper	Converts a string to uppercase
strtr	Translates certain characters
substr_compare	Binary-safe (optionally case-insensitive) comparison of 2 strings from an offset
substr_count	Counts the number of substring occurrences
substr_replace	Replaces text within part of a string
substr	Returns part of a string
trim	Strips white space from the beginning and end of a string
ucfirst	Makes a string's first character uppercase
ucwords	Uppercases the first character of each word in a string
vprintf	Outputs a formatted string
vsprintf	Returns a formatted string
wordwrap	Wraps a string to a given number of characters

Interpolating Variables in Strings

As discussed earlier in this chapter, you can display the values of variables like this in PHP:

```
$sandwiches = 1;
echo "Number of sandwiches: ", $sandwiches, ".";
```

However, there's a shortcut that you can use here. The values in variables are *interpolated* if you put them into double-quoted (not single-quoted) strings, which means that their values are inserted directly into the string. You can do that this way to convert the example from the previous code:

```
$sandwiches = 1;
echo "Number of sandwiches: $sandwiches.";
```

As you'd expect, this example displays Number of sandwiches: 1.

Here's a more complete example of variable interpolation, interpolation.php:

```html
<html>
    <head>
        <title>
            Interpolating variables with PHP
        </title>
    </head>

    <body>
        <h1>
            Interpolating variables with PHP
        </h1>
        <?
            echo "Setting number of sandwiches to 2.<br>";

            $sandwiches = 2;

            echo "Number of sandwiches: $sandwiches <BR>";

            echo "Adding 2 more sandwiches.<BR>";

            $sandwiches = $sandwiches + 2;

            echo "Number of sandwiches now: $sandwiches <BR>";
        ?>
    </body>
</html>
```

You can see the results in Figure 12.6.

FIGURE 12.6

Using interpolation

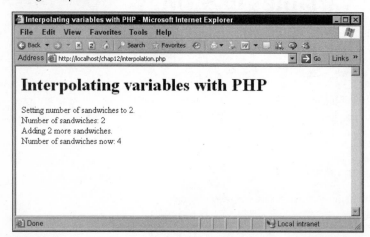

Interpolating can be useful, but it should be used with caution. What if you wanted to interpolate a variable named $data containing the word hot to the text dog? That might look like this:

```
<?
    $data = "hot";

    echo "Want a $datadog? <br>";
?>
```

This is not going to work, however, because PHP is going to start looking for a variable named $datadog, as you see here:

```
PHP Notice:  Undefined variable:  datadog in hotdog.php on line 3
```

Instead, the way to do this is to enclose the variable you're interpolating, $text, in curly braces, { and }, like this:

```
<html>
    <head>
        <title>
            Interpolating variables with PHP
        </title>
    </head>

    <body>
        <h1>
            Interpolating variables with PHP
        </h1>
        <?
            $data = "hot";

            echo "Want a ${data}dog? <br>";
        ?>
    </body>
</html>
```

You do indeed get Want a hotdog? from this example. In general, variable interpolation is a handy shortcut, and one you'll see often in PHP.

Working with Arrays

The next step up in PHP data handling from simple variables is to work with arrays, which are collections of data items stored under a single name, just as in JavaScript. Each element in an array can be addressed easily, by index.

487

Creating arrays

It's easy to create arrays in PHP. Just as you can assign values to variables to create those variables, so you can assign values to the elements of an array to create that array. PHP knows that if you use the array index operator [ ] after a variable's name, you're working with an array.

For example, take a look at this PHP statement:

```
$sandwiches[1] = "ham";
```

This statement actually creates an array named $sandwiches and sets the element at index 1 to ham. From now on, you can refer to this element as you would any simple variable; you just use the index value to make sure you reference the data you want, like this:

```
echo $sandwiches[1];
```

This statement would echo ham. You can add new values with different numeric indexes:

```
$sandwiches[2] = "turkey";
$sandwiches[3] = "roast beef";
```

Now you can refer to $sandwiches[1] (which is ham), $sandwiches[2] (which is turkey), and $sandwiches[3] (which is roast beef).

And, of course, you can store numeric values as well:

```
$sandwiches[2] = 200;
$sandwiches[3] = 300;
```

So far, the code you've seen has stored strings using numeric indexes, but, interestingly, you can also use string indexes. Here's an example:

```
$sandwich_inventory["Pittsburgh"] = 2343;
$sandwich_inventory["Albany"] = 5778;
$sandwich_inventory["Houston"] = 18843;
```

You can refer to the values in this array by string, as $sandwich_inventory["Pittsburgh"] (which holds 2343), $sandwich_inventory["Albany"] (which holds 5778), and $sandwich_inventory["Houston"] (which holds 18843). In fact, in PHP, the same array can use both numeric and text indexes.

You can also create arrays with the array statement. Here's an example showing how that works:

```
$data = array(15, 18, 22);
```

This creates an array named $data, with the contents 15, 18, 22.

By default, PHP starts the numbering of array elements with 0. What if you wanted to start with an index value of 1? You could specify that with the => operator like this:

```
$sandwiches = array(1 => "ham", "turkey", "roast beef");
```

Now the array would look like this:

```
$sandwiches[1] = "ham";
$sandwiches[2] = "turkey";
$sandwiches[3] = "roast beef";
```

You can also create arrays with text as index values in the same way:

```
$sandwich_inventory = array("Pittsburgh" => 2343,
"Albany" => 5778, "Houston"] => 18843);
```

This creates the following array:

```
$sandwich_inventory["Pittsburgh"] = 2343;
$sandwich_inventory["Albany"] = 5778;
$sandwich_inventory["Houston"] = 18843;
```

The => operator lets you specify key/value pairs. For example, "Pittsburgh" is the key for the first element, and 2343 is the value.

In fact, there's another shortcut for creating arrays. If you have a well-defined range of data, you can automatically create array elements to match with the range function, such as the numbers 1 to 10 or characters a to z like this:

```
$values = range("a", "z");.
```

As in JavaScript, you can modify the values in arrays as easily as other variables. For example, say you have this array:

```
$sandwiches[1] = "ham";
$sandwiches[2] = "turkey";
$sandwiches[3] = "roast beef";
```

Now say you want to change the value of $sandwiches[2] to egg. You could do that like this:

```
$sandwiches[1] = "ham";
$sandwiches[2] = "turkey";
$sandwiches[3] = "roast beef";

$sandwiches[2] = "egg";
```

Now say that you wanted to add a new element, `pastrami`, to the end of the array. You could do that by referring to `$sandwiches[]`, which is PHP's shortcut for adding a new element:

```
$sandwiches[0] = "ham";
$sandwiches[1] = "turkey";
$sandwiches[2] = "roast beef";

$sandwiches[2] = "egg";

$sandwiches[] = "pastrami";
```

Want to verify that this array now holds what you think it should? You can loop over that array using the PHP `for` loop, which will be introduced later, but which works just like a JavaScript `for` loop.

Here's how to use a `for` loop to loop over the array, in array.php:

```
<html>
    <head>
        <title>
            Displaying an array
        </title>
    </head>

    <body>
        <h1>
            Displaying an array
        </h1>

    <?
        $sandwiches[0] = "ham";
        $sandwiches[1] = "turkey";
        $sandwiches[2] = "roast beef";

        $sandwiches[2] = "egg";

        $sandwiches[] = "pastrami";

        for ($index = 0; $index < count($sandwiches);
          $index++){
            echo $sandwiches[$index], "<br>";
        }
    ?>
    </body>
</html>
```

The results are shown in Figure 12.7. As you can see, the code was not only able to modify `$sandwiches[2]`, it was also able to add `pastrami` to the end of the array.

Using arrays

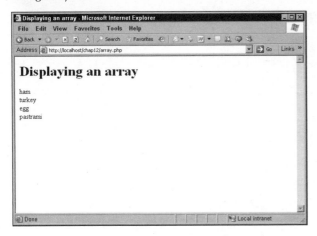

Copying arrays

In addition to creating arrays, you can also copy arrays. For example, you can copy a whole array at once by assigning it to another array, like this:

```
<html>
    <head>
        <title>
            Copying an array
        </title>
    </head>

    <body>
        <h1>
            Copying an array
        </h1>

        <?
          $sandwiches[0] = "ham";
          $sandwiches[1] = "turkey";
          $sandwiches[2] = "roast beef";
          $sandwiches[2] = "egg";
          $sandwiches[] = "pastrami";
          $lunch = $sandwiches;
          echo $lunch[2];
        ?>
    </body>
</html>
```

This code, copyArray.php, echoes egg, as shown in Figure 12.8.

FIGURE 12.8

Copying arrays

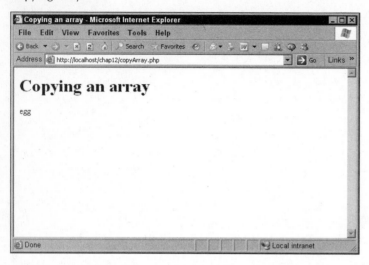

That's a good overview on storing data in PHP, including variables, strings, and arrays. Now how about doing something with the data? That brings up the topic of PHP operators.

Handling Your Data with Operators

There are many operators in PHP, and most of them do the same thing they do in JavaScript. Following is a list of the PHP operators:

- `new`
- `[`
- `! ~ ++ --`
- `* / %`
- `+ - .`
- `== !=`
- `&`
- `|`
- `&&`
- `||`
- `? :`
- `= += -= *= /= .= %= &= |= ^= <<= >>=`

The example, operators.php, puts some of these operators to work:

```html
<html>
    <head>
        <title>
            Using PHP operators
        </title>
    </head>

    <body>
        <h1>
            Using PHP operators
        </h1>
        <?
            echo "4 + 6 = ", 4 + 6, "<br>";

            echo "4 - 6 = ", 4 - 6, "<br>";

            echo "4 * 6 = ", 4 * 6, "<br>";

            echo "4 / 6 = ", 4 / 6, "<br>";

        ?>
    </body>
</html>
```

The results of operators.php are shown in Figure 12.9, where you can see that the PHP operators have done what they should.

FIGURE 12.9

Using PHP operators

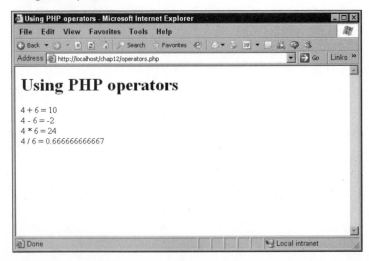

Making Choices with the if Statement

Just as in JavaScript, PHP supports an if statement:

```
if (expression)
    statement
```

As with JavaScript, in the previous code, *expression* is a true/false expression. If it evaluates to true, *statement* (which is usually enclosed in curly braces) is executed; otherwise, *statement* is not executed.

Here's an example. The following code checks $temperature to make sure it's below 80 degrees, and since it is, displays the text "Not too hot.":

```
<html>
    <head>
        <title>
            Using the if statement
        </title>
    </head>

    <body>
        <h1>
            Using the if statement
        </h1>
        <?
          $temperature = 75;

          if ($temperature < 80)
            echo "Not too hot.";
        ?>
    </body>
</html>
```

What if you want to execute multiple statements? You enclose them in curly braces, { and }:

```
<html>
    <head>
        <title>
            Using the if statement
        </title>
    </head>

    <body>
        <h1>
            Using the if statement
        </h1>
```

```
<?
    $temperature = 75;

    if ($temperature < 80){
        echo "Not ";
        echo "too ";
        echo "hot.";
    }
?>
</body>
</html>
```

As you can see, you can use comparison operators like < in `if` statements. Table 12.2 lists all the available PHP conditional operators.

TABLE 12.2

The Comparison Operators

Operator	Operation	Example	Result
==	Equal	$a == $b	true if $a is equal to $b
===	Identical	$a === $b	true if $a is equal to $b, and they are of the same type
!=	Not equal	$a != $b	true if $a is not equal to $b
<>	Not equal	$a <> $b	true if $a is not equal to $b
!==	Not identical	$a !== $b	true if $a is not equal to $b, or they are not of the same type
<	Less than	$a < $b	true if $a is less than $b
>	Greater than	$a > $b	true if $a is greater than $b
<=	Less than or equal to	$a <= $b	true if $a is less than or equal to $b
>=	Greater than or equal to	$a >= $b	true if $a is greater than or equal to $b

For example, if you wanted to check whether the value in the variable $temperature was exactly 75 degrees, you could use the equality operator (==):

```
<html>
    <head>
        <title>
            Using the if statement
        </title>
    </head>
```

```
<body>
    <h1>
        Using the if statement
    </h1>
    <?
      $temperature = 75;

      if ($temperature == 75){
        echo "Not ";
        echo "too ";
        echo "hot.";
      }
    ?>
</body>
</html>
```

As with JavaScript, you can also use logical operators to connect the conditions you test. For example, if you wanted to make sure the temperature was between 70 and 80, you could do this in your code:

```
<html>
    <head>
        <title>
            Using the if statement
        </title>
    </head>

    <body>
        <h1>
            Using the if statement
        </h1>
        <?
          $temperature = 75;

          if ($temperature >= 70 && $temperature <= 80){
            echo "Not ";
            echo "too ";
            echo "hot.";
          }
        ?>
    </body>
</html>
```

Table 12.3 lists the logical operators available in PHP.

TABLE 12.3

The Logical Operators

Operator	Operation	Example	Result
and	And	$a and $b	True if both $a and $b are true
or	Or	$a or $b	True if either $a or $b is true
xor	Xor	$a xor $b	True if either $a or $b is true, but not both
!	Not	! $a	True if $a is not true
&&	And	$a && $b	True if both $a and $b are true
||	Or	$a || $b	True if either $a or $b is true

Using else statements

You can also use else statements with if statements in PHP. An else statement contains code that will be executed if the if statement's statement isn't executed. For example, if the temperature is less than 80, you might display Not too hot, but if it's 80 or above, you might display Too hot. Here's what that looks like in code, in ifelse.php:

```
<html>
    <head>
        <title>
            Using the if statement
        </title>
    </head>

    <body>
        <h1>
            Using the if statement
        </h1>
        <?
          $temperature = 85;

          if ($temperature < 80){
            echo "Not too hot.";
          }
          else {
            echo "Too hot.";
          }
        ?>
    </body>
</html>
```

The results are shown in Figure 12.10, where, as you can see, the weather's too hot.

FIGURE 12.10

Using if/else statements

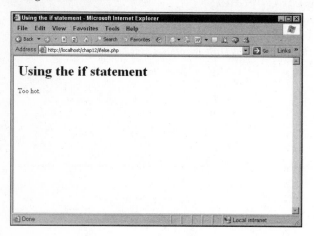

Using elseif statements

There's even more power built in to PHP if statements. You can also use elseif statements in PHP, something you can't do in JavaScript. The elseif statement lets you test additional conditions — additional to the main condition in the if statement, that is — and execute code to match.

For example, what if you wanted to execute some code if the temperature was below 80, other code if the temperature was below 85, and so on? You could do that as in this code, elseif.php:

```
<html>
    <head>
        <title>
            Using the elseif statement
        </title>
    </head>

    <body>
        <h1>
            Using the elseif statement
        </h1>
        <?
            $temperature = 85;

            if ($temperature < 80){
                echo "Not too hot.";
            }
```

```
      elseif ($temperature < 85) {
        echo "Still not too bad.";
      }
      elseif ($temperature < 90) {
        echo "Getting pretty hot.";
      }
      else {
        echo "Definitely too hot.";
      }
    ?>
  </body>
</html>
```

You can see the results in Figure 12.11, which shows that it's getting pretty hot.

Using `elseif` statements

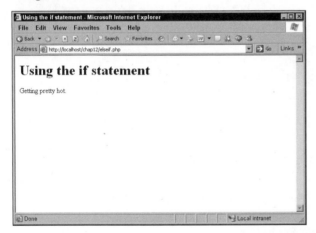

But what if you have dozens of conditions you want to test? It would get a little tedious to test them all, one by one, with `elseif` statements. That's why the `switch` statement exists.

Using Switch Statements

You create a `switch` statement with the keyword `switch`, and you indicate the item you're testing by placing it in parentheses. You create multiple tests using the `case` statement, specifying a value for each such statement. If the switch's test value matches a case statement's value, the internal statements in the `case` statement are executed up to a `break` statement, which ends the `case` statement. If no case matches, the statements in a default statement, if present, are executed.

Here's what the switch statement looks like:

```
switch (expression){
  case data:
    statement
    break;
  case data:
    statement
    break;
  case data:
    statement
    break;
  [default:
    statement]
  }
```

> **NOTE** If the value of expression doesn't match any data item, the code in the optional default statement will be executed.

In this example, different text based on the temperature, switch.php, is displayed:

```html
<html>
    <head>
        <title>
            Using the switch statement
        </title>
    </head>

    <body>
        <h1>
            Using the switch statement
        </h1>
        <?
          $temperature = 75;

          switch ($temperature){
            case 75:
              echo "Nice weather.";
              break;
            case 76:
              echo "Still nice weather.";
              break;
            case 77:
              echo "Getting warmer.";
              break;
            default:
              echo "Temperature outside the range.";
            }
        ?>
```

```
        </body>
    </html>
```

You can see switch.php at work in Figure 12.12, which shows that it's nice weather.

FIGURE 12.12

Using switch statements

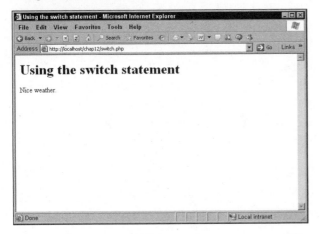

Using loop Statements

In addition to conditional statements like if/else and switch, PHP also supports loops.

Looping with the for loop

The for loop, which repeatedly executes a statement, looks like this in PHP:

```
for (expression1; expression2; expression3)
    statement
```

Here, as in JavaScript, *expression1* lets you initialize your loop, often by initializing a loop counter, also called a loop index, that tracks how many times the loop has executed. The next expression, *expression2*, is the test expression; the loop keeps going while this expression remains true. You usually test the value in your loop counter here. The final expression, *expression3*, is executed after the loop is executed, each time through the loop. You usually increment your loop counter variable in that expression. Every time through the loop, *statement*, which can be a compound statement consisting of many single statements enclosed in curly braces, is executed.

Here's an example, for.php. In this example, the code uses a `for` loop to display a line of text six times. The loop starts by setting a loop counter variable named $loop_counter to 0, incrementing it each time after the loop runs, and testing to make sure the loop counter doesn't exceed 6:

```
<html>
    <head>
        <title>
            Using the for loop
        </title>
    </head>

    <body>
        <h1>
            Using the for loop
        </h1>

        <?
            for ($loop_counter = 0; $loop_counter < 6;
              $loop_counter++){
                 .
                 .
                 .
            }
        ?>
    </body>
</html>
```

Then you add the body of the loop, which is what displays the text in the Web page:

```
<html>
    <head>
        <title>
            Using the for loop
        </title>
    </head>

    <body>
        <h1>
            Using the for loop
        </h1>

        <?
            for ($loop_counter = 0; $loop_counter < 6;
              $loop_counter++){
                echo "You're going to see this six times.<BR>";
            }
        ?>
    </body>
</html>
```

The results of this code appear in Figure 12.13, where, as you can see, the text was displayed six times.

Using the `for` loop

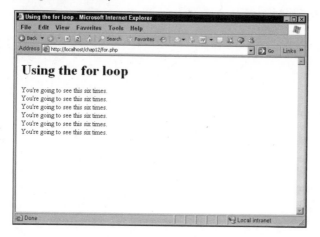

Looping with the while loop

The `while` loop keeps executing its code while an expression remains true. Here's what this loop looks like:

```
while (expression)
    statement
```

In this case, *statement* can be a compound statement, surrounded in curly braces. This loop keeps going as long as the condition *expression* remains true.

Here's an example, while.php. This example displays the value in a variable and increments it until it becomes greater than 8.

The `while` loop is set up like this:

```
<html>
    <head>
        <title>
            Using the while loop
        </title>
    </head>
```

```
<body>
    <h1>
        Using the while loop
    </h1>
    <?
        $data = 1;

        while ($data < 8){
            .
            .
            .
        }
    ?>
</body>
</html>
```

then you can display the current value of the variable and increment that value like this:

```
<html>
    <head>
        <title>
            Using the while loop
        </title>
    </head>

    <body>
        <h1>
            Using the while loop
        </h1>
        <?
            $data = 1;

            while ($data < 8){
                echo "New data:", $data, "<br>";
                $data += 1;
            }
        ?>
    </body>
</html>
```

The results are shown in Figure 12.14, where the loop terminates when the value in the variable reaches 8.

FIGURE 12.14

Using the while loop

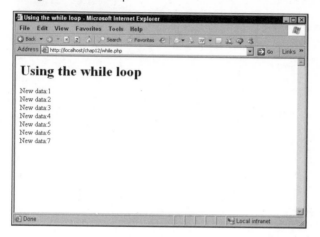

Looping with the do...while loop

There's another version of the while loop: the do...while loop, which checks its condition at the end of the loop, not the beginning. That means the loop's statement is always executed at least once (which is good if that statement sets the condition you want to test to see whether the loop should keep looping):

```
do
    statement
while (expression)
```

Here's what the previous while loop example would look like as a do...while loop instead, dowhile.php:

```
<html>
    <head>
        <title>
            Using the do...while loop
        </title>
    </head>

    <body>
        <h1>
            Using the do...while loop
        </h1>
```

```
      <?
          $data = 1;

          do {
              echo "New data:", $data, "<br>";
              $data += 1;
          } while ($data < 8)
      ?>
    </body>
  </html>
```

You can see the results in Figure 12.15.

Using the `do...while` loop

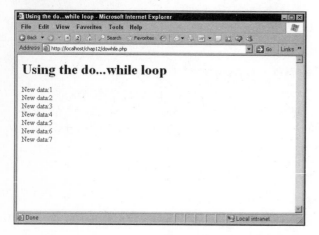

There's one more loop in PHP as well, and it's an important one: the `foreach` loop, which you use with collections of data items like arrays.

Looping with the foreach loop

The PHP `foreach` loop is designed to be used with collections of data items, like arrays. Here's one way to use this loop:

```
foreach (array as $value)
    statement
```

In this case, *array* is an array, and *$value* a variable. Each time through the loop, *$value* holds the next element from the array.

Here's an example, foreach.php. In this example, you can create an array that the foreach loop will loop over, and set up the foreach loop like this:

```
<html>
    <head>
        <title>Using the foreach loop</title>
    </head>

    <body>
        <h1>Using the foreach loop</h1>
            <?
                $array = array("ham", "turkey", "tuna",
                    "cheese");

                foreach ($array as $sandwich) {
                    .
                    .
                    .
                }
            ?>
        </body>
</html>
```

Now each time through the loop, $sandwich will hold the next successive element from $array, so you can display the current sandwich like this:

```
<html>
    <head>
        <title>Using the foreach loop</title>
    </head>

    <body>
        <h1>Using the foreach loop</h1>
            <?
                $array = array("ham", "turkey", "tuna",
                    "cheese");

                foreach ($array as $sandwich) {
                    echo "Current sandwich: $sandwich <br>";
                }
            ?>
        </body>
</html>
```

That's all you need. The results are shown in Figure 12.16. As you can see, the foreach loop was able to loop over all the items in the array automatically.

FIGURE 12.16

Using the `foreach` loop

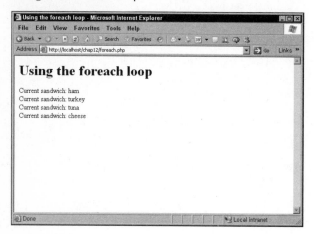

The `foreach` loop is a good one to use with collections like arrays because you don't have to worry about making sure you set up the loop index in a `for` loop just right, so the loop terminates after you've looped over every item in the collection.

Summary

In this chapter, the basics of PHP as it pertains to Ajax were introduced. You saw how to write PHP pages and how to use its basic syntax. You worked with PHP operators, `if` statements, and `elseif` statements. You also saw how to work with loops in PHP, and how to read data sent from the server. And you also saw how to work with data structures like arrays.

Chapter 13

PHP: Functions and HTML Controls

This chapter continues your guided tour of PHP with handling PHP functions and HTML controls. PHP functions are just as important in PHP as in JavaScript, but there's some added power in PHP compared to JavaScript. And working with HTML controls is the whole main point of using server-side scripting for many developers. You're going to see both in this chapter.

CROSS-REF For an introduction to using PHP with Ajax, see Chapter 12.

Working with Functions

On the face of it, functions work much the same in PHP as in JavaScript. Here's how a function is set up:

```
function function_name([argument_list...])
{
    [statements;]
    [return return_value;]
}
```

It's easiest to see this with examples. For instance, you might want to use a function to display a copyright symbol at the bottom of your Web pages. You would start by displaying the Web page content like this:

```
<html>
  <head>
    <title>Using functions to create a copyright
mark</title>
  </head>
```

```
        <body> ·
          <h1>Using functions to create a copyright mark</h1>

          <?
            echo "<h3>Welcome to my web page!</h3>";
            echo "<br>";
            echo "How do you like it?";
            echo "<br>";
            echo "<br>";
                .
                .
                .
          ?>
        </body>
      </html>
```

Then you call the function in this example, print_copyright, to print the copyright symbol:

```
      <html>
        <head>
          <title>Using functions to create a copyright mark</title>
        </head>

        <body>
          <h1>Using functions to create a copyright mark</h1>

          <?
            echo "<h3>Welcome to my web page!</h3>";
            echo "<br>";
            echo "How do you like it?";
            echo "<br>";
            echo "<br>";

            print_copyright();
                .
                .
                .
          ?>
        </body>
      </html>
```

The print_copyright function prints the copyright to the Web page when called, as you see here:

```
      <html>
        <head>
          <title>Using functions to create a copyright mark</title>
        </head>
```

```
<body>
  <h1>Using functions to create a copyright mark</h1>

  <?
    echo "<h3>Welcome to my web page!</h3>";
    echo "<br>";
    echo "How do you like it?";
    echo "<br>";
    echo "<br>";

    print_copyright();

    function print_copyright()
    {
      echo "<hr>";
      echo "<center>";
      echo "&copy; 2007 PHP Masters, Inc.";
      echo "</center>";
    }
  ?>
</body>
</html>
```

You can see the copyright mark at the bottom of the Web page, functions.php, shown in Figure 13.1.

The functions.php application

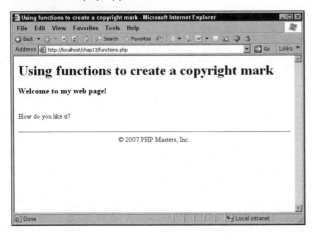

And, as with JavaScript, you can pass data to functions in PHP as well, which is discussed in the next section.

Passing data to functions

Arguments are passed to functions in the argument list, which is a comma-separated list of data items, as shown here:

```
function function_name([argument_list...])
{
    [statements;]
    [return return_value;]
}
```

For example, let's say you wanted to customize the copyright message you display, passing the date and copyright holder to the function. You could pass that data to the function like this in passData.php:

```
<html>
  <head>
    <title>Passing data to functions</title>
  </head>

  <body>
    <h1>Passing data to functions</h1>

    <?
      echo "<h3>Welcome to my web page!</h3>";
      echo "<br>";
      echo "How do you like it?";
      echo "<br>";
      echo "<br>";

      $date = "2007";
      $holder = "PHP Masters, Inc.";

      print_copyright($date, $holder);
         .
         .
         .
    ?>
  </body>
</html>
```

and you can read the passed data in the print_copyright function this way:

```
<html>
  <head>
    <title>Passing data to functions</title>
  </head>
```

```
<body>
  <h1>Passing data to functions</h1>

  <?
    echo "<h3>Welcome to my web page!</h3>";
    echo "<br>";
    echo "How do you like it?";
    echo "<br>";
    echo "<br>";

    $date = "2007";
    $holder = "PHP Masters, Inc.";

    print_copyright($date, $holder);

    function print_copyright($copyright_date,
      $copyright_holder)
    {
      echo "<hr>";
      echo "<center>";
      echo "&copy; $copyright_date $copyright_holder";
      echo "</center>";
    }
  ?>
</body>
</html>
```

The results are shown in Figure 13.2.

FIGURE 13.2

The passData.php application

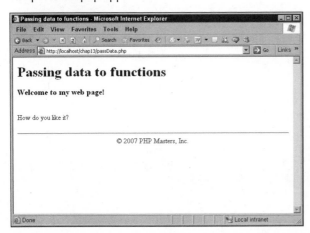

Setting up default arguments

In PHP, you can also set up *default* arguments.

The `print_copyright` function displays two items, `$copyright_date` and `$copyright_holder`:

```
function print_copyright($copyright_date,
  $copyright_holder)
{
  echo "<hr>";
  echo "<center>";
  echo "&copy; $copyright_date $copyright_holder";
  echo "</center>";
}
```

But what if you were to pass only one data item to the function, such as only the date?

```
<html>
  <head>
    <title>Passing data to functions</title>
  </head>

  <body>
    <h1>Passing data to functions</h1>

    <?
      echo "<h3>Welcome to my web page!</h3>";
      echo "<br>";
      echo "How do you like it?";
      echo "<br>";
      echo "<br>";

      $date = "2007";

      print_copyright($date);
         .
         .
         .
    ?>
  </body>
</html>
```

Normally, that would be a problem, of course, but not if you set up a default argument for the copyright holder. You do that in the argument list with an equal sign and the default value you want the argument to have if no other argument was assigned, like this:

```
<html>
  <head>
    <title>Passing data to functions</title>
  </head>
```

```
<body>
  <h1>Passing data to functions</h1>

  <?
    echo "<h3>Welcome to my web page!</h3>";
    echo "<br>";
    echo "How do you like it?";
    echo "<br>";
    echo "<br>";

    $date = "2007";

    print_copyright($date);

    function print_copyright($copyright_date,
      $copyright_holder = "PHP Masters, Inc.")
    {
      echo "<hr>";
      echo "<center>";
      echo "&copy; $copyright_date $copyright_holder";
      echo "</center>";
    }
  ?>
  </body>
</html>
```

The results are the same as the results shown in Figure 13.2, but this time, the copyright holder is supplied by the default argument.

> **NOTE** You can supply default values for as many arguments as you want, but if you supply a default value for a particular argument, you must supply a default argument for all the following arguments in the argument list as well; otherwise, PHP would not be able to figure out which argument your default value is meant for.

Creating variable-length argument lists

You can also pass variable-length argument lists to functions. This is not the same as setting up default arguments; in this case, you can call the same function with a different number of arguments, and you can retrieve all the arguments using special functions instead of giving each argument a default value. You can pass as many arguments as you want.

For example, if you have a function named combiner that joins strings together, you might call it like this:

```
combiner("No", "problems");
combiner("No", "problems", "here.");
combiner("No", "problems", "at", "all.");
```

In the combiner function, you can use three PHP functions to get the number of arguments passed to you, a single argument that you specify by number, and an array that holds all the arguments passed to you. Here are those functions:

- func_num_args: Returns the number of arguments passed
- func_get_arg: Returns a single argument
- func_get_args: Returns all arguments in an array

Here's what the combiner function might look like using func_get_args to get all the passed arguments in an array:

```
function combiner()
{
    $arg_list = func_get_args();
    .
    .
    .

}
```

Then you can loop over the number of arguments passed, which you can find with func_num_args this way:

```
function combiner()
{
    $arg_list = func_get_args();

    for ($loop_index = 0;$loop_index < func_num_args();
      $loop_index++) {          .
        .
        .
    }
}
```

You can combine the passed text into a single text string:

```
function combiner()
{
    $text_string = "";
    $arg_list = func_get_args();

    for ($loop_index = 0;$loop_index < func_num_args();
      $loop_index++) {
      $text_string .= $arg_list[$loop_index] . " ";
    }
    .
    .
    .

}
```

and all that's left is to echo the combined text string:

```
function combiner()
{
    $text_string = "";
    $arg_list = func_get_args();

    for ($loop_index = 0;$loop_index < func_num_args();
      $loop_index++) {
      $text_string .= $arg_list[$loop_index] . " ";
    }

    echo $text_string;
}
```

You can see this function at work in variableArguments.php:

```
<html>
  <head>

    <title>
      Using variable-length argument lists
    </title>

  </head>

  <body>
    <h1>Using variable-length argument lists</h1>
            <?
    echo "combiner(No, problems) =  ", combiner("No",
      "problems"), "<br>";

    echo "combiner(No, problems, here.) =  ",
      combiner("No", "problems", "here."), "<br>";

    echo "combiner(No, problems, at, all.) =  ",
      combiner("No", "problems", "at", "all."), "<br>";

    function combiner()
    {
      $text_string = "";

      $arg_list = func_get_args();

      for ($loop_index = 0;$loop_index < func_num_args();
        $loop_index++) {
        $text_string .= $arg_list[$loop_index] . " ";
      }

      echo $text_string;
    }
```

```
      ?>
    </body>
</html>
```

The results appear in Figure 13.3, where all the arguments passed to the combiner function are used.

FIGURE 13.3

The variableArguments.php application

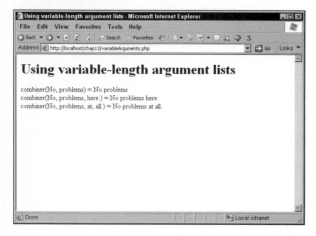

Returning values from functions

You can also return values from functions in PHP. To return a value from a PHP function, all you have to do is to use the `return` statement, which looks like this:

```
return (value);
```

The parentheses are optional; you can also use the `return` statement like this:

```
return value;
```

For example, you might have a function named `adder` that takes two numbers and returns their sum; here's what that looks like in adder.php:

```
<html>
  <head>

    <title>
      Returning values from functions
    </title>

  </head>
```

```
<body>
  <h1>Returning values from functions</h1>
  <?
    echo "adder(3, 2) = ", adder(3, 2), "<br>";

    echo "adder(5, 7) = ", adder(5, 7), "<br>";

    echo "adder(9, 17) = ", adder(9, 17), "<br>";


    function adder($operand_1, $operand_2)
    {
      return $operand_1 + $operand_2;
    }
  ?>
</body>
</html>
```

You can see what this application looks like in Figure 13.4.

FIGURE 13.4

The adder.php application

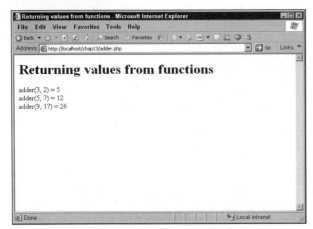

Returning multiple values from a function

Here's something you might not expect: You can return multiple values from a function in PHP. For example, you might have a function, `returner`, that returns six different colors: red, green, yellow, and so on. How could you handle all six return values?

You can handle them with the PHP `list` function, which lets you work with a data construct called a `list` in PHP. Here's how you would accept all six return values from the `returner` function, assigning them to variables `$first`, `$second`, and so on:

```
<html>
  <head>
    <title>
      Returning multiple values from functions
    </title>
  </head>

  <body>
    <h1>
      Returning multiple values from functions
    </h1>

    <?

      list($first, $second, $third, $fourth, $fifth,
        $sixth) = returner();
          .
          .
          .

    ?>
  </body>
</html>
```

then you could echo the multiple returned values this way:

```
<html>
  <head>
    <title>
      Returning multiple values from functions
    </title>
  </head>

  <body>
    <h1>
      Returning multiple values from functions
    </h1>

    <?

      list($first, $second, $third, $fourth, $fifth,
        $sixth) = returner();

      echo "\$first: $first<BR>";
      echo "\$second: $second<BR>";
      echo "\$third: $third<BR>";
      echo "\$fourth: $fourth<BR>";
      echo "\$fifth: $fifth<BR>";
```

```
      echo "\$sixth: $sixth<BR>";
                    .
                    .
                    .

    ?>
  </body>
</html>
```

How do you return multiple values from a function in PHP? One way is to simply place them into an array and to return that array, which looks like this:

```
<html>
  <head>
    <title>
      Returning multiple values from functions
    </title>
  </head>

  <body>
    <h1>
      Returning multiple values from functions
    </h1>

    <?

      list($first, $second, $third, $fourth, $fifth,
        $sixth) = returner();

      echo "\$first: $first<BR>";
      echo "\$second: $second<BR>";
      echo "\$third: $third<BR>";
      echo "\$fourth: $fourth<BR>";
      echo "\$fifth: $fifth<BR>";
      echo "\$sixth: $sixth<BR>";

      function returner()
      {
        $array = array("Red", "Green", "Yellow", "Blue",
          "Orange", "Magenta");

        return $array;
      }
    ?>
  </body>
</html>
```

You can see the results of this application, multipleReturns.php, in Figure 13.5.

FIGURE 13.5

The multipleReturns.php application

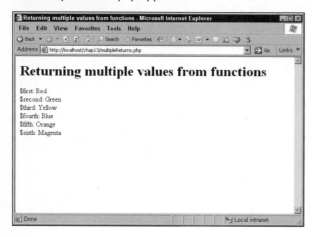

Now it's time to turn to one of the most powerful parts of working with PHP: handling HTML controls.

Handling HTML Controls

This is the section where your PHP-based Web pages start becoming interactive. This is where you start being able to take credit card numbers, user names, feedback, and more. You're going to see HTML controls like text fields, checkboxes, radio buttons, list boxes, and so on.

To read data from HTML controls, you need to put those controls in HTML forms, using the `<form>` element. Here are the important attributes of that element:

- `action`: This attribute gives the URL that will handle the form data. Note that you can omit this attribute, in which case its default is the URL of the current document.
- `method`: Specifies the method or protocol for sending data to the target action URL. If you set it to GET (the default) this method sends all form name/value pair information in a URL that looks like:

  URL?name=value&name=value&name=value

  If you use the POST method, the contents of the form are encoded as with the GET method, but are sent in hidden header variables.
- `target`: Indicates a named frame for the browser to display the form results in.

For example, say that you wanted to read data that the user entered into the controls in a Web page using a PHP script named reader.php in the same directory as reader.html. To handle that, you could set the form's `action` attribute to `reader.php` as shown here:

```
<html>
    <head>
        <title>
            Using HTML forms
        </title>
    </head>

    <body>
        <h1>
            Using HTML forms
        </h1>
        <form method="post" action="reader.php">
            .
            .
            .
        </form>
    </body>
</html>
```

If reader.php were not in the same directory, you'd have to give its URL, either relative to the current page, or absolute such as `http://the_isp.com/php/reader.php`.

Now you can place controls in your form, such as text fields and list boxes. You'll also need a Submit button that will send all the data in the form back to reader.php on the server when clicked; here's what that Submit button might look like:

```
<html>
    <head>
        <title>
            Using HTML forms
        </title>
    </head>

    <body>
        <h1>
            Using HTML forms
        </h1>
        <form method="post" action="reader.php">
            .
            .
            .
            <input type="submit" value="Submit">
        </form>
    </body>
</html>
```

In addition to Submit buttons, you can also display a Reset button, which resets the data in the form's controls to their default values (which usually means blank). Here's what a Reset button would look like in this case:

```html
<html>
    <head>
        <title>
            Using HTML forms
        </title>
    </head>

    <body>
        <h1>
            Using HTML forms
        </h1>
        <form method="post" action="reader.php">
            .

            .

            .
            <input type="submit" value="Submit">
            <input type="reset" value="Reset">
        </form>
    </body>
</html>
```

On the PHP side of things, how do you get the data the user entered? As you're going to see, you can use an array named $_POST if you've used the POST method, and an array named $_GET if you've used the GET method. You can also use the $_REQUEST array, which holds the data in both the $_GET and $_POST arrays.

It's time to see some HTML controls at work, starting with text fields.

Working with text fields

To create an HTML text field, you use the <input type="text"> element enclosed in an HTML <form> element. This example centers around two Web documents: an HTML page that contains the text field, and a PHP page that reads the data the user enters into that text field.

In the HTML page, you start with the HTML form, indicating that the data in the form should be sent to text.php:

```html
<html>
    <head>
        <title>
            Using Text Fields
        </title>
    </head>
```

```
<body>
    <center>

        <h1>
            Using Text Fields
        </h1>

        <form method="post" action="text.php">
        .
        .
        .
        </form>

    </center>
</body>
</html>
```

then you add the text field and a prompt asking for the user's name, as well as a Submit button:

```
<html>
    <head>
        <title>
            Using Text Fields
        </title>
    </head>

    <body>
        <center>

            <h1>
                Using Text Fields
            </h1>

            <form method="post" action="text.php">
                Please enter your name:

                <input name="name" type="text">

                <br>
                <br>

                <input type="submit" value="Submit">
            </form>

        </center>
    </body>
</html>
```

How can you retrieve the data from the text field? That's the job of text.php, which starts this way:

```
<html>
    <head>
        <title>
            Reading data from text fields
        </title>
    </head>

    <body>
        <center>

            <h1>
                Reading data from text fields
            </h1>
            Your name is
                .
                .
                .

        </center>
    </body>
</html>
```

To actually retrieve the text from the text field, you just need to use the name of the text field, which is name, as an index into the $_POST or $_REQUEST array. Here's what that looks like in text.php:

```
<html>
    <head>
        <title>
            Reading data from text fields
        </title>
    </head>

    <body>
        <center>

            <h1>
                Reading data from text fields
            </h1>
            Your name is
            <?
                echo $_REQUEST["name"];
            ?>
        </center>
    </body>
</html>
```

The text.html Web page is shown in Figure 13.6. After the user enters a name and clicks the Submit button, that name is displayed by text.php, as shown in Figure 13.7.

FIGURE 13.6

FIGURE 13.6

The text.html Web page

FIGURE 13.7

The text.php application at work

Working with checkboxes

Checkboxes are another fundamental HTML control that you should know how to use with PHP. In this example, checkboxes.html sends its data to the page checkboxes.php:

```html
<html>
    <head>
        <title>Using Checkboxes</title>
    </head>

    <body>
        <center>
        <h1>Using Checkboxes</h1>
```

```
                <form method=post action="checkboxes.php">
                    .
                    .
                    .
                    <input type="submit" value="Submit">
                </form>
                </center>
            </body>
        </html>
```

You might ask the user "Do you want fries with that?", and add two checkboxes, check1 and check2, to the page:

```
<html>
    <head>
        <title>Using Checkboxes</title>
    </head>

    <body>
        <center>
        <h1>Using Checkboxes</h1>
        <form method=post action="checkboxes.php">
            Do you want fries with that?
            <input name="check1" type="checkbox" value="Yes">
            Yes
            <input name="check2" Type="checkbox" value="No">
            No
            <br>
            <br>
            <input type="submit" value="Submit">
        </form>
        </center>
    </body>
</html>
```

What about the PHP page checkboxes.php, that will read the checkbox data? Here's the key: you can't just use an expression like $_REQUEST["check1"], because if the check1 checkbox was not selected, trying to access $_REQUEST["check1"] would give you an error. So you have to first test whether check1 was selected with the expression isset($_REQUEST["check1"]), which returns true if check1 was selected:

```
<html>
    <head>
        <title>
            Reading data from checkboxes
        </title>
    </head>

    <body>
        <center>
            <h1>Reading data from checkboxes</h1>
```

```
            You checked
            <?
                if (isset($_REQUEST["check1"]))
                    .
                    .
                    .
            ?>
        </center>
    </body>
</html>
```

If check1 was checked, you can report the text associated with that checkbox (which is "Yes"):

```
<html>
    <head>
        <title>
            Reading data from checkboxes
        </title>
    </head>

    <body>
        <center>
            <h1>Reading data from checkboxes</h1>

            You checked
            <?
                if (isset($_REQUEST["check1"]))
                    echo $_REQUEST["check1"], "<br>";
                    .
                    .
                    .
            ?>
        </center>
    </body>
</html>
```

and you do the same with the second checkbox, check2:

```
<html>
    <head>
        <title>
            Reading data from checkboxes
        </title>
    </head>

    <body>
        <center>
            <h1>Reading data from checkboxes</h1>

            You checked
            <?
```

```
                    if (isset($_REQUEST["check1"]))
                        echo $_REQUEST["check1"], "<br>";
                    if (isset($_REQUEST["check2"]))
                        echo $_REQUEST["check2"], "<br>";
            ?>
        </center>
    </body>
</html>
```

The two checkboxes are shown in Figure 13.8. After the user selects a checkbox and clicks the Submit button, the results appear, as shown in Figure 13.9.

NOTE This example presents two mutually exclusive options: either the user wants fries or he doesn't. Although checkboxes work here, it'd be a better idea to use radio buttons, which are designed for mutually exclusive options and are discussed in the next section.

FIGURE 13.8

The checkboxes.html Web page

FIGURE 13.9

The checkboxes.php application at work

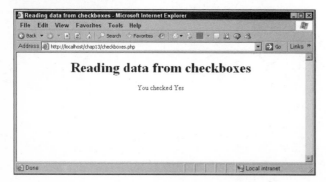

Working with radio buttons

You can easily convert the previous example to work with radio buttons instead of checkboxes. You start with the same basic HTML page as before, naming it radios.html:

```html
<html>
    <head>
        <title>Using radio buttons</title>
    </head>

    <body>
        <center>
        <h1>Using radio buttons</h1>
        <form method=post action="radios.php">
            Do you want fries with that?

            .

            .

            .
            <input type="submit" value="Submit">
        </form>
        </center>
    </body>
</html>
```

then you add the two radio buttons this way:

```html
<html>
    <head>
        <title>Using radio buttons</title>
    </head>

    <body>
        <center>
        <h1>Using radio buttons</h1>
        <form method=post action="radios.php">
            Do you want fries with that?
            <input name="radio1" type="radio" value="Yes">
            Yes
            <input name="radio1" Type="radio" value="No">
            No
            <br>
            <br>
            <input type="submit" value="Submit">
        </form>
        </center>
    </body>
</html>
```

NOTE This example gives the radio buttons the same name, `radio1`, which makes them operate together so that only one can be selected at a time.

To read which radio button was selected, you must first check whether either of the radio buttons were selected in radios.php:

```html
<html>
    <head>
        <title>
            Reading data from radio buttons
        </title>
    </head>

    <body>
        <center>
            <h1>Reading data from radio buttons</h1>

            You selected
            <?
                if (isset($_REQUEST["radio1"]))
                    .
                    .
                    .
            ?>
        </center>
    </body>
</html>
```

and if one of the radio buttons was indeed selected, you can display it like this:

```html
<html>
    <head>
        <title>
            Reading data from radio buttons
        </title>
    </head>

    <body>
        <center>
            <h1>Reading data from radio buttons</h1>

            You selected
            <?
                if (isset($_REQUEST["radio1"]))
                    echo $_REQUEST["radio1"], "<br>";
            ?>
        </center>
    </body>
</html>
```

You can see the two radio buttons in Figure 13.10.

FIGURE 13.10

The radios.html Web page

When the user selects a radio button and clicks the Submit button, you can see the results, as shown in Figure 13.11.

FIGURE 13.11

The radios.php application at work

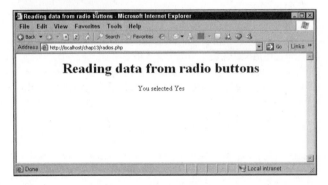

That's the basic HTML controls: text fields, checkboxes, and radio buttons. It's time to go to the next level of complexity, list boxes.

Working with list boxes

The HTML controls you've already seen — text fields, checkboxes, and radio buttons — can handle only single selections, but list boxes can handle multiple selections. How do you deal with multiple selections in PHP?

Here's an example, lists.html, which lets users select their favorite sandwich types. You start lists.html like this:

```
<html>
    <head>
        <title>Using Lists</title>
    </head>

    <body>
        <center>
            <h1>
              Using Lists
            </h1>

            <form method="get" action="lists.php">
                Select your favorite sandwiches(s):
                .
                .
                .
                <br>
                <br>
                <input type="submit" value="Submit">
            </form>
        </center>
    </body>
</html>
```

Then add the list box, which is an HTML <select> control, using the stand-alone attribute mul-tiple to let the user make multiple selections in this control. Note the name of the <select> control, sandwiches[], which tells PHP that this control can have multiple selections. Also note that this example uses the multiple attribute to allow the user to make multiple selections in the <select> control in the browser:

```
<html>
    <head>
        <title>Using Lists</title>
    </head>

    <body>
        <center>
            <h1>
              Using Lists
            </h1>

            <form method="get" action="lists.php">
                Select your favorite sandwiches(s):
                <br>
                <br>
```

```
                <select name="sandwiches[]" multiple>
                    .
                    .
                    .
                </select>
                <br>
                <br>
                <input type="submit" value="Submit">
            </form>
        </center>
    </body>
</html>
```

Then you can add the various items in the <select> control, using <option> elements:

```
<html>
    <head>
        <title>Using Lists</title>
    </head>

    <body>
        <center>
            <h1>
              Using Lists
            </h1>

            <form method="get" action="lists.php">
                Select your favorite sandwiches(s):
                <br>
                <br>
                <select name="sandwiches[]" multiple>
                    <option>Ham</option>
                    <option>Turkey</option>
                    <option>Salami</option>
                    <option>Chicken</option>
                </select>
                <br>
                <br>
                <input type="submit" value="Submit">
            </form>
        </center>
    </body>
</html>
```

And that completes the HTML for lists.html. The next step is to create the PHP that reads the selections in the list control.

Here's how you deal with a multiple-select control in PHP. You've named the control sand-wiches[], so you can't just recover selections like this: $_REQUEST["sandwiches"]. This expression actually returns an array of selected items, and you can recover the first selected item like this: $_REQUEST["sandwiches"][0]; the second like this: $_REQUEST["sand-wiches"][1]; and so on. To get all the selections, you can use a for or foreach loop.

Here's how the lists.php application, which reads the selections the user made, starts:

```
<html>
    <head>
        <title>Using Lists</title>
    </head>

    <body>
        <center>
            <h1>Retrieving Data From Lists</h1>
            You selected:
            <br>
            <?
                .
                .
                .
            ?>
        </center>
    </body>
</html>
```

To display the user's selections, you can use a foreach loop like this, which places the name of the current sandwich type in a variable named $sandwich:

```
<html>
    <head>
        <title>Using Lists</title>
    </head>

    <body>
        <center>
            <h1>Retrieving Data From Lists</h1>
            You selected:
            <br>
            <?
            foreach($_REQUEST["sandwiches"] as $sandwich){
                .
                .
                .
            }
            ?>
```

```
        </center>
    </body>
</html>
```

and you can display the current sandwich type this way:

```
<html>
    <head>
        <title>Using Lists</title>
    </head>

    <body>
        <center>
            <h1>Retrieving Data From Lists</h1>
            You selected:
            <br>
            <?
            foreach($_REQUEST["sandwiches"] as $sandwich){
                echo $sandwich, "<br>";
            }
            ?>
        </center>
    </body>
</html>
```

The lists.html Web page is shown in Figure 13.12, in which the user has made two selections.

FIGURE 13.12

The lists.html Web page

After users click the Submit button, the selections they've made are echoed in the list.php page, as shown in Figure 13.13.

FIGURE 13.13

The lists.php application at work

Working with password controls

Another common control in Web pages that work with PHP is the password control. This control lets the user enter a password, which you can check in PHP. The user sees only asterisks (*) in the password control, but you can read the text in a password control in PHP easily.

Here's an example, password.html, which lets the user enter a password in a password control:

```html
<html>
    <head>
        <title>
            Using Password Controls
        </title>
    </head>

    <body>

        <center>

            <h1>
                Using Password Controls
            </h1>

            <form method="post" action="password.php">
                Enter the password:

                <input name="password" type="password">

                <br>
                <br>

                <input type="submit" value="Submit">
```

```
                    </form>

                </center>

            </body>
        </html>
```

All you have to do is read the text from the password control in password.php:

```
<html>
    <head>
        <title>
            Reading data from password controls
        </title>
    </head>

    <body>
        <center>
            <h1>
                Reading data from password controls
            </h1>

            You entered:

            <?
                echo $_REQUEST["password"];
            ?>
        </center>
    </body>
</html>
```

The password.html Web page is shown in Figure 13.14, in which the user has entered a password.

The password.html Web page

Password.php reads the password and displays it on-screen, which is shown in Figure 13.15.

The password.php application at work

Working with Image Maps

You can also use image maps with PHP. An image map is a clickable image. With PHP you can recover the location at which the user clicked.

Here's an example, map.html, which connects to map.php:

```
<html>
    <head>
        <title>
            Using Image Maps
        </title>
    </head>

    <body>

        <center>

            <h1>
                Using Image Maps
            </h1>

            <form method="post" action="map.php">
            .
            .
            .
            </form>
```

```
            </center>

        </body>
    </html>
```

You create an image map with the `<input type="image">` element. This example uses a map image named map.jpg:

```
<html>
    <head>
        <title>
            Using Image Maps
        </title>
    </head>

    <body>

        <center>

            <h1>
                Using Image Maps
            </h1>

            <form method="post" action="map.php">
                Click anywhere in the image map.

                <br>
                <br>

                <input name="map" type="image" src="map.jpg">

            </form>

        </center>

    </body>
</html>
```

When the user clicks the image map, the mouse location is sent to map.php, which starts like this:

```
<html>
    <head>
        <title>Retrieving Image Map Data</title>
    </head>

    <body>

        <center>
```

```
                    <h1>Retrieving Image Map Data</h1>

                    <br>

                    You clicked the image map at location (
                        .
                        .
                        .
                        ).
                </center>

            </body>
        </html>
```

Now the question becomes: How do you read the x and y location of the mouse? The image map control is named map in this example, and in PHP, that means you can access the x coordinate of the mouse location as map_x, and the y coordinate as map_y (these coordinates are with respect to the map's upper left point) Here's what it looks like in code:

```
<html>
    <head>
        <title>Retrieving Image Map Data</title>
    </head>

    <body>

        <center>

            <h1>Retrieving Image Map Data</h1>

            <br>

            You clicked the image map at location (
            <?
                echo $_REQUEST["map_x"], ", ",
                    $_REQUEST["map_y"];
            ?>
            ).
        </center>

    </body>
</html>
```

Now to test it out. You can see the image map in map.html at work in Figure 13.16, where the user is about to click the image map.

FIGURE 13.16

The map.html Web page

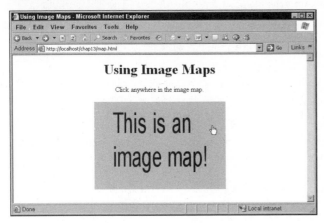

You can see the mouse location, given as (x, y), at which the user clicked the map reported by map.php, in Figure 13.17.

FIGURE 13.17

The map.php application at work

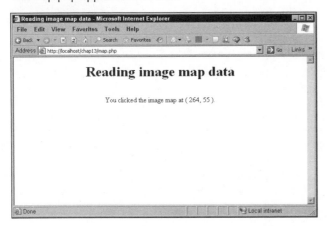

Uploading Files

It is common to upload files using PHP. After the file has been uploaded, its data is accessible to your PHP code.

For example, say that you wanted to upload a file named file.txt, which has these contents:

```
Now
is
the
time.
```

In order to make this work, you need a multi-part <form> element in the Web page that uploads this file, file.html. You create a multi-part form by setting the form's enctype attribute to multi-part/form-data:

```
<html>
    <head>
        <title>
            Uploading Files
        </title>
    </head>

    <body>
        <center>
            <h1>
                Uploading Files
            </h1>

            <form
                enctype="multipart/form-data"
                .
                .
                .
            </form>
        </center>
    </body>
</html>
```

then you set the action to the PHP application that will handle the uploaded file, and set the method to POST:

```
<html>
    <head>
        <title>
            Uploading Files
        </title>
    </head>
```

```
<body>
    <center>
        <h1>
            Uploading Files
        </h1>

        <form
            enctype="multipart/form-data"
            action="file.php" method="POST">
            .
            .
            .
        </form>
    </center>
</body>
</html>
```

Finally, you can add an HTML file-upload control, an `<input type="file">` element, like this (note that I named this control `userfile` in this example):

```
<html>
    <head>
        <title>
            Uploading Files
        </title>
    </head>

    <body>
        <center>
            <h1>
                Uploading Files
            </h1>

            <form
                enctype="multipart/form-data"
                action="file.php" method="POST">
                Upload this file: <input name="userfile"
                  type="file" />
                <br>
                <br>
                <input type="submit" value="Upload File" />
            </form>
        </center>
    </body>
</html>
```

Now you have to read the file's contents in PHP. You use the PHP array `$_FILES` to handle uploaded files. Following are the specific elements you can use and what they mean (note that the first index is the name of the file upload control, which is `userfile` here):

- `$_FILES['userfile']['name']`: The name of the file on the user's machine.

- `$_FILES['userfile']['type']`: The MIME type of the file. For example, this could be `image/gif` or `text/plain`.

- `$_FILES['userfile']['size']`: The size of the uploaded file, in bytes.

- `$_FILES['userfile']['tmp_name']`: The temporary file name of the file in which the uploaded file was stored on the server.

- `$_FILES['userfile']['error']`: The error code associated with this file upload.

To read the text from the file in file.php, start this way:

```
<html>
    <head>
        <title>Reading uploaded files</title>
    </head>

    <body>
        <center>
            <h1>Reading uploaded files</h1>
            <br>
            Here is what's in the file:
            <br>
            <br>
            <b>
                .
                .
                .
            </b>
        </center>

    </body>
</html>
```

When you upload a file, it's stored as a temporary file that you can access as `$_FILES['userfile']['tmp_name']`. Here's how you recover and display the contents of that file: you start by getting a file handle, which stands for the file, using the `fopen` function (file open — the `r` argument here means you want PHP to open the file for reading):

```
<html>
    <head>
        <title>Reading uploaded files</title>
    </head>

    <body>
        <center>
            <h1>Reading uploaded files</h1>
            <br>
            Here is what's in the file:
```

```
            <br>
            <br>
            <b>

            <?
                $handle = fopen($_FILES['userfile']['tmp_name'],
                 "r");
                    .
                    .
                    .
            ?>
            </b>
        </center>

    </body>
</html>
```

Now that you've got a file handle for the temporary file, you can loop over the lines in that file. You do that with a `while` loop, which keeps executing until you reach the end of the file — something you can test with the PHP function `feof`, which returns true when you're at the end of the file:

```
<html>
    <head>
        <title>Reading uploaded files</title>
    </head>

    <body>
        <center>
            <h1>Reading uploaded files</h1>
            <br>
            Here is what's in the file:
            <br>
            <br>
            <b>

            <?
                $handle = fopen($_FILES['userfile']['tmp_name'],
                 "r");

                while (!feof($handle)){
                    .
                    .
                    .
                }
            ?>
            </b>
        </center>

    </body>
</html>
```

You can read the current line of text with the PHP `fgets` (file get string) function, and echo that line to the browser like this:

```html
<html>
    <head>
        <title>Reading uploaded files</title>
    </head>

    <body>
        <center>
            <h1>Reading uploaded files</h1>
            <br>
            Here is what's in the file:
            <br>
            <br>
            <b>

            <?
                $handle = fopen($_FILES['userfile']['tmp_name'],
                    "r");

                while (!feof($handle)){
                    $text = fgets($handle);
                    echo $text, "<BR>";
                }
            ?>
            </b>
        </center>

    </body>
</html>
```

When you're done, you can close the file with the `fclose` function this way:

```html
<html>
    <head>
        <title>Reading uploaded files</title>
    </head>

    <body>
        <center>
            <h1>Reading uploaded files</h1>
            <br>
            Here is what's in the file:
            <br>
            <br>
            <b>
```

```
<?
    $handle = fopen($_FILES['userfile']['tmp_name'],
      "r");

    while (!feof($handle)){
        $text = fgets($handle);
        echo $text, "<BR>";
    }

    fclose($handle);
?>
</b>
</center>

</body>
</html>
```

That's all you need. The file.html Web page is shown in Figure 13.18, where you can use the Browse button to locate the file you want to upload.

FIGURE 13.18

The file.html Web page

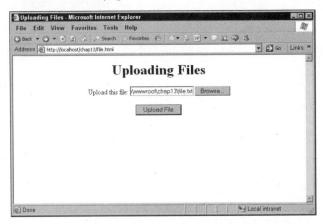

When the user clicks the Upload File button, the file uploads and its contents appear, as shown in Figure 13.19.

FIGURE 13.19

The file.php application at work

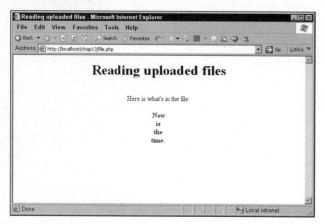

Summary

This chapter covered PHP functions and the use of HTML controls in PHP. You saw how to create functions, pass data to functions, return data from functions, and more — all the way up to using default values. You also saw how to work with HTML controls and PHP in this chapter, which covered all the standard controls from text fields to checkboxes and radio buttons.

Chapter 14

Handling User Input in PHP

This chapter contains two main parts: using the built-in support in PHP for handling user input (such as working with the powerful server variables that come with PHP and how to determine which browser the user has), and writing code to validate user input.

There's a lot of built-in support in PHP for handling user input, and you're going to see that support in this chapter. Validating user input is also an important part of online programming—checking to make sure what should be an integer really is an integer, or what should be a text string really is a text string, and so on.

Here's the way it'll work in outline. You call a function named `validate_data` to validate the user's input. If there are any errors, they're stored in an array named `$errors`. If that array contains any errors, you can call another function, `show_errors`, to display the errors, and then a `display_welcome` function to display the application's welcome page so that the user can start over. Otherwise, there are no errors and you can get on with the rest of the application:

```
validate_data();

if(count($errors) != 0){
    show_errors();
    display_welcome();
}
else {
    handle_data();
}
```

But more about this later in the chapter. The chapter starts by displaying all of the data in a form, a great topic for debugging and developing your PHP pages.

Displaying All the Data in a Form

You can use PHP to display all a form's data. Following is an example, formdata.html, which includes a form containing a text field:

```html
<html>
  <head>
    <title>Reading All Form Data</title>
  </head>

  <body>
    <center>
      <h1>Reading All Form Data</h1>

      <form method="post" action="formdata.php">

        Please enter your name:
        <input name="name" type="text">
        .
        .
        .
        <br>
        <br>

        <input type="submit" value="Submit">
      </form>
    </center>
  </body>
</html>
```

as well as a `<select>` control:

```html
<html>
  <head>
    <title>Reading All Form Data</title>
  </head>

  <body>
    <center>
      <h1>Reading All Form Data</h1>

      <form method="post" action="formdata.php">

        Please enter your name:
        <input name="name" type="text">

        <br>
        <br>
        Select your favorite sandwiches(s):
        <br>
        <br>
```

```
         <select name="sandwiches[]" multiple>
           <option>Ham</option>
           <option>Turkey</option>
           <option>Salami</option>
           <option>Chicken</option>
         </select>

         <br>
         <br>

         <input type="submit" value="Submit">
       </form>
     </center>
   </body>
 </html>
```

To read all the data in this form, you use a special form of the `foreach` loop in a new PHP page, formdata.php:

```
<html>
  <head>
    <title>
      Reading all form data
    </title>
  </head>

  <body>
    <center>
      <h1>Reading all form data</h1>

      Here is the form's data:
      <br>
         .
         .
         .
    </center>
  </body>
</html>
```

You can loop over an array with string indices rather than numeric indices, such as the `$_REQUEST` array, using a `foreach` loop like this: `foreach($_REQUEST as $index => $value)`, which places the index in `$index` and the associated value in `$value` each time through the loop:

```
<html>
  <head>
    <title>
      Reading all form data
    </title>
  </head>
```

```
<body>
  <center>
    <h1>Reading all form data</h1>

    Here is the form's data:
    <br>
    <?
      foreach($_REQUEST as $index => $value){
        .
        .
        .
      }
    ?>
    </center>
</body>
</html>
```

Note that some values in the $_REQUEST array can be arrays themselves (as with multiple-selection <select> controls), in which case you need another foreach loop:

```
<html>
  <head>
    <title>
      Reading all form data
    </title>
  </head>

  <body>
    <center>
      <h1>Reading all form data</h1>

      Here is the form's data:
      <br>
      <?
        foreach($_REQUEST as $index => $value){
          if(is_array($value)){
            foreach($value as $item){
              echo $index, " => ", $item, "<br>";
            }
          }
          .
          .
          .
        }
      ?>
      </center>
  </body>
</html>
```

Otherwise, you can just display the current $index/$value pair:

```html
<html>
  <head>
    <title>
      Reading all form data
    </title>
  </head>

  <body>
    <center>
      <h1>Reading all form data</h1>

      Here is the form's data:
      <br>
      <?
        foreach($_REQUEST as $index => $value){
          if(is_array($value)){
            foreach($value as $item){
              echo $index, " => ", $item, "<br>";
            }
          }
          else {
            echo $index, " => ", $value, "<br>";
          }
        }
      ?>
    </center>
  </body>
</html>
```

Formdata.html, crammed full of data, is illustrated in Figure 14.1.

FIGURE 14.1

The formdata.html page

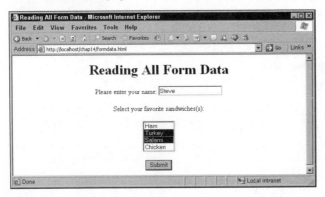

When you click the Submit button, all the form's data appears, as shown in Figure 14.2.

The formdata.php application

Looking at Server Variables

PHP has a special array built in called $_SERVER, which contains a lot of useful information, such as $_SERVER['PHP_SELF'], which holds the name of the current script, and $_SERVER['REQUEST_METHOD'], which holds the request method that was used (GET, POST, and so on).

The most useful server variables available in $_SERVER are listed in Table 14.1.

The Server Variables

Server Variable	Description
AUTH_TYPE	When operating under Apache and using authenticated HTTP this variable holds the authentication type.
DOCUMENT_ROOT	Contains the document root directory under which the script is executing.
GATEWAY_INTERFACE	Contains the revision of the CGI specification the server is using.
HTTP_ACCEPT	Contains the text in the Accept: header from the current request.
HTTP_ACCEPT_CHARSET	Contains the text in the Accept-Charset: header from the current request.
HTTP_ACCEPT_ENCODING	Contains the text in the Accept-Encoding: header from the current request.
HTTP_ACCEPT_LANGUAGE	Contains the text in the Accept-Language: header from the current request.

Server Variable	Description
`HTTP_CONNECTION`	Contains the text in the Connection: header from the current request.
`HTTP_HOST`	Contains the text in the Host: header from the current request.
`HTTP_REFERER`	Contains the address of the page (if any) that referred the user agent to the current page. Set by the browser.
`HTTP_USER_AGENT`	Contains the text in the User-Agent: header from the current request.
`PATH_TRANSLATED`	Specifies the file system-based path to the script.
`PHP_AUTH_PW`	When running under Apache using HTTP authentication, this variable holds the password the user provides.
`PHP_AUTH_USER`	When running under Apache using HTTP authentication, this variable holds the username the user provides.
`PHP_SELF`	Contains the filename of the currently executing script, relative to the document root.
`QUERY_STRING`	Contains the query string, if there was any.
`REMOTE_ADDR`	Contains the IP address from which the user is viewing the current page.
`REMOTE_HOST`	Contains the Host name from which the user is viewing the current page.
`REMOTE_PORT`	Contains the port being used on the user's machine to communicate with the Web server.
`REQUEST_METHOD`	Specifies which request method was used to access the page; such as `GET, HEAD, POST, PUT`.
`REQUEST_URI`	The URL that was given in order to access this page, such as /index.html.
`SCRIPT_FILENAME`	The absolute pathname of the currently executing script.
`SCRIPT_NAME`	Contains the current script's path. This is useful for pages that need to point to themselves.
`SERVER_ADMIN`	Contains the value given to the SERVER_ADMIN directive in the Web server configuration file.
`SERVER_NAME`	Contains the name of the server host under which the script is executing.
`SERVER_PORT`	Contains the port on the server machine being used by the Web server for communication.
`SERVER_PROTOCOL`	Contains the name and revision of the information protocol by which the page was requested.
`SERVER_SIGNATURE`	Contains the server version and virtual host name.
`SERVER_SOFTWARE`	Contains the server identification string.

Say you wanted to determine the type of browser the user has; you might want to use a <marquee> element, for example, which is supported only by Microsoft Internet Explorer. You could start with this page, browser.html:

```html
<html>
  <head>
    <title>
      Finding browser type
    </title>
  </head>

  <body>
    <center>

      <h1>Finding browser type</h1>

      <form method="post" action="browser.php">

        <input type="submit" value="Submit">

      </form>

    </center>
  </body>
</html>
```

In browser.php, you can check whether you're dealing with Internet Explorer by using the PHP strpos function to search $_SERVER["HTTP_USER_AGENT"] for the text MSIE, which that string contains if you're using Internet Explorer:

```html
<html>
  <head>
    <title>Finding browser type</title>
  </head>

  <body>
    <center>
      <h1>Finding browser type</h1>

      <br>
      <?
        if(strpos($_SERVER["HTTP_USER_AGENT"], "MSIE")){
          .
          .
          .
        }
      ?>

    </center>
  </body>
</html>
```

If you are using Internet Explorer, you can display a <marquee> element; otherwise, you might just display a message:

```
<html>
  <head>
    <title>Finding browser type</title>
  </head>

  <body>
    <center>
        <h1>Finding browser type</h1>

        <br>
        <?
          if(strpos($_SERVER["HTTP_USER_AGENT"], "MSIE")){
            echo("<marquee><h1>Welcome to my
              page!</h1></marquee>");
          }
          else {
              echo("<h1>Please get Internet Explorer</h1>");
          }
        ?>

    </center>
  </body>
</html>
```

The browser.html page is shown in Figure 14.3.

FIGURE 14.3

The browser.html page

When you click the Submit button, you see the marquee if you're using Internet Explorer, as shown in Figure 14.4.

FIGURE 14.4

The browser.php application

You can also group the data from a form into an array for easier handling in PHP, which is discussed in the next section.

Getting User Input in Arrays

It is easy to organize the data sent to you from an HTML form into a single array. For example, say you wanted to ask the user's name and age. You could store those items in an array named $data, as $data['name'] and $data['age']. You could create those array entries like this in formarray.html:

```
<html>
  <head>
    <title>
      Using form arrays
    </title>
  </head>

  <body>
    <center>
      <h1>
        Using form arrays
      </h1>

      <form method="post" action="formarray.php">

        Enter your name:
        <input name="data[name]" type="text">

        <br>
        <br>
```

```
        Enter your age:
        <input name="data[age]" type="text">

        <br>
        <br>
        <input type="submit" value="Submit">
      </form>

    </center>
  </body>
</html>
```

In formdata.php, you can get the $data array like this:

```
<html>
  <head>
    <title>
      Reading form data in arrays
    </title>
  </head>

  <body>
    <center>
      <h1>
        Reading form data in arrays
      </h1>

      Your name is
      <?
        $data = $_REQUEST['data'];
        .
        .
        .
      ?>

    </center>

  </body>
</html>
```

Now you can access the user's name as $data['name']. Here's how to do that and get the user's age as well, echoing them to the browser:

```
<html>
  <head>
    <title>
      Reading form data in arrays
    </title>
  </head>
```

```
<body>
  <center>
    <h1>
      Reading form data in arrays
    </h1>

    Your name is
    <?
      $data = $_REQUEST['data'];
      echo $data['name'], "<br>";
    ?>

    Your age is
    <?
      $data = $_REQUEST['data'];
      echo $data['age'], "<br>";
    ?>
  </center>

  </body>
</html>
```

You can see formarray.html, with the two text fields, in Figure 14.5.

The formarray.html page

In Figure 14.6, you can see the text recovered from those text fields in formarray.php, where the application has been able to read the text from the $data array.

FIGURE 14.6

The formarray.php application

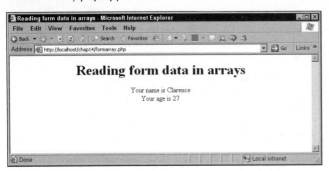

You've gotten some good expertise with PHP now, but each application so far has relied on two pages: an HTML starting page, and a PHP page that handles user input. Can't you do everything in a single PHP page?

Wrapping PHP Applications in a Single Page

Say, for example, you want to use a single page to both get the user's name and display that name. The text field in this example will be named "text," so you might start by checking whether there is some data waiting for you under the name "text" (that is, the user has already entered his or her name) in this Web page, single.php:

```
<html>
    <head>
        <title>
            Putting everything in a single page
        </title>
    </head>

    <body>
        <center>
            <h1>Putting everything in a single page</h1>
            <?
              if(isset($_REQUEST["name"])){
            ?>
              .
              .
              .
        </center>
```

563

```
        </body>
    </html>
```

If there is data waiting for you — that is, the user's name — you can display it like this:

```
<html>
    <head>
        <title>
            Putting everything in a single page
        </title>
    </head>

    <body>
        <center>
            <h1>Putting everything in a single page</h1>
            <?
              if(isset($_REQUEST["name"])){
            ?>
              Your name is
            <?
              echo $_REQUEST["name"];
              }
              .
              .
              .
            ?>
        </center>
    </body>
</html>
```

On the other hand, if there is no data waiting for you, you can display an HTML form to get the user's name:

```
<html>
    <head>
        <title>
            Putting everything in a single page
        </title>
    </head>

    <body>
        <center>
            <h1>Putting everything in a single page</h1>
            <?
              if(isset($_REQUEST["name"])){
            ?>
              Your name is
            <?
              echo $_REQUEST["name"];
              }
              else {
```

```
    ?>
       <form method="post" action="single.php">
          .
          .
          .
       </form>
    <?
       }
    ?>
       </center>
    </body>
</html>
```

The action of this form is set to send the user's name back to the same PHP page, single.php.

And you could add the text field to that form, as well as a prompt to the user and a Submit button:

```
<html>
    <head>
       <title>
          Putting everything in a single page
       </title>
    </head>

    <body>
       <center>
          <h1>Putting everything in a single page</h1>
          <?
             if(isset($_REQUEST["name"])){
          ?>
             Your name is
          <?
             echo $_REQUEST["name"];
             }
             else {
          ?>
             <form method="post" action="single.php">
                Enter your name:

                <input name="name" type="text">
                <br>
                <br>
                <input type="submit" value="Submit">
             </form>
          <?
             }
          ?>
          </center>
       </body>
</html>
```

This page displays a text field if users haven't already entered their name; if they have, it displays their name. You can see what this page, single.php, looks like in Figure 14.7, where it's asking for your name.

FIGURE 14.7

The single.php page asks for your name.

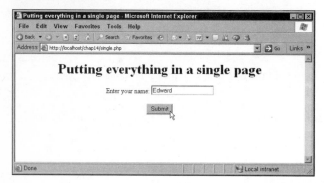

After entering a name and clicking the Submit button, the same page tells you what name you entered, as shown in Figure 14.8.

FIGURE 14.8

The single.php page displays your name.

There you have it, no HTML opening page needed — everything was done with PHP.

Using Hidden Controls to Check Whether a Page Has Been Seen Before

To check whether a page has been previously viewed, the example illustrated in the previous section can work, but it might not always give you correct results. For example, checking the data in a text field to see whether the user has seen the page already may work some of the time, but in some cases it may be a valid option to leave the text field blank.

To avoid using HTML controls that the user can work with to check whether that user has already seen the page, you can use hidden controls instead, which store hidden text in a page.

For example, you can modify the example, single.php, illustrated in the previous section, into single2.php, which looks and acts just the same as single.php, but uses a hidden control to determine whether the user has seen the page before. That means that you check the hidden control, which will be named `already_shown`, to see whether you should display the text field:

```
<html>
    <head>
        <title>
            Putting everything in a single page
        </title>
    </head>

    <body>
        <center>
            <h1>Putting everything in a single page</h1>
            <?
              if(isset($_REQUEST["already_shown"])){
            ?>
                .
                .
                .
            ?>
        </center>
    </body>
</html>
```

If you're supposed to show the text field, you can create and add the hidden control to the same form as the text field, placing the text `data` in the hidden control:

```
<html>
    <head>
        <title>
            Putting everything in a single page
        </title>
    </head>
```

```
<body>
    <center>
      <h1>Putting everything in a single page</h1>
      <?
        if(isset($_REQUEST["already_shown"])){
      ?>
        Your name is
      <?
        echo $_REQUEST["name"];
        }
        else {
      ?>
        <form method="post" action="single.php">
            Enter your name:

            <input name="name" type="text">
            <input name="already_shown" type="hidden"
              value="data">
            <br>
            <br>
            <input type="submit" value="Submit">
        </form>
      <?
        }
      ?>
    </center>
  </body>
</html>
```

This page, single2.php, works just as single.php did, but it has the advantage that the control you use to check whether the user has seen the page before is under your control, not the user's.

Validating User Input, Numbers, and Text

Validating user input is a big part of Web programming.

Validating user input

Following is an example showing how to validate user input; in this case, you can require the user to have entered some text in a text field. Everything starts with an array named $errors, which holds the validation error messages, if there are any:

```
<html>
  <head>
    <title>
      Validating user input
    </title>
  </head>
```

```
<body>
  <center>

    <h1>Validating user input</h1>
    <?
      $errors = array();
          .
          .
          .
    ?>

  </center>
  </body>
</html>
```

Next, you can check whether the user has already seen the Web page, in which case you're supposed to check the text he or she has entered. You can make that check by seeing whether the hidden control `already_shown` contains any data:

```
<html>
  <head>
    <title>
      Validating user input
    </title>
  </head>

  <body>
    <center>

      <h1>Validating user input</h1>
      <?
        $errors = array();

        if(isset($_REQUEST["already_shown"])){
            .
            .
            .
      ?>

    </center>
  </body>
</html>
```

If the user has already seen the page, there is, presumably, data waiting for you to check, so you can call a function named `validate_data`:

```
<html>
  <head>
    <title>
```

```
      Validating user input
   </title>
</head>

<body>
  <center>

    <h1>Validating user input</h1>
    <?
      $errors = array();

      if(isset($_REQUEST["already_shown"])){

        validate_data();
        .
        .
        .
        function validate_data()
        {
          .
          .
          .
        }
    ?>

  </center>
  </body>
</html>
```

You start the `validate_data` function with the line `global $errors`, which makes the global array `$errors` that you've created accessible inside that function — that's what you need to do in PHP to make global data available inside functions:

```
<html>
  <head>
    <title>
      Validating user input
    </title>
  </head>

<body>
  <center>

    <h1>Validating user input</h1>
    <?
      $errors = array();

      if(isset($_REQUEST["already_shown"])){
```

```
              validate_data();
              .
              .
              .
       function validate_data()
       {
         global $errors;
         .
         .
         .
       }
    ?>

    </center>
  </body>
</html>
```

Now you can check whether the text field is empty, and if it is, add an error message to the $errors array this way in validate_data:

```
<html>
  <head>
    <title>
      Validating user input
    </title>
  </head>

  <body>
    <center>

      <h1>Validating user input</h1>
      <?
        $errors = array();

        if(isset($_REQUEST["already_shown"])){

          .
          .
          .

        function validate_data()
        {
          global $errors;

          if($_REQUEST["name"] == "") {
            $errors[] = "<font color='red'>Enter your
              name</font>";
          }
        }
      ?>
```

```
      </center>
    </body>
  </html>
```

Having validated the user's input, you next check whether there were any errors, and if so, call a function named show_errors to display the errors, and then a function named display_welcome to display the starting page again so the user can start over. Otherwise, if the data the user entered was okay, you can call a function named handle_data to process the user-entered data:

```
<html>
  <head>
    <title>
      Validating user input
    </title>
  </head>

  <body>
    <center>

      <h1>Validating user input</h1>
      <?
        $errors = array();

        if(isset($_REQUEST["already_shown"])){

          validate_data();

          if(count($errors) != 0){
            show_errors();
            display_welcome();
          }
          else {
            handle_data();
          }
        }
        else {
         display_welcome();
        }

        function validate_data()
        {
          global $errors;

          if($_REQUEST["name"] == "") {
            $errors[] = "<font color='red'>Enter your
              name</font>";
          }
        }
        .
        .
        .
```

```
      ?>

   </center>
  </body>
 </html>
```

Next comes the show_errors function, which displays the errors in the $errors array by looping over them:

```
<html>
  <head>
    <title>
      Validating user input
    </title>
  </head>

  <body>
    <center>

      <h1>Validating user input</h1>
      <?
        $errors = array();

        if(isset($_REQUEST["already_shown"])){

          validate_data();

          if(count($errors) != 0){
            show_errors();
            display_welcome();
          }
          else {
            handle_data();
          }
        }
        else {
         display_welcome();
        }

          .
          .
          .
        function show_errors()
        {
          global $errors;

          foreach ($errors as $error){
            echo $error, "<br>";
          }
        }
```

```
            .
            .
            .
        ?>

    </center>
  </body>
</html>
```

The `handle_data` function, called if the user successfully entered the data, displays that data:

```
<html>
  <head>
    <title>
      Validating user input
    </title>
  </head>

  <body>
    <center>

      <h1>Validating user input</h1>
      <?
        $errors = array();

        if(isset($_REQUEST["already_shown"])){

          validate_data();

          if(count($errors) != 0){
            show_errors();
            display_welcome();
          }
          else {
            handle_data();
          }
        }
        else {
         display_welcome();
        }
        .

        .

        .

        function handle_data()
        {
          echo "Your name is ";
          echo $_REQUEST["name"];
        }
        .

        .

        .
```

```
       ?>

    </center>
   </body>
  </html>
```

Finally, the show_welcome function displays the Web page that asks the user for his or her name. Here's what the whole page looks like:

```
<html>
  <head>
    <title>
      Validating user input
    </title>
  </head>

  <body>
    <center>

      <h1>Validating user input</h1>
      <?
        $errors = array();

        if(isset($_REQUEST["already_shown"])){

          validate_data();

          if(count($errors) != 0){
            show_errors();
            display_welcome();
          }
          else {
            handle_data();
          }
        }
        else {
         display_welcome();
        }

        function validate_data()
        {
          global $errors;

          if($_REQUEST["name"] == "") {
            $errors[] = "<font color='red'>Enter your
              name</font>";
          }
        }

        function show_errors()
        {
```

```
        global $errors;

        foreach ($errors as $error){
          echo $error, "<br>";
        }
      }

      function handle_data()
      {
        echo "Your name is ";
        echo $_REQUEST["name"];
      }

      function display_welcome()
      {
        echo "<form method='post' action='validate.php'>";
        echo "Please enter your name";
        echo "<br>";
        echo "<input name='name' type='text'>";
        echo "<br>";
        echo "<br>";
        echo "<input type='submit' value='Submit'>";
        echo "<input type='hidden' name='already_shown' " ,
          "value='data'>";
        echo "</form>";
      }
    ?>

  </center>
  </body>
</html>
```

You can see the welcome page in Figure 14.9.

FIGURE 14.9
_____

The validation.php page asks for your name.

If you don't enter a name and click Submit, an error message appears, as shown in Figure 14.10.

The validation.php page displays an error.

If you do enter a name and click Submit, the page echoes the name, as shown in Figure 14.11.

The validation.php page displays your name.

Validating numbers

You've seen the validation framework you can use. Now how about putting it to work in requiring that the user enter particular kinds of data? For example, you could insist that the user enter an integer in a new page, validateinteger.php. This page starts by checking whether the user has already seen the page with the hidden control `already_shown`:

```
<html>
  <head>
    <title>Validating integers</title>
  </head>

  <body>
    <center>

      <h1>Validating integers</h1>

      <?
        if(isset($_REQUEST["already_shown"])){
          .
          .
          .
```

Then, if the user has already seen the page, you validate the data, and if there were any errors, you display them and then display the welcome page so the user can re-enter the data:

```
<html>
  <head>
    <title>Validating integers</title>
  </head>

  <body>
    <center>

      <h1>Validating integers</h1>

      <?
        $errors = array();

        if(isset($_REQUEST["already_shown"])){
          validate_data();

          if(count($errors) != 0){
            show_errors();
            display_welcome();
          }
          .
          .
          .
```

If there were no errors, you can handle the data the user entered:

```
<html>
  <head>
    <title>Validating integers</title>
  </head>
```

```
<body>
  <center>

    <h1>Validating integers</h1>

    <?
      $errors = array();

      if(isset($_REQUEST["already_shown"])){
        validate_data();

        if(count($errors) != 0){
          show_errors();
          display_welcome();
        }
        else {
          handle_data();
        }
      }
      else {
        display_welcome();
      }
        .
        .
        .
```

In the validate_data function, you can check whether the number the user entered — stored under the parameter number — is an integer. One way of doing that is by converting the data passed to you from the user into an integer using the PHP intval function. Then you can convert the integer back to a string using the strval function and compare that string to the original string from the $_REQUEST array.

For example, if the user entered "12.16", converting that to an integer would give you 12, and converting it back to a string would give you "12" — clearly not the same as "12.16".

You can compare the two strings with the PHP strcmp function like this:

```
function validate_data()
{
  if(strcmp($_REQUEST["number"],
    strval(intval($_REQUEST["number"])))) {
      .
       .
        .
  }
}
```

If there was an error, you can add it to the global $errors array:

```
function validate_data()
{
  global $errors;

  if(strcmp($_REQUEST["number"],
    strval(intval($_REQUEST["number"]))))  {
    $errors[] = "<font color='red'>Please enter an
    integer</font>";
  }
}
```

and display that error in the show_errors function:

```
function show_errors()
{
  global $errors;

  foreach ($errors as $err){
    echo $err, "<BR>";
  }
}
```

The show_errors function, called when the user has not yet seen the page or has made an error, displays a prompt asking the user to enter an integer and a text field:

```
function display_welcome()
{
  echo "<form method='post'
    action='validateinteger.php'>";
  echo "Please enter an integer.";
  echo "<br>";
  echo "<input name='number' type='text'>";
  echo "<br>";
  echo "<br>";
      .
      .
      .
}
```

Then you add a Submit button and the hidden control named already_shown:

```
function display_welcome()
{
  echo "<form method='post'
    action='validateinteger.php'>";
```

```
        echo "Please enter an integer.";
        echo "<br>";
        echo "<input name='number' type='text'>";
        echo "<br>";
        echo "<br>";

        echo "<input type='submit' value='Submit'>";
        echo "<input type='hidden' name='already_shown' " .
          "value='data'>";
        echo "</form>";
    }
```

If everything goes well, you can display in the handle_data function the integer the user entered:

```
        function handle_data()
        {
          echo "You entered ";
          echo $_REQUEST["number"];
        }
```

The validateinteger.php page is shown in Figure 14.12, where it's asking the user to enter an integer. As you can see, however, the user has entered the text hello? instead of an integer.

FIGURE 14.12

The validateinteger.php page asks for an integer.

When the user clicks the Submit button, the page displays an error, as shown in Figure 14.13.

FIGURE 14.13

The validateinteger.php page displays an error.

If you do enter an integer, the page displays the integer entered, as shown in Figure 14.14.

FIGURE 14.14

The validateinteger.php page displays your integer.

That validates integers. How about validating some text?

Validating text

Say that you wanted to make sure that the text the user enters follows a certain pattern, which you might check with regular expressions. Could you do that with PHP? You sure can, as you're going to see in a new page, validatetext.php.

PHP includes a function named `preg_match` whose job it is to look for regular expression matches. The validatetext.php example starts as usual — by validating the text the user sent, displaying errors if there were any, and displaying the welcome page as needed:

```html
<html>
  <head>
    <title>Validating text</title>
  </head>

  <body>
    <center>
      <h1>Validating text</h1>

      <?
        $errors = array();

        if(isset($_REQUEST["already_shown"])){

          validate_data();

          if(count($errors) != 0){
            show_errors();
            display_welcome();
          }
          else {
            handle_data();
          }
        }
        else {
          display_welcome();
        }
        .
        .
        .
```

The `show_errors` and `handle_data` functions work as usual:

```php
function show_errors()
{
  global $errors;

  foreach ($errors as $err){
    echo $err, "<br>";
  }
}
```

```
function handle_data()
{
  echo "You entered ";
  echo $_REQUEST["text"];
}
```

In the `display_welcome` function, you can ask the user to enter text containing the word `hello` like this:

```
function display_welcome()
{
  echo "<form method='post'
    action='validatetext.php'>";
  echo "Please enter text including 'hello'";
  echo "<br>";
  echo "<input name='text' type='text'>";
  echo "<br>";
  echo "<br>";
  echo "<input type='submit' value='Submit'>";
  echo "<input type='hidden' name='already_shown'
  value='hidden_data'>";
  echo "</form>";
}
```

Then, in the `validate_data` function, you can check whether the text entered included the text `hello`:

```
function validate_data()
{
  if(!preg_match('/hello/i', $_REQUEST["text"])){
    .
    .
    .
  }
}
```

and if the text did not include the string `hello`, you can add an entry to the `$errors` array:

```
function validate_data()
{
  global $errors;

  if(!preg_match('/hello/i', $_REQUEST["text"])){
  $errors[] = "<font color='red'>Please include
    'hello' " . "in your text.</font>";
  }
}
```

You can see this page, validatetext.php, in Figure 14.15. Note that the user has entered text that does not include the string `hello` in this case.

FIGURE 14.15

The validatetext.php page asks for text.

When you click the Submit button, an error message appears, as shown in Figure 14.16.

FIGURE 14.16

The validatetext.php page displays an error.

On the other hand, if your text does contain the string `hello`, the page displays your text, as shown in Figure 14.17.

FIGURE 14.17

The validatetext.php page displays your text.

Handling HTML Sent by the User

Here's another validation consideration: what if users include HTML in the data they're sending you, and you don't want them to do so? Such HTML can be malicious, as when it includes JavaScript to redirect the browser to other pages.

There are ways of stripping out unwanted HTML. For example, say that you ask the user for their comments on your Web page, and you want to display those comments — but not any HTML? You could do that in a new page, handlehtml.php. Everything is as you'd expect in this page, except when it is time to display the user's comments: at that point you can use the PHP `strip_tags` function to strip any HTML out, as shown here:

```
<html>
  <head>
    <title>Handling HTML</title>
  </head>

  <body>
    <center>
      <h1>Handling HTML</h1>
      <?
        $errors = array();
        if(isset($_REQUEST["already_shown"])){
          validate_data();
          if(count($errors) != 0){
            show_errors();
            display_welcome();
          }
          else {
            handle_data();
```

```
      }
    }
    else {
      display_welcome();
    }

    function validate_data()
    {
      global $errors;
      if($_REQUEST["comments"] == "") {
        $errors[] = "<font color='red'>Please enter your " .
          "comments</font>";
      }
    }

    function show_errors()
    {
      global $errors;

      foreach ($errors as $err){
        echo $err, "<br>";
      }
    }

    function handle_data()
    {
      echo "Your comments were ";
      $text = strip_tags($_REQUEST["comments"]);
      echo $text;
    }

    function display_welcome()
    {
      echo "<form method='post' action='handlehtml.php'>";
      echo "Enter your comments<br>";
      echo "<input name='comments' type='text'>";
      echo "<br><br>";
      echo "<input type='submit' value='Submit'>";
      echo "<input type='hidden' name='already_shown'
        value='hidden_data'>";
      echo "</form>";
    }
  ?>
  </center>
  </body>
</html>
```

Now users can enter HTML in their comments, as shown in Figure 14.18.

FIGURE 14.18

The handlehtml.php page accepts HTML.

And that HTML is stripped out in the final result, as shown in Figure 14.19.

FIGURE 14.19

The HTML has been stripped out.

In fact, there's another way of handling HTML text: you can use the `htmlentities` function, which renders HTML harmless. This function "escapes" HTML by converting sensitive characters such as < into <, > into >, and so on, which means that browsers will display characters such as < as <, not as the beginning of a tag.

Presently, the `handle_data` function looks like this:

```
function handle_data()
{
    echo "Your comments were ";
```

```
        $text = strip_tags($_REQUEST["comments"]);
        echo $text;
    }
```

You can use the `htmlentities` function in place of `strip_tags` like this:

```
    function handle_data()
    {
      echo "Your comments were ";
      $text = htmlentities($_REQUEST["comments"]);
      echo $text;
    }
```

Now when the user enters HTML, that HTML will be escaped and displayed out in the final result, as shown in Figure 14.20.

FIGURE 14.20

The HTML has been escaped.

Summary

This chapter gave you a guided tour of some new PHP techniques to handle user input and to validate user data. You saw how to display all the data in a form, how to read user input in custom arrays, and how to create single-page PHP applications. You also saw how to validate user input, including how to insist that data be present, or that it be a number or text.

Chapter 15

Ajax and Security

This chapter discusses Ajax and security, a particularly important topic because Ajax involves communicating with server-side programming, which lays it open for abuse. This chapter contains a discussion of security issues with Ajax, and what to do about them.

Protecting Against Malicious Users

Unfortunately, malicious users are out there, ranging from the casual to the very serious. If your Ajax application involves credit card use or other sensitive data, that application may be open to abuse.

The problem with Ajax applications is that the way you deal with the server is by using JavaScript, and that JavaScript is visible to all. Even placing that JavaScript in a .js file on the server offers no relief — those .js files are easily downloaded. Even if you create the JavaScript on the fly, as with a PHP script, it's still easily accessible by the user, who has only to view the page source.

That means you have to assume that, security-wise, users have access to your JavaScript, which means they can figure out how your application deals with the server. In simple terms, for example, you might access this URL on the server to record a user's score:

```
scorekeeper.cgi?score=21
```

Not much is stopping users from figuring this out and uploading fictitious scores, like this:

```
scorekeeper.cgi?score=2221
```

All of which means that you have to be very careful with the data sent to you from the browser—and never execute that data as code, which is one of the primary doors through which hackers enter.

 Not even appending a checksum, uniquely generated by some algorithm based on the score you've come up with, will help:

```
scorekeeper.cgi?score=2221;checksum=3949503
```

Appending a checksum doesn't help because the code you use to generate that checksum is in your application's JavaScript, in plain view, and easily copied and used.

The JavaScript in an Ajax application is always very public. For that reason, a primary rule of Ajax security is to keep the business rules code (that is, the in-depth, core code) on the server. You should never expose more code than necessary.

 **You can also try to make your JavaScript unreadable, a process known as *obfuscation*, which replaces characters with character codes, and so on. There's a limit to the obfuscation you can perform, of course, because the browser needs to read your JavaScript, but if you're interested, take a look at `www.semdesigns.com/Products/Obfuscators/ECMAScriptObfuscationExample.html`.**

JavaScript insertion

Another malicious technique is JavaScript insertion, where users insert JavaScript into their response, and when you display that response in the browser, that JavaScript executes. For example, Yahoo! Mail was hijacked by the Yamanner worm recently, which exploited the software's ability to include JavaScript in e-mail.

Following is an example, comments.html, which accepts and displays user comments and displays. To work through the examples in this chapter you need access to a Web server, because security solutions are often implemented on the server. A good Web server for this purpose is the Apache Tomcat server because it handles security in both a very powerful and easily generalized way.

 You can pick up a copy of Tomcat, which is a Java-based server, for free at `http://tomcat.apache.org/`.

Here's what comments.html looks like; it's just a straightforward Ajax application that reads and displays user comments:

```
<html>
  <head>
    <title>Display your comments</title>

    <script language = "javascript">
```

```
      var XMLHttpRequestObject = false;

      if (window.XMLHttpRequest) {
        XMLHttpRequestObject = new XMLHttpRequest();
      } else if (window.ActiveXObject) {
        XMLHttpRequestObject = new
        ActiveXObject("Microsoft.XMLHTTP");
      }

      function getData(dataSource, divID)
      {
        if(XMLHttpRequestObject) {
          var obj = document.getElementById(divID);
          XMLHttpRequestObject.open("GET", dataSource +
            "?text=" + escape(document.getElementById
              ("text").value));
          XMLHttpRequestObject.onreadystatechange = function()
          {
            if (XMLHttpRequestObject.readyState == 4 &&
              XMLHttpRequestObject.status == 200) {
                obj.innerHTML =
                  XMLHttpRequestObject.responseText;
            }
          }

          XMLHttpRequestObject.send(null);
        }
      }
    </script>
  </head>

<body>

  <H1>Display your comments</H1>

  <form>
    Enter your comments:
    <input type = "text" name="text">
    <br>
    <br>
    <input type = "button" value = "Display your comments"
      onclick = "getData('comments.jsp', 'targetDiv')">
  </form>

  <div id="targetDiv">
    <p>The fetched data will go here.</p>
  </div>

  </body>
</html>
```

The Tomcat Web server supports Java code in JavaServer Pages (JSP) and Java servlets. JSPs are easier to work with, and use this markup to enclose Java code:

```
<%
    .
    .
    .
%>
```

You can get the comments the user typed, sent to the server under the parameter name `text`, like this:

```
<%
    String text = request.getParameter("text");
        .
        .
        .
%>
```

That creates a Java String object containing the user's comments. To display those comments, you can use the JSP out object's `println` method, which sends text back to the browser:

```
<%
    String text = request.getParameter("text");

    out.println("You typed ");

    out.println(text);
%>
```

This works fine, but it does allow the user to insert HTML, as shown in Figure 15.1, where the user has entered some comments.

FIGURE 15.1

The comments.html page

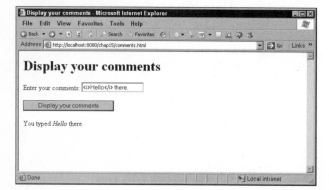

In this case, the user entered the relatively harmless HTML "<i>Hello</i> there." But what if he or she had entered HTML that included JavaScript code, such as this JavaScript, designed to redirect the browser to a malicious site:

```
<script>location.href=www.malicious-site.com</script>
```

That's an example of JavaScript insertion, and one way to fight against it is to convert sensitive HTML characters like < and > into their escaped and harmless equivalents, < and >. Escaping HTML characters like this renders HTML elements harmless.

You can perform this kind of conversion in Java using the String class's replaceAll method, like this:

```
<%
    String text = request.getParameter("text");

    text = text.replaceAll("<", "&lt;");

    text = text.replaceAll(">", "&gt;");

    out.println("You typed ");

    out.println(text);
%>
```

Now when you click the Display your comments button, you see the HTML itself, as shown in Figure 15.2.

FIGURE 15.2

Blocking HTML

The previous example demonstrated a way of defusing JavaScript insertion. Another type of malicious insertion you should guard against is SQL insertion. Believe it or not, some Ajax applications send SQL directly to the server, and, of course, it's easy to modify that SQL maliciously. The main solution for SQL insertion, like the solution for so many Ajax security issues, is to leave the business rules, including SQL generation, on the server.

You should carefully check all data coming from the browser; one way hackers break or control applications is by feeding them invalid data.

For example, take a look at array.html, which asks users what element they want to fetch from an array on the server. Here's what the code looks like:

```
<html>
  <head>
    <title>Display an array element</title>

    <script language = "javascript">
      var XMLHttpRequestObject = false;

      if (window.XMLHttpRequest) {
        XMLHttpRequestObject = new XMLHttpRequest();
      } else if (window.ActiveXObject) {
        XMLHttpRequestObject = new
          ActiveXObject("Microsoft.XMLHTTP");
      }

      function getData(dataSource, divID)
      {
        if(XMLHttpRequestObject) {
          var obj = document.getElementById(divID);
          XMLHttpRequestObject.open("GET", dataSource +
            "?index=" + escape(document.getElementById
              ("index").value));

          XMLHttpRequestObject.onreadystatechange = function()
          {
            if (XMLHttpRequestObject.readyState == 4 &&
              XMLHttpRequestObject.status == 200) {
                obj.innerHTML =
                  XMLHttpRequestObject.responseText;
            }
          }

          XMLHttpRequestObject.send(null);
        }
      }
    </script>
  </head>
```

```
<body>

  <H1>Display an array element</H1>

  <form>
    Which array element do you want?
    <input type = "text" name="index">
    <br>
    <br>
    <input type = "button" value = "Display the element"
      onclick = "getData('array.jsp', 'targetDiv')">
  </form>

  <div id="targetDiv">
    <p>The fetched data will go here.</p>
  </div>

  </body>
</html>
```

In the server-side script, array.jsp, you can create an array of strings like this in Java:

```
<%
  String[] array = {"tic", "tac", "toe"};
      .
      .
      .
%>
```

That creates the array ["tic", "tac", "toe"]. You can get the index of the element the user requested using the expression request.getParameter("index"), but that returns the index as a string. To convert that string to an integer array index you can work with, you can use the Integer class's parseInt method this way:

```
<%
  String[] array = {"tic", "tac", "toe"};

  int index = Integer.parseInt(request.getParameter("index"));
      .
      .
      .
%>
```

Now you can display the requested array element in the browser like this:

```
<%
  String[] array = {"tic", "tac", "toe"};

  int index = Integer.parseInt(request.getParameter("index"));
```

```
        out.println("The array element is ");

        out.println(array[index]);
    %>
```

That works fine as long as you enter an array index from 0 to 2, as shown in Figure 15.3.

FIGURE 15.3

The array.html page

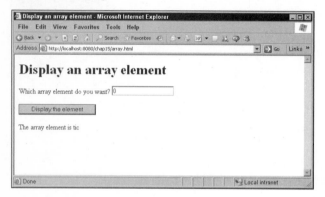

But if you enter an illegal value, you won't see any response from the server because an error occurred and the out.println statements weren't reached, as shown in Figure 15.4.

FIGURE 15.4

An error in the array.html application

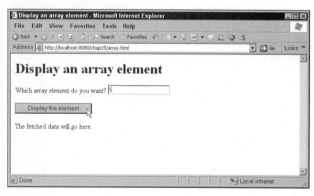

This kind of error is easily overlooked, but it's the source of some major problems. Until Microsoft patched the problem, Windows suffered from numerous array-overrun vulnerabilities where hackers used illegal array indices to overwrite legitimate Windows code.

The solution here is simply to do some bounds checking to make sure the index is legal for your array. Here's how you can check whether you're not dealing with a legal index and send an error message back to the browser:

```
<%
   String[] array = {"tic", "tac", "toe"};

   int index = Integer.parseInt(request.getParameter("index"));

   if(index < 0 || index > array.length){

     out.println("Sorry, that array element is out of bounds.");

   }
     .
     .
     .
%>
```

If the array index is legitimate, you can send back the array element, as shown here:

```
<%
   String[] array = {"tic", "tac", "toe"};

   int index = Integer.parseInt(request.getParameter("index"));

   if(index < 0 || index > array.length){

     out.println("Sorry, that array element is out of bounds.");

   }
   else {

     out.println("The array element is ");

     out.println(array[index]);
   }
%>
```

Now if you enter an illegal value, you'll get an error message, as shown in Figure 15.5.

FIGURE 15.5

FIGURE 15.5

Handling an error in the array.html application

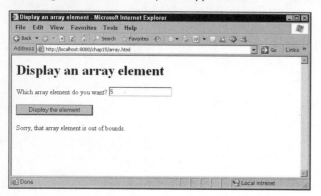

Looking at the Security Issues with Proxy Servers

As Ajax programmers, you first have to face the situation that browsers are attempting to protect their users from *us*. The biggest issue you have to face as an Ajax programmer is that browsers won't let you access domains other than your own. This is actually fairly unintelligently implemented, so you have to be careful. The browser does the checking solely based on domain name, which leads to some odd results. For example, you can access other accounts on the same domain, even if they're not yours, and the browser will be fine with that. On the other hand, if you substitute the IP address for the actual domain name, the browser won't let you access data that way.

Take a look at Table 15.1, which summarizes the rules a browser uses to determine whether you can access a server-side resource.

TABLE 15.1

Using Proxies on the Server

`www.ajaxsuperduperco.com/a www.ajaxsuperduperco.com/b`	OK
`www.ajaxsuperduperco.com:8080/a www.ajaxsuperduperco.com/b`	Not OK
`http://www.ajaxsuperduperco.com/a https://www.ajaxsuperduperco.com/b`	Not OK
`www.ajaxsuperduperco.com/a www.203.217.555.201/b`	Not OK
`www.ajaxsuperduperco.com/a dave.ajaxsuperduperco.com/b`	Not OK
`www.ajaxsuperduperco.com/sam/a www.ajaxsuperduperco.com/frank/b`	OK

Although you might look at Table 15.1 with annoyance because it puts restrictions on your code, it also helps preserve your Ajax applications from being hijacked by users who do some cross-server scripting, placing their URL in your applications. However, as you can also see from Table 15.1, the scheme is far from perfect. For example, the recent "Samy" worm used cross-server scripting to exploit the popular Web site MySpace, adding a million "friends" to the author's friends list.

There's not very much you can do about cross-server scripting because the hacker operates on client code. Probably the best thing you can do is restrict the users to those that have passwords, and log their activities if security becomes an issue.

Handling Security in Ajax Applications

So how do you handle security in Ajax applications? The general answer is that, if security is important, you ask the user to log in, giving username and password, and record both. You'll see a number of ways of doing that in Ajax applications in the following sections.

Easy password protection

The easiest way to implement password protection is to do it yourself, asking the user for a password and then checking it yourself on the server. Because the user can't download server-side scripts, your password-checking code is safe.

Here's an example, checker.html. This example displays a password field, asking the user for his or her password:

```
<body>

    <H1>Easy password protection</H1>

    <form>
      Enter your password:
      <input type = "password" name="text">
      <br>
      <br>
      <input type = "button" value = "Display Message"
        onclick = "getData('checker.jsp', 'targetDiv')">
    </form>

    <div id="targetDiv">
      <p>The fetched data will go here.</p>
    </div>

</body>
```

This example also displays a button, and when the user clicks that button, the JavaScript passes the password to the server-side script, a JavaServer Page, checker.jsp. Everything starts as usual, by getting an XMLHttpRequest object:

```
<html>
  <head>
    <title>Easy password protection</title>

    <script language = "javascript">
      var XMLHttpRequestObject = false;

      if (window.XMLHttpRequest) {
        XMLHttpRequestObject = new XMLHttpRequest();
      } else if (window.ActiveXObject) {
        XMLHttpRequestObject = new
          ActiveXObject("Microsoft.XMLHTTP");
      }

      function getData(dataSource, divID)
      {
        if(XMLHttpRequestObject) {
          var obj = document.getElementById(divID);
          .
          .
          .
        }

        XMLHttpRequestObject.send(null);
      }
    </script>
  </head>
```

The password is added to the end of the URL sent to the server like this:

```
<html>
  <head>
    <title>Easy password protection</title>

    <script language = "javascript">
      var XMLHttpRequestObject = false;

      if (window.XMLHttpRequest) {
        XMLHttpRequestObject = new XMLHttpRequest();
      } else if (window.ActiveXObject) {
        XMLHttpRequestObject = new
          ActiveXObject("Microsoft.XMLHTTP");
      }

      function getData(dataSource, divID)
      {
        if(XMLHttpRequestObject) {
          var obj = document.getElementById(divID);
          XMLHttpRequestObject.open("GET", dataSource
            + "?password=" +
```

```
              document.getElementById("text").value);

          XMLHttpRequestObject.onreadystatechange = function()
          {
            if (XMLHttpRequestObject.readyState == 4 &&
              XMLHttpRequestObject.status == 200) {
                obj.innerHTML =
                  XMLHttpRequestObject.responseText;
            }
          }

          XMLHttpRequestObject.send(null);
        }
      }
    </script>
  </head>
    .
    .
    .
  </html>
```

In the server-side script, checker.jsp, you need a way of recovering the password. You can recover the password, encoded under the parameter name `password`, using the expression `request.getParameter("password")` in JSP. And you can check whether that password equals the one you're expecting — say, opensesame — this way:

```
<%
  if(request.getParameter("password").equals("opensesame")){
        .
        .
        .
  }
%>
```

If the password matches, you can send back a confirming message using Ajax and the JSP `out.println` method, which sends text back to the browser:

```
<%
  if(request.getParameter("password").equals("opensesame")){
    out.println("You're in.");
  }
%>
```

Otherwise, you can let the user know he or she has not been accepted:

```
<%
  if(request.getParameter("password").equals("opensesame")){
    out.println("You're in.");
  }
  else {
    out.println("Wrong password");
```

```
    }
%>
```

You can see checker.html at work in Figure 15.6, where the user has entered the password.

FIGURE 15.6

The checker.html page

When you click the Display Message button, Ajax fetches the data, as shown in Figure 15.7.

FIGURE 15.7

The checker.html application lets you in.

On the other hand, if you enter the incorrect password, you're not admitted, as shown in Figure 15.8.

FIGURE 15.8

The checker.html application says no way.

That's one way to support passwords in Ajax applications. But there are many other ways as well.

Server-side user authentication

Another way to support passwords in Ajax applications is by implementing server-side user authentication, so that users are asked for their names and passwords when they interact with your site. The normal way of doing this is to have the server ask the browser to display that familiar login dialog that asks the user for their username and password.

That login dialog normally appears when you first navigate to a page, but it turns out that accessing a site using an XMLHttpRequest object can also trigger the dialog. To see this in action, you must first create a login name and password for a fictitious user, and you do that in Tomcat by editing the file tomcat-users.xml, which is in the Tomcat conf directory.

Presently, this file looks like this:

```
<!--
  NOTE:  By default, no user is included in the "manager" role
required
  to operate the "/manager" web application.  If you wish to use
this app,
  you must define such a user - the username and password are
arbitrary.
-->
<tomcat-users>
  <user name="tomcat" password="tomcat" roles="tomcat" />
  <user name="role1"  password="tomcat" roles="role1"  />
  <user name="both"   password="tomcat" roles="tomcat,role1" />
</tomcat-users>
```

Here, users have a name and a password, and a *role*. A role corresponds to a region on the server that users are admitted to when they log on, and you'll see how to set a role in the next page or two. To create new users, you might give them the password `tomcat` and the role `ajax`:

```
<!--
  NOTE:  By default, no user is included in the "manager" role
required
  to operate the "/manager" web application.  If you wish to use
this app,
  you must define such a user - the username and password are
arbitrary.
-->
<tomcat-users>
  <user name="tomcat" password="tomcat" roles="tomcat" />
  <user name="role1" password="tomcat" roles="role1" />
  <user name="steve"  password="tomcat" roles="ajax"  />
  <user name="both"   password="tomcat" roles="tomcat,role1" />
</tomcat-users>
```

Next, you have to restrict the data you want to download using Ajax to that new ajax role. You do that in a file called web.xml, which configures Java-enabled Web applications. You can divide up Web applications by folder, such as placing this chapter's examples in a folder named chap15:

```
tomcat
  |
  |__chap15
```

Inside the chap15 folder, you need a directory named WEB-INF, which contains configuration data, and which has two required subfolders named classes and lib (which must be present, even if they're empty):

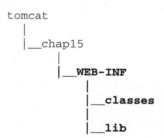

```
tomcat
  |
  |__chap15
        |
        |__WEB-INF
              |
              |__classes
              |
              |__lib
```

The web.xml file goes in the WEB-INF directory, and you can use this file to specify which parts of your Web application are parts of a particular role. For example, say that you have a file named data.txt that you want to restrict access to, in a folder named data:

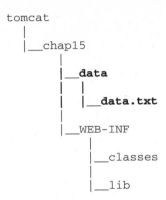

```
tomcat
  |
  |__chap15
       |
       |__data
       |   |
       |   |__data.txt
       |
       |__WEB-INF
            |
            |__classes
            |
            |__lib
```

How could you restrict access to that file to users logged in under the ajax role? You can do that in web.xml. Here's how web.xml starts, with a `<web-app>` element that configures your Web application:

```
<?xml version="1.0" encoding="ISO-8859-1"?>

<!DOCTYPE web-app
    PUBLIC "-//Sun Microsystems, Inc.//DTD Web Application
      2.3//EN"
    "http://java.sun.com/j2ee/dtds/web-app_2_3.dtd">

<web-app>
         .
         .
         .
</web-app>
```

To specify that you want to configure the role for the data folder's contents, you can use a `<security-constraint>` element, containing a `<web-resource>` element like this:

```
<?xml version="1.0" encoding="ISO-8859-1"?>

<!DOCTYPE web-app
    PUBLIC "-//Sun Microsystems, Inc.//DTD Web Application
      2.3//EN"
    "http://java.sun.com/j2ee/dtds/web-app_2_3.dtd">

<web-app>

  <security-constraint>
    <web-resource-collection>
      <web-resource-name>Secure Area</web-resource-name>
         .
         .
         .
```

```
      </web-resource-collection>
                .
                .
                .
      </security-constraint>

   </web-app>
```

and you can specify the data folder's contents with a `<url-pattern>` element:

```
<?xml version="1.0" encoding="ISO-8859-1"?>

<!DOCTYPE web-app
    PUBLIC "-//Sun Microsystems, Inc.//DTD Web Application
       2.3//EN"
    "http://java.sun.com/j2ee/dtds/web-app_2_3.dtd">

<web-app>

   <security-constraint>
     <web-resource-collection>
       <web-resource-name>Secure Area</web-resource-name>
       <url-pattern>/data/*</url-pattern>
     </web-resource-collection>
            .
            .
            .
   </security-constraint>

   <login-config>
     <auth-method>BASIC</auth-method>
     <realm-name>Ajax Area</realm-name>
   </login-config>

</web-app>
```

Finally, you can specify the role that the contents of the data folder are in, the ajax role, with an `<auth-constraint>` element:

```
<?xml version="1.0" encoding="ISO-8859-1"?>

<!DOCTYPE web-app
    PUBLIC "-//Sun Microsystems, Inc.//DTD Web Application
       2.3//EN"
    "http://java.sun.com/j2ee/dtds/web-app_2_3.dtd">

<web-app>

   <security-constraint>
     <web-resource-collection>
       <web-resource-name>Secure Area</web-resource-name>
```

```
          <url-pattern>/data/*</url-pattern>
        </web-resource-collection>
        <auth-constraint>
          <role-name>ajax</role-name>
        </auth-constraint>
      </security-constraint>
              .
              .
              .
    </web-app>
```

Next, you indicate that you want the browser to ask for the username and password using a dialog box — a process known as "basic" authentication — with a <login-config> element:

```
    <?xml version="1.0" encoding="ISO-8859-1"?>

    <!DOCTYPE web-app
        PUBLIC "-//Sun Microsystems, Inc.//DTD Web Application
        2.3//EN"
        "http://java.sun.com/j2ee/dtds/web-app_2_3.dtd">

    <web-app>

      <security-constraint>
        <web-resource-collection>
          <web-resource-name>Secure Area</web-resource-name>
          <url-pattern>/data/*</url-pattern>
        </web-resource-collection>
        <auth-constraint>
          <role-name>ajax</role-name>
        </auth-constraint>
      </security-constraint>

      <login-config>
              .
              .
              .
      </login-config>

    </web-app>
```

Inside the <login-config> element, you specify that you want to use basic authentication this way:

```
    <?xml version="1.0" encoding="ISO-8859-1"?>

    <!DOCTYPE web-app
        PUBLIC "-//Sun Microsystems, Inc.//DTD Web Application
        2.3//EN"
        "http://java.sun.com/j2ee/dtds/web-app_2_3.dtd">
```

```
<web-app>

  <security-constraint>
    <web-resource-collection>
      <web-resource-name>Secure Area</web-resource-name>
      <url-pattern>/data/*</url-pattern>
    </web-resource-collection>
    <auth-constraint>
      <role-name>ajax</role-name>
    </auth-constraint>
  </security-constraint>

  <login-config>
    <auth-method>BASIC</auth-method>
    <realm-name>Ajax Area</realm-name>
  </login-config>

</web-app>
```

That sets up the login username and password. Now even if you use an XMLHttpRequest object to access data.txt in the data folder, you'll still be asked for your username and password.

You can see this at work in a new example, password.html, which starts simply by displaying a button, letting the user fetch data using Ajax:

```
<body>

  <H1>Ajax security at work</H1>

  <form>
    <input type = "button" value = "Display Message"
      onclick = "getData('data/data.txt', 'targetDiv')">
  </form>

  <div id="targetDiv">
    <p>The fetched data will go here.</p>
  </div>

</body>
```

When the user clicks the button, the getData function connects to the server and attempts to download data/data.txt:

```
<html>
  <head>
    <title>Ajax security at work</title>

    <script language = "javascript">
      var XMLHttpRequestObject = false;
```

```
    if (window.XMLHttpRequest) {
      XMLHttpRequestObject = new XMLHttpRequest();
    } else if (window.ActiveXObject) {
      XMLHttpRequestObject = new
        ActiveXObject("Microsoft.XMLHTTP");
    }

    function getData(dataSource, divID)
    {
      if(XMLHttpRequestObject) {
        var obj = document.getElementById(divID);
        XMLHttpRequestObject.open("GET", dataSource);

        XMLHttpRequestObject.onreadystatechange = function()
        {
          if (XMLHttpRequestObject.readyState == 4 &&
            XMLHttpRequestObject.status == 200) {
              obj.innerHTML =
                XMLHttpRequestObject.responseText;
          }
        }

        XMLHttpRequestObject.send(null);
      }
    }
  </script>
</head>

</html>
```

However, as you know, this is not going to be successful until the user enters his or her username and password. You can see password.html in Figure 15.9.

FIGURE 15.9

The password.html page

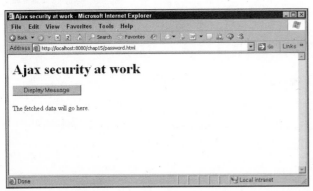

611

When you click the Display Message button, the login dialog box appears, as shown in Figure 15.10.

FIGURE 15.10

The password.html application's login dialog box

After entering the username and password into the login dialog box, you gain access to the Ajax data, which is downloaded as shown in Figure 15.11.

FIGURE 15.11

Downloading password protected Ajax data

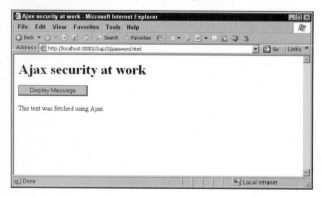

As you can see, access can be password protected, even if you're dealing with XMLHttpRequest objects.

You can do more with Java-enabled Web applications as well: you can track who is logging in, as shown in a new example, password2.html, which calls a JSP page, user.jsp, to report the current user's username:

```
<html>
  <head>
    <title>Ajax security at work</title>

    <script language = "javascript">
      var XMLHttpRequestObject = false;

      if (window.XMLHttpRequest) {
        XMLHttpRequestObject = new XMLHttpRequest();
      } else if (window.ActiveXObject) {
        XMLHttpRequestObject = new
          ActiveXObject("Microsoft.XMLHTTP");
      }

      function getData(dataSource, divID)
      {
        if(XMLHttpRequestObject) {
          var obj = document.getElementById(divID);
          XMLHttpRequestObject.open("GET", dataSource);

          XMLHttpRequestObject.onreadystatechange = function()
          {
            if (XMLHttpRequestObject.readyState == 4 &&
              XMLHttpRequestObject.status == 200) {
                obj.innerHTML =
                  XMLHttpRequestObject.responseText;
            }
          }

          XMLHttpRequestObject.send(null);
        }
      }
    </script>
  </head>

  <body>

    <H1>Ajax security at work</H1>

    <form>
      <input type = "button" value = "Display Message"
        onclick = "getData('data/user.jsp', 'targetDiv')">
    </form>

    <div id="targetDiv">
      <p>The fetched data will go here.</p>
    </div>

  </body>
</html>
```

The user.jsp page starts by including the java.security package to give the code in the page access to the methods it will need to recover the user's username:

```
<%@ page import="java.security.*" %>
        .
        .
        .
```

Then the code in user.jsp uses the `request` object's `getUserPrincipal` method to get data about the user in a `Principal` object this way:

```
<%@ page import="java.security.*" %>

<%
    Principal principal = request.getUserPrincipal();
        .
        .
        .
%>
```

Now the code can use the Principal object's `getName` method to return the user's username to the browser:

```
<%@ page import="java.security.*" %>

<%
    Principal principal = request.getUserPrincipal();

    out.println("Your username is: " + principal.getName());
%>
```

That's all it takes. Now when a user logs in, you can echo his or her username back to the browser, as shown in Figure 15.12.

FIGURE 15.12

Echoing the user's username

In fact, you can avoid the whole login dialog completely when using the XMLHttpRequest object. Here's what that object's open method looks like in general:

```
open("method", "URL"[, asyncFlag[, "userName"[, "password"]]])
```

Here are what these various parameters mean — note in particular that you can specify the login username and password:

- method: This is the HTTP method used to open the connection, such as GET, POST, PUT, HEAD, or PROPFIND.
- URL: This is the requested URL.
- asyncFlag: A Boolean value indicating whether the call is asynchronous. The default is true.
- userName: The username.
- password: The password.

Here's an example, password3.html, which starts by asking the user for his or her username:

```
<body>

    <H1>Ajax security at work</H1>

    <form>
      Enter your username:
      <input type = "text" name = "username">
      <br>
      <br>
        .
        .
        .
      <input type = "button" value = "Display Message"
        onclick = "getData('data/user.jsp', 'targetDiv')">
    </form>

    <div id="targetDiv">
      <p>The fetched data will go here.</p>
    </div>

</body>
```

and then asks for the user's password in a password control:

```
<body>

    <H1>Ajax security at work</H1>

    <form>
```

```
      Enter your username:
      <input type = "text" name = "username">
      <br>
      <br>
      Enter your password:
      <input type = "password" name = "password">
      <br>
      <br>
      <input type = "button" value = "Display Message"
        onclick = "getData('data/user.jsp', 'targetDiv')">
    </form>

    <div id="targetDiv">
      <p>The fetched data will go here.</p>
    </div>

  </body>
```

Then the code creates an XMLHttpRequest object in the usual way:

```
<html>
  <head>
    <title>Ajax security at work</title>

    <script language = "javascript">
      var XMLHttpRequestObject = false;

      if (window.XMLHttpRequest) {
        XMLHttpRequestObject = new XMLHttpRequest();
      } else if (window.ActiveXObject) {
        XMLHttpRequestObject = new
          ActiveXObject("Microsoft.XMLHTTP");
      }

      function getData(dataSource, divID)
      {
        .
        .
        .
        }
      }
    </script>
  </head>
```

In the getData function, you can configure the open method call by including the user's username and password like this:

```
<html>
  <head>
    <title>Ajax security at work</title>
```

```
<script language = "javascript">
  var XMLHttpRequestObject = false;

  if (window.XMLHttpRequest) {
    XMLHttpRequestObject = new XMLHttpRequest();
  } else if (window.ActiveXObject) {
    XMLHttpRequestObject = new
      ActiveXObject("Microsoft.XMLHTTP");
  }

  function getData(dataSource, divID)
  {
    if(XMLHttpRequestObject) {
      var obj = document.getElementById(divID);
      XMLHttpRequestObject.open("GET", dataSource, true,
      document.getElementById("username").value,
      document.getElementById("password").value);
        .
        .
        .
    }
  }
</script>
</head>
```

Having configured the XMLHttpRequest object to include the username and password, you can set up the Ajax callback and send a value of null to the server:

```
<html>
  <head>
    <title>Ajax security at work</title>

    <script language = "javascript">
      var XMLHttpRequestObject = false;

      if (window.XMLHttpRequest) {
        XMLHttpRequestObject = new XMLHttpRequest();
      } else if (window.ActiveXObject) {
        XMLHttpRequestObject = new
          ActiveXObject("Microsoft.XMLHTTP");
      }

      function getData(dataSource, divID)
      {
        if(XMLHttpRequestObject) {
          var obj = document.getElementById(divID);
          XMLHttpRequestObject.open("GET", dataSource, true,
          document.getElementById("username").value,
          document.getElementById("password").value);
```

```
XMLHttpRequestObject.onreadystatechange = function()
{
  if (XMLHttpRequestObject.readyState == 4 &&
     XMLHttpRequestObject.status == 200) {
       obj.innerHTML =
         XMLHttpRequestObject.responseText;
  }
}

XMLHttpRequestObject.send(null);
    }
  }
 </script>
</head>
```

On the server side, you can use the same password-protected JSP as before, user.jsp:

```
<%@ page import="java.security.*" %>

<%
  Principal principal = request.getUserPrincipal();

  out.println("Your username is: " + principal.getName());
%>
```

Now users can enter their username and password in your application, as shown in Figure 15.13.

FIGURE 15.13

Entering the user's username and password

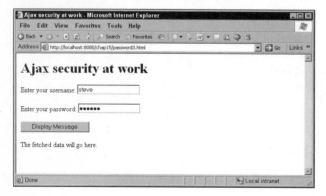

And this login process works, as you see in Figure 15.14, where the user's username is echoed to the browser.

FIGURE 15.14

Echoing the user's username

Using usernames and passwords is one of the strongest techniques you have of ensuring security in Ajax applications, especially if you record who's logging in when. But who's going to protect the password? When your users log in over the Internet, their usernames and passwords are freely accessible, and so security could be a serious concern.

To protect username and password, you can use a secure protocol, such as HTTPS. HTTPS involves some extra setup, however, and is not available on all Web servers. An easily implemented alternative is to use public and private keys, which are discussed in the next section.

Protecting Passwords Using Public and Private Keys

Passwords are freely viewable over the Internet, and can be skimmed easily. Public/private key encryption helps out by creating an encrypted code at the time the user wants to log in.

Two keys are involved in this process. In this discussion, the password is the private key and the public key is a random string sent from the server. Here's how it works: Say the password is opensesame. When the user logs in, that password could simply be sent, using the GET or POST method, to the server, which exposes it publicly. That means malicious persons could skim it and use it to log in themselves.

However, you could change that exposure cleverly at login time by having the code on the server send a random text string, say, abcd. Then you combine the password and the random string to get, for example, opensesameabcd. Next, you can use an algorithm, such as the MD5 algorithm, to encrypt the resulting string, opensesameabcd. That gives you a string of bytes that you can send to the server.

That string of bytes may be skimmed as well, but it won't do malicious people much good because the next time they try to log in, the random string will have changed, so the string of bytes they've skimmed won't work.

It's not a perfect scheme — especially if the malicious entity can read the random string public key and figure out how it's used — but it does provide some measure of protection.

Here's an example showing how to work with MD5-encoded text strings in the browser and server. This example takes a simple text string — test — and encodes it, sending it up to the server. The server also encodes the same text string and compares the two strings; if they match, a confirming message is sent to the browser.

There are various MD5 encryption tools available on the Internet. This example uses the JavaScript library, webtoolkit.md5.js (available at www.webtoolkit.info/javascript/utils/md5/index.html), which it includes in the page md5.html:

```
<html>
  <head>
    <title>Using public and private keys</title>

    <script src="webtoolkit.md5.js"></script>
        .
        .
        .
```

Then md5.html displays a button with the caption Check encrypted text:

```
<body>

    <H1>Using public and private keys</H1>

    <form>
      <input type = "button" value = "Check encrypted text"
        .
        .
        .
    </form>

    <div id="targetDiv">
      <p>The fetched message will appear here.</p>
    </div>

  </body>
</html>
```

and that button is connected to a function named getData, which calls the JSP document md5.jsp on the server:

```
    <body>

      <H1>Using public and private keys</H1>

      <form>
        <input type = "button" value = "Check encrypted text"
          onclick = "getData('md5.jsp', 'targetDiv')">
      </form>

      <div id="targetDiv">
        <p>The fetched message will appear here.</p>
      </div>

    </body>
  </html>
```

The JavaScript part of the page starts by using the webtoolkit.md5.js library's MD5 method to encode the text string test into a string of 32 bytes, md5String:

```
  <html>
    <head>
      <title>Using public and private keys</title>

      <script src="webtoolkit.md5.js"></script>

      <script language = "javascript">
        var md5String = MD5("test");

             .
             .
             .
```

Then the code creates the XMLHttpRequest object it uses to communicate with the server:

```
  <html>
    <head>
      <title>Using public and private keys</title>

      <script src="webtoolkit.md5.js"></script>

      <script language = "javascript">
        var md5String = MD5("test");

        var XMLHttpRequestObject = false;

        if (window.XMLHttpRequest) {
          XMLHttpRequestObject = new XMLHttpRequest();
        } else if (window.ActiveXObject) {
          XMLHttpRequestObject = new
            ActiveXObject("Microsoft.XMLHTTP");
        }
```

.
.
.

The getData function, called when the button is clicked, sets up the call to md5.jsp, using the POST method:

```
function getData(dataSource, divID)
{
  if(XMLHttpRequestObject) {
    var obj = document.getElementById(divID);
    XMLHttpRequestObject.open("POST", dataSource);
    XMLHttpRequestObject.setRequestHeader('Content-Type',
      'application/x-www-form-urlencoded');

    XMLHttpRequestObject.onreadystatechange = function()
    {
      if (XMLHttpRequestObject.readyState == 4 &&
        XMLHttpRequestObject.status == 200) {
          obj.innerHTML =
            XMLHttpRequestObject.responseText;
      }
    }
      .
      .
      .
  }
}
```

The data to send is the MD5-encoded string, which the getData function sends under the parameter name data:

```
function getData(dataSource, divID)
{
  if(XMLHttpRequestObject) {
    var obj = document.getElementById(divID);
    XMLHttpRequestObject.open("POST", dataSource);
    XMLHttpRequestObject.setRequestHeader('Content-Type',
      'application/x-www-form-urlencoded');

    XMLHttpRequestObject.onreadystatechange = function()
    {
      if (XMLHttpRequestObject.readyState == 4 &&
        XMLHttpRequestObject.status == 200) {
          obj.innerHTML =
            XMLHttpRequestObject.responseText;
      }
    }
```

```
          XMLHttpRequestObject.send("data=" + md5String);
      }
  }
```

Now it's up to the JSP page, md5.jsp, to encrypt the text string `test` and compare it to what's been sent from the browser. In Java, you can use the `java.security.MessageDigest` package to encrypt MD5 strings, so you first start by importing that package to make it available to your code:

```
<%@ page import="java.security.MessageDigest" %>

<html>
  <head>
    <title>
      Using public and private keys
    </title>
  </head>
        .
        .
        .
```

Next, you recover the MD5 string the browser sent, storing it in a variable named `browserString` like this:

```
<%@ page import="java.security.MessageDigest" %>

<html>
  <head>
    <title>
      Using public and private keys
    </title>
  </head>

  <body>

    <%
       String browserString = request.getParameter("data");
        .
        .
        .
```

Now it's time to encode the text `test`, which you start by getting a `MessageDigest` object — you enclose this code in a Java `try` block, which is used to contain sensitive code that could cause problems:

```
    <%
       String browserString = request.getParameter("data");

       try
       {
```

623

```
        MessageDigest md = MessageDigest.getInstance("MD5");
           .
           .
           .
    }
       .
       .
       .
```

You can encode the string `test` into an MD5 string using the `MessageDigest` object's `digest` method. To do that, you need to convert the string `test` into an array of bytes, which you can do with the Java String class's `getBytes` method this way:

```
<%
  String browserString = request.getParameter("data");

  byte[] bytes = {0, 0, 0};

  try
  {
    MessageDigest md = MessageDigest.getInstance("MD5");

    bytes = md.digest("test".getBytes());
  }
     .
     .
     .
```

If there was an error, you can handle it with a `catch` block, which follows the `try` block and displays an error message like this:

```
  String browserString = request.getParameter("data");

  String serverString = new String("");

  byte[] bytes = {0, 0, 0};

  try
  {
    MessageDigest md = MessageDigest.getInstance("MD5");

    bytes = md.digest("test".getBytes());
  }

  catch(Exception ex)
  {
    out.println("Error.");
  }
     .
     .
     .
```

That stores the MD5 string as an array of bytes. Now you've got to compare those bytes against the string of bytes sent to you from the browser. For example, the text sent to you from the browser might look like this: 09F8E3..., where you have byte values that have been converted to hexadecimal, then to strings, and concatenated together. On the server, you have the bytes 09, F8, E3, and so on, in an array of *numerical*, not string, bytes.

One way of comparing these two sets of data is to convert the array of bytes into a string like the one sent from the browser. To do that, you might start by creating such a string, serverString, like this, where you loop over all the bytes in the byte array:

```
<%
    String browserString = request.getParameter("data");

    String serverString = new String("");

    byte[] bytes = {0, 0, 0};

    try
    {
        MessageDigest md = MessageDigest.getInstance("MD5");

        bytes = md.digest("test".getBytes());
    }

    catch(Exception ex)
    {
        out.println("Error.");
    }

    for (int loopIndex = 0; loopIndex < bytes.length;
        loopIndex++){
        .
        .
        .
    }
        .
        .
        .
```

Converting an array of bytes to a string of hexadecimal entries takes some work in Java. You can start by getting the current byte from the byte array and converting it into an Integer object:

```
<%
    String browserString = request.getParameter("data");

    String serverString = new String("");

    byte[] bytes = {0, 0, 0};

    try
    {
```

```
    MessageDigest md = MessageDigest.getInstance("MD5");

    bytes = md.digest("test".getBytes());
  }

  catch(Exception ex)
  {
    out.println("Error.");
  }

  for (int loopIndex = 0; loopIndex < bytes.length;
    loopIndex++){
    byte b  = bytes[loopIndex];

    Integer i = new Integer(b);
      .
      .
      .

  }
      .
      .
      .
```

What does that buy you? The Integer class has a handy method named toHexString that converts an integer into a hexadecimal string, so here's how you convert the current byte into hex string representation (for example, the numeric byte 4D will be converted into the text 4D):

```
  <%
    String browserString = request.getParameter("data");
      .
      .
    for (int loopIndex = 0; loopIndex < bytes.length;
      loopIndex++){
      byte b  = bytes[loopIndex];

      Integer i = new Integer(b);

      String s = Integer.toHexString(i.intValue());
        .
        .
        .
    }
        .
        .
```

You have to be a little careful here because each byte must make up two characters in the serverString variable, and the current byte might be 9 or less — which means its string would only be one character (for example, 9 would be translated into 9, not 09). To get around that, you add a leading 0 if needed:

```
<%
  String browserString = request.getParameter("data");
    .
    .
    .
  for (int loopIndex = 0; loopIndex < bytes.length;
    loopIndex++){
    byte b  = bytes[loopIndex];

    Integer i = new Integer(b);

    String s = Integer.toHexString(i.intValue());

    if(java.lang.Math.abs(i.intValue()) < 10){
      s = "0" + s;
    }
    .
    .
    .
  }
    .
    .
    .
```

In fact, there's something else to be careful about: if the current byte holds a value greater than 7F, it'll be treated as a negative value by the toHexString, which means that the string returned by that method will end up containing six leading hex F digits — for example, E8 would be converted to the string FFFFFFE8, following the standard binary representation for negative numbers. To fix that, you can strip off the leading hex F digits this way:

```
<%
  String browserString = request.getParameter("data");
    .
    .
    .
  for (int loopIndex = 0; loopIndex < bytes.length;
    loopIndex++){
    byte b  = bytes[loopIndex];

    Integer i = new Integer(b);

    String s = Integer.toHexString(i.intValue());

    if(java.lang.Math.abs(i.intValue()) < 10){
      s = "0" + s;
    }

    if(s.indexOf("ffffff") >= 0){
      s = s.substring(6);
    }
```

```
        .
        .
        .
    }
        .
        .
        .
```

You can then append the current byte's string representation to the `serverString` variable, finishing the `for` loop. Then you check whether the resulting string, `serverString`, matches the `browserString` variable, using the Java String class's `equals` method:

```
String browserString = request.getParameter("data");
    .
    .
    .
for (int loopIndex = 0; loopIndex < bytes.length;
  loopIndex++){
  byte b  = bytes[loopIndex];

  Integer i = new Integer(b);

  String s = Integer.toHexString(i.intValue());

  if(java.lang.Math.abs(i.intValue()) < 10){
    s = "0" + s;
  }

  if(s.indexOf("ffffff") >= 0){
    s = s.substring(6);
  }

  serverString += s;
}


if(browserString.equals(serverString)){
    .
    .
    .
}
```

If the browser string matches the server string, you can display the confirming text `You're in` in the browser; otherwise, you can display an error:

```
String browserString = request.getParameter("data");
    .
    .
    .
```

```
for (int loopIndex = 0; loopIndex < bytes.length;
  loopIndex++){
  byte b  = bytes[loopIndex];

  Integer i = new Integer(b);

  String s = Integer.toHexString(i.intValue());

  if(java.lang.Math.abs(i.intValue()) < 10){
    s = "0" + s;
  }

  if(s.indexOf("ffffff") >= 0){
    s = s.substring(6);
  }

  serverString += s;
}


if(browserString.equals(serverString)){
  out.println("You're in.");
}
else {
  out.println("No go.");
}
```

Now md5.html in the browser will encrypt the string test and send it to the server, which will check to see whether that string matches the MD5 encryption of test as it should.

You can see md5.html at work in Figure 15.15. When the user clicks the Check encrypted text button, this page MD5-encrypts test and sends it to the JSP md5.jsp.

The md5.html page

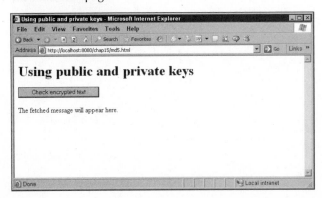

After the encrypted string is sent to md5.jsp, that JSP returns the text `You're in`, as shown in Figure 15.16.

FIGURE 15.16

The two MD5 strings agree.

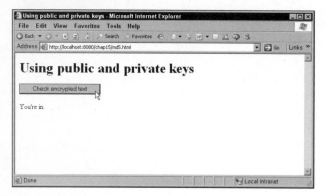

This example demonstrates a way to send MD5 data between browser and server. In practice, you use this technique to handle passwords. The server sends a random string to the browser, which combines that string with the password, encrypts it, and sends the result back to the server for checking—which means that the naked password is never sent over the Internet.

Summary

This chapter discussed Ajax and security, including how to handle malicious users and withstand JavaScript and SQL injection. You saw how to implement password protection, both in your code and in the server. You also saw how to send the username and password to the server using the `XMLHttpRequest` object, as well as using public/private key encryption to protect passwords.

Chapter 16

Filters, MVC, and Ajax

This chapter covers some advanced Ajax techniques: using filters and model-view-controller (MVC) architecture.

You can use filters with Ajax to restrict access to resources on the server. Filters can get control of the user's request before that request is passed on to the Web resource the user is trying to get to; so you can use filters for password checking, user logging, even restricting access to Web resources based on the time of day.

The MVC architecture is designed to be used as your Web applications become larger and larger. This architecture provides a way of dividing up your application into distinct parts, following the divide-and-conquer strategy. By separating your Web application into well-defined parts, you can make it easier to maintain and debug.

Restricting Access with Filters

Filters give you control both before and after a user accesses a Web resource on Java-enabled servers. Usually, you get a direct connection between the browser and a Web resource such as an HTML page, Java servlet, or JSP page:

```
 --------------           --------------
|              |         |  Web         |
|              |-------->|  resource    |
|    browser   |         |  (HTML page, |
|              |<--------|  servlet,    |
|              |         |  JSP, etc.)  |
 --------------           --------------
```

However, filters you install get control before and after the Web resource gets a chance to respond:

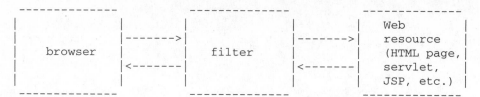

That makes filters very useful in restricting access to Web resources in Ajax applications. Here's an example, password.html, which restricts access based on a password. This application starts by displaying a password field and asking users to enter their password — note that the button passes the name of the JSP page to call, password.jsp, to the `getData` function:

```
<body>

    <H1>Using a filter for authentication</H1>

    <form>
      Enter your password:
      <input type = "password" name="password">
      <br>
      <br>
      <input type = "button" value = "Get the message"
        onclick = "getData('password.jsp', 'targetDiv')">
    </form>

    <div id="targetDiv">
      <p>The fetched message will appear here.</p>
    </div>

</body>
```

The `getData` function uses the POST method to access password.jsp, sending the password to the server as the parameter named `password`:

```
<html>
  <head>
    <title>Using a filter for authentication</title>

    <script language = "javascript">
      var XMLHttpRequestObject = false;

      if (window.XMLHttpRequest) {
        XMLHttpRequestObject = new XMLHttpRequest();
      } else if (window.ActiveXObject) {
        XMLHttpRequestObject = new
          ActiveXObject("Microsoft.XMLHTTP");
      }
```

```
function getData(dataSource, divID)
{
  if(XMLHttpRequestObject) {
    var obj = document.getElementById(divID);
    XMLHttpRequestObject.open("POST", dataSource);
    XMLHttpRequestObject.setRequestHeader('Content-Type',
      'application/x-www-form-urlencoded');

    XMLHttpRequestObject.onreadystatechange = function()
    {
      if (XMLHttpRequestObject.readyState == 4 &&
        XMLHttpRequestObject.status == 200) {
          obj.innerHTML =
            XMLHttpRequestObject.responseText;
      }
    }

    XMLHttpRequestObject.send("password=" +
      document.getElementById("password").value);
  }
}
</script>
</head>
```

The password.jsp file is a simple one, simply displaying a welcoming message:

```
<html>
    <head>
        <title>Filters And User Authentication</title>
    </head>

    <body>
        Congratulations, you're in!
        <br>
    </body>
</html>
```

If this were all there were to the story, users would get in every time, no matter what password they entered:

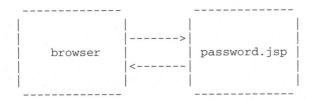

This is where the filter, named PasswordFilter here, comes in, because it's inserted between the browser and password.jsp:

The PasswordFilter filter is supported with a Java file, PasswordFilter.java, which starts by importing the Java packages it's going to use:

```
import java.io.*;
import javax.servlet.*;
import javax.servlet.http.*;
        .
        .
        .
```

To create a Java-enabled filter class, you must implement the Filter interface:

```
import java.io.*;
import javax.servlet.*;
import javax.servlet.http.*;

public final class PasswordFilter implements Filter
{
        .
        .
        .
}
```

To implement the Filter interface, you must add three methods: doFilter, init, and destroy:

```
import java.io.*;
import javax.servlet.*;
import javax.servlet.http.*;

public final class PasswordFilter implements Filter
{
  public void doFilter(ServletRequest request, ServletResponse
    response,
    FilterChain chain)
    throws IOException, ServletException
  {
        .
        .
        .
```

```
    }

    public void destroy()
    {
    }

    public void init(FilterConfig filterConfig)
    {
    }
}
```

In the doFilter method, you need to check the password before letting the user access password.jsp. You can get the password this way, using the request object's getParameter method:

```
import java.io.*;
import javax.servlet.*;
import javax.servlet.http.*;

public final class PasswordFilter implements Filter
{
  public void doFilter(ServletRequest request, ServletResponse
    response,
    FilterChain chain)
    throws IOException, ServletException
  {
    String password = ((HttpServletRequest)
      request).getParameter("password");
      .
      .
      .

  }

  public void destroy()
  {
  }

  public void init(FilterConfig filterConfig)
  {
  }
}
```

If the password is correct — say, opensesame — then you can pass control on to password.jsp, which returns the welcome message that the Ajax application displays.

You can pass control on to password.jsp by connecting the filter to that JSP page in the web.xml file, which is in the Tomcat WEB-INF directory. This directory is a subdirectory of the chap16 directory, which itself is in the Tomcat webapps directory:

```
webapps
   |
   |__chap16
       |
       |__WEB-INF
           |    |
           |    |__web.xml
           |
           |__classes
           |
           |__lib
```

Here's what web.xml looks like now:

```xml
<?xml version="1.0" encoding="ISO-8859-1"?>

<!DOCTYPE web-app
    PUBLIC "-//Sun Microsystems, Inc.//DTD Web Application
      2.3//EN"
    "http://java.sun.com/j2ee/dtds/web-app_2_3.dtd">

<web-app>

</web-app>
```

The goal is to connect the compiled PasswordFilter.java file, which is named PasswordFilter.class, to password.jsp. You start by giving the new filter a name, like `Authentication`, and connecting it to the .class file PasswordFilter.class:

```xml
<?xml version="1.0" encoding="ISO-8859-1"?>

<!DOCTYPE web-app
    PUBLIC "-//Sun Microsystems, Inc.//DTD Web Application
      2.3//EN"
    "http://java.sun.com/j2ee/dtds/web-app_2_3.dtd">

<web-app>

  <filter>
    <filter-name>Authentication</filter-name>
    <filter-class>PasswordFilter</filter-class>
  </filter>
        .
        .
        .
</web-app>
```

Then you connect that new filter to password.jsp:

```
<?xml version="1.0" encoding="ISO-8859-1"?>

<!DOCTYPE web-app
    PUBLIC "-//Sun Microsystems, Inc.//DTD Web Application
      2.3//EN"
    "http://java.sun.com/j2ee/dtds/web-app_2_3.dtd">

<web-app>

  <filter>
    <filter-name>Authentication</filter-name>
    <filter-class>PasswordFilter</filter-class>
  </filter>

  <filter-mapping>
    <filter-name>Authentication</filter-name>
    <url-pattern>/password.jsp</url-pattern>
  </filter-mapping>

</web-app>
```

That inserts `PasswordFilter` as a filter on password.jsp, which means that in PasswordFilter.java, you can pass control on to password.jsp by calling the `doFilter` method of the `chain` object, passed to the `doFilter` method in PasswordFilter.java:

```
import java.io.*;
import javax.servlet.*;
import javax.servlet.http.*;

public final class PasswordFilter implements Filter
{
  public void doFilter(ServletRequest request, ServletResponse
    response,
    FilterChain chain)
    throws IOException, ServletException
  {
    String password = ((HttpServletRequest)
      request).getParameter("password");

    if(password.equals("opensesame")) {
        chain.doFilter(request, response);
    }
          .
          .
          .
  }
```

```
        public void destroy()
        {
        }

        public void init(FilterConfig filterConfig)
        {
        }
    }
```

On the other hand, if the password was not correct, you need some way of sending an error message back to the browser. You start that process by setting the response object's content type header to text/html — the response object is what will be sent back to the browser, so this tells the browser you're sending back a text-based response. You can also get a PrintWriter object, out, which is what you'll use to place text in the response object:

```
    import java.io.*;
    import javax.servlet.*;
    import javax.servlet.http.*;

    public final class PasswordFilter implements Filter
    {
      public void doFilter(ServletRequest request, ServletResponse
        response,
        FilterChain chain)
        throws IOException, ServletException
      {
        String password = ((HttpServletRequest)
          request).getParameter("password");

        if(password.equals("opensesame")) {
            chain.doFilter(request, response);
        }
        else {
            response.setContentType("text/html");
            PrintWriter out = response.getWriter();
            .
            .
            .
        }
      }

      public void destroy()
      {
      }

      public void init(FilterConfig filterConfig)
      {
      }
    }
```

Now you can use the out object's println method to display HTML in the browser indicating that the password was incorrect:

```java
import java.io.*;
import javax.servlet.*;
import javax.servlet.http.*;

public final class PasswordFilter implements Filter
{
  public void doFilter(ServletRequest request, ServletResponse
    response,
    FilterChain chain)
    throws IOException, ServletException
  {
    String password = ((HttpServletRequest)
      request).getParameter("password");

    if(password.equals("opensesame")) {
        chain.doFilter(request, response);
    }
    else {
        response.setContentType("text/html");
        PrintWriter out = response.getWriter();
        out.println("<html>");
        out.println("<head>");
        out.println("<title>");
        out.println("Incorrect Password");
        out.println("</title>");
        out.println("</head>");
        out.println("<body>");
        out.println("<H1>Incorrect Password</H1>");
        out.println("Sorry, that password was incorrect.");
        out.println("</body>");
        out.println("</html>");
    }
  }

  public void destroy()
  {
  }

  public void init(FilterConfig filterConfig)
  {
  }
}
```

To compile PasswordFilter.java, you need to make either servlet.jar or servlet-api.jar, depending on your version of Tomcat, accessible to Java. You'll find this .jar file — either servlet.jar or servlet-api.jar — in Tomcat's common\lib directory. You can copy that .jar file to the directory in which you're copying PasswordFilter.java and add the .jar file to the `classpath` environment variable. That works like this in Windows:

```
set classpath=servlet.jar
```

If you don't want to copy the .jar file to the directory in which you're compiling PasswordFilter.java, you can give the fill path to the .jar file like this:

```
set classpath=C:\[Tomcat path including
version]\coom\lib\servlet.jar
```

Next, you compile PasswordFilter.java using the Java compiler tool, javac:

```
javac PasswordFilter.java
```

If javac is not in your path, you have to give the path to it, something like this in Windows (change this path to match your Java installation — the javac tool is in the Java installation's bin directory):

```
C:\jdk\bin\javac PasswordFilter.java
```

That compiles PasswordFilter.java and creates PasswordFilter.class, which is what you want.

The PasswordFilter.class file should be placed in the webapps\chap16\WEB-INF\classes directory, like this, to make it accessible to the server:

```
webapps
   |
   |__chap16
        |
        |__WEB-INF
             |   |
             |   |__web.xml
             |
             |__classes
             |   |
             |   |__PasswordFilter.class
             |
             |__lib
```

That sets up the application. Now you should restart Tomcat if you're working with a local installation of that server (you should restart Tomcat if you've changed an XML file and/or added a .class file — you can configure Tomcat to notice if you've made such changes, but it doesn't do so by default).

The password.html page is shown in Figure 16.1.

FIGURE 16.1

The password.html page

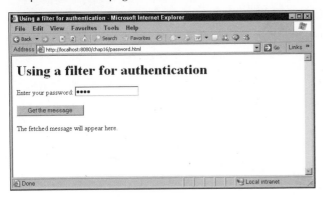

If you enter the wrong password, it's sent to password.jsp using Ajax techniques. But the filter, PasswordFilter, intercepts that password and returns an error message, as shown in Figure 16.2.

FIGURE 16.2

An incorrect password

On the other hand, if you enter the right password, a welcoming message appears, as shown in Figure 16.3.

FIGURE 16.3

Using the right password

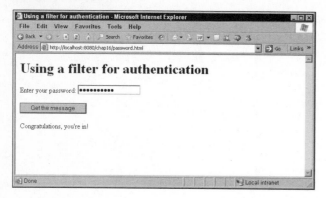

As you can see, filters work even when you're using an XMLHttpRequest object.

Logging User Access with Filters

One of the primary uses of filters in Ajax applications is to log user accesses, something that's particularly important if security is an issue. Here's an example, log.html, which accesses log.jsp on the server:

```
<html>
  <head>
    <title>Using a filter for user logging</title>

    <script language = "javascript">
      var XMLHttpRequestObject = false;

      if (window.XMLHttpRequest) {
        XMLHttpRequestObject = new XMLHttpRequest();
      } else if (window.ActiveXObject) {
        XMLHttpRequestObject = new
          ActiveXObject("Microsoft.XMLHTTP");
      }

      function getData(dataSource, divID)
      {
        if(XMLHttpRequestObject) {
          var obj = document.getElementById(divID);
          XMLHttpRequestObject.open("GET", dataSource);

          XMLHttpRequestObject.onreadystatechange = function()
          {
```

```
              if (XMLHttpRequestObject.readyState == 4 &&
                XMLHttpRequestObject.status == 200) {
                  obj.innerHTML =
                    XMLHttpRequestObject.responseText;
              }
            }

            XMLHttpRequestObject.send(null);
          }
        }
      </script>
    </head>

    <body>

      <H1>Using a filter for user logging</H1>

      <form>
        <input type = "button" value = "Get the message"
          onclick = "getData('log.jsp', 'targetDiv')">
      </form>

      <div id="targetDiv">
        <p>The fetched message will appear here.</p>
      </div>

    </body>
  </html>
```

Here's what the accessed JSP, log.jsp looks like:

```
<html>
    <head>
        <title>Logging user access</title>
    </head>
    <body>
        <h1>Logging user access</h1>
        You have been logged.
        <br>
    </body>
</html>
```

The trick here is to use a filter, called LogFilter in this case, to log the user access. Here's how you connect LogFilter to log.jsp in web.xml:

```
<?xml version="1.0" encoding="ISO-8859-1"?>

<!DOCTYPE web-app
    PUBLIC "-//Sun Microsystems, Inc.//DTD Web Application
      2.3//EN"
    "http://java.sun.com/j2ee/dtds/web-app_2_3.dtd">
```

```
<web-app>

  <filter>
    <filter-name>Log Filter</filter-name>
    <filter-class>LogFilter</filter-class>
  </filter>

  <filter>
    <filter-name>Authentication</filter-name>
    <filter-class>PasswordFilter</filter-class>
  </filter>

  <filter-mapping>
    <filter-name>Log Filter</filter-name>
    <url-pattern>/log.jsp</url-pattern>
  </filter-mapping>

  <filter-mapping>
    <filter-name>Authentication</filter-name>
    <url-pattern>/password.jsp</url-pattern>
  </filter-mapping>

</web-app>
```

Now it's time to write the filter in Java, LogFilter.java. That filter starts as you'd expect:

```
import java.io.*;
import javax.servlet.*;
import javax.servlet.http.*;

public final class LogFilter implements Filter
{
        .
        .
        .
}
```

As you know, you have to support three methods in a filter: doFilter, init, and destroy:

```
import java.io.*;
import javax.servlet.*;
import javax.servlet.http.*;

public final class LogFilter implements Filter
{
  public void doFilter(ServletRequest request, ServletResponse
    response,
    FilterChain chain)
    throws IOException, ServletException
```

```
    {

            .

            .

            .

    }



    public void destroy() { }

    public void init(FilterConfig filterConfig) {

            .

            .

            .

    }
}
```

This filter differs from PasswordFilter in that it's going to need the FilterConfig object passed to the init method in order to write to a log file. That means you should save the FilterConfig object this way to make it accessible in the doFilter method — the Java this keyword points to the current object, so this.filterConfig refers to the filterConfig variable stored in the filter; the filterConfig variable is also declared private, which makes it inaccessible outside the current filter object:

```
import java.io.*;
import javax.servlet.*;
import javax.servlet.http.*;

public final class LogFilter implements Filter
{
  private FilterConfig filterConfig = null;

  public void doFilter(ServletRequest request, ServletResponse
    response,
    FilterChain chain)
    throws IOException, ServletException
  {

            .

            .

            .

  }



            .

            .

            .

  public void destroy() { }
```

```
   public void init(FilterConfig filterConfig)
   {
     this.filterConfig = filterConfig;
   }
 }

 import java.io.*;
 import javax.servlet.*;
 import javax.servlet.http.*;

 public final class LogFilter implements Filter
 {
   private FilterConfig filterConfig = null;

   public void doFilter(ServletRequest request, ServletResponse
     response,
     FilterChain chain)
     throws IOException, ServletException
   {

     long start = System.currentTimeMillis();
         .
         .
         .
   }

   public void destroy() { }

   public void init(FilterConfig filterConfig)
   {
     this.filterConfig = filterConfig;
   }
 }
```

This filter logs users' IP addresses (you can log users' usernames as well, as described in Chapter 15, but that means your users must be logged in first), the resource they're accessing (such as a JSP page), and the amount of time they spend with the resource. To track the amount of time, begin by getting the current system time, in milliseconds, before transferring control to the resource users want to look at:

```
 import java.io.*;
 import javax.servlet.*;
 import javax.servlet.http.*;

 public final class LogFilter implements Filter
 {
   private FilterConfig filterConfig = null;

   public void doFilter(ServletRequest request, ServletResponse
     response,
```

```
      FilterChain chain)
      throws IOException, ServletException
   {

      long start = System.currentTimeMillis();
               .
               .
               .
   }

   public void destroy() { }

   public void init(FilterConfig filterConfig)
   {
      this.filterConfig = filterConfig;
   }
}
```

Next, you can get the user's IP address with the `request` object's `getRemoteAddr` method this way:

```
import java.io.*;
import javax.servlet.*;
import javax.servlet.http.*;

public final class LogFilter implements Filter
{
   private FilterConfig filterConfig = null;

   public void doFilter(ServletRequest request, ServletResponse
      response,
      FilterChain chain)
      throws IOException, ServletException
   {

      long start = System.currentTimeMillis();

      String address =  request.getRemoteAddr();
               .
               .
               .
   }

   public void destroy() { }

   public void init(FilterConfig filterConfig)
   {
      this.filterConfig = filterConfig;
   }
}
```

You can also get the URL of the Web resource (JSP page, servlet, HTML page, and so on) that the user is trying to access using the `request` object's `getRequestURI` method:

```
import java.io.*;
import javax.servlet.*;
import javax.servlet.http.*;

public final class LogFilter implements Filter
{
  private FilterConfig filterConfig = null;

  public void doFilter(ServletRequest request, ServletResponse
    response,
    FilterChain chain)
    throws IOException, ServletException
  {

    long start = System.currentTimeMillis();

    String address =  request.getRemoteAddr();

    String file = request.getRequestURI();
        .
        .
        .

  }

  public void destroy() { }

  public void init(FilterConfig filterConfig)
  {
    this.filterConfig = filterConfig;
  }
}
```

> **NOTE** URI stands for universal resource indicator, which in practice currently means a URL, or universal resource locator.

However, the code is not going to work as written because as things stand, the `request` object is an object of the Java `ServletRequest` class, as you can see in the declaration of the `doFilter` method:

```
public void doFilter(ServletRequest request, ServletResponse
    response,
    FilterChain chain)
    throws IOException, ServletException
  {
        .
        .
        .

  }
```

The `ServletRequest` class does not support the `getRequestURI` method, so you have to change the code here to avoid a compiler error. In fact, because our filter is online, the `request` object passed to the `doFilter` method is of a class based on the `ServletRequest` class, the `HttpServletRequest` class, and the `HttpServletRequest` class does support the `getRequestURI` method. So you can tell Java that you're really dealing with an `HttpServletRequest` object this way:

```java
import java.io.*;
import javax.servlet.*;
import javax.servlet.http.*;

public final class LogFilter implements Filter
{
  private FilterConfig filterConfig = null;

  public void doFilter(ServletRequest request, ServletResponse
    response,
    FilterChain chain)
    throws IOException, ServletException
  {

    long start = System.currentTimeMillis();

    String address =  request.getRemoteAddr();

    String file = ((HttpServletRequest) request).getRequestURI();
         .
         .
         .

  }

  public void destroy() { }

  public void init(FilterConfig filterConfig)
  {
    this.filterConfig = filterConfig;
  }
}
```

Now you have the user's IP address and requested URL, as well as the start time of his or her Web resource access. Now it's time to pass control on to that Web resource with `chain.doFilter`:

```java
import java.io.*;
import javax.servlet.*;
import javax.servlet.http.*;

public final class LogFilter implements Filter
{
  private FilterConfig filterConfig = null;
```

```
public void doFilter(ServletRequest request, ServletResponse
  response,
  FilterChain chain)
  throws IOException, ServletException
{

  long start = System.currentTimeMillis();

  String address =  request.getRemoteAddr();

  String file = ((HttpServletRequest) request).getRequestURI();

  chain.doFilter(request, response);
      .
      .
      .
  );
}

public void destroy() { }

public void init(FilterConfig filterConfig)
{
  this.filterConfig = filterConfig;
}
}
```

That calls the Web resource the user was trying to access, and after that resource does its thing, control returns to you in the filter, where you can write to the log. To do that, you can use the `FilterConfig` object's `getServletContext` method to get the current servlet context (the servlet context of a Web application lets you store data and share that data between servlets and between JSPs, among other things). The servlet context object has a method that lets you write to a log file, the `log` method, and you can use that method like this:

```
import java.io.*;
import javax.servlet.*;
import javax.servlet.http.*;

public final class LogFilter implements Filter
{
  private FilterConfig filterConfig = null;

  public void doFilter(ServletRequest request, ServletResponse
    response,
    FilterChain chain)
    throws IOException, ServletException
  {

    long start = System.currentTimeMillis();

    String address =  request.getRemoteAddr();
```

```
      String file = ((HttpServletRequest) request).getRequestURI();

      chain.doFilter(request, response);

      filterConfig.getServletContext().log(
            .
            .
            .
      );
  }

  public void destroy() { }

  public void init(FilterConfig filterConfig)
  {
     this.filterConfig = filterConfig;
  }
}
```

To write to the log method, you pass it a string. In this case, that string contains the URL the user was accessing, the user's IP address, and the time he or she took on the Web resource, which you can get by subtracting the starting time from the current time, like this:

```
import java.io.*;
import javax.servlet.*;
import javax.servlet.http.*;

public final class LogFilter implements Filter
{
  private FilterConfig filterConfig = null;

  public void doFilter(ServletRequest request, ServletResponse
    response,
    FilterChain chain)
    throws IOException, ServletException
  {

    long start = System.currentTimeMillis();

    String address =  request.getRemoteAddr();

    String file = ((HttpServletRequest) request).getRequestURI();

    chain.doFilter(request, response);

    filterConfig.getServletContext().log(
        "User access! " +
        " User IP: " + address +
        " Resource: " + file +
```

```
                   " Milliseconds used: " + (System.currentTimeMillis() -
                   start)
           );
       }

       public void destroy() { }

       public void init(FilterConfig filterConfig)
       {
           this.filterConfig = filterConfig;
       }
   }
```

That completes LogFilter.java. After compiling it, place it in the application's WEB-INF\classes directory:

```
webapps
   |
   |__chap16
         |
         |__WEB-INF
               |    |
               |    |__web.xml
               |
               |__classes
               |    |
               |    |__LogFilter.class
               |
               |__lib
```

You can see the HTML page in this application, log.html, in Figure 16.4. When you click the "Get the message" button in log.html, your access to log.jsp is logged, and log.jsp tells you so, as shown in Figure 16.5.

FIGURE 16.4

The log.html page

FIGURE 16.5

The log.jsp page

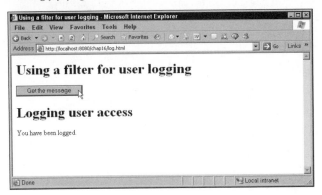

So where did the log text go? That varies by server. On Tomcat, it goes into a log file in the Tomcat logs directory, whose name depends on the date. In this case, the log file written to is localhost_log.2006-10-26.txt, and here's what you find in it:

```
2006-10-27 11:51:04 invoker: init
2006-10-27 11:51:04 jsp: init
2006-10-27 11:51:04 StandardHost[localhost]: Installing web
application at context path /webdav from URL
file:C:\tomcat\jakarta-tomcat-4.0.3\webapps\webdav
2006-10-27 11:51:04 WebappLoader[/webdav]: Deploying class
repositories to work directory C:\tomcat\jakarta-tomcat-
4.0.3\work\localhost\webdav
2006-10-27 11:51:04 StandardManager[/webdav]: Seeding random
number generator class java.security.SecureRandom
2006-10-27 11:51:04 StandardManager[/webdav]: Seeding of random
number generator has been completed
2006-10-27 11:51:04 ContextConfig[/webdav]: Added certificates ->
request attribute Valve
2006-10-27 11:51:04 StandardWrapper[/webdav:default]: Loading
container servlet default
2006-10-27 11:51:04 default: init
2006-10-27 11:51:04 StandardWrapper[/webdav:invoker]: Loading
container servlet invoker
2006-10-27 11:51:04 invoker: init
2006-10-27 11:51:04 jsp: init
2006-10-27 11:52:00 jsp: init
2006-10-27 11:52:00 User access!  User IP: 127.0.0.1 Resource:
/chap16/log.jsp Milliseconds used: 672
```

As you can see, the text you wanted logged has indeed been logged, and users need not know they've been logged, which is useful for security purposes.

Restricting Access Based on Time of Day

You can also use filters to restrict access to Web pages based on time of day; for example, you can restrict access to a game, data that needs to be updated, and so on.

Here's an example, time.jsp, which you can access if the time of day is right:

```html
<html>
    <head>
        <title>Using Filters to Restrict Access</title>
    </head>

    <body>

        <h1>Using Filters to Restrict Access</h1>

        Congratulations, you're in!
        <br>

    </body>
</html>
```

To write the time-based filter TimeFilter.java, you start like this, declaring the `TimeFilter` class:

```java
import java.io.*;
import java.util.*;
import javax.servlet.*;
import javax.servlet.http.*;

public final class TimeFilter implements Filter
{
  public void doFilter(ServletRequest request, ServletResponse
    response,
    FilterChain chain)
    throws IOException, ServletException
  {
        .
        .
        .

  }

  public void destroy()
  {
  }

  public void init(FilterConfig filterConfig)
  {
  }
}
```

In the doFilter method, you need to start by getting the current time. Say that you want to restrict access to time.jsp such that it wasn't available between the hours of 9 to 5. You start that process in Java by creating a GregorianCalendar object and a Date object:

```
import java.io.*;
import java.util.*;
import javax.servlet.*;
import javax.servlet.http.*;

public final class TimeFilter implements Filter
{
  public void doFilter(ServletRequest request, ServletResponse
    response,
    FilterChain chain)
    throws IOException, ServletException
  {

    GregorianCalendar calendar = new GregorianCalendar();

    Date date1 = new Date();
        .
        .
        .
  }

  public void destroy()
  {
  }

  public void init(FilterConfig filterConfig)
  {
  }
}
```

Then you set the time in the GregorianCalendar object with the setTime method, passing the Data object to that method, and get the current hour of the day with the GregorianCalendar object's get method:

```
import java.io.*;
import java.util.*;
import javax.servlet.*;
import javax.servlet.http.*;

public final class TimeFilter implements Filter
{
  public void doFilter(ServletRequest request, ServletResponse
    response,
    FilterChain chain)
    throws IOException, ServletException
  {
```

```
    GregorianCalendar calendar = new GregorianCalendar();

    Date date1 = new Date();

    calendar.setTime(date1);

    int hour = calendar.get(Calendar.HOUR_OF_DAY);
         .
         .
         .
  }

  public void destroy()
  {
  }

  public void init(FilterConfig filterConfig)
  {
  }
}
```

If the hour is not between 9 and 5, you can call the next link in the chain, which is time.jsp:

```
import java.io.*;
import java.util.*;
import javax.servlet.*;
import javax.servlet.http.*;

public final class TimeFilter implements Filter
{
  public void doFilter(ServletRequest request, ServletResponse
    response,
    FilterChain chain)
    throws IOException, ServletException
  {

    GregorianCalendar calendar = new GregorianCalendar();

    Date date1 = new Date();

    calendar.setTime(date1);

    int hour = calendar.get(Calendar.HOUR_OF_DAY);

    if(hour < 9 || hour > 17) {
        chain.doFilter(request, response);
    }
         .
         .
         .
```

```
      }

    public void destroy()
    {
    }

    public void init(FilterConfig filterConfig)
    {
    }
}
```

Otherwise, you want to restrict access to time.jsp, which you can do by sending a nasty page back to the browser, like this:

```
import java.io.*;
import java.util.*;
import javax.servlet.*;
import javax.servlet.http.*;

public final class TimeFilter implements Filter
{
  public void doFilter(ServletRequest request, ServletResponse
    response,
    FilterChain chain)
    throws IOException, ServletException
  {

    GregorianCalendar calendar = new GregorianCalendar();

    Date date1 = new Date();

    calendar.setTime(date1);

    int hour = calendar.get(Calendar.HOUR_OF_DAY);

    if(hour < 9 || hour > 17) {
        chain.doFilter(request, response);
    }

    else {
        response.setContentType("text/html");
        PrintWriter out = response.getWriter();
        out.println("<html>");
        out.println("<head>");
        out.println("<title>");
        out.println("Get Back to Work!");
        out.println("</title>");
        out.println("</head>");
        out.println("<body>");
        out.println("<H1>Get Back to Work!</H1>");
```

```
        out.println("Sorry, that resource is not available
          now.");
        out.println("</body>");
        out.println("</html>");
    }
  }

  public void destroy()
  {
  }

  public void init(FilterConfig filterConfig)
  {
  }
}
```

That completes TimeFilter.java. After compiling it, place it in the application's WEB-INF\classes directory:

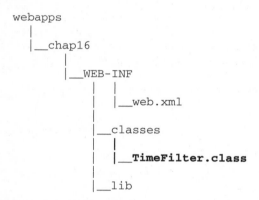

```
webapps
  |
  |__chap16
  |     |
  |     |__WEB-INF
  |           |  |
  |           |  |__web.xml
  |           |
  |           |__classes
  |           |  |
  |           |  |__TimeFilter.class
  |           |
  |           |__lib
```

You also need to install TimeFilter in web.xml, as a filter for the time.jsp page, and you do that like this:

```
<?xml version="1.0" encoding="ISO-8859-1"?>

<!DOCTYPE web-app
    PUBLIC "-//Sun Microsystems, Inc.//DTD Web Application
      2.3//EN"
    "http://java.sun.com/j2ee/dtds/web-app_2_3.dtd">

<web-app>

  <filter>
    <filter-name>Log Filter</filter-name>
    <filter-class>LogFilter</filter-class>
  </filter>
```

```
<filter>
  <filter-name>Authentication</filter-name>
  <filter-class>PasswordFilter</filter-class>
</filter>

<filter>
  <filter-name>Time</filter-name>
  <filter-class>TimeFilter</filter-class>
</filter>

<filter-mapping>
  <filter-name>Log Filter</filter-name>
  <url-pattern>/log.jsp</url-pattern>
</filter-mapping>

<filter-mapping>
  <filter-name>Authentication</filter-name>
  <url-pattern>/password.jsp</url-pattern>
</filter-mapping>

<filter-mapping>
  <filter-name>Time</filter-name>
  <url-pattern>/time.jsp</url-pattern>
</filter-mapping>

</web-app>
```

You can see the results when you navigate to time.jsp during the middle of the day, as shown in Figure 16.6, where the filter is blocking access.

FIGURE 16.6

The Time filter at work

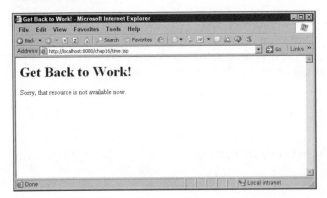

Model-View-Controller Applications

When your Web applications get larger, dividing their parts can make them more manageable. One way of doing that is to separate your application into model-view-controller (MVC) parts. The user interacts with the controller, which in turn calls the model to do data crunching, and the view to display results to the user.

Here's an overview of these three parts:

- Model: Implements the data crunching of the application. This is the code that actually does the in-depth (non-presentation) work, such as checking tax rater and so on. The model doesn't know anything about the view. The model is often implemented using JavaBeans.

- View: Implements the presentation of data to the user. The view takes and displays the data supplied to it (usually from the controller). The view is often implemented in JSP.

- Controller: Oversees the model and the view by reacting to the data the user sends. Accepts input from the user, calls the appropriate bean methods in the model, and sends data to the view for presentation. Often implemented as a servlet.

There are several ways to implement MVC architecture with Ajax. For example, you can think of the model as being on the server, the browser as the view, and the JavaScript in the browser as the controller. That's one way to implement MVC in Ajax applications; however, it's more usual to host the model, view, and controller on the server, and that's the way you'll see it here.

Here's an example showing how this works. The controller is a Java servlet on the server, and it calls a method in the model, which is implemented as a JavaBean. After retrieving data from the model, the controller passes that data on to the view, which is a JSP page. The view won't be directly visible in the browser; instead, the JSP is accessed via an XMLHttpRequest object from the browser, and displayed using JavaScript.

It all starts with the controller.

The controller

The controller in this example is a Java servlet named Controller. A *servlet* is Java code that's directly accessible by navigating to it in a browser, and the Controller servlet starts like this:

```
import java.io.*;
import javax.servlet.*;
import javax.servlet.http.*;

public class Controller extends HttpServlet
{
        .
        .
        .
}
```

When the user navigates to the controller, the controller creates an object of the Model class, which is simply named Model, and calls that object's msg method to read the text it must send back to the browser. The model is implemented as a Java file named Model.java, and it'll be a JavaBean in a directory below the directory in which the Controller servlet resides, named beans. To access that bean class, you import it as beans.Model, and then you can create an object of the Model class in your code:

```
import java.io.*;
import javax.servlet.*;
import javax.servlet.http.*;
import beans.Model;

public class Controller extends HttpServlet
{

    Model model = new Model();
        .
        .
        .

}
```

When the Ajax part of this application calls the controller, it uses the GET method, which you handle in servlets with the doGet method:

```
import java.io.*;
import javax.servlet.*;
import javax.servlet.http.*;
import beans.Model;

public class Controller extends HttpServlet
{

    Model model = new Model();

    public void doGet(HttpServletRequest request,
      HttpServletResponse response)
        throws ServletException, IOException
    {
        .
        .
        .

    }
}
```

In the doGet method, you can set an attribute of the request object named message to the message retrieved from the model that the view is supposed to display. Setting a request object attribute is the way you pass data around in an MVC application — the request object is sent to all the application components you forward from the controller, and those components can retrieve the data you're sending to them from the request object — and you store data in the request object using attributes.

Here's how you store the message — fetched from the model to send back to the browser — in the request object under the attribute name message:

```
import java.io.*;
import javax.servlet.*;
import javax.servlet.http.*;
import beans.Model;

public class Controller extends HttpServlet
{

    Model model = new Model();

    public void doGet(HttpServletRequest request,
      HttpServletResponse response)
        throws ServletException, IOException
    {
        request.setAttribute("message", model.msg());
        .
        .
        .
    }
}
```

Now you have to forward the request object on to the view, which sends the data currently in the request object's message attribute back to the browser. The view in this example is a JSP named view.jsp, and you can forward the request object on to it using a RequestDispatcher object:

```
import java.io.*;
import javax.servlet.*;
import javax.servlet.http.*;
import beans.Model;

public class Controller extends HttpServlet
{
    String target = "view.jsp";

    Model model = new Model();

    public void doGet(HttpServletRequest request,
      HttpServletResponse response)
        throws ServletException, IOException
    {
        request.setAttribute("message", model.msg());

        RequestDispatcher dispatcher =
            request.getRequestDispatcher(target);
```

```
            .
            .
            .
    }
}
```

Now you can forward the `request` — and `response` (which you use to configure the data you send back to the browser — object to the view like this:

```java
import java.io.*;
import javax.servlet.*;
import javax.servlet.http.*;
import beans.Model;

public class Controller extends HttpServlet
{
    String target = "view.jsp";

    Model model = new Model();

    public void doGet(HttpServletRequest request,
      HttpServletResponse response)
        throws ServletException, IOException
    {
        request.setAttribute("message", model.msg());

        RequestDispatcher dispatcher =
            request.getRequestDispatcher(target);

        dispatcher.forward(request, response);
    }
}
```

That finishes the controller, which the `XMLHttpRequest` object in the browser interacts with. Because this is a Java servlet, you have to add `<servlet>` and `<servlet-mapping>` elements to web.xml so the server will know how to deal with this servlet; that looks like this:

```xml
<?xml version="1.0" encoding="ISO-8859-1"?>

<!DOCTYPE web-app
    PUBLIC "-//Sun Microsystems, Inc.//DTD Web Application
      2.3//EN"
      "http://java.sun.com/j2ee/dtds/web-app_2_3.dtd">

<web-app>
    .
    .
    .
  <servlet>
```

```
  <servlet-name>Controller</servlet-name>
  <servlet-class>Controller</servlet-class>
</servlet>

<servlet-mapping>
  <servlet-name>Controller</servlet-name>
  <url-pattern>/Controller</url-pattern>
</servlet-mapping>

</web-app>
```

Next you create the view.

The view

The view is fairly simple. Its job is simply to retrieve the data stored by the controller in the `request` object's message attribute and send that back to the browser. The view can display any HTML you want:

```
<html>
  <head>
    <title>Using MVC Architecture</title>
  </head>

  <body>
    <h1>Using MVC Architecture</h1>
    Here is the message:
         .
         .
         .
  </body>
</html>
```

Here's the Java code that retrieves the message from the `request` object and sends it back to the browser:

```
<html>
  <head>
    <title>Using MVC Architecture</title>
  </head>

  <body>
    <h1>Using MVC Architecture</h1>
    Here is the message:
    <% out.println(request.getAttribute("message")); %>
  </body>
</html>
```

That completes the controller and the view. Next comes the model.

The model

The model is where the data-crunching goes on in an MVC application. Ideally, the model has no idea what the view is — it's entirely separate from the presentation logic, which is an important part of separating the pieces of your application along the MVC architecture lines. The model in this example is a class named `Model`, in the Java package named `beans`:

```
package beans;

public class Model
{
    .
    .
    .
}
```

As all JavaBeans must have, the model has a Java constructor that takes no arguments:

```
package beans;

public class Model
{
    public Model()
    {
    }
}
```

You also need to add the `msg` method that the controller can call to get the `Hello from Ajax!` message:

```
package beans;

public class Model
{
    public String msg()
    {
        return "Hello from Ajax!";
    }

    public Model()
    {
    }
}
```

That completes the model, the view, and the controller. The next step is to get this MVC application installed on the server.

Installing the MVC Application

To install the MVC application on the server, start by placing the view JSP, view.jsp, in the chap16 folder on the server:

```
chap16                                   view.jsp
|_____WEB-INF
          |_____classes
                    |_____beans
```

Next, place Model.java in the classes\beans directory and compile it there to create Model.class this way:

```
chap16                                   view.jsp
|_____WEB-INF
          |_____classes
                    |_____beans          Model.class
```

To compile the Controller servlet, you set the `classpath` so that Java can find servlet.jar (or servlet-api.jar, depending on your version of Tomcat) as well as the Model.class file in the beans directory. To do this, place the servlet's Java code, Controller.java, in the classes directory, and copy servlet.jar (or servlet-api.jar) to the classes directory as well. Then set the `classpath` to `servlet.jar;.` on the command line:

```
set classpath=servlet.jar;.
```

The dot on the end of the `classpath` means that Java should include the current directory, and tells Java that when it's looking for the `beans.Model` class to try to find a directory named beans that contains a class named `Model`. After you compile Controller.java in the classes directory, you'll have Controller.class in the same directory, which is where you need it:

```
chap16                                   view.jsp
|_____WEB-INF
          |_____classes                  Controller.class
                    |_____beans          Model.class
```

That sets up the code on the server. Now it's time to call that code from the browser.

Accessing MVC with Ajax

Interacting with the MVC code you've set up on the server is not difficult — you just have to access the controller using Ajax code. Here's what that looks like in an Ajax-enabled page, mvc.html, which goes in the chap16 directory on the server. Note that because you set things up appropriately in web.xml, you can refer to the controller servlet simply as Controller:

```html
<html>
  <head>
    <title>Ajax and MVC</title>

    <script language = "javascript">
      var XMLHttpRequestObject = false;

      if (window.XMLHttpRequest) {
        XMLHttpRequestObject = new XMLHttpRequest();
      } else if (window.ActiveXObject) {
        XMLHttpRequestObject = new
          ActiveXObject("Microsoft.XMLHTTP");
      }

      function getData(dataSource, divID)
      {
        if(XMLHttpRequestObject) {
          var obj = document.getElementById(divID);
          XMLHttpRequestObject.open("GET", dataSource);

          XMLHttpRequestObject.onreadystatechange = function()
          {
            if (XMLHttpRequestObject.readyState == 4 &&
              XMLHttpRequestObject.status == 200) {
                obj.innerHTML =
                  XMLHttpRequestObject.responseText;
            }
          }

          XMLHttpRequestObject.send(null);
        }
      }
    </script>
  </head>

  <body>

    <H1>Ajax and MVC</H1>

    <form>
      <input type = "button" value = "Display Message"
        onclick = "getData('Controller', 'targetDiv')">
    </form>

    <div id="targetDiv">
      <p>The fetched data will go here.</p>
    </div>

  </body>
</html>
```

The results are shown in Figure 16.7. When you click the Display Message button, the XMLHttpRequest GET request is sent to the controller, which calls the model to get the data to send back, which the controller forwards to the view. The view sends the message back to the browser, which displays the message, as shown in Figure 16.7. Mission accomplished.

FIGURE 16.7

The MVC application at work

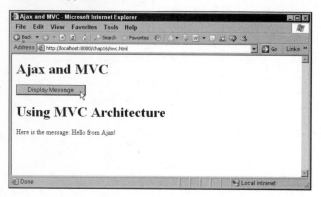

That's it for putting MVC architecture to work, and that's it for this book. Happy Ajax programming!

Summary

The chapter introduced some advanced Ajax topics: working with filters and MVC architecture. You saw how to create basic filters. You saw how to enforce passwords using filters and how to create logging filters as well as time-of-day filters. You also got the basics of MVC architecture down, complete with a working example.

Index

I

O